EV
W....,

ONE YEAR DEVOTIONAL

Hope Everlasting

SELWYN HUGHES
Further Study: Trevor J Partridge

Copyright © CWR 2006

Published 2006 by CWR, Waverley Abbey House, Waverley Lane, Farnham, Surrey GU9 8EP, UK. Registered Charity No. 294387. Registered Limited Company No. 1990308. Reprinted 2008.

Issues of *Every Day with Jesus* were previously published as follows: *Preparing for Revival*, Jan/Feb 1984; *The Crimson Trail in Scripture*, Mar/Apr 1983; *The Divine Gardener*, Sep/Oct 1983; *The Letters of James and John*, Nov/Dec 1983; *The Cross in Modern Life*, Mar/Apr 1984; *Faith Thriving Under Persecution*, Jul/Aug 1984.

See back of book for list of National Distributors.

Unless otherwise indicated, all Scripture references are from the Holy Bible: New International Version (NIV), copyright © 1973, 1978, 1984 by the International Bible Society.

KJV: The King James Version
Moffatt: The Moffatt Translation of the Bible, © 1987, Hodder & Stoughton
NKJV: New King James Version, © 1982, Thomas Nelson Inc.
Phillips: J.B. Phillips *The New Testament in Modern English*, © 1960, 1972, J.B. Phillips, Fount Paperbacks
RSV: Revised Standard Version, © 1965, Division of Christian Education of the National Council of the Churches of Christ in the United States of America
TLB: The Living Bible, © 1971, 1994, Tyndale House Publishers
Amp: The Amplified Bible Old Testament © 1965, 1987 by the Zondervan Corporation
The Amplified New Testament © 1958 by the Lockman Foundation. Used by permission
GNB: Good News Bible © American Bible Society 1966, 1971, 1976, 1992, 1994

Concept development, editing, design and production by CWR

Cover image: Digitalvision

Printed in Finland by WS Bookwell

ISBN: 978-1-85345-408-0

CONTENTS

Foreword

One of the primary calls of God on the life of Selwyn Hughes was to write *Every Day with Jesus*, which he did faithfully for over forty years.

In this one-year edition, *Hope Everlasting*, you will find some key themes covered by Selwyn over the years, encapsulating his heart for us all to meditate on the Word of God each day, open our hearts and minds before Him, and develop our devotional life.

Hope is one of the three elements of ideal Christian character, and has been defined as a 'trustful expectation'. To believers, hope is a trust in God's Word, which leads to eternal life: 'those who hope in me will not be disappointed' (Isa. 49:23). Hope is an essential and fundamental element of Christian life, so essential indeed, that, like faith and love, it can itself designate the essence of Christianity.

One of the six themes included – *Preparing for Revival* was very dear to Selwyn's heart. His continual hope was to see the Church pray for – and be prepared for – revival. May his words in the opening pages of this book inspire in you a passion and hope for that revival to come; and as you read through the other themes, may your hope be placed in the eternal, living God. 'For in this hope we were saved. But hope that is seen is no hope at all. Who hopes for what he already has? But if we hope for what we do not yet have, we wait for it patiently' (Rom. 8:24–25).

How to use the Bible

A question I am often asked, especially by young Christians, is this: why do I need to read the Bible?

We need to read the Bible in order to know not only God's mind for the future but how to develop a daily walk with Him. God uses His Word to change people's lives and bring those lives into a deeper relationship with Himself and a greater conformity to His will. For over four decades now I have spent hours every week reading and studying the Scriptures. God has used this book to transform my life and to give me a sense of security in a shifting and insecure world.

How do we read the Bible? Do we just start at Genesis and make our way through to the book of Revelation? There are many ways to go about reading the Scriptures; let me mention the three most popular approaches.

One is to follow a reading plan such as is included in the *Every Day with Jesus Devotional Bible* or *Through the Bible in One Year*. The great advantage of following a reading plan is that your reading is arranged for you; in a sense you are being supervised. You are not left to the vagaries of uncertainty: what shall I read today, where shall I begin, at what point shall I end?

A second approach is to thread your way through the Scriptures by following a specific theme. It is quite staggering how many themes can be found in Scripture and what great spiritual rewards can be had by acquainting yourself with them. When I started writing *Every Day with Jesus* in 1965 I decided to follow the thematic approach and I wondered how long I would be able to keep it up. Now, nearly forty years later, I am still writing and expounding on different themes of the Bible, and the truth is that I have more biblical themes and subjects than it is possible to deal with in one lifetime!

A third approach is by reading through a book of the Bible. This enables you to get into the mind of the writer and understand his message. Every book of the Bible has something unique and special to convey and, as with any book, this can only be understood when you read it from start to finish.

How to use the Bible

It is important to remember that all reading of the Bible ought to be preceded by prayer. This puts you in a spiritually receptive frame of mind to receive what God has to say to you through His Word. The Bible can be read by anyone but it can only be understood by those whose hearts are in tune with God – those who have come into a personal relationship with Him and who maintain that relationship through daily or regular prayer. This is how the Bible puts it: "The man without the Spirit does not accept the things that come from the Spirit of God, for they are foolishness to him, and he cannot understand them, because they are spiritually discerned" (1 Cor. 2:14).

Praying before you open your Bible should not be a mere formality. It is not the *act* that will make the Bible come alive but the *attitude*. Prayer enables us to approach the Scriptures with a humble mind. The scientist who does not sit down before the facts of the universe with an open mind, is not prepared to give up every preconceived idea and is not willing to follow wherever nature will lead him, will discover little or nothing. It is the same with the reading of the Scriptures; we must come to it with a humble and receptive mind or we too will get nowhere. Prayer enables us to have the attitude that says, "Speak, for your servant is listening" (1 Sam. 3:10).

If we are to grow in the Christian life then we must do more than just *read* the Bible – we must *study* it. This means that we must give time to poring over it, considering it, thinking about what it is saying to us and assimilating into our hearts and minds its doctrines and its ideas.

I have already pointed out that one of the ways of reading the Bible is by taking a theme and tracing it through the various books of the Bible. The pleasure this brings can be greatly enhanced by using this as a regular means of Bible study. When we study the Bible with the aid of concordances, lexicons and so on, we feed our minds, but when we study the Bible devotionally, we apply the Word of God to our hearts. Both exercises are necessary if we are to be completely rounded people but we must see that it is at the place of the devotional that we open up our hearts and expose ourselves to God's resources.

How to use the Bible

Let me encourage you also to take advantage of a reading plan as a further basis of study. Following this will enable you to cover the whole of the Bible in a set period. Those who have used this method tell of the most amazing spiritual benefits. One person who had read through the whole of the Bible in a year said to me, "It demanded more discipline than I thought I was capable of, but the rewards have been enormous." When I asked her what these rewards were, she said, "I used to have a partial view of God's purposes because I dipped into my Bible just here and there as it suited me. Now, however, I feel as if I have been looking over God's shoulder as He laid out the universe, and I feel so secure in the knowledge that He found a place for me in that marvellous plan." There can be no doubt that reading through the entire Bible in a set period enables one to gain a perspective that has tremendous positive spiritual consequences.

The third form of study – reading through a book of the Bible at a time – has the advantage of helping you understand the unity and diversity of the Bible. It is quite incredible how so many writers sharing their thoughts at different times of history combine to say similar things and give a consistent emphasis. Reading and pondering on this gives you such an appreciation of the wisdom of God in putting together this marvellous volume that it fires your soul and quickly brings praise and adoration to your lips.

I have found the best way to study a book of the Bible is to read it through once for a sense of the whole, and then to read it again, making a note of anything that strikes me, such as a principle to be applied, an insight to be stored away in my heart, or a thought to be shared with someone who is struggling.

One thing is sure, time spent with the Bible is not wasted. The more one loves God the more one will love the Bible. And the more one loves the Bible the more one will love God. Always remember this unique volume – God's one and only published work – yields its treasures only to those who read it, study it and obey it.

Selwyn Hughes

Preparing
for
Revival

A new day dawns

For reading & meditation – Esther 4:1–17

*'... who knows whether you have not come to the kingdom
for such a time as this?' (v.14, RSV)*

A re we on the verge of one of the greatest spiritual revivals the world has ever seen? There are evidences that this is so. In all the years that I have been a Christian I have never witnessed such a burden and expectancy for revival as I do at this moment among the true people of God. The last part of the twentieth century was characterised by the word 'renewal', but now the word is slowly losing currency, and another is taking its place – 'revival'. And why? Because great and wonderful though renewal is, many are beginning to see that there are greater things in our Father's storehouse.

Many years ago, CWR was founded in order to become a voice for revival. Some said at that time that the emphasis was ill-timed as the breath of the risen Christ was already blowing upon the Church in charismatic renewal. Thankful though I was for the showers of renewal that were falling, I still felt that God's call to me was to elevate the spiritual vision of the Church to focus its gaze on revival. At times, the message I preached seemed to fall on deaf ears. Now, however, things are different.

Now CWR receives letters from ministers or church leaders that say something like this: 'Our church is burdened for revival – how can we prepare ourselves for it?' Hence this theme: God, so I believe, is about to send revival to His people – our task is to provide the prayer ramp over which His purposes can pass.

FURTHER STUDY
Deut. 11:1–17;
Jer. 3:1–25;
Joel 2:23–27
1. To what do we
equate the latter rain?
2. Why had God
withheld the latter
rain from the children
of Israel?

Prayer

O God, I begin this theme with a sense of great anticipation. This matter of revival has the feel of the real and the eternal upon it. Lead on: I follow – follow with all my being. Amen.

What is revival?

For reading & meditation – Habakkuk 3:1–19

'… O LORD, revive thy work in the midst of the years …'
(v.2, KJV)

We said yesterday that the Holy Spirit is witnessing to many parts of His Church that a spiritual revival is on the way. Probably no greater issue faces the Church at this moment than this issue of revival. Many are very confused about the subject so we must begin by carefully defining the term. We ask ourselves, therefore: What is revival? Before coming to a definite conclusion, it might be helpful if we were to look first at what it is not. Revival is not evangelism. Great damage has been done by people who insist on placing it in this category.

During my first visit to the United States in 1961, I was asked by one group if I would preach at the 'revival' they would be having in their church in a few months' time. I was overwhelmed by what I thought was the faith of the leaders in believing that a revival would take place at a certain time in a certain week until I was informed that, in most American churches, the term 'revival' meant a series of evangelistic meetings, such as I am often invited to preach at in England. But to place revival on a par with evangelism is to misunderstand both its nature and its purpose.

FURTHER STUDY

Isa. 32:1–33:24;
Psa. 80:18;
119:25,40,50,88

1. What will happen when God's Spirit moves in revival?
2. How will this affect evangelism?

Evangelism is the expression of the Church – something brought about by a combination of human and divine effort, but revival is an experience in the Church – something brought about by God alone. Evangelism is the work men do for God: revival is the work God does for men.

Prayer

O Father, help me to clarify the true nature of revival in these weeks that lie ahead, for unless I see clearly, how can I pray clearly? Help me, dear Lord. In Jesus' name. Amen.

What revival is not

For reading & meditation – Isaiah 64:1–8

'Why don't you tear the sky apart and come down …'
(v.1, GNB)

Revival is not evangelism or the restoration of backslidden Christians. There are times in church life when large numbers of lethargic Christians make a new and deeper commitment to Jesus Christ. This, of course, is highly desirable, and worthy of much praise and gratitude to God – but it is not revival. In one meeting at which I was present, about 500 Christians responded to an invitation to make a total commitment to Christ. Later, a report in a Christian newspaper stated: 'Revival breaks out at a Deeper Life Conference'. It was true that Christians had been individually revived, but in the classic sense of the word, it was not strictly a revival.

Revival is not an unusual sense of God's presence resting upon a particular church or fellowship for a number of weeks or months. I have known churches where a great sense of God's presence predominates for a few weeks more than usual, and they come to speak of it as revival. Supernatural things may happen but in the strictest sense of the word, it cannot be described as revival. While the salvation of sinners, the restoration of backsliders, and an unusual sense of God's presence hovering over a congregation for a period of time are by-products of revival, these experiences by themselves do not necessarily constitute it. You can see people converted, renewed, restored, and yet fall short of revival. Revival includes all these things, yet it surpasses them all.

FURTHER STUDY

1 Kings 18:1–39;

Isa. 35:6–7;

Lam. 3:40–42

1. In what way is Elijah's experience a picture of revival?
2. Write out your own definition of revival.

Prayer

O Father, already I feel something happening to my spirit as I contemplate the glory and wonder of true revival. Fan this desire into a powerful flame. For Jesus' sake. Amen.

Wake up and live

For reading & meditation – Isaiah 52:1–15

'Awake, awake, O Zion, clothe yourself with strength. Put on your garments of splendour …' (v.1)

We ended yesterday's meditation by looking at the many things that revival is not. Today, by studying the Bible and looking at Church history we will attempt to define what revival really is. It is important to remember that any definition can never adequately describe the true nature of revival. 'Revival in a definition,' said one preacher, 'is like David in Saul's armour – it just does not fit.' Revival, like salvation, is grander and greater and more glorious than anything that can be said or written about it.

Having said that, however, we must still struggle to find a working definition of the term. From the Old Testament we see that the word comes from the root meaning 'to live'. The basic idea contained in the word is the return of something to its true nature and purpose. G. Campbell Morgan put it this way:

> Revival is the re-animation of the life of the believer (not the unregenerate as they are 'dead in sin') … there can only be revival where there is life to revive.

FURTHER STUDY

Hos. 6:1–11;
Isa. 35:6;
Psa. 80:7; 85:6

1. What was Hosea's exhortation?
2. What two things happen when God revives us?

A revival, then, is for Christians, not sinners. Sinners don't need revival: they need a resurrection. Based on these thoughts, I believe the definition of Christmas Evans, the famous Welsh preacher, is the most effective I have ever heard. It is this: 'Revival is God bending down to the dying embers of a fire that is just about to go out, and breathing into it, until it bursts again into flame.' In revival, men and women come alive to the life of God.

Prayer

O Father, breathe on any dying embers in Your Church this day – myself included – until out of the ashes rises a new and living flame. In Jesus' name I ask it. Amen.

Patterned after Pentecost

For reading & meditation – Acts 3:19–26

*'... that times of refreshing may come from the presence
of the Lord.' (v.19, RSV)*

Revival, we said yesterday, means 'wake up and live'. D.M. Panton describes it as 'the inrush of divine life into a body threatening to become a corpse'. The very word 'revival' suggests that once life existed in all its fullness, but, for some reason, it waned and became moribund. When the prefix 're' is used in a word, such as revival, re-animation, return, and so on, it simply means 'back again'. Revival, then, is the Christian Church going back again to the God-given norm. And what is that 'norm'? Nothing less than the experience of Pentecost.

Peter made it clear that when God's people repented of their sin, this would be followed by 'times of refreshing from the presence of the Lord'. 'This phrase,' says J. Edwin Orr 'is one of the best definitions of revival in the Bible.' Isn't this what happens when true revival takes place? The Church returns to the glory and power that prevailed at Pentecost.

Picture the scene described in Acts chapter 3. Except, of course, for the ministry of Jesus, no prophet had spoken in the nation of Israel for four hundred years. Spiritually the people were at an all-time low – broken, beggared and bankrupt. Then the Spirit came. Thousands were brought into a new and living relationship with God. It was a 'time of refreshing from the presence of the Lord'. Every revival contains some feature of the Day of Pentecost, for Pentecost is God's pattern of blessing for His Church.

FURTHER STUDY

Acts 2:1–47;

Zech. 4:6;

Isa. 40:31

*1. List seven results
of the outpouring of
the Holy Spirit.
2. How do these
relate to revival?*

Prayer

Gracious Father, send us, I pray, another 'time of refreshing from the presence of the Lord', for Your Church is patterned after Pentecost and we cannot live effectively without it. Amen.

The pattern for revival

For reading & meditation – John 7:37–44

*'… Up to that time the Spirit had not been given since Jesus
had not yet been glorified.' (v.39)*

Why is the pattern for revival based on Pentecost? Why couldn't it be based on an Old Testament revival such as took place under the leadership of Nehemiah, Hezekiah or King David?

Old Testament revivals did not contain enough ingredients upon which to construct a norm. The Holy Spirit – always the prime agent in any revival – worked in a limited capacity in Old Testament times. He came and went, providing temporary infusions of power for temporary tasks. Then again, He came upon people from the outside as opposed to residing permanently on the inside. He could never fully reveal His true nature, for there was no perfect vehicle through whom He could manifest Himself.

John draws all these strands of thought together into a single statement when he says that the Spirit could not be given until Jesus had been glorified. Only through the life and death of Jesus could God's power be properly seen and understood. Eternal power must be seen not only in the context of signs, wonders and miracles, but at work on a cross, forgiving its enemies and triumphing over denial, betrayal and an ugly death. It must be seen in supreme modesty and humility as Jesus showed, when, after triumphing over those who brought about His crucifixion, He chose not to appear in all His glory to make them cower before Him. The power that fell at Pentecost was Christlike power, which became, from that point, the pattern for all future manifestations of power.

FURTHER STUDY

John 16:1–16;
15:26; 6:63;
Rom. 8:11

1. What do you understand by the word 'quicken'?
2. List several things Jesus said concerning the Holy Spirit.

Prayer

O Father, I am so thankful that You have fixed the pattern for all revivals at Pentecost. And because it is built around Jesus, I know it can never be changed or superseded. I am so thankful. Amen.

The pattern fixed – yet continuous

For reading & meditation – Acts 2:29–41

'The promise is for you and your children and for all who are far off ...' (v.39)

Many Christians, when praying for revival, set their sights only on the Old Testament pattern. We can certainly learn many valuable lessons and find many challenges from the record of Old Testament revivals but we must not make them our pattern. The pattern for revival, as we saw yesterday, is Pentecost.

The Spirit could not have been fully given in the Old Testament dispensation because this would have set the wrong pattern. The Spirit could not have been fully given in the day of Jesus' humiliation (His birth, life and death), for that, too, would have set the wrong pattern. He could only be given in the day of Christ's triumph – His arrival on the throne – for that alone could set the right pattern.

Before we move into the weeks that lie ahead, let's settle this matter once and for all. Our prayers and expectations for revival must be based upon the greatest manifestation of the Holy Spirit the world has ever known – Pentecost. Don't be intimidated by theologians who tell you that Pentecost was simply a one-off experience which God will never want to repeat. The revivals that have taken place in the last few hundred years all contain one or more of the ingredients that were present at Pentecost. In some, the dominant feature has been conviction of sin, in others, abounding joy, and in others, amazing supernatural events. Perhaps the next revival will contain all the ingredients of Pentecost. Somehow, I think it will.

FURTHER STUDY
Acts 19:1–41;
Ezek. 36:27;
Acts 10:44
1. List some of the results when the Holy Spirit descended at Ephesus.
2. How did this affect the community?

Prayer

O Spirit of God, take from my heart any tendency or desire to limit You and Your power. Help me see that Pentecost is not the most You can do – but the least. For Your own dear name's sake, I pray. Amen.

Too big a gap

For reading & meditation – James 5:7–11

'… See how the farmer waits … how patient he is for the autumn and spring rains.' (v.7)

It has been a long time since Britain and the English-speaking world have been visibly shaken by an extraordinary outpouring of the Spirit of God. Most of us have to acknowledge that we have never been part of a deep and powerful revival. That, however, should not stop us desiring it, for, with the Acts of the Apostles before us, together with the records of history, we are able to see that God has greater things in store for us than we are presently witnessing and experiencing.

Our purpose this week then is to examine in more detail the ingredients of that first outpouring at Pentecost for there, as we said, we have the model of what God wants His Church to be.

A young Christian said to me some years ago, 'I've been a Christian for three months, and as I read the Acts of the Apostles, I sense that something is wrong.' 'What do you think it is?' I asked. He said, 'There seems to be too wide a gap between the Church of that day and the Church of today.' He had spotted it. There is! 'All revivals,' said Dr Martyn Lloyd-Jones, 'are in some way a return to Pentecost. Every revival in history repeats some aspect of that first great outpouring.'

The more clearly we understand what happened at Pentecost, the deeper our desire will be for a revival based on God's great pattern.

FURTHER STUDY

Acts 8; 11:19;13:3;
10:44–48

1. How did the coming of the Holy Spirit to Jerusalem spread further?
2. What were the results?

Prayer

O God, how foolish we are to be playing in puddles when we have the whole ocean of Your Spirit before us. Our hearts desire fullness. May it come in our day as it did at Pentecost. For Jesus' sake I ask it. Amen.

Unusual physical phenomena

For reading & meditation – Acts 2:1–13

'… a rushing mighty wind … And there appeared … tongues
like as of fire …' (vv.2–3, KJV)

W e continue focusing our thoughts on that first great outpouring
at Pentecost, in order to identify some of the ingredients
present in a mighty move of God.

The first thing that strikes even the most casual reader of
the second chapter of Acts is that the descent of the Spirit is
accompanied by extraordinary physical occurrences. We read that
God sent a 'mighty rushing wind' and caused 'tongues of fire' to rest
on the disciples. Why, we ask ourselves, did God cause such strange
physical occurrences to accompany the descent of the Spirit?

The answer is quite clear – God called attention to Himself and
His work through unusual physical phenomena.

Some say, of course, that the wind and fire were occurrences that
took place only on the Day of Pentecost and were never repeated.
That may be so, but similar supernatural happenings took place later
in the book of Acts – events that were most certainly on a par with
what happened at Pentecost (see further study section).

The history of revivals, subsequent to the Acts of the Apostles,
show that whenever God floods His Church with
extraordinary power He usually accompanies
it with unusual physical phenomena. Why He
should do so is His own business: ours is to
make sure that we do not quench the Spirit by
our intellectualism and unwillingness to accept
the supernaturalism that generally accompanies
revival.

FURTHER STUDY

Acts 16:25–40;
4:31; 8:39; 9:3;
12:7

1. List the
extraordinary events
that occurred in the
Early Church.
2. What is the last
supernatural event
you remember
witnessing?

Prayer

O God, my Father, I am so thankful that You are opening my eyes to the
greatness of Your power. Now that I have seen what You can do, help me not
to settle for anything less. In Jesus' name. Amen.

Extraordinary preaching

For reading & meditation – Acts 2:22–41

'When the people heard this, they were cut to the heart and said ... "Brothers, what shall we do?"' (v.37)

A nother ingredient present at the outpouring of the Spirit at Pentecost was that of extraordinary preaching. One sermon, preached by Peter, resulted in three thousand souls coming into the kingdom of God. Richard Owen Roberts, in one of his books, says that there are three kinds of preaching.

(1) Mouth to ear preaching. This takes place when the words from the mouth of the preacher enter the ears of the hearer but go no further.

(2) Head to head preaching. This is where the thoughts of the preacher influence the thoughts of the hearer, affecting the mind, but nothing more.

(3) Heart to heart preaching. This is where something happens in the preacher's heart of so compelling a nature that it runs like quicksilver into the heart of the hearer, producing great and wonderful results.

FURTHER STUDY

Acts 7; 9:29–31;
10:44; 13:38–43;
17:22–34

1. What were some responses to the apostles' preaching?
2. What was its main emphasis?

That was the kind of preaching that took place at Pentecost.

In revival, preachers experience an extra-ordinary dynamic flowing through their words. Simple statements and sentences bristle with a strange and unusual power. Men and women are cut to the quick with conviction. You may have heard preaching that has come very close to this, but, believe me, it is nothing compared to what one hears in revival.

Prayer

O Father, hasten the day, I pray, when once again Your servants will preach, not mouth to ear, or head to head, but heart to heart. In Jesus' name. Amen.

Extraordinary awesomeness

For reading & meditation – Acts 2:42–47

'And fear came upon every soul; and many wonders and signs were done through the apostles.' (v.43, RSV)

T oday we look at another ingredient of revival – an extraordinary sense of God's holiness. Something of this is undoubtedly present in the Church at all times, but when revival comes, the sense of God's holiness is greatly heightened. Such was the sense of God's holiness in the early Church that on one occasion we read: 'No-one else dared join them, even though they were highly regarded by the people' (Acts 5:13).

Every great move of God since Pentecost has contained this impressive ingredient. It is probably true to say that the very first evidence that revival is present is when men and women are gripped by a heightened sense of God's awesomeness and holiness.

Conduct, that hitherto appeared respectable, now seems unbelievably wicked. Prejudices that characterised professing Christians for years are seen as grievous sins. Private indulgences, upon which people have looked with favour, suddenly seem to merit all the wrath of God. Prayerlessness, ignorance of Scripture, sins of omission, pride, self-centred living, long-forgotten sins against members of the Body of Christ, words carelessly spoken are no longer defended by a myriad of excuses, but are laid open before the God 'with whom we have to do'. People who thought themselves worthy of heaven stand amazed that they are not in hell.

FURTHER STUDY

Acts 5:1–11;
8:9–25; 9:31; 10:2

1. What was Ananias and Sapphira's sin?
2. How did the apostles maintain holiness in the Church?

Prayer

Father, one thing seems clear – in an age which fails to see the heinousness of sin, nothing can help us except a revelation of Your majesty and holiness. Let it happen, dear Lord, in this generation. For Jesus' sake. Amen.

Extraordinary insight

For reading & meditation – Acts 2:14–24

*'… and you, with the help of wicked men, put him to death
by nailing him to the cross.' (v.23)*

I doubt whether Peter really understood the meaning of the cross until it was revealed to him by the Spirit on the Day of Pentecost. Doubtless its meaning deepened for him as he waited with the others those ten days in the Upper Room, but the full understanding of it came only as the Holy Spirit revealed it to him on that first Day of Pentecost. Empowered by the Spirit, he was able to make its meaning clear to the crowd gathered before him some of whom, no doubt, had actually been present at the Saviour's crucifixion. After Peter's sermon, such was their understanding of the cross, they were 'cut to the heart and said 'Brothers, what shall we do?' (Acts 2:37).

The cross of Christ always takes on a new and precious meaning in times of revival. Awakened hearts see the cross, not in general terms, but in personal terms. It is no longer 'He died for the sins of the world', but 'He died for me'. The cross becomes so personal that the wounds, bruises and stripes Jesus received, along with the insults, the taunts and the jeers, provoke deep personal sorrow that He had to endure such agony for 'such a one as me'. These stirrings in the hearts of revived Christians drive the soul to contemplate the cross in a way never before known. All the devils in hell and all the wickedness on earth do not have the power to keep the awakened Christian from deeper consecration and devoted love to such a Saviour.

FURTHER STUDY

Acts 26:1–23;
Gal. 6:14;
Eph. 2:16;
Col. 1:20

1. How did Paul respond to Agrippa?
2. When was the last time you spoke to someone about the cross?

Prayer

Lord Jesus, relentless Lover and Redeemer, corner my soul until I see Your cross in a new and glorious light. My view of it tends to be so general: make it personal, dear Lord, today. Amen.

Extraordinary spiritual interests

For reading & meditation – Acts 6:1–7
'... and will give our attention to prayer and the ministry of the word.' (v.4)

Prior to Pentecost, the disciples no doubt spent a good deal of their time praying and pondering the Scriptures. After Pentecost, however, both prayer and the study of God's Word took on a new and greater meaning. So important did this become that they decided to abstain from their administrative tasks in order to give themselves continually to prayer and the ministry of the Word. If it be said that these men were the ministers of the Early Church, and as such were obligated to spend their time in this way, then consider the Christians of Berea of whom it was said that they 'examined the Scriptures every day to see if what Paul said was true' (Acts 17:11).

In today's Church, many Christians are content to let their pastors or elders do the praying and studying for them, but in revival each Christian finds their heart leaping toward prayer and the perusal of the Word of God. They learn to appreciate not only the 'sincere milk of the word' but the 'strong meat' also, and delight in lengthy, reverent, searching study of God's Word, and in the application of its truths to their lives. Prayer, too, which prior to revival might have seemed a drudgery becomes pure delight. And when the allotted time for prayer is up, instead of relief that the chore is over, there is sorrow that the time has passed so swiftly. In revival, men and women enjoy, as Moffatt puts it in 1 Samuel 21:7 – being 'detained in the presence of the Eternal'.

FURTHER STUDY

Acts 3:1–10; 4:24;
12:12; 21:5

*1. Where were Peter and John going after the Holy Spirit fell?
2. What was the result?*

Prayer

O Father, the more I ponder this great subject of revival, the more I see that at present Your Church is like a car working on only half its cylinders. We can't go on running a stalling car. Help us, Lord. For Jesus' sake. Amen.

Extraordinary excitement

For reading & meditation – Acts 8:1–8

'So there was great joy in that city.' (v.8)

A nother ingredient of revival is extraordinary fervour and excitement. One has only to read the pages of the Acts of the Apostles to feel the throb of excitement and joy that characterised the early disciples.

The Early Church was excited about everything that was connected with God and His kingdom. They were excited about Jesus, about the coming of the Spirit, about the establishing of His kingdom, and about His coming again. The dull apathetic attitude, which is present in so many churches today, was a thing unknown in the first-century Christian community. They were gripped by intense earnestness and a spirit of expectation. The God that raised up Jesus from the dead had raised them also from their own graves of sin. The power that had elevated Christ to the heavens and placed Him at the right hand of the Father was working in them with all its quickening might.

In revival, Christians often have to defend themselves against the charge that they are drunk. And what are the marks of a man who is a little drunk? He is happy, hearty, jocular, exhilarated, genial and exuberant. Most of today's Christians do not come under the same dark suspicion as did our first-century brothers and sisters, but it is hardly to our credit to stress such a distinction. We are more dignified, more sophisticated, more respectable and more sober – and more in need of revival.

FURTHER STUDY

Acts 4; 15:3; 16:25;
Rom. 14:17

1. How did Peter and John stir things up?
2. What was the response?

Prayer

O Father, one thing urges me on – You are a relentless and inexorable Lover, and You will not let Your Church settle down this side of victory. So deepen my desire for a return to Pentecost. For Jesus' sake. Amen.

'What mean these stones?'

For reading & meditation – Joshua 4:14–24

'... when your descendants ask their fathers, "What do these stones mean?" tell them ...' (vv.21–22)

C an we expect these same ingredients of revival to be seen in the Church after Pentecost? I believe we can. In fact, God has been pleased to show us, in almost every century of the Church, that what He did at Pentecost, He can do again.

This week I want to examine with you, therefore, some of the great revivals of history with a view to identifying in them the same characteristics that were present on the Day of Pentecost and in the life of the Early Church. Some might feel hesitant about looking outside the Bible for confirmation of what we are saying, but I believe there is a clear biblical principle we can follow here which is seen in the passage we are looking at today. God, knowing how easy it is for the human mind to forget even as great and significant an event as the crossing of the Jordan, commanded Joshua to raise up a memorial of twelve stones, so that when future generations asked what they meant, they could be told precisely what happened.

How sad it is that the great events of the past – even spiritual events – can be so easily forgotten. God has done great things for us in the past and if we ignore them, we do so to our peril. I propose to raise up before you this week some 'memorial stones' from some of the great revivals of history, in the hope that as you gaze at what God has done, you will draw fresh inspiration from it and move forward with renewed faith and greater expectancy.

FURTHER STUDY

Heb. 1; 8:5;
1 Cor. 10:11;
2 Pet. 2:6

1. Why has God given us historical records?
2. What can we learn from them?

Prayer

Gracious Father, I want to have an informed and reflective mind. As I look back at the 'stones' of revival You have set up in history, deepen my desire to see You do it again. For Jesus' sake. Amen.

Strange happenings in Ulster

For reading & meditation – Joel 2:21–32

'… I will pour out my Spirit on all people.' (v.28)

L ooking back can sometimes be a wasteful exercise, but not when we focus upon the great spiritual events of history. Dr Martyn Lloyd-Jones once said, 'So dulled is the human mind by sin that we would forget the death of Christ were it not for the fact that God has commanded us to remind ourselves of it regularly by breaking bread and drinking wine.' Today, therefore, we shall begin to look at revivals of the past in order to see how every revival is, to some extent at least, a return to Pentecost. We said previously that one of the first noticeable features in an extraordinary move of God was *strange and unusual physical manifestations*. The chief characteristic of the 1859 revival in Ulster was, what has come to be called, the 'strikings down'. People would fall to the ground in the streets or in the fields and would lie there motionless for hours. When they recovered, they sensed that God had visited them, and they would worship Him and praise Him with great fervour and excitement.

So astonishing was this physical phenomenon that crowds of non-Christians gathered where believers were present just to see these physical manifestations take place. Many were converted as they sensed that God was at work. Our human minds may find it difficult to accept such strange happenings, but we must face the fact that, in revival, God draws attention to Himself by unusual and inexplicable physical manifestations.

FURTHER STUDY

Dan. 3:13–30;
Num. 22:28–30;
Exod. 7:20–21;
Acts 28:1–6

1. How did Nebuchadnezzar respond to the manifestation of God's power?
2. In what ways did God reveal Himself?

Prayer

O Father, there is something in me that fears the unusual and the inexplicable. But enlarge my understanding and my faith that I might not hinder Your power or quench Your Spirit. In Jesus' name I pray. Amen.

David Davies – a man ablaze

For reading & meditation – 1 Corinthians 2:1–10

'My message and my preaching were … with a demonstration of the Spirit's power.' (v.4)

Today we look at the second of these characteristics of revival – *extraordinary preaching*. Almost every revival carries evidence of very ordinary preachers being transformed as the Spirit came upon them, but perhaps the most conclusive evidence of this is the record of what happened in 1904 to David Davies, a minister in the town of Swansea, South Wales. Prior to the revival, David Davies was known to be a fine Christian minister, but he was regarded by most as an extremely poor speaker. He would cough and splutter his way through a sermon, and were it not for the consistent Christian character he bore, many would not have gone to listen to him. Then one day revival hit Swansea, and David Davies became a man transformed. He went into his pulpit the next Sunday, and the people could hardly believe their ears. Gone was the hesitancy and stuttering; instead he spoke with the most amazing authority and power. Following his message that Sunday, hundreds of men and women were converted to Christ, and week by week thereafter David Davies wielded an exceptional ministry in the power and demonstration of the Spirit.

When the revival simmered down the following year, the strange thing was that David Davies reverted to his previous hesitant style of preaching. This underlined, even more clearly, the fact that his anointed preaching was not the result of human effort, but a mighty manifestation of the Living God.

FURTHER STUDY

Acts 3:11–26; 4:13;
9:29; 14:3; 19:8;
Matt. 7:29

1. What characteristic did Peter display?
2. What was his message?

Prayer

O Father, You know my tendency to analyse things and to want to explain them. Show me that there are some inexplicable things that belong to You, and help me to accept them. For Jesus' sake. Amen.

Glorious in holiness

For reading & meditation – Psalm 93:1–5

'… holiness adorns your house for endless days, O LORD.'
(v.5)

The third ingredient in revival is *an extraordinary sense of God's majesty and holiness*. Just as God's awesomeness and holiness were made known to the Early Church, so they have been made known in every great spiritual awakening since.

One example is found in the great revival under Charles Finney in America during the mid-eighteenth century. As Finney preached on such subjects as 'The holiness of God' or 'Sinners in the hands of an angry God', men and women were given such a revelation of God's holiness that the thought of remaining in a state of sinfulness became intolerable, and they would cry out: 'O God, save me from myself and from my sin. Slay me, but do not let me persist another day in this awful condition.' Some have put this down to Finney's eloquence and logic, but eloquence and logic apart from the anointing of the Spirit are utterly powerless to bring about lasting change in a human heart.

In one service in Northampton, Massachusetts, such was the anointing on Finney's message that the whole congregation of about 500 people rose up as one man crying out: 'O God, we are not worthy to stand in Your presence. Save us – or destroy us.' Such was the revelation of God's holiness during the days of Finney that anyone who committed sin would make an instant confession of it. Christians, particularly, feared to enter a church with unconfessed sin in their hearts, unless, in front of the congregation, their sin might be made known.

FURTHER STUDY

Acts 16:25–34;
2 Chron. 7.1-3;
Exod. 40:34;
1 Kings 8:11

1. How did the jailer respond to God's presence?
2. What is 'the glory of the Lord'?

Prayer

O Father, I am almost afraid to ask You to reveal Your holiness to me, for I know then that I will have to break with all sin. Help me overcome this reluctance. In Jesus' name. Amen.

The glory of the cross

For reading & meditation – Galatians 6:11–18

*'… God forbid that I should glory except in the cross of our
Lord Jesus Christ …' (v.14, NKJV)*

A nother ingredient found in revival is *a new insight into the
cross*. One such revival in which the work of Christ on the
cross was most significantly underlined was that which took place
under the ministry of Christmas Evans in North Wales during
the mid-eighteenth century. Christmas Evans had always been an
eloquent and forceful speaker, but when the revival came, it touched
his tongue with an even greater eloquence and power. The main
emphasis in all his preaching was the work of Christ on the cross.
When he came to the part of his message that dealt with Christ's
death on the cross, his rugged features would take on a softness and
a gentleness that had to be seen to be believed, and his voice, usually
stern and demanding, became soft, mellow and persuasive.

A biographer says of him: 'Thousands who heard Christmas
Evans, having been content to wear the Cross as an ornament, now
found themselves viewing it as the place on which Christ bore their
own personal sins. The conviction was borne home to every man
and woman, that their very own sins put Christ there. In every place
he preached, multitudes would weep at the foot of
the cross, and end up wholly saved and redeemed.'
Can there be any movement of the Holy Spirit in
which the cross is not made prominent? Such a
thing is unthinkable. It is as impossible as a river
without a source, or a day without light.

FURTHER STUDY

Matt. 27:26–61;
1 Cor. 2:1-2, 9:16;
Col. 2:13–14

1. What was Paul's
declaration?
2. Why is the cross so
central?

Prayer

O Father, I knew all the time that my sins hurt You, but I never understood the
full extent of that hurt until I saw You dying for me on the cross. Illuminate its
meaning even more fully – to me and the whole world. In Jesus' name. Amen.

In love with Jesus

For reading & meditation – Song of Solomon 1:1–7

'... we will remember thy love more than wine ...' (v.4, KJV)

Another common element in any revival is that of *an intense interest in prayer and the reading of the Scriptures*. A classic example is the revival which happened in Wales at the beginning of this century. When the fire fell, as the Welsh like to put it, one of the first indications that God was at work was evidenced by people's intense desire to pray and read the Bible. Meetings lasted from ten in the morning until twelve at night. There was little preaching. Singing, testimony, prayer and reading the Bible aloud were the predominant features. Coal miners, thousands of feet below the earth would gather together during their food breaks, not to eat, but to pray and read the Scriptures aloud. Some would even gather at the pithead an hour before work in order to sing and pray. Often the manager and officials of the mine would join in.

This is characteristic not only of the Welsh revival, but of every revival. When God comes down upon His people in the way we are describing, it invariably happens that, instead of excuses for not praying and reading the Scriptures, revived Christians find no other activity so delightful and beneficial. Why should this be so? Simply because the revived Christian has fallen in love. The prime desire of every lover is to be with his beloved. He delights to talk to her, to spend time with her, to listen to her voice, to focus on her endless charm. And so it is with revival.

FURTHER STUDY

Psa. 119:1–16;
97–107;
Acts 2:42;
2 Tim. 2:15

1. What was Paul's exhortation to Timothy?
2. What did the Early Church continue to do?

Prayer

O Lord Jesus, how I long that once again Your Church might know You in this way. Bring us soon to the place where we cannot think apart from You, love apart from You or be apart from You. For Your own dear name's sake. Amen.

An exciting Church

For reading & meditation – Psalm 30:1–12

'… weeping may remain for a night, but rejoicing comes in the morning.' (v.5)

We consider now the last characteristic of revival – *extraordinary fervour and excitement*. We have already spoken of the 1859 revival which, measured by its impact on both the Church and the world, was one of the greatest outpourings of God's Spirit since the Day of Pentecost. The 1859 revival is sometimes called the 'International Revival' because it broke out simultaneously in America, Ulster and many other places. Once people had repented of their sins, and had found perfect peace with God, it invariably happened that they would be filled to overflowing with deep and lasting joy.

Let no one think that revival is associated with gloom and heaviness and a downcast spirit. There is always a period of mourning for sin, but this is soon followed by waves of endless delight and joy. It is surely amongst the most tragic misrepresentations of truth when historians write that, in times of revival, Christians act like 'dejected melancholiacs'. It is a travesty of the true tradition of revival. Revival imparts an immense sense of wellbeing. It produces a witness in the hearts of believers that all is well within. It makes music inside the soul, and bestows a glad exuberance. Compare what I am saying with the dull, apathetic attitude which is common in many parts of today's Church. Only the Almighty can produce the change. O God, send a revival.

FURTHER STUDY

Acts 5:12–42; 8:6;
Isa. 61:10;
1 Pet. 1:8

1. What does revival bring with it?
2. How did the apostles answer the Sanhedrin?

Prayer

Father, day by day, my appetite for revival is being whetted. I see that only an invasion from heaven can change things. And so with all my heart, I echo that cry: O God, send a revival. For Jesus' sake. Amen.

The 'when' of revival

For reading & meditation – Hosea 10:8–12

'… for it is time to seek the LORD, until he comes …' (v.12)

W hen does revival usually come? The answer is simple – when the Church is at a low ebb spiritually. It is my belief that we are at such a place right now. 'But surely that cannot be,' says someone. 'After several decades of charismatic Christianity, when thousands of Christians have been renewed, the Church at last has turned a corner. She is on the way to spiritual greatness and supremacy.' Not so. Despite the renewal that has taken place and the great activity in the realm of evangelism – things for which we are indeed thankful – the reality is that, generally speaking, the Church in the West is on the decline. Every year denominations report great reductions in numbers, and the Church's influence in the world grows less and less.

The patient may have all the outward signs of good health, but when proper tests are given, the results show cause for deep concern. Don't be misled, I beg you, by the sabre rattling that goes on in today's Church. We sing, we shout, we hold occasional large meetings and conferences, but when it is all over, what impact have we made on society? Some perhaps, but far less than we ought. 'Success,' said someone, 'is measured not by what we are, but by what we are, compared to what we could be.' All the good we accomplish is nothing compared to what needs to be accomplished. The world laughs at our attempts to influence it. It sees us as weak, feeble and ineffectual. It is time to seek the Lord.

FURTHER STUDY

Luke 11:1–13;

2 Chron. 7:14;

Deut. 4:29;

Isa. 55:6

1. What has God promised to those who seek?
2. How did Jesus illustrate this?

Prayer

O Father, I realise that the problem is not that the Church isn't strong enough, but that it isn't weak enough. For when we are weak, we are strong, strong in Your strength and not our own. Bring us to this point, gracious Father – now. Amen.

Why no travail?

For reading & meditation – Isaiah 66:1–11

'... *Yet no sooner is Zion in labour than she gives birth to her children.*' (v.8)

The Church of today, generally speaking, is a prayerless Church. Many churches in Great Britain go from week to week without a public prayer meeting of any kind. More upsetting is the fact that many individual Christians have no regular times of private prayer when they commune alone with God. There are exceptions, of course, but in general there is such a perfunctory attitude toward prayer that it is little less than scandalous. The public prayer meeting has often been called 'The Cinderella of the Church', and how fitting that description is of contemporary Christianity. How many churches do you know where as many attend the prayer meeting as the Sunday morning worship service?

'We wish revival would come to us as it came in the Hebrides,' said a pastor to Leonard Ravenhill – author of *Why Revival Tarries*. 'But revival didn't come to the Hebrides by wishing,' said Ravenhill. 'The heavens were opened and the mighty power of the Lord shook those islands because a group of people waited, tear-stained and travailing, before the throne of the living God.'

The birth of a child is preceded by months of burden and days of travail: so is the birth of revival. Jesus prayed for His Church, but then, to bring it to birth, He gave Himself in death. It was when Zion travailed that she brought forth children.

FURTHER STUDY
Rom. 8:22–39;
Luke 18:1;
John 16:24;
Eph. 6:18

1. When do 'all things work together for good'?
2. How does this apply to revival?

Prayer

My Father, deepen my conviction that prayer is not just a duty but a necessity. If I, and my brothers and sisters, fail here then anaemia spreads through our whole being. Give me the mind to pray, the desire to pray, the will to pray. In Jesus' name. Amen.

Will the real Church stand up?

For reading & meditation – Revelation 3:14–22

'I know your deeds, that you are neither cold nor hot … I am
about to spit you out of my mouth' (vv.15–16)

A nother reason why the Church in the West is in a state of decline
is because it has compromised its convictions. Bonhoeffer said,
'Suffering is the badge of the Christian.' Luther said, 'Suffering is
one of the marks of the true Church.' Paul said, '… all who desire
to live a godly life in Christ Jesus will be persecuted' (2 Tim. 3:12,
RSV). And Jesus said, 'If they persecuted me, they will persecute
you' (John 15:20).

In the light of these statements, I ask: why does the Church here
in the West not suffer for the faith? The ugly truth is that we tend to
avoid suffering by compromise. Our moral lives are often not much
higher than the standards of the world. Our lives do not challenge
and rebuke unbelievers by their integrity and purity. We are seldom
bold to rebuke vice or speak out against the injustices in society.
Issues like abortion on demand and other unbiblical practices
deserve our united condemnation, but many Christians mind their
own business lest people are offended. The Christian message is so
diluted that we escape suffering by compromise.

Suppose we raised our standards, tightened
our disciplines, and spoke out against the breaking
of God's laws without fear or favour – what would
happen? There would be a huge public outcry. We
would be ridiculed, scorned and vilified in the
press, on radio and on television. But, at the same
time, the Church would be carried by God into a
place of mighty spiritual revival.

FURTHER STUDY

Matt. 5:1–16;

Heb. 11:36;

Acts 4:3, 8:1

1. What qualities
should be the
hallmark of the
Church?
2. What are the
two results when
these qualities are
demonstrated?

Prayer

O Lord, forgive us that we have become ensnared by the fear of people, that
we love the praise of men more than the praise of God. Help us to break with
compromise, and to stand up and be counted. For Jesus' sake. Amen.

Church robbers

For reading & meditation – Deuteronomy 14:22–29

'Thou shalt truly tithe ... And I will rebuke the devourer for your sakes ...' (Deut. 14:22; Mal. 3:11, KJV)

T he Church will never be powerful until Christians understand and apply the principles of financial giving. Giving must begin with tithes and offerings to God. No Christian can afford to neglect this. If we give to Him, He has promised that He will 'open ... the windows of heaven' (Mal. 3:10, KJV). I am convinced that multitudes of Christians in our land are robbing God through neglect of tithes and offerings.

What is the tithe? It is the first ten percent of our income. This belongs to the Lord. God encourages us to give offerings to meet special needs, but these offerings are above and beyond the tithe. Those who say that tithing is part of the law and does not apply today are quite wrong as the tithe was established before the law was given by Moses (Gen. 14:20), and tithing was reaffirmed by Christ in the New Testament (Matt. 23:23). God also promises that when we are faithful in our tithes and offerings, He 'will prevent pests from devouring ... crops, and the vines ...' (Mal. 3:11).

I am convinced that many of the financial difficulties in which Christians find themselves are due to their failure to tithe. This might sound harsh and legalistic to some, but don't, I beg you, dismiss the principle on those grounds. I have seen it working in my own life and in the lives of many others. Our failure to give tithes and offerings to the Lord will prevent Him from 'rebuking the devourer' for our sakes. We will be left to fend for ourselves.

FURTHER STUDY

2 Cor. 9:1–15;

Prov. 3:9;

Deut. 16:17;

Matt. 10:8;

1 Cor. 16:2

1. What sort of giver does God love?
2. What is the law of action and reaction here?

Prayer

O Father, I see even more clearly why Your Church, despite all its efforts and activities, is so powerless. Lord, help me, as well as my brothers and sisters, to pay back what I have robbed – and to begin today. In Jesus' name. Amen.

Brainwashed believers

For reading & meditation – Romans 12:1–8

'Don't let the world around you squeeze you into its own mould …' (v.2, Phillips)

Another evidence of the fact that the Church is spiritually declining is its worldliness. You can refrain from wordly pursuits, and still be wordly: or you can fully participate in what some might consider wordly pursuits, and still be deeply spiritual in character.

Worldliness is an attitude of mind – it means thinking like the world. Many Christians have allowed themselves to be squeezed into the mould of the world. Instead of letting Scripture be our standard and guide, we tend to form conclusions based on humanistic thinking. For example, take this issue – one supported not only by the world, but by large numbers of Christians also – that husbands and wives have equal rights and responsibilities in society. Not so, says the Bible. Both are equal before God, but both do not have equal responsibilities (Eph. 5:22–25). Another view held by the world and also by many Christians is that the standard for all behaviour is love. No, says the Bible, the standard for behaviour is truth (Rom. 2:2). Yet another popular view of life, and one supported by many Christians – marriages that are unhappy qualify for divorce. The answer, according to Scripture, is to overcome self-centredness and put one's own interests last (Phil. 2:3–4).

Slowly but surely the Church in this generation is allowing its thinking to be cast in the mould of the world. In revival, the Church influences the world.

FURTHER STUDY

Matt. 13:18–52;

Luke 21:34;

Col. 3:2;

1 John 2:15

1. What chokes God's Word?

2. What is your definition of 'worldliness'?

Prayer

O God, save us from the subtle influences of the world which brainwash us into believing things that are contrary to truth. Help us see that it is only when we take Your way that we can find ours. Amen.

Repentance – a missing note

For reading & meditation – Hebrews 6:1–12

'... *not laying again the foundation of repentance from acts that lead to death* ...' (v.1)

What characterised New Testament Christianity, but is scarcely heard in the Church today? Why, repentance of course! Time after time, in the Acts of the Apostles, the call to repentance was sounded. The mandatory nature of repentance was woven throughout the entire fabric of the life and ministry of Jesus Himself, and its urgent necessity repeatedly proclaimed. But repentance is a missing note in today's Church. 'Nowadays,' says James Robinson, an American evangelist, 'there is abroad an "easy believism". We tell people, "Say this prayer after me and you will have the gift of eternal life, a mansion on the main street of heaven, a diamond-studded crown, and you will be ruler over five cities in the Millennium."' An exaggeration? Well maybe, but there is still enough truth in it to hurt.

When men and women are not challenged to repent as they come into the Christian life, then they enter it with their ego still intact and dominant. Is it any wonder that we have so many Christians in the Church today who are argumentative, self-centred and rebellious? They never really surrendered their will when they entered the Christian life, and when any issue comes up between their will and God's will, they, never having learned the way of obedience and repentance, take a self-centred stance – one that is usually in opposition to the Almighty. A church which does not recognise the importance of repentance is a church that is rapidly in decline.

FURTHER STUDY

Rev. 2:1–29;

Acts 3:19; 8:22; 17:30;

Luke 15:21

1. What was Jesus' message to the Ephesian church?
2. What does 'repentance' mean?

Prayer

O Father, help Your Church to get its values and its allegiances straight. Left to ourselves, we tend to go astray. Save us, Lord Jesus – or else we perish. Amen.

The biggest scandal of all

For reading & meditation – John 13:31–35

'By this all men will know that you are my disciples, if you love one another.' (v.35)

Although there is a great deal of zeal and activity in today's Church, it has, nevertheless, the smell of decay upon it. This is evidenced in its general prayerlessness, its tendency to adopt worldly attitudes, its willingness to compromise, its disregard of God's principles of finance, and its failure to preach and practise the truth of wholehearted repentance.

Yet another of these signs is the unloving attitudes of Christians toward one another. I wrote to ten Christian leaders in Great Britain, asking where they saw the greatest need for concern in today's Church. All, with one exception, put at the top of his list the harsh, critical and unloving attitudes which Christians have one toward the other. A man I know, who travels the country visiting churches of all denominations, said: 'The biggest single issue that muffles the voice of the Church in Great Britain is the hostile and unloving attitudes Christians have one toward another.'

The truth is that such unloving attitudes can never be entirely eliminated from the Church by powerful preaching, expert counselling, or by writing about it in *Every Day with Jesus*! These things can help, but the real answer lies in a mighty Holy Spirit revival that cleanses the Church of all its blemishes and impurities, and gives it once again a powerful voice in the world. Our condition is desperate, but take heart, for, as Peter Lewis says, 'Revival comes to a desperate church not a triumphalist one.'

FURTHER STUDY

1 John 4:7–21;

Matt. 22:39;

John 15:12;

1 Thess. 3:12;

James 2:8

1. What is the royal law?

2. What is the standard for our love?

Prayer

O Father, Your Church may be busy and active at this time but it is obvious that only a mighty Holy Spirit revival can turn the tide. Let it come, dear Lord – and soon. For Jesus' sake. Amen.

How do revivals begin?

For reading & meditation – Psalm 85:1–13

'Will you not revive us again, that your people may rejoice in you?' (v.6)

Revivals begin in the sovereign purposes of God. Man has little to do with them: they are initiated not on earth, but in heaven. There are many things that Christians, by dedicated and spiritual effort, can bring to pass in the Church, but revival is not one of them. Evangelism, counselling, teaching and so on are work that men and women do for God. Revival is work that God does for men and women.

It is at this point – the sovereignty of God – that Christians tend to differ in their thinking about revival. One school of thought says: 'Revival is a sovereign act of God, and there is absolutely nothing that man has to do with it. God sends revival when He wills and does not consult or confer with any of His creation.' Another school of thought says: 'Revival can happen any time the Church wants it – providing she is willing to pay the price.' Charles Finney believed this. 'Revival,' he said, 'can happen in the Church the moment we are prepared to meet God's conditions.'

The truth, as is so often the case, is found, I believe, somewhere between these opposing views. Revival is a sovereign act of God in the sense that He alone can produce it, but it is transported to earth on the wings of fervent, believing prayer. Every revival in history – Pentecost included – began in heaven, but flowed into the Church across the ramp of intercessory prayer. This view, I believe, neither robs God of His sovereignty, nor man of his responsibility.

FURTHER STUDY

2 Kings 19:1–37;
Prov. 21:1;
Exod. 15:18;
Rev. 19:6

1. What caused Hezekiah to act as he did?
2. How did God show His sovereignty?

Prayer

Father, I know that revival can only begin with You, but I know, too, that it enters the world through earthly channels. Let me be one of those channels. In Jesus' name. Amen.

Two rails in Scripture

For reading & meditation – Matthew 18:15–20

'… if two of you on earth agree about anything you ask for, it will be done for you by my Father in heaven.' (v.19)

We continue meditating on the important issue of divine sovereignty. I have thought long and hard on this matter, and I have come to the conclusion that there are two rails running through Scripture – one is the sovereignty of God and the other is the responsibility of man. If you keep to just one of those rails, you end up being derailed. Those who talk only of the sovereignty of God end up minimising the responsibility of man. Those who talk only of the responsibility of man end up minimising the sovereignty of God. When we move along both rails, making sure that we do not place a disproportionate emphasis on either truth, then we are more likely to arrive at sounder conclusions.

How can we balance these great truths of the sovereignty of God and the responsibility of man? John Wesley said, 'God does nothing redemptively in the world – except through prayer.' Can you see what he is saying? Whenever God wants to bring His redemptive purposes to pass here on earth, He does not move arbitrarily but respects the principle of prayer, which He Himself has established. He, therefore, touches the hearts of certain of His people to pray – it may only be a few – and thus proceeds to transmit His purposes along the ramp that prayer has built. God never acts against His nature. He would cease to be God if He did so. And His nature is to use, not ignore, the great principle of prayer which He has so wonderfully established in His universe.

FURTHER STUDY

Acts 12:1–19;

Luke 1:10;

Acts 1:14; 4:24

1. What was the result of corporate prayer?

2. How did the believers respond to Peter's appearing?

Prayer

Gracious Father, my being is tingling to find out the way to revival. Help me move along both these rails of Scripture, keeping them in a balanced perspective. And save me from derailment. In Jesus' name. Amen.

The burden of revival

For reading & meditation – Jeremiah 23:33–40

'... "the burden of the Lord" ...' (v.36, RSV)

Although, from the divine point of view, revival begins in the sovereign purposes of God, it would be true to say, so I believe, that from the human point of view, it begins in the hearts of those who are burdened to see God work in an extraordinary way.

John Wallace, Principal of the Bible College I attended in my youth, used to say: 'Before there can be a blessing, somebody has to bear a burden.' He went on to illustrate it in this way: 'Before deliverance came to the nation of Israel in Egypt, Moses had to bear a burden. Before the great temple of God was built, Solomon had to bear a burden. Before the sins of the world could be removed, Jesus had to bear a burden. Before there can be a blessing, somebody has to bear a burden.'

This is one of the great principles of Scripture which can be traced right through the Bible from Genesis to Revelation. It can be seen at work, too, in the history of revival. Before God comes from heaven to work in extraordinary ways, He places the burden of revival on the hearts of certain of His people. Why some should be selected to carry this burden and others not, I cannot say, except that it is a mystery we must ascribe to the sovereignty of God. One thing is sure, however, God never goes behind the back of His Church to introduce redemptive changes in His universe. When revival comes, it will come through the hearts of those who have been greatly burdened to pray.

FURTHER STUDY

Psa. 21:1–13; 38:9;
73:25;
Isa. 26:9;
Mark 11:24

1. What will God grant to us?
2. How can a desire become a burden?

Prayer

O God, if before there can be a blessing someone has to bear a burden, then burden my heart this day for a mighty Holy Spirit revival in Your Church. In Jesus' name I ask it. Amen.

Closer than we think

For reading & meditation – Malachi 3:1–6

'... *Then suddenly the Lord you are seeking will come to his temple ...*' (v.1)

Revival is not only a sovereign work of God: it is a sudden work of God. Revival begins without much preamble and without warning. Pentecost began in this way you remember: 'When the day of Pentecost had come ... suddenly a sound came from heaven like the rush of a mighty wind' (Acts 2:1–2, RSV). This is brought out very clearly in the book of Habakkuk (3:1–3). After the prophet has prayed for revival: 'O Lord, revive thy work in the midst of the years', the next verse goes on to say: 'God came from Teman, the Holy One from Mount Paran.' The original Hebrew here, so I am told, conveys the impression of suddenness. Following Habakkuk's prayer, God came suddenly, and without warning, to revive and reinvigorate His people.

When revival came to Ulster in the nineteenth century – it came suddenly. When revival came to Wales in 1904 – it came suddenly. When revival came to the Hebrides in the middle of the twentieth century – it came suddenly. Study the record of any revival throughout history and you will find that God came to His people unheralded and unannounced. It sometimes happens that He imparts to a few people a sense of His approaching presence, but the actual breakthrough always comes with startling suddenness. Tonight we may go to sleep aware that the Church desperately needs revival, and wake up tomorrow to find ourselves right in the middle of it. Oh, that it may be so.

FURTHER STUDY

John 3:8;

Acts 16:25–40;

2:2, 9:3;

Num. 12:4–5

1. What was Jesus saying to Nicodemus?
2. How was this fulfilled?

Prayer

O Father, from the very bottom of my heart, I pray that You will break in upon us, as You did at Pentecost, in power, in majesty and in glorious suddenness. For Jesus' sake. Amen.

'The least likely place'

For reading & meditation – Exodus 3:1–6

'There the angel of the LORD appeared to him in flames of fire from within a bush …' (v.2)

Revival begins in the most unlikely places. Pentecost, you remember, began not in the majestic atmosphere of Solomon's Temple, but in an upper room. For some reason, God seems to delight in bypassing the places where we might expect revival to break out – in a splendid cathedral or at a large Christian conference – and causes His fire to burst out in a small prayer meeting where only a few are present. In fact, no revival has been an official movement of the Church. This is why revival always astonishes the Church – it flares up where it is least expected.

The Primitive Methodist revival in the 1800s began not on the historic sites of former Methodist accomplishments, but in a tiny hamlet on the hillside of Mow Cop near Stoke-on-Trent. Someone described it as 'the least likely place in which a revival has ever broken out'. And why? Because there were only a few grey, roughly-built cottages situated there, inhabited by people with little intellectual ability or learning. The area was bleak, rugged and uninteresting. Nevertheless, this is the place God chose in which to manifest His power and glory. If ever the Church receives a blow to its pride it is when God breaks forth in revival. He shows, in that act, how unimpressed He is with ornate buildings or exquisite architecture. When God came down to meet Moses in Midian, did He do so because Midian was a holy and sanctified place? No, He came not because it was holy, but to make it holy.

FURTHER STUDY

Acts 9:1–21;

Gen. 32:24–30;

1 Sam. 16:12–13

1. Why was Saul an unlikely candidate to meet with God?

2. Why was the Damascus road an unlikely place?

Prayer

O God, help me learn this secret – that Your decisions are based not on material or aesthetic values, but on the condition of the heart. Make my heart a fit receptacle for Your presence. In Jesus' name I pray. Amen.

In unexpected ways

For reading & meditation – Judges 6:11–24

'… how can I save Israel? My clan is the weakest … and I am the least …' (v.15)

Revivals begin in the most unexpected ways. One revival in North Wales in the eighteenth century began with the death of a highly respected minister. As the crowds gathered at his funeral service, the Holy Spirit broke in and produced a mighty revival. The 1904 revival is connected with the name of Evan Roberts, but it really began in a meeting at which Evan Roberts was present, when a shy and timid 16-year-old girl stood up and blurted out, 'I love Jesus Christ with all my heart.'

Consider the great revival which took place in New York in 1847. A businessman, Jeremiah Lanphier, advertised a midday prayer meeting in his office. At the first meeting, six people were present. So mightily did the Spirit work amongst those six, that within six months more than 100,000 businessmen were crowding into prayer meetings all over the city. In Uganda, a revival broke out when one Christian walked more than a hundred miles to ask the forgiveness of a Christian whom he had wronged twenty years previously.

The question is often asked by those who study the origin of revival: Why does God bypass organisations, committees and the well-oiled machinery of the Church in order to bring a revival to birth? He does it, as this passage before us today shows, that the glory might not be man's, but God's. The Almighty delights to be involved in situations where there is no doubt who is responsible for the victory which has been achieved. And revival is such a situation.

FURTHER STUDY

Isa. 48:1–11;
1 Cor. 1:29;
1 Pet. 1:24–25

1. Why was the Lord angry with Israel?
2. What is He not willing to give up?

Prayer

O Father, when will we learn that You desire the glory for Yourself? Drive this truth deep into my spirit, for I see that unless I live by it, I just won't get very far spiritually. Amen.

The people He uses

For reading & meditation – 1 Corinthians 1:18–31

'He has chosen a plan ... and used it to bring down to nothing those the world considers great.' (v.28, TLB)

Revivals begin with the most unassuming people. Don't think, when you read of famous names such as Charles Finney, Christmas Evans, and so on, that all revivals begin with such outstanding personalities. In fact, although revivals have marked the history of the Church throughout its long course of almost 20 centuries, most of these began with unknown individuals. And those who were well known, generally speaking, played little part in the revival until they themselves had passed through a time of deep repentance and inner cleansing.

Ever heard of James McQuilkee? I'll be surprised if you have. Yet he was a man whom God used mightily in the Ulster revival in 1859. Have you heard of David Morgan? God used him greatly in one of the revivals that shook Wales, yet prior to the revival he was known to no more than the 500 or so people who lived in the small village where he was brought up. In researching this subject, I came up with names of men who never merited a mention in the usual books on revival, but who were used by God nevertheless to bring about His mighty purposes here on earth.

I am conscious, as I write, that within me is a tendency to try to explain why God works in this strange way, but the Spirit seems to be saying to my heart: 'Don't try to explain my ways, for they are higher than your ways, and my thoughts higher than your thoughts. If you can explain a revival – then it is not a revival.'

FURTHER STUDY

Jer. 1:1–10;
Hag. 2:23;
John 15:16;
Acts 9:15

1. How did Jeremiah respond when God called him?
2. How are you responding to God's moving in your life?

Prayer

O God, help me to lay aside all my critical faculties, and come, like a child, to the holy fountain of Your Word, believing that with You all things are possible. Amen.

God's purpose in revival

For reading & meditation – Isaiah 42:8–17

'I am the LORD; that is my name! I will not give my glory to another ...' (v.8)

Those who have made a special study of revival tell us that in every century of the Church, somewhere or other in the world, a revival containing one or more of the features of the first Pentecost has taken place. Why does God send these periodic awakenings of revival? The primary purpose behind every spiritual revival is to bring glory to God's name. Lose sight of this and you can miss your way regarding this great and important subject.

Many Christians are motivated to pray for revival because they are tired of the dull, apathetic condition of the Church, and long for the kind of meetings revival produces – meetings in which there is great spiritual fervour and excitement. There is no doubt that revival creates such an atmosphere, but if that is our primary motivation, then we have simply fallen prey to the age-old problem – self-centred interests.

But someone asks: Isn't it legitimate for Christians to enjoy themselves in God's presence, and to long for services which pulsate with divine power? Yes, of course it is – this is certainly a legitimate desire. The problem arises when that desire takes priority, for then your interests, and not God's, take pre-eminence. I say again, the primary purpose behind every spiritual revival is to bring glory to God's name. When we make His goal, our goal then we bring ourselves in line with His infinite purposes. And when we are linked to His purposes, we are linked to His power.

FURTHER STUDY

Acts 12:18–25;
Phil. 4:20;
1 Pet. 5:1;
Luke 2:14;
John 8:50

1. What did the angels proclaim?
2. Why did Herod come to an untimely end?

Prayer

Dear Father, drain all self-interest from my heart so that my primary goal, too, is Your honour and glory. Then my purposes will coincide and not conflict with Yours. Thank You, Father. Amen.

'What is the chief end of man?'

For reading & meditation – Psalm 72:1–19

*'Praise be to his glorious name for ever; may the whole earth
be filled with his glory …' (v.19)*

The main purpose of our being in the world, and in the Church, is not to enjoy ourselves, but to glorify God. God's glory is to be the goal – enjoyment the result. Reverse the order and you end up in conflict with God, and with the structure of the universe.

Great theologians of the past, when laying down guidelines for the worship of the Church, asked the question: 'What is the chief end of man?' With absolute accuracy they answered: 'Man's chief end is to glorify God, and to enjoy Him forever.' Any pursuit of pleasure, even spiritual pleasure, apart from God who made us, is a violation of God's purpose in the creation of man, and a travesty of man's best interests. Man was not made for himself but for God.

'To pursue self-gratification to the abandonment of God', the theologians went on to say, 'is to guarantee immediate disappointment and eventually total ruin.' The greatest need of the Church at this moment is to put God's interests first, and other interests second. Some may be prepared to pray earnestly for revival, fearing that if it doesn't come, their very way of life will be undermined or destroyed. Others may pray for revival motivated by a concern for loved ones who are in sin. Still others may pray for revival out of a concern for the bankrupt condition of the Church. But worthy as such aims may be, let it be understood that the primary reason why we should pray for and desire a spiritual revival is for the glory of God.

FURTHER STUDY

1 Kings 8:1–11;
Exod. 24:17; 40:34;
John 1:1–18

1. What happened when the glory of God filled the Temple?
2. What are two characteristics of God's glory?

Prayer

O Father, again I ask You to help me bring my priorities in line with Your priorities. Fill my heart with such a vision of Your glory that all self-centred interest will be crowded out. For Jesus' sake. Amen.

The peaks and troughs

For reading & meditation – Jeremiah 17:5–14

'The heart is deceitful above all things, and beyond cure ...'
(v.9)

A second purpose for which God sends revival is to elevate His Church to the level of power it was always intended to enjoy. The history of the Church has been one of 'peaks and troughs'. At times it soars in the chariot of revival with the world at its feet. Other times it is beggared and bankrupt – the laughing-stock of society. History records that 50 years after Pentecost, the Church began to lapse into lukewarmness and infidelity, and by the end of the first century had lost much of its spiritual supremacy. Then at the beginning of the third century, God stepped in to revive His people. In subsequent centuries, this pattern of 'peaks and troughs' is clearly traceable. During one period the Church is up, in the next, it is down. Then when it looks as if it is finished and will never rise again, God graciously steps in and touches the hearts of His people in revival power.

Why should it be that with all the great ministries which God sets in the Church – gifted pastors, teachers, prophets, etc. – it should fall into periods of lukewarmness and decline? There can

FURTHER STUDY

Mark 7:14–23;
Eccl. 8:11; 9:3;
Matt. 23:25;
Heb. 3:15

1. What did Jesus say about the heart?
2. List some of the characteristics of the human heart.

only be one answer – the waywardness of the human heart. Such is the human condition that even the most spiritual people can allow their hearts to be turned away from God by things such as materialism, humanism and so on. So wilful are their desires that the ordinary ministries of the Church cannot move them. It is at such times that God sends revival.

Prayer

Father, this little glimpse You have given me today into the waywardness of the human heart, pulls me up with a jerk. Can it be that my own heart is capable of playing truant from You? Help me, dear Lord, or I am sunk. Amen.

The sleeping giant

For reading & meditation – Song of Solomon 6:4–12

'Who is this that appears like the dawn, fair as the moon, bright as the sun, majestic as the stars in procession?' (v.10)

Revival elevates the Church to the position it was always intended to enjoy. Is the Church at present experiencing all that God intends for her? Hardly. Someone has described the Church here in Great Britain as 'a sleeping giant'. 'But how can that be,' asks someone, 'when at this moment the Church in general is caught up in a tremendous amount of activity, including evangelism programmes such as Alpha courses? Isn't this evidence that the "sleeping giant" has awakened?' Not necessarily. An evangelistic concern is good and proper and I support evangelism one hundred percent. When I use the term 'sleeping giant', I am using it in relation to what the Church could be doing, not in relation to what it is doing. When revival comes, the 'sleeping giant' will not just stir and awaken, but will move with such dynamic power and impact that it will make a mass evangelistic crusade look like a Sunday School picnic.

Imagine your church with every member living together in harmony, with not one sleeping Christian left, with every individual on fire for God, and with everyone intent on seeing the will of Christ accomplished. To this startling picture, add the power that produced such astonishing scenes on the Day of Pentecost. Now multiply this until it fills every church in every community, every town, and every city in the nation. Unleash all this mighty power against the forces of sin and evil. That is revival!

FURTHER STUDY

Prov. 6:1–11;

Eph. 5:14;

Rom. 13:11;

1 Thess. 5:6

1. What can we learn from the ant?
2. What has produced spiritual poverty in the Church?

Prayer

O God, now that I am beginning to see more clearly the vision of what You want Your Church to be, grant that it may be fulfilled and be fulfilled soon. In Jesus' name. Amen.

Mockery from the world

For reading & meditation – Judges 16:6–31

'But the hair on his head began to grow again ...' (v.22)

God sends revival in order to arrest the attention of an unbelieving world. We have to face the fact that, at the moment, the world hardly recognises the presence of the Church. It pays lip service to it, of course, but deep down unbelievers regard the Church as a relic of the past – archaic and ineffectual. This finds expression in many ways. When a minister is portrayed in a play, he is invariably a stilted caricature, who speaks in a silly, affected voice, and who is more non-Christian than Christian. It would be impossible to deny, of course, that occasionally one meets members of the clergy who come close to the caricature, but this is the exception not the rule.

Another idea the world has of the Church is that we are a group of psychologically immature people needing a religious prop in order to face the challenge of living in a strife-torn world. But that isn't the worst of it. Men and women in the world project the weaknesses, the mistakes, the inadequacies of the Church on to God, and say: 'If there is a God, what kind of God can He be to give His name to such a motley crowd as this?' Revival changes all that. It puts God right in the middle of His people, giving them a voice so powerful that when the Church speaks – the world sits up and listens. To those who say that the Church of Jesus Christ is weak and enervated, we can reply: 'That is how it may look at present. But just wait – our God is on the way.'

FURTHER STUDY

Acts 4:13–22;
5:12–16; 14:1–17

1. How did people react to the early disciples?
2. What effect did their ministry have upon the community?

Prayer

O Father, when I pause to think how ineffectively we, Your people, reflect Your power and Your purity, it is no wonder the world laughs at us. But be gracious to us, and, as You did with Samson, reveal Your power and glory one last time. For Jesus' sake. Amen.

'Be still and know'

For reading & meditation – Psalm 46:1–11

'Be still, and know that I am God ...' (v.10)

Does it grieve you, my friend, that we are living in a godless and morally bankrupt age? Does it grieve you that the name of our God is ridiculed and blasphemed in almost every section of society? Does it grieve you that men scoff at the Bible, this matchless book which God brought into being by the power of His Holy Spirit, and regard it with no more interest than the works of Shakespeare?

The more I see and hear arrogant men denying or blaspheming the very God who gave them breath, the more I can understand and identify with the psalmist in the psalm before us today. The writer penned these words because he was conscious that all around him godless men were repudiating the Almighty by their blasphemous utterances and sinful lives, and he petitions God that such men might be silenced. The psalmist implores God to do something, to come from heaven and stop the mouths of those who are ridiculing Him. He wants God to rise up and confront an unbelieving world and say: 'Be still, and know that I am God'.

Do not you, too, when you hear the Lord's name taken in vain, spiritual concerns mocked and eternal issues flippantly treated, feel the way this psalmist felt? If you are a Christian, and you don't, then, believe me, there is something deeply wrong with you. To hear sacred things treated with contempt and eternal matters trivialised without indignation is not possible to those who truly love God and serve His Son, the Lord Jesus Christ.

FURTHER STUDY

Phil. 2:1–30;
Isa. 9:6;
Luke 1:31;
Rev. 19:16

1. Why do men disregard the name of God?
2. Share with someone today about the name that is above all names.

Prayer

Gracious Father, every time I hear Your name blasphemed or Your cause ridiculed, give me, I pray, a deeper desire than before to see a spiritual revival that will not only transform the Church, but make the world, too, sit up and take notice. Amen.

Apprehended and arrested

For reading & meditation – Acts 2:1–13

'Amazed and perplexed, they asked one another, "What does this mean?"' (v.12)

When the Holy Spirit fell on the Day of Pentecost, the people who were in Jerusalem, together with all the strangers gathered there for the feast, came to where the disciples were, and said, 'What does this mean?' They were arrested by the mighty outpouring of God's eternal power. The world sat up and took notice. That is always the case in revival – unbelievers, albeit out of curiosity, gather in the presence of the unusual and ask the question: 'What does this mean?'

As a boy I remember hearing a great preacher, who was converted in the 1904 Welsh revival, recounting his experience of conversion. 'I was a drunkard and a down-and-out,' he said, 'but one night someone came into the pub where I was drinking and said, "There's some strange things going on in the church down the road. People are crying, falling on the floor, and all kinds of things are happening." My friends and I went down to the church to scoff and have some fun. But when I entered the door it was as if I had been arrested. I sobered up immediately, and fell to my knees calling upon God to have mercy on my soul.' And then he added some words which I have heard on numerous occasions in connection with revival: 'I went to scoff but I stayed to pray.'

Clearly, there is nothing the Church can do to produce such an impact and an effect. Evangelistic crusades, rallies, concerts can attract and appeal to the world, but only revival can arrest it.

FURTHER STUDY

Luke 4:20–36; 2:47–48;

Matt. 13:54; 15:31; 22:22;

Mark 2:12

1. What kind of impact did Jesus have on people?
2. Does your life astonish anyone?

Prayer

O God, I feel I am coming to a crisis point. I want nothing less than You. You in all Your fullness. You in all Your glory. You in all Your restoring and reviving power. In Jesus' name I ask it. Amen.

Glorious upheaval

For reading & meditation – Proverbs 14:1–14

'Where no oxen are, the crib is clean ...' (v.4, KJV)

W hat are the results of revival? Revival, as we have seen, results in greater power and purity in the Church. But what does this mean in practical terms? First, it means that long-standing habits of self-indulgence, that surrender neither to reason nor to God, will be broken when revival comes. The doors and walls of the prison of self, in which so many Christians are incarcerated, will be broken down by revival. The Lord who came to declare freedom to the captive will enable His people to be free indeed. Unconfessed sins that have been covered over for years will be brought to light. The interesting thing about the exposure of sin in times of revival is that the fear and shame which usually accompany such moments are thought of as nothing in comparison with the prospect of forgiveness and cleansing.

Second, it means that the plans and strategies of the Church are thrown into upheaval and disarray. Goals and ambitions once thought to be of the utmost spiritual importance are seen to be but temporal. God's timing, God's purpose, God's plans rule the day. Some church structures may collapse when revival comes, but are then rebuilt – 'according to the pattern shown in the Mount'. Traditions may perish. Programmes may have to be abandoned and schedules rearranged. Well-rehearsed choir numbers may remain unsung for ever. Nothing is ever the same again in the Church when revival comes.

FURTHER STUDY

James 4:1–17;

Mal. 3:2–3;

Titus 2:14;

1 Pet. 1:22

1. Where does
striving come from?
2. What does
purification bring?

Prayer

O God, the thought of a Church rising like a lion from the thicket, noble and puissant, quickens my pulse and excites my spirit. Let the day soon dawn that sees such power and glory. For Jesus' sake. Amen.

'In the day of thy power'

For reading & meditation – Psalm 110:1–7

'Thy people shall be willing in the day of thy power …'
(v.3, KJV)

A third result of revival is the breaking of the will. When God moves from heaven in extraordinary power, all that stands in opposition to Him may be expected to be broken and cast aside. Pastors, elders and leaders will be broken by revival. Men who have preached interesting and eloquent sermons may discover that their ministry has the value of 'wood, hay and stubble'. Sermons and messages which seemed satisfactory enough in previous days will never do for revival. God, the Master Workman, will break the congregation, too. Men and women, who had resisted Him and His Word, now find themselves pliant and ready to do His bidding. But the breaking always leads to a remaking. God not only pulls down – He builds up.

A fourth result of revival among the people of God is that holiness becomes the prime object of their lives. To be like Jesus often becomes the theme song of a revival. Christians are consumed with a desire to conform to Christ's image, and the principle of Romans 8:29 – 'God decided that those who came to him … should become like his Son' (TLB) – becomes the dominating passion of their lives. The great truths of Scripture are no longer relegated to group discussions in church on a Sunday or in a mid-week house group, but are lived out on a daily basis and applied in every exigency of life. Revived people are truly a holy people.

FURTHER STUDY

Eph. 5:15–33;
Heb. 12:10–14;
Psa. 47:8;
Rom. 6:19;
2 Cor. 7:1

1. What does 'without spot or wrinkle' mean?
2. Write out your definition of holiness.

Prayer

O Father, as I see the picture of the Church as You destined it to be, my heart is almost breaking with a desire to witness a great outpouring of revival power. Grant it, dear Lord, in my day. For Jesus' sake. Amen.

Poor at loving

For reading & meditation – John 15:1–17

'My command is this: Love each other as I have loved you.'
(v.12)

A fifth result of revival is that Christians become greatly burdened
for the souls of unbelievers. Prayer for the eternal welfare of
those outside of Christ becomes a passion. Someone said that the
word that is characteristic of revival is the word 'Oh'. It comes out
continually in the prayers of those who agonise for the lost. 'Oh
God,' they cry, 'save those who are dying in sin.' Nothing short of
lasting conversions will satisfy the saints in a time of revival. They
pray that the same liberating Spirit that broke and remade them will
do the same in the hearts of their friends, families, acquaintances
and people throughout the world. New converts are made without
arm-twisting. No elaborate plans for follow-up are necessary as new
converts stand on their own feet from the moment of conversion.

Sixthly, Christians begin to manifest the love of Christ toward
one another. Those who have borne grudges or have gossiped about
other Christians go to those they have wronged and ask for their
forgiveness. Maintaining a clear conscience becomes a matter of
paramount importance. Those who have sinned privately make their
confession to God whom they have wronged.
Those who have sinned publicly find the grace
and strength to make a public confession. A
watching world will look on in amazement
as it sees Christians who had hitherto lived
hypocritical lives, now taking their faith seriously.
The light that shines in a revived Church cannot
be put out.

FURTHER STUDY

Luke 10:25–37;

Matt. 9:36; 14:14;

Luke 15:20

1. *What moved Jesus
to take action?*
2. *List seven things
the Samaritan did.*

Prayer

O Father You have shown me before that the Church's way of life will not work
unless it works by love. But despite our best efforts we are still so poor at loving.
Come and revive us, dear Lord. Amen.

The revival we need

For reading & meditation – Isaiah 41:1–13

'The islands have seen it and fear; the ends of the earth tremble … each helps the other …' (vv.5–6)

Today we consider how revival affects the wider community and ultimately the nation. Some people say that revival is completely irrelevant to such issues as politics and socio-economics, but to hold such a view is to fly in the face of the facts. J. Edwin Orr in his book, *The Second Evangelical Awakening in Britain* (now out of print), says that when revival came to Wales 'drunkenness was immediately cut by half and many public houses went bankrupt'. Crime was so diminished that the judges were presented with white gloves signifying that there were no cases of murder, assault, rape, robbery, or such like, to consider. The police became 'unemployed' in many districts. Stoppages occurred in coal mines, not due to unpleasantness between management and workers, but because so many miners became converted and stopped using foul language that the horses which hauled the coal trucks in the mines could no longer understand what was being said to them, and transportation ground to a halt.

In an age when so much is being said about the Church's duty to

FURTHER STUDY

Acts 19:17–41;
17:6–8; 13:44–52

1. How did Paul's ministry affect the community?
2. What does revival bring with it?

become involved in bringing about positive social and political changes, it is salutary to observe the tremendous effects which God's people have had upon society when they were in a state of revival. When the Church communicates her unique message in the power of the Holy Spirit, an improved society is always an early and inevitable result.

Prayer

Lord, thank You for showing me a little glimpse of what Your power can do and achieve. Deepen my concern and increase my desire for a great spiritual revival, I pray. In Jesus' name. Amen.

Our need – a stronger Voice

For reading & meditation – Isaiah 30:27–33

'The LORD will cause men to hear his majestic voice ...' (v.30)

We saw yesterday that revival has a salutary effect upon society and a heightening of morality. At this moment, thousands of Christians throughout the world are deeply concerned over the high rate of abortion. Despite our strongest protests, we seem powerless to get people to see that life begins at the moment of conception, and that to abort a fetus for any other reason than danger to the life of the mother is an offence in the eyes of God. Though the problem is one that did not affect previous generations to such a degree, and we have no statistics against which we can measure it, I believe, nevertheless, that revival in the Church would greatly affect the thinking of society in relation to this issue. The Holy Spirit flowing out from the Church into the world with power would, in my judgment, cause men and women to feel deeply uncomfortable about abortion. In no time, the laws governing abortion on demand would be changed.

Today subjectivism has taken the place of fixed principles of moral law. Instead of judging conduct on the basis of what God says, we now say: 'Let your conscience be your guide.' But conscience, without the reinforcement of God's Word and the Holy Spirit, can excuse just as easily as it can accuse. Revival would not force men and women to act in ways that are consistent with God's demands in Scripture, but the light it would cast would make men think twice before embarking upon deeds of darkness.

FURTHER STUDY

2 Cor. 3:1–18;
Heb. 10:16;
Rom. 2:15; 7:22

1. Where does God want to write His law?
2. How does He do it?

Prayer

O Father, I see more clearly than ever, that only revival will give Your Church the voice it needs to speak powerfully into these vitally important social issues. So we pray and wait – in eager anticipation. For Jesus' sake. Amen.

The break-up of marriage

For reading & meditation – Psalm 127:1–5

'Unless the Lord builds the house, its builders labour in vain ...' (v.1)

We are seeing that although revival will not force unbelievers to conform to biblical principles, it will, nevertheless, produce an atmosphere in which the standards of right and wrong are more sharply differentiated. Consider yet another social problem – divorce. Prior to the 1960s, the figures for divorce in the United Kingdom were published for five-yearly periods. During the period 1951–56 there were 146,186 divorces – an average of approximately 29,000 a year. Now, because divorce is a matter of immense social concern, the statistics are published annually. By 1982 the number of divorces in the UK was 150,000. In two decades, the divorce rate had rocketed and it is even worse now!

What can be done about this problem? Very little, it seems. The Church can teach about the sanctity of marriage for all it is worth, but this seems to make little difference to a secular society. Newspapers report celebrity marriage break-ups on an almost daily basis. Although these issues can be complex and sensitive, how it highlights the fact that the Church's teaching on marriage seems to make little impression on the world. The community, as a whole, tends to make divorce easier and easier. Revival in the Church would, I believe, curb the rising divorce rate. Such would be the power that would flow through the Church that its voice would be heeded, and its standards recognised and upheld.

FURTHER STUDY

Gen. 2:18–25;
Eph. 5:22–28;
Col. 3:18-21;
1 Cor. 11:3

1. How many families do you know which are breaking up?
2. What message of reconciliation can you share with them?

Prayer

Lord, the more I look at society with its increasing problems, the more convinced I am that only an extraordinary move of Your Spirit can right its wrongs. Again I pray – let it come, dear Lord. And soon. For Jesus' sake. Amen.

Britain – a nation of destiny

For reading & meditation – Proverbs 14:26–34

'Righteousness exalts a nation, but sin is a disgrace to any people.' (v.34)

Revival would restore to Britain a sense of destiny. Once the British people believed that they had a special destiny in the world. Some aspects of the idea were, of course, quite insupportable. Those who said that whoever resisted Britain resisted heaven, and old memorial tablets in churches to admirals and generals declare this, were speaking from an imperialistic and not a spiritual perspective. Thankfully, most of that imperial pride has gone. Discerning people know that the only country with a future is the country which sets out to bring its purposes in harmony with the purposes of God.

One Christian historian believes that Britain could do that more swiftly than most other countries. The reasons given are these: 'She has a longer history and experience of self-government, and long enjoyment of civil, political and religious liberty has given her a maturity of judgment in all these fields, which is still rare among men. Britain has had no civil war for 300 years. Tolerance, fair play and a freedom from frenzy mark the people. The nation has a high destiny still.' A revival in the House of God would inevitably overflow into the Houses of Parliament. Revived Christians in Parliament, and other high places, would speak with new power and new authority. How many, I wonder, would be able to resist the call to biblical standards and morality? Yes, Britain can be a great nation still – but nothing short of revival in the Church can accomplish it.

FURTHER STUDY

Josh. 1; 24:31;

Prov. 11:11; 16:2;

Isa. 54:14

1. What was the key to Joshua's leadership?

2. What was the tribute to Joshua's leadership?

Prayer

Gracious Father, I see that the greatness of a nation depends not merely on what goes on in its 'Houses of Parliament', but what goes on in the House of God. Fill Your House with Your glory, I pray – then let it overflow. For Jesus' sake. Amen.

God's formula for revival

For reading & meditation – 2 Chronicles 7:11–22

'... if my people ... will humble themselves and pray ... and turn from their wicked ways, then will I hear ...' (v.14)

We come now to what is perhaps the most important question of all: What is the way to revival? We said that revival is a sovereign act of God, and that the Church is unable to produce it, unable to explain it, and unable to control it. It is a glorious, majestic, mighty, awesome act of God in which He sweeps His Church from spiritual bankruptcy into spiritual riches.

The impression you may have got is that as revival is a sovereign act of God, and cannot be produced by anyone on earth, then the only thing the Church can do is sit back and wait for God to send it. Nothing could be further from the truth. Revival is most certainly a sovereign act of God, in the sense that only He can initiate it, but whenever God gets ready to revive His Church, He approaches those who are ready to listen to His voice, and instructs them on how to be the channel through whom His Spirit can flow from heaven to earth.

The instructions God gives to His people, when preparing them for revival, are crystallised in the text before us today. This verse has

FURTHER STUDY

Gal. 6:1–10;
John 12:24;
Eccl. 11:1;
2 Cor. 9:6

1. What is the principle of sowing and reaping?
2. How does this relate to revival?

been described as 'the final and finished formula on how to prepare for revival'. It is so important that I propose to draw our attention to it daily for the next few days. Before we begin to look at it clause by clause, let me urge you to spend a few minutes today memorising it. If you do, I promise you that this text will make more of an impact upon your life than anything else you have ever experienced!

Prayer

Lord, help me to hide Your Word in my heart, and enable me to memorise and meditate on this verse so that, from today on, it will not just be a text but a testimony. For Jesus' sake. Amen.

Where revival begins

For reading & meditation – Psalm 79:1–13

'Then we your people, the sheep of your pasture, will praise you for ever ...' (v.13)

We begin studying 2 Chronicles 7:14 by looking at the opening clause: 'If my people, who are called by my name ...' The truth we have been stressing over and over again in our daily meditations is, once again, brought to our attention – revival begins with the people of God. To criticise and condemn unbelievers for their unbiblical standards and practices is beginning at the wrong place. Revival relates first to the people of God. Some believe that the term 'people of God' refers to all who have some kind of religious inclination. But the Almighty leaves us in no doubt as to whom He is addressing: 'If my people, who are called by my name'. He is talking to those who know Him intimately, who have taken His name upon themselves, and who are linked with Him in a family relationship.

What a responsibility it is to belong to the people of God. After all, whether we like it or not, people judge God by the impression we make upon them. If we fail, they don't reason with themselves and say: 'He is only one in a million Christians – the others are a good deal better.' No, they observe our way of life, evaluate our actions and our behaviour, and say: 'If that's what serving God is like, then I want nothing to do with it.' This is why God chooses to begin with His own people when He is about to bring His redemptive purposes to pass in history. Once the people of God are right, then it won't take long to put the world right.

FURTHER STUDY

Eph. 1:1–23;

Psa. 4:3;

1 Cor. 1:26;

James 2:5;

1 Pet. 2:10

1. For what purpose has God chosen us?
2. With what have we been sealed?

Prayer

O God, forgive us that we, Your people, give such a poor impression to the world of Your love, Your power and Your glory. Things must change. So begin that change with me – today. In Jesus' name, I pray. Amen.

Humility comes first

For reading & meditation – 2 Chronicles 12:1–8

'When the LORD saw that they humbled themselves, this word of the LORD came ...' (v.7)

We come now to the third clause: 'will humble themselves'. Humble themselves? Shouldn't prayer take priority of place here? There is good reason why God puts humility first. It is because pride is one of the biggest barriers to God having His way in His Church. Not for nothing did the old theologians put pride at the head of the list of the 'seven deadly sins'. 'Pride,' said one preacher, 'is the primal sin. Little as we know of the life of the angels, there is evidence for believing that pride led to the revolt of Satan in heaven.'

Self-centredness, self-promotion and self-interest are a blight that affects both the redeemed and the unredeemed. Because we are Christians, it does not mean that we are automatically protected from the disease of self-interest. How many times have you, even though you are a Christian, allowed yourself rather than God to have the benefit of the doubt over some spiritual challenge He gave you? When pride is present, then everything which comes up has an immediate self-reference. There can be no real victory in any Christian's life until they have found victory over pride. The phrase, 'humble yourself', suggests that an act of the will is necessary. God can humble us, but how much more meaningful it becomes when we do it ourselves. Are you a proud person? Then do something today to trample on your pride. Pride has many evil characteristics, but its greatest evil is this – it blocks the way to revival.

FURTHER STUDY

Joel 2:1–13;

Psa. 34:18, 51:17;

Isa. 66:2;

2 Cor. 7:10

1. How should we turn to the Lord?
2. What does it mean to 'rend your heart'?

Prayer

O God, I realise how much Your work in me has been frustrated by my pride. Help me to take the first step down from my pride this day – and then keep going. In Jesus' name. Amen.

Striking the same chimes

For reading & meditation – Zechariah 10:1–5

'Ask the LORD for rain in the springtime ...' (v.1)

The next clause is 'and pray'. But Christians do pray! Ah, but how much? How sincerely? How unselfishly? When did we last stay up late just to pray? When did we last get up early simply to pray? Many Christians go through their Christian life praying by rote, or praying only when they want something for themselves. This isn't the kind of praying God means when He lays down the conditions for revival.

One of the greatest definitions of prayer I know is this – Prayer is co-operation with God. Consider what is meant by this phrase – co-operation with God. It is an exercise that links our faculties to our Maker to work out the intentions He had in mind in their creation. Prayer isn't bending God's will to ours, but bending our will to His. We work out the purposes which God has worked out for us.

A man sat and listened to an organist playing a beautiful melody. He said that, behind the organ, he could see a man striking upon bells the same notes the organ was playing. So in addition to the tones of the organ were the tones of the chimes, forming a beautiful accompaniment. Prayer is like that – it means we are striking the same notes as God. We thus become a part of a universal harmony – the music of the spheres. Our little notes are caught up and universalised. Prayer puts us in tune with the Infinite, and then Infinite power works through our finiteness. Milton summed it up when he said, 'By small accomplishing great things.'

FURTHER STUDY
John 15:1–17;
Jer. 29:13;
Mark 11:24;
1 John 3:21-22
1. When can we ask
for whatever we
want?
2. What is one of
the conditions of
answered prayer?

Prayer

Gracious Father, my feet often stumble on this path of prayer. I have learned much – but there is still much more to learn. Help me not just to say prayers – but really pray. For Your own dear name's sake. Amen.

Seek my face

For reading & meditation – Isaiah 63:15–49

'Look down from heaven and see from your lofty throne, holy and glorious ...' (v.15)

G od invites us not merely to pray, but to make our prayer time a deep encounter with Him. The kind of praying God looks for is not the brief, eager-to-get-it-over-with type, but the unhurried waiting before Him – the true seeking of His face. The Old Testament prophets knew how to pray like this. They came before God and laid hold on Him until something great and mighty happened.

Some time ago, when studying the great biblical prayers such as the prayers of Moses, Abraham and Daniel, I made a fascinating and interesting discovery. I found that in all these prayers there were common elements. The prophets, when they prayed, all used the same principles to get God to respond. Now it follows that if we can discover these common elements, and weave them into our prayers, then their presence will greatly strengthen our petitions.

The first ingredient was selflessness. They put others first – themselves last. The second – boldness. They were so convinced of their cause that they had no fear in coming into His presence. The third ingredient was that of reasoned argument. Taking God's own words, and quoting them back to Him, was one of their greatest strategies. God loves to be reasoned with – Isaiah 1:18. A fourth ingredient of the great biblical prayers was that of being specific. They knew what they wanted, and they asked God straight out for it. All of these ingredients are in this great prayer of Isaiah which we read today. Can you spot them?

FURTHER STUDY

Hos. 10:1–15;

Deut. 4:29;

Psa. 105:4;

Isa. 55:6

1. What did the prophet exhort the children of Israel to do?

2. How can we break up our fallow ground?

Prayer

Father, one thing is certain, I cannot pray effectively unless I am Spirit-taught. Inspire prayer within me so that I may pray according to Your will – and hence be answered according to Your power. In Jesus' name. Amen.

God's wicked people

For reading & meditation – Ezekiel 18:25–32

'... Repent and turn from all your transgressions ...'
(v.30, RSV)

'**I**f my people will turn from their wicked ways' – can it be true that God's people have wicked ways? Perhaps the Lord meant careless ways, or formal ways – surely not wicked ways? The Bible says wicked ways.

Perhaps we Christians have learned to so rationalise some of our actions and our behaviour that we do not realise quite how wicked they really are. The tendency in this day and age is to let ourselves off lightly whenever we have done wrong. We use such euphemisms as: 'Well, the only one I hurt was myself', or: 'It isn't all that important.' But any violation of a biblical principle is immensely serious. When we pass on a juicy bit of gossip concerning someone who has erred and strayed – that is a wicked way. When we criticise and condemn those who have the spiritual oversight over us, rather than bring them before God in prayer – that is a wicked way. When we wound others by our words or actions, and fail to ask their and God's forgiveness – that is a wicked way. When the acquisition of money dominates our thinking and crowds out eternal things – that is a wicked way. When we watch degrading films or read morally debilitating literature – that is a wicked way.

Can these things, and there are many others, go on in the hearts of those who claim to know the Way – God's own people, called by His name? I am sorry to say they can. If we are guilty of any of these wicked ways, then let us, here and now, repent of them and have done with them.

FURTHER STUDY

Ezek. 18:1–32;

Isa. 55:7;

Acts 17:30

1. How does Ezekiel define revival?
2. How is this achieved?

Prayer

O Master of my heart, I turn away from all that would divide my heart. Class consciousness, jealousy, love of money, anger, and many other things have silently entered and set up their shrine within me. I tear out these altars to make You, O Christ, my sole Lord and Liege. Amen.

The sure and certain promise

For reading & meditation – 2 Chronicles 6:18–31

'When ... your people have sinned ... when they pray ... and turn from ... sin ... then hear from heaven and forgive ...' (vv.26–27)

We come now to the last clause of 2 Chronicles 7:14;

'then will I hear from heaven and will forgive their sin and will heal their land.'

What a hope-filled promise! What a healing word! 'I will hear ... forgive ... and heal.' Do you believe that? Do you believe that as you prepare your heart through repentance and prayer, God will come again and restore the Church to its former glory?

It may be a lot for some of you to believe, especially those of you who find yourselves in a lethargic local church. But not to believe it would make God a liar. Believe it then! With all your heart. Put your whole weight behind the promise. Humble yourself before God. Pray more – in private and in the public prayer meeting. If your church doesn't have a prayer meeting, then gently ask why this is so. Lay hold of the grace of God to get rid of everything in your life of which you know He disapproves. Hear His promise again. Even though you have memorised it, it will do you good to see it spelt out in full:

FURTHER STUDY

Zech. 13:1–9;
Psa. 91:15;
Isa. 58:9, 65:24;
Luke 11:9

1. Write out 2 Chronicles 7:14 in your own words.
2. What does it mean in terms of your own personal life?

'If my people, who are called by my name, will humble themselves and pray and seek my face and turn from their wicked ways, then will I hear from heaven and will forgive their sin and will heal their land' (2 Chron. 7:14).

Prayer

O God, I would live in this text and have it live in me. You who have breathed into words and made them Your Word, let the message of this glorious text fasten on my spirit, and change me hour by hour, day by day and week by week. In Jesus' name. Amen.

It's time for a checkup

For reading & meditation – Psalm 139:1–24

*'Search me, O God, and know my heart; test me and know my
anxious thoughts.' (v.23)*

Having explored the thrilling and important subject of revival over the past eight weeks, it is now time to give ourselves a spiritual checkup. Remember God's love for you remains constant and certain whatever your condition but if we are to be agents of revival we must be revived ourselves.

I must ask myself:

- How long is it since I became a Christian?

- Have I grown steadily in that time?

- Was I ever further forward than I am now?

- Can I measure a degree of steady progress in my spiritual understanding?

- Is my reading of the Scriptures a mere duty, or is it a delight?

- Am I deeply conscious of the need for more private and corporate prayer?

- Do I think more of a larger income than I do of my spiritual development?

- Am I a *deeply* spiritual person?

FURTHER STUDY

2 Tim. 2:1–26;
1 Chron. 28:9;
Jer. 17:10;
Rom. 8:27

1. What was Paul's exhortation to Timothy?
2. What has God given us?

Prayer

Heavenly Father, as I undertake this spiritual check-up, I need, more than ever, to feel Your reassuring love encircling and surrounding me. Don't let me be devastated – let me be developed. For Jesus' sake. Amen.

Further examination

For reading & meditation – Psalm 26:1–12

'Test me, O LORD, and try me, examine my heart and my mind.' (v.2)

Wcontinue our spiritual checkup, for, as someone has said, 'The unexamined life is not worth living.'

- Do I live day by day in conscious dependence on the Lord?

- Does the need for revival have much place in my prayer life?

- Have I hurt or wounded anyone and not yet apologised?

- Do I give myself to God, then draw back when I realise just how much is involved?

- How do I feel about undertaking this spiritual check-up – challenged, bored, unconcerned?

- Do I grieve when I hear the name of Christ blasphemed, or have I grown insensitive to such things?

- When my non-Christian friends ask me about my interests do I take the opportunity to share Christ?

- How long is it since I last shed tears over the condition of the world and the Church?

- Am I fighting a losing battle with evil thoughts?

- When did I last undertake a spiritual fast?

FURTHER STUDY

Matt. 7:1–12;
1 Cor. 11:28;
2 Cor. 13:5;
Lam. 3:40

1. What is a danger, when we hear the truth?
2. How did Jesus illustrate this?

Prayer

O Father, even if the corporate Church is not where it should be, I want to be my spiritual best. Help me to make a clean sweep, and put right every wrong. In Christ's name I ask it. Amen.

The search continues

For reading & meditation – Romans 13:7–14

'The night is nearly over; the day is almost here. So let us put aside the deeds of darkness …' (v.12)

I ask myself some more searching questions:

- If I was arrested for being a Christian, would there be enough evidence to convict me?

- Am I a faithful steward of the money that flows through my hands?

- Do I give at least one-tenth of my income to God?

- What do other members of my family think about my Christian life at home?

- Does my conscience function in the way God designed it – by objecting to evil and approving good?

- Do I watch degrading films in the cinema or on television?

- Am I dependent on alcohol to see me through life's problems and difficulties?

- Have I debts which are outstanding and well overdue?

- Am I honest in relation to my employer – giving my whole energy to my responsibilities, and remembering that I am not employed by an earthly employer, but by God? (Rom. 13:1)

- Am I eager for revival?

FURTHER STUDY

Psa. 51:1–19;
Gal. 6:3–4;
James 1:22

1. What did David say about truth?
2. When do we deceive ourselves?

Prayer

Father, I have put my hand to the plough and I am not going to look back. I am going to be all out for You. Forgive me for every failure, and let me know personal revival this very hour. In Jesus' name. Amen.

'Preparing the way'

For reading & meditation – Luke 3:1–6

'… *Prepare the way for the Lord, make straight paths for him.*' (v.4)

The conclusion of our studies on 'Preparing for Revival' is this: nothing else but an extraordinary move of God can meet the urgent need of the Church and the world at this hour. Evangelism, conferences, seminars, rallies, and the other activities of the Church, while important and necessary, are, however, inadequate in themselves to arrest the attention of an unbelieving world. God must come down from heaven and visit us in mighty Holy Spirit power. My personal conviction is that, in conjunction with His prepared people – He will.

Bishop Wilberforce wrote many years ago: 'We look at some mighty estuary which the retiring tide has left bare of water. We see a vast expanse of sand and mud, with little trickling rivulets weaving their scarcely appreciable way through the resisting banks of that yielding ooze. The man who knows not the secrets of the tide, and the influence by which God governs nature would say: How can you expect to see that great expanse covered? But high in the heavens, the unseen Ruler has set the orb, which shall bring in her time, the tides of the surrounding ocean and when the appointed moment comes, suddenly and sufficiently, the whole is covered by the rejoicing water, and again it is one silvery surface, sandless and mudless – because the Lord has willed it.'

My Christian friend, take heart. The unseen Ruler has willed the revival of His people. The day of His power is not far distant. But He looks to you and me to 'prepare the way'.

FURTHER STUDY

Ezek. 47:1–12;
2 Kings 3:16–17;
Isa. 40:3–5;
Rev. 22:1

1. Write out your own definition of revival.
2. How will you make it a reality?

Prayer

Gracious Father, You have given me a commission – a commission to 'prepare the way' for the coming revival. I am the wire along which Your power runs. Keep me connected and insulated. For Your praise and honour and glory. Amen.

The Crimson
Trail in
Scripture

No blood – no forgiveness

For reading & meditation – Hebrews 9:11–28

'*… without the shedding of blood there is no forgiveness of sins.*' (v.22, RSV)

The 'crimson trail' in Scripture refers to references to blood that begin in Genesis and end in Revelation. The Bible has been described by someone as being much like the human body – wherever you cut it, it bleeds. Open the Bible at almost any point and you are not very far from some reference to blood. The Old Testament pages are so stained with blood that some critics have referred to the religion of the Bible as a 'slaughterhouse gospel'. Why does the Bible place so much emphasis upon blood? The answer is given in the words of our text for today: '… without the shedding of blood there is no forgiveness of sins.' God wanted to teach His people in the Old Testament (and, through them, the other nations of the world) that sin was such a heinous offence, the only way it would be expunged was through the sacrifice of another life. The blood of animals could not take away sin, of course, but God used the ritual to lay deep in human minds the truth of atonement by substitution.

In an age when references to Christ's blood and atoning sacrifice are being dropped from our hymn books and from our pulpits, we must walk once again the crimson trail that runs from one end of the Bible to the other, and remind ourselves that it is by the innocent sufferings of Christ we are saved, and by His blood we are redeemed. We sing with delight: 'Oh, precious is the flow that makes me white as snow; No other fount I know, nothing but the blood of Jesus.'

FURTHER STUDY

1 Pet. 1:1–25.
Matt. 26:28;
Rom. 5:9

1. By what are we redeemed?
2. What was the price of our salvation?

Prayer

Lord Jesus Christ, help me, I pray, never to be moved from the foundation of my faith, and deepen my understanding over these next two months of the meaning and power of Your precious blood. For Your own dear name's sake. Amen.

The beginning of the trail

For reading & meditation – Genesis 3:8–24

'The Lord God made garments of skin for Adam and his wife and clothed them.' (v.21)

Robert Coleman tells the story of a boy who appeared at a mission hospital in Kenya with a gaping wound in his foot. He, together with the help of a companion, started out to the mission hospital many miles away. The child's mother, hearing that her boy had been injured, set out to find him. Eventually she reached the mission hospital, and the superintendent asked her, 'How did you find us so quickly?' 'Oh, it was easy,' she said, 'I just followed the trail of blood.' In a much more profound sense, this is how we come to find Jesus Christ in the Bible – we follow the trail of blood.

When Adam and Eve defied God, and asserted their independence, they were stripped of the glory that surrounded them, and stood naked and exposed before the Almighty. How deeply God must have suffered at that moment. Before Him stood the couple whom He had designed to be the reflection of His eternal glory, now broken, beggared and bankrupt. I am astonished that He did not destroy them. Infinite love, however, reaches down: God slays an animal, skins it, and from the skin provides a covering for His naked children.

FURTHER STUDY

Luke 15:11–32;

Isa. 61:10;

Zech. 3:4;

2 Cor. 5:20–21

1. What did the father give to the repentant son?

2. What has become ours through the shed blood?

The first shedding of blood that took place in the universe was a portrayal to Adam and Eve, and to their offspring, of the cost to God for their wilful wrongdoing. An innocent animal had to die. Blood had to be spilled. God becomes the first High Priest of the universe, and takes the initiative in providing a covering for sin!

Prayer

O Father, how can I ever sufficiently thank You for making the truth so clear to me: that it is only, always and ever shall be, what You have done that can suffice to pay the price for human sin. Help me never to forget it. Amen.

The better word

For reading & meditation – Genesis 4:1–16

'... *Your brother's blood cries out to me from the ground.*' (v.10)

Today we look at the first instance in history when human blood was shed: the world's first murder. Cain, overcome by jealousy turned upon his brother and slew him. As the warm blood emptied out of Abel's veins and trickled onto the ground, it reached up into heaven and cried out to God for vengeance and retribution. Immediately God confronted Cain, claiming that Abel's blood had cried out to Him from the ground. As a result of this act, Cain was punished and cursed by the Almighty, and, in fact, little more is said of him until we come to this reference in the book of Hebrews. The passage says: 'You have come to God, the judge of all men ... to Jesus the mediator of a new covenant and to the sprinkled blood that speaks a better word than the blood of Abel' (12:23–24).

Here the writer draws a fascinating comparison between the blood of Christ and the blood of Abel. Both Christ and Abel were victims of hatred and jealousy, and, in both cases, their blood cried out to God from the ground. When Abel's blood was spilled, God came down to pronounce a swift judgment on his murderer. If this was God's attitude toward the assassination of Abel, then what would be His attitude towards the murderers of His own dear Son? But listen! Listen! The voice of Christ's blood cries not for vengeance or retribution. It cries for forgiveness: 'Father, forgive them, for they do not know what they are doing' (Luke 23:34). And that, indeed, is a better word.

FURTHER STUDY

Rom. 5:1–21;

1 John 1:7;

Matt. 26:28

1. What does Christ's shed blood do for us?

2. What is the atonement?

Prayer

Blessed Lord Jesus, when I realise that my sins put You to death on the cross, yet Your atoning blood cried out, not for my judgment, but for my salvation, my feelings just won't go into words. Thank You for loving me so much. Amen.

Noah offers a sacrifice

For reading & meditation – Genesis 8:15–9:17

'Then Noah built an altar to the LORD ...' (8:20)

When the Flood had subsided, however, and Noah once again emerged into the world, one would have thought that his first concern would have been to build a house for himself. But what do we read? 'Then Noah built an altar to the LORD ... he sacrificed burnt offerings on it.' Though Noah's stock of cattle was small and preserved with great care, yet he did not hesitate to present a blood sacrifice to the Lord.

Isn't it interesting that the first action in the new world was an act of sacrifice and worship? The Flood had washed away the whole of the human race (with the exception of Noah and his family), but it could not remove the sin from man's nature. And as a new age dawns, it must be seen by both Noah and his descendants that God's continuance with the human race is not because of human merit but because of divine mercy.

As the Almighty smelled the sweet fragrance that arose from the burning sacrifice, He graciously declares that never again will the world be covered with water. And while the earth remains, and man upon it, there shall be summer and winter. In confirmation of the blood that flowed upon the altar, God then set a rainbow in the sky. A rainbow appears, so I am told, when we have the most reason to think that the rain will continue and prevail. The blood on the altar and the rainbow in the sky are evidence of a God who hates sin but loves the sinner.

FURTHER STUDY

Heb. 6:1–20;
13:20–21;

2 Sam. 23:5;

Isa. 54:10;

Heb. 10:35–36

1. What does Hebrews say about God's promises?
2. How have they been sealed?

Prayer

O Father, what joy fills my heart when I realise that You fellowship with me, not on the basis of my merit, but on the basis of Your mercy. If You love me in spite of what I am, then help me to love others in spite of what they are. Amen.

Pledged in blood

For reading & meditation – Genesis 15:1–21

'When the sun had set ... a blazing torch appeared and passed between the pieces.' (v.17)

Today we see that momentous occasion when God made a covenant with Abraham. God promised Abram (Abraham) that he would have an heir, and that one day the nation that came from him would come into a new land. Here again, we see the shedding of blood as a confirmation of the divine promise. Abram is instructed to cut in half a three-year-old heifer, a female goat and a ram. The divided animals were then arranged with the halves opposite each other, forming a wall, much like the sides of a door. The shedding of blood here symbolised the fact that God's covenant was rooted in sacrifice. When the sun set, a flaming torch, representing the divine presence and approval, passed through the blood-soaked sacrifice, no doubt burning and consuming it. God accepted the sacrifice, and the covenant was now ratified forever.

Did God keep His covenant with Abraham? You only have to study Bible history to see how God fulfilled His promise to His servant. And what is more, one has merely to look to present-day Israel to see how God has once again brought the nation into its 'promised land'. All that God was to Abraham, on the basis of His great covenant, He will be to us, on the grounds of the shed blood of our Lord Jesus Christ. Wonder not, my dear friend, if you encounter times of darkness and distress. God has pledged Himself to you through the innocent sufferings of His Son on Calvary, and every one of His promises will be vouchsafed. His pledge is written in blood.

FURTHER STUDY

Jer. 31:27–34;
Matt. 26:28;
Heb. 12:22–24;
13:20

1. What was God's promise in Jeremiah?
2. When was the start of its fulfilment?

Prayer

O Father, what unspeakable blessedness it is to know that, through the cross, You have committed Yourself to me in an act that can never be undone. What glorious security this gives me! I am so grateful. Amen.

Sealed with blood

For reading & meditation – Genesis 17:1–14

'You are to undergo circumcision, and it will be the sign of the covenant between me and you.' (v.11)

Here Abraham is given specific instructions by God that every male child born into the nation of Israel must be circumcised. Characteristically, Abraham is prompt to obey, and proceeds to apply God's command both to himself and to his sons. What a trusting and obedient servant of the Lord was Abraham! He did what God asked of him without so much as a question. And he did it promptly, without delay. No wonder he appears high on the list of the heroes of faith as recorded in Hebrews chapter 11. The rite of circumcision became the sign of God's covenant with Abraham. Those who did not receive the operation had no part in the promise, for God said, 'He has broken my covenant' (v.14).

The importance of circumcision can be glimpsed from a later incident in the life of Moses. Moses had neglected to circumcise his son, and when God approached him about the matter, Moses feared for his life (Exod. 4:24). Catastrophe was averted only when his wife took a flint knife and quickly performed the operation on her son.

It is difficult to understand why God should insist on circumcision as a sign of His covenant with Abraham, but simply believing that God had good reason for it, Abraham accepted it by faith. How different our own lives would be if we followed the great patriarch's example. Why do we question God so much when our own common sense ought to tell us that God knows best? In this life we are not called to understand – just to stand.

FURTHER STUDY

Rom. 2:17–29;
15:8;

Gal. 5:6;

Col. 2:11–13

1. What is circumcision of the heart?
2. What corresponds to circumcision for us?

Prayer

Gracious Father, I see I have my life strategy wrong. I expect to understand before I stand. Help me to exercise the faith Your servant Abraham demonstrated, by trusting You even though I cannot comprehend Your reasons. For Jesus' sake I ask it. Amen.

A dress rehearsal

For reading & meditation – Genesis 22:1–14

*'… Take your son, your only son Isaac, whom you love …
Sacrifice him … as a burnt offering …' (v.2)*

What a marvellous picture this is of the substitutionary work of our Lord Jesus Christ on the cross. Abraham receives the divine command to take his only son, Isaac, and offer him as a human sacrifice. Whatever the reason for the strange request, Abraham is quick to obey. The patriarch could have been forgiven if he had waited a few days to think through God's command, but Abraham got up early the next morning in determined obedience.

When Abraham and Isaac arrive at the place where the sacrifice is to be carried out, Isaac raises the question: 'The fire and wood are here but where is the lamb for the burnt offering?' Abraham replies, 'God himself will provide the lamb for the burnt offering' (vv.7–8). Those words roll down the centuries to remind us that the lamb sacrifice was not an invention of human imagination, a device to appease an angry God, rather, God Himself provides the Lamb.

A few minutes later Isaac is placed upon the altar, and just as Abraham takes the knife in his hand, and is ready to plunge it into the body of his dear son, God intervenes. Enough has been accomplished to depict to Abraham, and, through him, to succeeding generations, that this was a dress rehearsal for a greater sacrifice that one day would take place, not on Mount Moriah, but on Mount Calvary. On Mount Moriah the substitute for Isaac was the ram caught in the thicket. But on Calvary there was no substitute: Jesus became the atoning sacrifice.

FURTHER STUDY

Isaiah 53:1–12;
John 1:29;
1 Pet. 1:19; 2:21–25

1. What did Isaiah prophesy?
2. How did John and Peter confirm this?

Prayer

O God, my Father and my Redeemer, how can I thank You enough for allowing Your Son to be the sacrifice for my sin. May I express my heartfelt thanks today, not only with my lips, but also with my life. For Your own dear name's sake. Amen.

'I will pass over you'

For reading & meditation – Exodus 12:1–13

'… when I see the blood, I will pass over you …' (v.13)

Today we move into the book of Exodus, where we meet the children of Israel who, labouring under the cruel lash of their Egyptian taskmasters, cry out to God for their freedom and deliverance. God heard the cry of His people and raised up Moses to be their deliverer. Despite the plagues that God sent to the land of Egypt, Pharaoh remained stubborn and resistant: he would not let the Israelites leave the land and head for Canaan. God then decreed that on a certain night the firstborn of every family would die. Only those sheltered behind a blood-sprinkled door would survive. The way of deliverance was portrayed so clearly that no one could mistake it. A lamb was to be slain and its blood sprinkled on the doorposts and the lintels of each house. In this way the Israelites would suffer no loss while the firstborn of the Egyptians would die. Had the Israelites decided to ignore God's precise instructions and decorate their doorposts with gold, silver or other precious materials, their firstborn would have also perished. Had rubies gleamed like red flames from every door and diamonds shone like miniature stars, it would not have saved them. God said, 'When I see the blood, I will pass over you.'

Today, as in every generation, there are many who would prefer a gospel that has no mention of blood. However, the solemn fact remains: there is just no other way by which the sin of mankind can be covered except by blood – Christ's blood.

FURTHER STUDY

Matt. 26:17–30;

1 Cor. 5:7;

Rev. 5:6; 15:3

1. What did Jesus institute at the Passover?
2. What does 'new testament' mean?

Prayer

Lord Jesus, You are my Passover – and I am so thankful. My hope is indeed built on nothing less than Your blood and righteousness. Blessed be Your name for ever. Amen.

The Passover Feast

For reading & meditation – Exodus 12:14–20

'This is a day you are to commemorate ... you shall celebrate it as a festival to the LORD ...' (v.14)

In order to impress deeply into the hearts of His people the importance of their deliverance from Egypt, God decreed that they should observe a Passover Feast each year when they entered the promised land. There can be no doubt that the Passover Feast has grown to become one of the most important Jewish festivals. The date of the Passover was determined by the first full moon after the spring equinox. It was followed by the Feast of Unleavened Bread, which lasted for seven days (Exod. 13:3–10), and so closely were the two associated that before long they came to be regarded as one.

In the early part of Israel's history, the Passover sacrifice was killed by the head of the family in front of his dwelling, but later the animal was taken to a central place where all gathered together. Other adaptations of the ritual took place as the years passed, but its basic meaning remains unchanged – a celebration of deliverance from Egypt. In the afternoon before the Passover meal, the lambs were killed and the blood of each sacrifice offered to God on the altar. One census, reported by Flavius Josephus, claims that on one Passover occasion more than a quarter of a million lambs were slain. As one pictures the bleating animals, the flash of knives, and the rivers of blood, one wonders how many grasped the fact that this ritual had a wider meaning.

As William Cowper put it:

'The paschal sacrifice ...
Seen with enlightened eyes
Would teach the need of other blood
To reconcile the world to God.'

FURTHER STUDY

Luke 22:1–20;
1 Cor. 5:7-8;
1 Pet. 1:18-19

1. What was the significance of Christ's Passover meal?
2. When does the Christian celebrate his 'Passover'?

Prayer

O Father, I am so glad that I have been washed by that 'other blood'. Your nail-pierced hands have passed over my life, and I am clean – clean in You. And Your continual cleansing keeps me clean. Thank You, Father. Amen.

A marriage union

For reading & meditation – Exodus 24:1–18

'Moses then took the blood, sprinkled it on the people and said, "This is the blood of the covenant …"' (v.8)

A blood covenant in the Bible carries with it sacred obligations. Nowhere is this more clearly seen than in the giving and receiving of the Law at Sinai.

When Moses told the people of Israel 'all the LORD's words and laws, they responded with one voice, "Everything the LORD has said we will do."' What a commitment. But the matter did not end there. The following morning, Moses got up early and built an altar at the foot of Mount Sinai. 'And he sent young men of the people of Israel, who offered burnt offerings and sacrificed peace offerings of oxen to the LORD' (v.5, RSV). Then, to emphasise the sacredness of the bond made between God and His people, Moses took the blood of the sacrifices, and with it he sprinkled the altar and the people. Every aspect of the covenant was thus brought under this sacred seal.

Following this formal ratification of the Law, Moses, with the leading priests and 70 elders of Israel, participated in a communion meal. The celebration described here has all the ingredients of a wedding. God covenants to fulfil all the words written in His book, and the people promise to obey all that God says. The blood, like a wedding ring, becomes the symbol of the marriage. So it is with God's New Testament people. Christ's blood becomes the wedding band. As God's people, in the past, confirmed the old covenant at Sinai, so we, His present-day people, are joined to Christ in a new covenant at the cross.

FURTHER STUDY

Rev. 19:1–10;
Rom. 7:4;
1 Cor. 6:17;
1 John 2:24

1. How is the Church related to Christ?
2. What scene is John describing?

Prayer

O Father, with all my heart and with all the enthusiasm I can muster, I promise to love You, honour You and obey You, both in time and in eternity. Amen.

A clearer focus

For reading & meditation – Leviticus 1:1–9

'… the priests shall bring the blood and sprinkle it against the altar …' (v.5)

The spiritual significance of blood is brought more clearly into focus in Leviticus than in any other book in the Old Testament. The offering of the blood of a sacrificed animal to God expressed the highest devotion of which a man was capable. In the shed blood of that animal, the life was poured out – nothing more could man give and yet nothing less could God accept.

In order for a sacrifice to be acceptable to God, there were several conditions. First, it had to be the rightful property of the person offering the sacrifice. If the person did not own an animal to sacrifice, he could purchase one for the occasion. Second, whatever kind of animal was offered, it had to be free of defects and considered 'perfect' (Lev. 22:21–25). Third, the person had to bring the sacrifice to the door of the tabernacle 'before the LORD' (Lev. 1:3, KJV), and there place the sacrifice upon the altar so that it faced the holy place.

Fourth, he then placed his hands upon the head of the animal, while stating the reason for his sacrifice. This meant that the person had put away the sin from himself and transferred it to the helpless animal. Fifth, the animal was then violently killed, and the shed blood offered to God by the officiating priest.

It becomes immediately apparent how Christ's atoning sacrifice is reflected in the blood-soaked altars of the Old Testament. As someone said: 'The Old Testament is the New concealed. The New Testament is the Old revealed.'

FURTHER STUDY

John 19:1–42;
Luke 22:44;
Heb. 11:28; 12:24;
1 Pet. 1:2

1. In what ways did Christ fulfil the requirement of the sin offering?
2. How was the Scripture fulfilled through His death?

Prayer

Blessed Lord Jesus, as the trail of blood deepens and widens, give me, I pray, an increasing awareness of the debt I owe to You for shedding Your own precious blood for me on the cross of Calvary. I am eternally grateful. Amen.

The sin offering

For reading & meditation – Numbers 15:22–29

'… if just one person sins … he must bring a … sin offering.'
(v.27)

The sacrifices offered in the tabernacle fell into three types: the sin offering, the burnt offering and the peace offering. The sin offering was the most basic of these offerings and was a sacrifice for sins that had been committed through ignorance or weakness. We sometimes forget, when considering these Old Testament sacrifices, that a genuine spirit of repentance was expected to accompany a ceremonial offering in order for sin to be removed.

In the Mishna, a Jewish document of olden times, it was said: 'If a man says, "I will sin and repent and sin again and repent," he will be given no chance to repent. If he says, "I will sin and the Day of Atonement will effect atonement," then the Day of Atonement effects no atonement.'

This document also contained a typical prayer, used in Old Testament times, which goes like this: 'O God, I have sinned. I have committed (naming the specific sin) but I return in repentance, and let this be for my atonement.' An animal was then killed and its blood applied to the brazen altar, after which the fat part of the animal would be burned on the altar, signifying the putting away of sin. Even so, the deeper sins of the human heart (pride, envy, lust, etc) could not be dealt with by such an offering. Not until Christ died on Calvary was a full sin offering provided. His blood avails for the deepest sin.

FURTHER STUDY

Psa. 32:1–11;
Eph. 1:7;
Col. 1:14;
Acts 13:38–39

1. When are we blessed?
2. What is the message of Calvary?

Prayer

O Father, I cannot thank You enough for the revelation of Your love expressed in the cross. Through Your Son's sacrifice on Calvary, the deepest stains of my sin are cleansed and cancelled. Blessed be Your name forever. Amen.

The burnt offering

For reading & meditation – Leviticus 1:10–17

'… It is a burnt offering, an offering made by fire, an aroma pleasing to the LORD.' (v.17)

The burnt offering derived its name from a word meaning 'to go up'. A burnt offering was a sacrifice, the smoke of which ascended to God as it was burned on the altar. The main feature of this offering was that the whole animal was consumed by fire after its blood had been shed. Nothing was left of the animal that had been sacrificed, and for this reason it was sometimes called a 'whole' sacrifice (Deut. 33:10; 1 Sam. 7:9 and Psa. 51:19). The main purpose of the burnt offering was to express consecration. This was the normal sacrifice of an Israelite who was living in a proper relationship with God and was the only sacrifice in which a non-Israelite could not participate. Those who had sinned could present a sin offering, and then follow it up with a burnt offering to express their personal consecration and desire for purity and worship.

Fire, as you know, not only consumes inwardly but aspires upwardly, giving the person who offers the sacrifice the symbolic picture of an offering that reaches upward to God. The smoke of such a sacrifice was said to be 'an aroma pleasing to the LORD' (Lev. 1:9, 4:31 and Gen. 8:21). How beautifully typical of the fact that Jesus has given Himself for us 'as a fragrant offering and sacrifice to God' (Eph. 5:2). By the offering of Himself on the cross, He has filled the universe with the fragrance of His grace. Now, as partakers of that grace, we, too, are 'to God the aroma of Christ' (2 Cor. 2:15).

FURTHER STUDY

Heb. 10:1-23;
13:16;
John 15:13;
1 John 3:16-18

1. Why were the OT sacrifices insufficient?
2. What has God accomplished through one offering?

Prayer

O Father, what a revelation! Once my life came up before You as an offence. But now, through the sacrifice of Jesus, I am sweeter to You than the fragrance of a million flowers. Eternal praise and glory be to Your wonderful name. Amen.

The peace offering

For reading & meditation – Leviticus 3:1–17

*'If a man's offering is a sacrifice of peace offering ... he shall
offer it without blemish ...' (v.1, RSV)*

The sin offering was one in which an individual sought
communion with God. The burnt offering was one in which
an individual consecrated themselves to God. The peace offering
was so called because that is precisely what happened to those who
participated – they were at peace with God.

As with the other sacrifices, the ritual of the peace offering
called for the person to lay his hands on the animal about to be
offered, whereupon the animal was sacrificed and its blood applied
to the brazen altar. The main point of this offering was the symbolic
sharing of the offering between God, the priest and the person
making the sacrifice. The fat of the animal, representing God's part,
was burned on the altar (Lev. 3:16 and 7:22–24). The breast and
the right thigh of the animal were kept by the priest as his part of
the sacrifice (7:31–34). Symbolically these portions were presented
to God and then returned by God to the priest. This was done by
the priest placing his hands under the hands of the person offering
the sacrifice, and together they moved the sacrifice up and down,
right and left – actually in the sign of the cross.
The remainder of the flesh belonged to the person
making the offering. This he could eat and share
with his family.

The peace offering was always a joyous one.
The people sang and praised the Lord. Sin had
been put away; God was reconciled to them. With
such an assurance, what could be more appropriate
than to respond with praise?

FURTHER STUDY

Eph. 2:1–22;

Col. 1:20;

Isa. 53:5;

Rom. 5:1

1. What is the
'middle wall of
partition'?
2. What has this now
made us?

Prayer

My Father and my God, when I ponder the fact that You have done all that is
necessary to take away my sin, the only appropriate response is to magnify You
and praise Your glorious name. I do so now – with all my heart, Hallelujah!
Amen.

Chosen for a special purpose

For reading & meditation – Leviticus 8:1–29

'Moses ... took some of its blood and put it on the lobe of Aaron's right ear, on the thumb ... on the big toe ...' (v.23)

T he word 'priest' means 'one that takes the place of another', and, as such, every priest was a mediator between men and God. Prior to the giving of the laws of Moses, the father was the priest in his own family and officiated at the domestic altar. When the father died, he was succeeded by his firstborn son. When the tabernacle was constructed, a special order of men were selected who became the official representatives of the people, empowered to present the blood to God on their behalf. These men had to remain detached from profane things and were subject to very strict rules concerning purity, for nothing could be allowed to bring reproach upon the ministry of sacrifice and worship.

When the priests were ordained, the whole ritual of ordination was saturated with blood. After an animal had been sacrificed, blood was taken from the altar and put on the tip of the priest's right ear, on the thumb of his right hand and on the big toe of his right foot. This signified that a priest needed a special anointing from God for what he was to hear, what he would handle and where he would walk. Now, of course, all true Christians are consecrated to be spiritual priests. We should seriously ask ourselves, therefore, whether, in our daily walk, we seek to maintain the dignity of our high calling; whether, in the things we touch and handle, we reflect Christ's grace and whether, in the things we listen to, we demonstrate Christian judgment.

FURTHER STUDY

Rom. 12:1–21;

Exod. 32:29;

Phil. 3:7–8;

Rev. 5:10

1. What do you understand by 'consecrate'?
2. How did Paul apply this?

Prayer

O Father touch my ears with Your blood so that I might listen as You want me to listen. Touch my hands so that I might reach out and touch others. Touch my feet so that I might walk in Your way and Your way alone. For Christ's sake I ask it. Amen.

A naked priest

For reading & meditation – Leviticus 8:30–36

'Then Moses took … some of the blood from the altar and sprinkled them on Aaron and his garments …' (v.30)

We said yesterday that the whole ritual of ordination was saturated with blood. In fact, so much so, that on one occasion the sons of Levi were said to have ordained themselves, because of the way they had slain three thousand rebellious Israelites! (Exod. 32:25–29).

In addition to the application of blood to the right ear, the right thumb and the big toe of the priest, it was also necessary for him to put on special robes when ministering at the altar. Nudity was never permitted in ancient Israel, least of all when it came to the matter of approaching the altar. The early altar in the tabernacle did not have steps for this reason: to avoid the possibility of the high priest exposing part of his flesh when bending over it (Exod. 20:26). In later times, when a larger altar was constructed, which required steps, this type of exposure was prevented by the wearing of linen undergarments (Exod. 28:42). To approach God with some part of the body exposed was regarded as offensive and brought fearful judgment.

FURTHER STUDY

Heb. 7:1–28; 2:17;
4:14–15; 8:1

1. How has the Levitical priesthood been superseded?
2. What is Jesus' position now?

There was only one occasion in history when a naked priest offered a sacrifice that was acceptable to God. It happened at Calvary, and the name of that priest was Jesus. When our Lord died on the cross, He was stripped of His clothes (John 19:23), yet, despite His nakedness, He was clothed with a worthiness which was His by right. As the Great High Priest of heaven, He offered up His own blood – for you and me.

Prayer

O God, what lessons leap out of these Old Testament pages when they are touched by Your Holy Spirit. When I see how Jesus has superseded all the rituals of the past, my heart is lost in wonder, love and praise. Thank You, Father. Thank You, Jesus. Amen.

The altar made ready

For reading & meditation – Leviticus 8:10–17

*'Moses ... took ... blood, and ... put it on all the horns of the
altar to purify the altar ... So he consecrated it ...' (v.15)*

T he altar was in use continually, and was the means by which
individuals in the nation could approach a holy God. In order
for the altar to be a means through which God could be approached,
a ceremony was performed known as 'sanctifying the altar'. The task
took seven days, during which time Moses took the blood of a sin
offering and ceremonially cleansed the altar whereupon the altar
obtained such a holiness that it had the power to sanctify everything
that was laid on it. No Israelite need fear that his offering might be
too small or unworthy; the altar sanctified the gift that was laid upon
it. Our Lord referred to this fact when He said: 'Which is greater:
the gift, or the altar that makes the gift sacred?' (Matt. 23:19).
The scripture says: 'Then the altar will be most holy, and whatever
touches it will be holy' (Exod. 29:37).

We, too, have an altar (Heb. 13:10). It is the cross of our Lord
Jesus Christ. By the shedding of His blood upon the cross, He has
made that altar a place on which we can offer our own sacrifice, or
as Paul puts it: '... offer your bodies as living sacrifices, holy and
pleasing to God' (Rom. 12:1). Do not fear lest
your self-sacrifice be imperfect, or that there are
spots and blemishes upon your dedication. The
cross on which Jesus died and shed His blood
becomes a daily altar which sanctifies everything
that touches it. The altar, sanctified by blood, now
sanctifies the gift and the giver.

FURTHER STUDY

Gal. 6:1–18; 2:20;

Heb. 12:2;

Phil. 2:8;

Eph. 2:16

1. How did the cross
differ from the mercy
seat?
2. What does the
cross represent
for us?

Prayer

O Father, as I trace the trail of blood laid down in the Old Testament, I can't help
but lift up my eyes and see where it finally brings me – to the cross. And where
else could it lead? Thank You, Father. Amen.

Not 'do' but 'done'

For reading & meditation – Leviticus 16:1–10

'… the goat chosen by lot as the scapegoat shall be … used for making atonement …' (v.10)

God's laws covered many topics, but by far the most important laws covered the issue of removal of sin. God wanted to teach them that whenever they violated His laws, they could find forgiveness and remission through a blood sacrifice.

There were different types of sacrifices that could be offered, the most meaningful and dramatic of which was the one presented annually on the Day of Atonement. Two young goats were brought before the high priest, and, by the casting of lots, one would be selected for sacrifice as a sin offering and the other, for a scapegoat. The one chosen for sacrifice would be slain, and its blood taken into the Holy of Holies and sprinkled on the mercy seat. This was a public demonstration that the sins of the nation were covered, and that God had met them in mercy. Returning from the Holy of Holies, the high priest then laid his blood-stained hands on the head of the second goat, symbolically transferring to it all the sins of Israel (v.21). The sin-bearing scapegoat would then be sent out into the wilderness never to be seen again.

FURTHER STUDY

Col. 2:1–15;

Heb. 8:12; 10:17;

Isa. 43:25

1. What does forgiveness include?
2. What does 'blotting out' mean?

How beautifully did our Lord fulfil this Old Testament picture through His sacrifice on the cross. His blood became the full payment for sin, which He offered in the presence of God. And as I reach out my hands in faith, and lay them in quiet trust upon Him, He assures me that my sin will be carried away into the wilderness of oblivion, never to be remembered any more.

Prayer

O Lord Jesus, as I gaze upon Your surpassing merit and worth, my heart is overwhelmed with gratitude and praise. How glad I am that while other religions stress the word 'Do', mine stresses the word 'Done'. Thank You, dear Lord. Amen.

The poured-out blood

For reading & meditation – Leviticus 17:10–16

*'Any Israelite … who hunts any animal or bird … must drain
out the blood and cover it with earth.' (v.13)*

T hose who have studied the subject meticulously, tell us that
in the Bible there are over 460 specific references to blood,
and that if related concepts are counted – such as altar, sacrifice,
offering, covenant, atonement and so on – the total would be over
a thousand. 'It is the scarlet thread,' says one writer, 'which weaves
the whole scope of revelation into one harmonious witness to the
drama of redemption.'

Today's text shows us that not only was the blood to be taken
from any beast or bird before it could be eaten, but the law decreed
that the blood must be poured out upon the earth like water and
then covered with the soil (see Deut. 12:16, 15:23 and Ezek. 24:7).
Returning the blood to the earth suggests that while the body of the
animal was to be eaten by man, the life that was in it, by virtue of its
blood, was being given back to God. The Almighty evidently wanted
to teach His people, early in their history, that blood had a divine
essence. It was the physical symbol of created life.

The Israelites were unable to visualise the full meaning of the
message contained in that mysterious substance
called blood, but they knew, nevertheless, that
the blood belonged to God, and that somehow it
was the means of their salvation and redemption.
Today, as you probably know, orthodox Jews still
eat only kosher meat: that is, meat which is without
blood, and which has been slaughtered according
to the method described here in Leviticus.

FURTHER STUDY

James 1:1–15;
Gen. 2:17;
Rom. 6:23;
John 19:34

1. *What is the
penalty for sin?*
2. *What did shed
blood represent?*

Prayer

O Father, how glad I am that I am living in the light of full revelation. In the past
Your people had just a glimpse of the truth, but now, in Jesus, I have it in all its
fullness. And what fullness! Amen.

The sanctity of blood

For reading & meditation – Leviticus 17:1–11

'For the life of the flesh is in the blood ...' (v.11, RSV)

A s all life flows from God, it is natural that blood (without which there is no life) be regarded with great reverence. God commanded the Israelites not to take blood into their system, and they were to eat animal flesh only after the blood had been completely drained from it (Lev. 19:26). God wanted to emphasise to His people in those early days that blood had a special significance and a special sanctity. It was the physical symbol of created life, and spoke of Him who would one day come to give His life for the sins of the world.

The Israelites knew that the life, which was in the blood, belonged to God, and that somehow, when the blood was poured out for them in sacrifice, it was the means of their redemption. Of course, it was not until Christ came and shed His blood upon the Cross that the world could see the full meaning of what God had tried to show His people in the Old Testament.

One writer, expounding on the theme of the blood, said, 'At the creation God came down to earth to give His breath to man, but at Calvary He came down to give His blood for man.' In each act, of course, God gave something of His own life in order that man might be brought into a proper relationship with Himself. The whole purpose of the Old Testament is to lay down in the minds of men and women a deep respect for blood, and thus prepare them for the highest expression of love as demonstrated in the giving of Christ's blood on Calvary.

FURTHER STUDY

Col. 1: 1–23;

Acts 20:28;

Rev. 1:5

1. What five things are ours 'through the blood of the cross'?
2. What do these things mean to you?

Prayer

O Father, these words of Scripture, even in the Old Testament take me by the hand and lead me to Jesus. New light breaks out from Your Word all the time. I am so grateful. Amen.

Defilement by death

For reading & meditation – Numbers 19:1–22

'Whoever touches the dead body of anyone and fails to purify himself defiles the LORD's tabernacle ...' (v.13)

There was a special ceremony to cleanse anyone who had been in contact with someone who had just died. A red heifer was sacrificed and its blood sprinkled seven times toward the sanctuary, after which the whole animal was burned. Some of the ashes were mixed with water; hyssop was then dipped into the solution and it was sprinkled on the unclean person. They were then deemed to be free of any defilement.

Why did the law regard a corpse as a defiling thing? Doubtless because death, which entered the world through sin, is a defilement that affects every member of the human race. The law could not conquer death, nor abolish it; whereas the gospel brings 'life and immortality to light' (2 Tim. 1:10). This ceremony must have been in the mind of the writer to the Hebrews, when he wrote: 'the ashes of a heifer sprinkled on those who are ceremonially unclean sanctify them ... How much more, then, will the blood of Christ ... cleanse our consciences' (Heb. 9:13–14).

In this ceremony, we have a picture of how important it is for us to experience day by day the cleansing application of Christ's blood to our consciences. Despite the fact that we have been saved and our sins forgiven, we still have a corrupt carnal nature, and live in a depraved world, which makes it necessary for us to walk moment by moment in the light of Christ, applying the power of His blood to our hearts and lives so that we might continually be kept pure.

FURTHER STUDY

1 Tim. 1:1–20;
Acts 24:16;
Rom. 9:1;
1 Pet. 3:16

1. What did Paul exhort Timothy to do?
2. Is your conscience clear today?

Prayer

O crucified Redeemer, I realise that although I have been cleansed from the past, I need continual cleansing in the present. You shared my defilement. Now I share Your purity. Blessed exchange! I am so thankful. Amen.

The blood covenant ritual

For reading & meditation – 1 Samuel 18:1–4

'And Jonathan made a covenant with David because he loved him ...' (v.3)

In the Bible the word 'covenant' implies a binding agreement between two parties. The word literally means 'cutting an agreement by shedding blood'. When two Hebrew men entered into a covenant, they embarked upon a ceremony that involved nine steps. Today we shall look at the first four steps.

First, each would take off his coat or robe, symbolising the giving of themselves to each other. Second, each would take off his belt, indicating (as the belt contained weapons of warfare) that 'your battles are now my battles'. Third, they sacrificed an animal, cut it in half and stood together between the divided portions. Fourth, they raised their right arms, and after cutting their palms placed both of them together. At this moment, as their blood intermingled, they would swear their undying allegiance to each other.

The depth of this covenant ritual becomes shallow by the side of the covenant Christ seeks to make with us. The Bible says that He stands knocking at the door of our hearts, desiring to enter into a blood covenant with us by sharing His life with us (Rev. 3:20). Way back in eternity, He divested Himself of His glory, and came to this earth that He might take our sin and shame upon Himself. Early believers recognised this, and spoke of Him as Immanuel – 'God with us'. On the cross, He gave Himself as our sacrifice, and when we receive Him, He pledges that our names are written on the palms of His hands for all eternity (Isa. 49:16).

FURTHER STUDY

2 Sam. 9:1–13; 4:4;
1 Sam. 20:16–17

1.Why did Mephibosheth become like one of the king's sons?
2. Who does Mephibosheth typify,

Prayer

O Jesus, You are the One through whom I see right into the heart of God. And what I see there sets my heart on fire, for I see Love seeking me, finding me, saving me, bleeding for me. All honour and glory be to Your peerless name. Amen.

He planted a tree

For reading & meditation – 1 Samuel 20:1–17

'So Jonathan made a covenant with the house of David ...'
(v.16)

The fifth step was to exchange names. Each took part of the other's name, symbolising their newly established bond. Sixth, they made a scar in each other's palms by rubbing their wounds together. The scar would remind them of their covenant responsibilities. Seventh, they identified their assets and said, at the same time, 'From now on all that I own is yours.' Eighth, they then shared a memorial meal by cooking the flesh of the sacrificed animal and eating it together. Finally they planted a tree as a perpetual memorial to their covenant, and sprinkled it with the blood of the sacrificed animal.

When placed against the background of this ancient Hebrew ritual, the life and death of our Lord Jesus Christ comes alive with new and special meaning. Not only, as we saw yesterday, did He divest Himself of His robes of glory and take upon Himself a state of weakness and humiliation, but He gave us His name. For all who enter into covenant with Him, He sends the Holy Spirit, and through the Holy Spirit, we become partakers of His nature. The Holy Spirit is like the scar that seals us into the body of Christ (Eph. 1:13–14). Prior to going to the cross, Jesus ate a covenant meal with His disciples. The bread, He said, represented His body and the wine, His blood. After that meal, Jesus went out and left a memorial to that covenant. He planted a tree (the cross) and poured out His blood upon it. What a covenant! What a Saviour!

FURTHER STUDY

Rev. 21:1–27; 3:5;
Luke 10:20;
Phil. 4:3

1. Where are our names written?
2. To what does this give us access?

Prayer

Lord Jesus, how can I ever sufficiently thank You for making a covenant with me that will outlast time and go on through eternity. My heart pillows itself on that wondrous and glorious fact. Amen.

The crucifixion psalm

For reading & meditation – Psalm 22:1–31

'They divide my garments among them and cast lots for my clothing.' (v.18)

Psalm 22 has rightly been called the crucifixion psalm. Look at the way in which the writer, under the inspiration of the Holy Spirit, paints a word picture of Christ's death on the cross. 'They divide my garments among them and cast lots for my clothing.' Isn't this what happened at Calvary? Then what about this? 'My tongue sticks to the roof of my mouth; you lay me in the dust of death' (v.15). Did not our Lord cry out on the cross: 'I thirst'? A more exact expression of our Lord's thoughts and feelings during the hours He spent on the cross could not be found anywhere in the Bible: 'I am a worm and not a man, scorned by men and despised by the people. All who see me mock me; they hurl insults … "He trusts in the Lord … Let him deliver him …"' (vv.6–8). Isn't this fulfilled in Matthew's words: 'He trusts in God. Let God rescue him now if he wants him, for he said, "I am the Son of God"' (27:43)?

It seems that in Psalm 22, the Holy Spirit draws aside the veil of the future, and gives a sure and certain hope to those who recognised that the temple sacrifices were woefully inadequate to really take away sin. It is as if the Holy Spirit is saying: 'The day will come when a man will die upon a Cross, will be humiliated, spat upon, mocked at, scoffed and ridiculed. But His death, violent and brutal as it will be, will be God's way of dealing with sin – once and for all.'

FURTHER STUDY

Psa. 23:1–6; 24:1–10

1. What picture do these three psalms show, taken together?
2. Select three words to describe Christ, one for each psalm.

Prayer

O Father, like the watermark in paper which I see only when I hold it up to the light, so is the stain of Your shed blood on Calvary written into the very texture of the Old Testament. I can but stand in awe at the wonder of Your developing revelation. Amen.

The Lamb of God

For reading & meditation – Isaiah 53:1–12

'... *he was wounded for our transgressions, he was bruised for our iniquities ...*' (v.5, RSV)

Here, centuries before Christ came, Isaiah prophesies, through the Spirit, the sacrifice of Christ upon the cross. In the Old Testament, the saints and prophets seem almost to stand on tiptoe as they peer forward into the future, straining through the mists of time to catch sight of the event toward which the ages moved, namely the sacrifice of the Lamb of God, on Calvary's tree. We, in this age, can look back to the cross, and view it as an historical fact, but they (the Old Testament saints) could only look through a glass darkly, and reach out toward it in faith. Whichever way Calvary is viewed, however, it is the axis of the universe. On its hinges, the door of eternity swings wide open. Calvary is where time and eternity intersect, and in the flowing blood that streams from the cross lies the answer to the ages.

Dr Robert G. Lee tells the unforgettable story of his first visit to Gordon's Calvary in Jerusalem. He was so excited at seeing the skull-like hill that he outran his guide in getting to the top. As he reached the summit, he paused, and, with tears running down his face, gave thanks to God for the death of His Son. The guide looked nonplussed and said, 'Sir, have you been here before?' 'Yes,' said Dr Lee, 'I was here two thousand years ago.' In a sense we were all there two thousand years ago. Jesus died in our place, 'the just for the unjust, that he might bring us to God' (1 Pet. 3:18, KJV).

FURTHER STUDY

1 Pet. 3:1–18;
Psa. 69:9;
Gal. 3:13;
Heb. 2:9;
1 Pet. 2:24

1. What did Christ become for us?
2. How should we now live?

Prayer

O Father, I am so thankful that, because Your death brought me my salvation, Calvary is not a tragedy but a glorious victory. Others may see it in gloom but I see it in glory. I am so thankful. Amen.

The deciding mark

For reading & meditation – Ezekiel 9:1–11

'… but do not touch anyone who has the mark …' (v.6)

In this chapter the prophet Ezekiel is visualising the destruction of Jerusalem and the dispersion of God's people, the Jews. The reason for this destruction is quite clear – the people of God had become idolators. The word comes to the prophet that the idolators will be slaughtered, God's glory will depart from the sanctuary and Judah's leaders will watch helplessly as the city is overthrown and destroyed.

However, there is a ray of hope – those who carry in their hearts a deep desire to break with idolatry, 'those who grieve and lament over all the detestable things that are done' (v.4), will be preserved and protected from destruction. A man clothed in fine linen, representative of Christ, is told to put a mark on the foreheads of those who share God's concern over the state of the nation. And what was that mark? Many Jewish commentators believe it to be a mark of blood. We are not told this expressly, and, therefore, we can only conjecture, but from my own research into the subject, I am convinced it was so.

FURTHER STUDY

1 Cor. 1:17–31;

Titus 2:14;

John 15:16;

Eph. 1:4

1. What sort of people does God select?

2. What characterises God's 'very own' people?

Jerome, one of the early Church Fathers, believed that, not only was the mark one of blood, but that it was the letter *tau* from the Hebrew alphabet, which was, at that time, written like a cross. But whatever the nature of the sign, it did, for those thus marked, what the blood sprinkled on the doorposts did for the earlier Israelites. Those who were marked by the special sign were protected and delivered.

Prayer

O God my Father, I am so thankful that I am one of those marked with Your blood, not upon my forehead but upon my heart. This guarantees me a safe passage through death and a glorious welcome in eternity. What a prospect! Glory! Amen.

Jesus is the Messiah

For reading & meditation – Zechariah 13:1–9

*'Awake, O sword, against my shepherd … Strike the shepherd,
and the sheep will be scattered …' (v.7)*

There are many other scriptures in the Old Testament we could have looked at, but I chose to select only the ones which I considered had clear reference to the covenant of blood which was established by our Lord Jesus Christ. Although the actual word 'blood', or 'sacrifice', does not appear in this passage, a clear picture is given of a shepherd being subjected to a violent death: 'Awake, O sword … Strike the shepherd.' This text takes on added significance when we remember that it was quoted by our Lord on the night in which He was betrayed (Matt. 26:31).

Many years ago a Russian Jew, by the name of Joseph Rabinowitz, visited the Holy Land and sat on the summit of the Mount of Olives, reading the prophecy of Zechariah. His eye fell on this passage and, as he read, the same thing happened to him that had happened to Saul of Tarsus on the road to Damascus. The scales fell from his eyes, and it became clear to him that Jesus Christ, the crucified one, was none other than the promised Messiah. He returned to Russia and became a powerful witness for Christ. He used to say, 'We Jews are like a farmer on his way to market. However, a wheel comes off the wagon, but we struggle on, hoping we will find a wheel further up ahead. But we will never find one ahead. We must turn back to find the wheel. Jews are looking ahead for their Messiah. We must turn back to the one we rejected – Jesus.'

FURTHER STUDY

Luke 22:63–71:

John 18:22:

Matt. 27:30:

Luke 6:29

1. What did Jesus teach about smiting?
2. How did He demonstrate this?

Prayer

Gracious Father, I feel today I must pray for Your people – the Jews. Help them to see, as I have seen, that the one who was crucified at Calvary is truly the Messiah – both the Son of God and God, the Son. For Your own dear name's sake. Amen.

'Look, the Lamb!'

For reading & meditation – John 1:19–29

'... Look, the Lamb of God, who takes away the sin of the world!' (v.29)

I s the crimson trail as visible in the New Testament as it is in the Old? Most definitely. There are about one hundred references to blood in the New Testament, most of which refer directly to the blood of our Lord Jesus Christ. Here, in the passage before us today, we come face to face with a phrase that speaks of the fact of atoning sacrifice: 'Look, the Lamb of God, who takes away the sin of the world!'

The whole of the Old Testament can be summed up in the words of Isaac on Mount Moriah: 'Where is the lamb?' This was the cry of all the Old Testament priests and prophets as they looked beyond the ancient tabernacle and temple sacrifices for One who would come and make a final and perfect offering for sin. If the Old Testament can be summed up in the question: 'Where is the Lamb?', then the New Testament can be summed up in this answer of John's: 'Look, the Lamb.' This is, in fact, the main thesis of the Bible. In the Old, Christ is the Lamb portrayed; in the New, He is the Lamb displayed.

FURTHER STUDY

Rev. 7; 5:8–14;
13:8; 22:1–3

1. What was happening around the throne?
2. What were they all saying?

In the lives of the Israelites, a lamb made atonement for an individual. Then later, as in the Exodus from Egypt, a lamb made atonement for a family. In the tabernacle sacrifices, a lamb made atonement for the whole nation. But see now how the value of God's Lamb is so beautifully expressed by John. Here is a Lamb whose sacrifice covers not merely the sin of an individual, a family, or even a nation: His sacrifice takes away the sin of the whole world.

Prayer

Blessed Lord Jesus, stepping into the New Testament is like stepping from darkness into light, from gloom to glory. What need have I of attempting to work my way to heaven when You have paid my passage – in full. I am deeply thankful. Amen.

No diversion

For reading & meditation – Matthew 16:21–28

*'... Jesus began to explain ... that he must go to Jerusalem
and suffer many things ... and ... be killed ...' (v.21)*

Early in His ministry, Jesus began to make clear to His disciples
that it was foreordained that He should go to Jerusalem and
be crucified upon a cross. Peter, acting as their spokesman, pleads
with the Master to reject the possibility. Peter must have been deeply
shocked by Christ's reply: 'Get away from me, you Satan! You are a
dangerous trap to me. You are thinking merely from a human point
of view, and not from God's' (v.23,TLB).

When Jesus called Simon Peter 'you Satan' was He being too
harsh? No. Here the greatest issue of all times was at stake – Christ's
going to the cross – and nothing, absolutely nothing, must interfere
with it. Of course, Peter had confessed that Jesus Christ was truly
the Son of God, but when he rejected the idea of the cross, Jesus
had to identify where those thoughts came from. They came from
Satan, for that is exactly how Satan became Satan, by putting his
own interests before God's.

This incident took place in a very significant spot. At Caesarea
Philippi there was a grotto where an image of Caesar was worshipped
as God. Against this background, the issue
becomes clear: Is the message of Jesus a Caesar-
like power force? Or is it the force of suffering
love? Jesus knew that the only way God could
truly be revealed in this world was through a
cross, and the only way sinners could be redeemed
was by His shed blood. And nothing, no nothing,
must be allowed to interfere with His reaching
that momentous goal.

FURTHER STUDY

John 18; 20:1–10;
21:15–17

1. What was Peter's
first response to the
Lord?
2. In what ways can
we be like Peter?

Prayer

Lord Jesus, I am increasingly amazed at the solid determination that lay behind
Your intentions to go to the cross. Nothing diverted You, and because of that, I
now share the benefits of Your redemptive death. I am so grateful. Amen.

Partaking of His blood

For reading & meditation – John 6:35–58

'Whoever eats my flesh and drinks my blood has eternal life ...' (v.54)

The question must be faced: Why did Christ invite us to drink His blood? How are we to understand this strange command? The mystery deepens even further when we consider that under the laws of Moses the drinking of blood was strictly forbidden, and was regarded as an offence and an abomination.

Well, to understand this statement of Jesus' we must first understand who He is, and the purpose of His mission to this world. Someone said, 'We can only understand the pronouncements of Christ when we understand the person of Christ.' We ask ourselves: Who then is Jesus? He is the Son of God who came to this world for the express purpose of giving His life for us on the cross. The giving of His life, symbolised in the blood that emptied from His veins at Calvary, is the only way mankind can be saved. When we receive that poured-out life into our own beings, then we receive the life-renewing power of His sacrifice for us on the cross.

When Jesus asked us to drink His blood and eat His flesh, He was using this as an analogy to show us that what eating and drinking is to the body (energy and nourishment), so is His life to our spirit and soul. Jesus, unlike the leaders of other religions, does not just give us a code of ethics or a moral structure – He gives us Himself. And, partaking of His poured-out sacrifice, is the secret of life, real life, life now and life forever.

FURTHER STUDY

2 Pet. 1:1–20;

Heb. 3:14;

Phil. 1:7

1. Of what are we partakers?
2. List some characteristics of this.

Prayer

O Father, I have one request: show me more clearly how I can draw from You the substance and nourishment I need to live a full and effective life for You here on this earth. In Jesus' name I ask it. Amen.

The new Passover Lamb

For reading & meditation – Luke 22:7–20

'... This cup is the new covenant in my blood, which is poured out for you.' (v.20)

J esus participated in a Passover meal the night before His death. In it, He declared Himself to be another Passover Lamb, by whose death an exodus would be achieved far greater than that of the children of Israel from the land of Egypt. What a moving moment this must have been.

A Passover ceremony began with the leader of the household drinking a cup of blood-red wine, which was then passed around the other members of the family. Next a roasted paschal lamb would be brought in and eaten, along with other portions of a meal. Next came the drinking of a second cup, at which point the leader of the household would explain the meaning of the Passover. They would then join in singing the first part of the Hallel, Psalms 113 and 114. After this, the unleavened bread would be broken and distributed, followed by the third cup of blessing. The meal would then conclude by singing the second part of the Hallel, Psalms 115–118.

What a moving experience it must have been as Jesus drew the parallel between the ancient Exodus, and its Passover lamb, and His own mission: 'This is my blood of the covenant, which is poured out for many for the forgiveness of sins' (Matt. 26:28). And what meaning the words of the Hallel would have had for Him as He sang such words as: 'This is the day which the Lord has made', or, 'Bind the sacrifice with cords to the altar'. When this Passover ended, a greater one was about to begin.

FURTHER STUDY
John 6:32–58;
1 Cor. 11:23–32;
10:16–17
1. Why is Holy Communion so important?
2. What is Paul's teaching about it?

Prayer

Blessed Lord Jesus, as I sense the pathos and beauty of that moment in the Upper Room, my heart is moved more than ever at the wonder of Your love for me and determination to die for my sin. I am eternally grateful. Thank You, dear Lord Jesus. Amen.

Calvary – a blood bank

For reading & meditation – Matthew 27:11–31

'… he had Jesus flogged, and handed him over to be crucified.' (v.26)

The shedding of our Saviour's blood began many hours prior to His crucifixion on the cross. It started, as you know, in the Garden of Gethsemane when, in the midst of His anguish His 'sweat was like great drops of blood falling to the ground' (Luke 22:44). It continued later when He was brutally flogged. The whip with its sharp pieces of bone would have ripped the flesh from His back (Psa. 129:3). Victims often died under such vicious scourging. And, adding insult to injury, the Roman soldiers brought a crown of thorns and placed it on His head; so again the blood flowed freely.

At Calvary the blood spurts yet again as huge iron nails are hammered into His hands and feet. But look at the last final detail. As Christ's blood must be completely shed in order that He might be a perfect sin offering, a soldier thrusts a spear into His side and out gushes blood and water. His life is now fully poured out. Blessed Jesus!

Myron L. Morris, a medical doctor, tells how a little boy once saved his sister's life by giving her his blood. As the transfusion took place, the little boy's lips began to tremble. It was many minutes later that the doctor realised what the trembling lips signified, when the boy said, 'Doctor, when do I die?' We hear a lot today about blood banks and blood donors, but how much more wonderful is the blood bank of Calvary. There our Saviour gave His blood for us, and became the greatest blood donor in history.

FURTHER STUDY

Acts 2:22–36;

Isa. 53:3;

Phil. 2:7-8

1. Who crucified Christ?
2. Where did you stand?

Prayer

Lord Jesus, as I stand again at the foot of Your cross, my heart is filled with deepest love and gratitude that You shed Your precious blood – just for me. Thank You, Lord Jesus. Thank You. Amen.

The torn curtain

For reading & meditation – Luke 23:44–49

'... the curtain of the temple was torn in two' (v.45)

T he Passover service would have been well under way, when thousands of men, bringing with them a lamb for sacrifice, slowly made their way to the temple on Mount Moriah where the animals were put to death by the priests. No doubt some of the blood had already been taken into the Holy Place and sprinkled before the curtain – a finely woven fabric of blue, purple and scarlet which separated the Holy Place from the Holy of Holies. The curtain served to hide the inner sanctuary from everyone except the high priest, and he could only enter it once a year on the Day of Atonement. At the moment Jesus died on the cross, the earth began to shake, and suddenly the curtain of the temple was tom from the top to the bottom. The barrier to the Holy of Holies fell in two limp heaps on the marble floor. It must have been a sobering moment for the priest who ministered there, for clearly no human hand could have tom the heavy fabric. Now the mercy seat was in full view, and the inner heart of the Holy of Holies laid bare for all to see.

Little did those priests realise that not very far away on another mount, Mount Calvary, the sacrifice of God's Lamb would make all other sacrifices irrelevant and unnecessary. The curtain is a symbol of our Lord's body, which when rent asunder opened a highway for us into the very heart of God. At Calvary the very heart of God lies exposed. And what do we see? His heart is a mercy seat stained by the blood of His own dear Son.

FURTHER STUDY

Heb. 10:1–23; 9:24;
Eph. 2:13,18

1. What has Christ opened up for us?
2. How can we now approach God?

Prayer

O Father, I am so excited at the thought that the curtain between Your heart and mine has been torn asunder. When I look through the lens of Calvary, I see straight into Your heart. And I see love – suffering, redeeming love. I am so grateful. Amen.

And then . . .

For reading & meditation – Mark 16:1–7

'... *He has risen! He is not here. See the place where they laid him.*' (v.6)

C hrist's sacrifice on the cross was the full and final atonement for sin. No longer was the offering of an animal needed to atone for sin. The true Lamb of God, by His sacrifice on the cross, had taken away the sins of the whole world.

However, in order for salvation to be complete, it was necessary that Christ must also be a Great High Priest. If He had died as an offering for sin, and had not risen to present the benefits of His death before God in heaven, then His sufferings on the cross would have been to no avail. No one else but a sinless High Priest could stand before the majestic presence of God, and so, by virtue of the resurrection, the offering now becomes the offerer.

The Living Bible puts it beautifully: 'He came as High Priest ... and once for all took blood into that inner room, the Holy of Holies, and sprinkled it on the mercy seat; but it was not the blood of goats and calves. No, he took his own blood, and with it he, by himself, made sure of our eternal salvation' (Heb. 9:11–12, TLB). And so, once again, as we, in our imagination, follow the women into the tomb, that great hole in the side of the rock, we remind ourselves that there is nothing to be seen. Nothing. It's empty! It is just the place where they laid Him. The genius of Christianity is that its followers get their greatest joy out of seeing nothing. We have looked into the tomb where they laid Him and we have discovered nothing. Nothing! Are you satisfied?

FURTHER STUDY

Exod. 26:26–37;
Matt. 27:51;
Heb. 6:19; 10:20

1. What separated us from the most holy place?
2. How was the curtain torn?

Prayer

Yes, blessed Lord, the discovery that the tomb in which You were laid now contains nothing, is the foundation on which I stand eternally secure. Satisfied? – I feel like shouting it from the rooftops! He is risen! Amen.

What happened at the cross?

For reading & meditation – Luke 24:36–49

'… *It is I myself! Touch me and see; a ghost does not have flesh and bones, as you see I have.*' (v.39)

Today we ask ourselves an intriguing question: What happened to Christ's blood after it was poured out at Calvary? Did it return supernaturally into His veins (as some believe) at the moment of the resurrection? Was it caught up by God (as others believe) and carried into heaven? I think not. It is interesting to note that in the passage before us today, Christ does not refer to His resurrection body as having blood. Omissions, of course, prove nothing, but I am satisfied in my own heart that Christ's resurrection body was bloodless.

I have thought long and hard about this matter of Christ's blood which was shed at Calvary, and, for what it is worth, this is my view on the matter. I believe that Christ's blood was of such immense value to God that, when it was shed on the cross, God literally froze eternity at that point, so that the shed blood of the Lord Jesus became the focal point of the ages. Just as we can 'freeze' a crucial moment on a video screen, so that we can hold it before us, so God froze the moment when Christ's blood drained from His body, and this moment has, by reason of its spiritual significance, become the most important moment of eternity. Nothing greater or more wonderful has ever taken place in the universe than the shedding of Christ's blood on the cross. It is an event that affects the eternal ages.

FURTHER STUDY

Phil. 2:1–11;
John 1:14;
Rom. 8:3;
1 Pet. 4:1

1. What does Paul say about the humanity of Christ?
2. What does the cross bring to an end?

Prayer

O Father, whatever may be men's theories regarding Christ's blood, I am thankful above all that it was shed – and shed for me. Thank You, dear Father. Amen.

The Blood of God

For reading & meditation – Acts 20:17–38

'... Be shepherds of the church of God, which he bought with his own blood.' (v.28)

John Stott tells how he received an angry letter from a lady who had been at one of the services in All Souls, London, when they had sung a hymn about Christ's blood. She referred to the service as 'a hangover from primitive blood rituals'. But there is all the difference in the world between the way blood is seen in the Bible and the way it is used in other religions. One great difference is this: in other religions, blood is brought to an idol or image as a libation or a sacrifice. In Christianity, blood is not brought to an image, but blood flows from the image. Christ is referred to in Hebrews as 'the express image' of God (KJV), the perfect representation of the Father (1:3). Blood to the image (or idol) is the cry of the heathen; blood from the Image (Christ) is the cry of the Christian.

It is true that, in the Old Testament, blood was offered before God as a sacrifice for sin, but the Almighty took great care to teach men that it was but a temporary procedure. The day would come when, instead of them offering blood to Him, He would offer it to them. The phrase before us today is, to my mind, one of the most moving in the whole Bible – the blood of God. Can you see what this means? The blood that flows from Christ is also the blood of God. And that can mean only one thing – God, in Christ, gave His life for us. No wonder Wesley sang: 'With what rapture, with what rapture, Gaze we on those glorious scars!'

FURTHER STUDY

Heb.1:1–2:18;

2 Cor. 4:4;

Col. 1:15

1. Of what did Christ become a partaker?
2. What is His exalted position?

Prayer

Yes, dear Lord, with what rapture! I am lost in wonder, love and praise. Amen.

Propitiation

For reading & meditation – Romans 3:21–31

'whom God set forth to be a propitiation by his blood through faith …' (v.25, NKJV)

We come today to a new and interesting word – propitiation. The word means to conciliate, to gain the favour of, to overcome someone's indignation. In pagan religions, propitiation referred to what men did to appease an offended deity. In the Bible, the word refers to the provision made on the cross, by which God could show mercy to a sinner.

Sin is an offence to God, an insult to His holiness, so awful and so affronting that no mortal can conceive how great the insult is. Anything that offends a holy God as deeply as sin cannot lightly be tossed aside and ignored. Something must be done to remove the divine wrath, and make it possible for God to demonstrate His love and mercy. Here human language breaks down, for through the shedding of Christ's blood, we see that it is God Himself who takes the initiative in removing His own wrath. A gift is offered, but it is God who gives it – in Christ. Blood is shed, but it is the blood of His own dear Son. God is seen, therefore, as both requiring yet offering propitiation. God's wrath against sinners is removed, not because of what we have done, but because of what He has done.

The Hebrew word for propitiation literally translated is 'mercy seat'. The mercy seat covered the ark of the covenant which contained the Law, and was the place where the blood of the atoning sacrifice was sprinkled. In Christ, and through His shed blood, the wrath of the law is covered by His mercy. What justice! What mercy!

FURTHER STUDY

Rom. 8:1–17;
1 John 2:2; 4:10

1. What is it that condemns and separates?
2. Why can we cry Abba, Father?

Prayer

Gracious God, I see so clearly that the cross, from beginning to end, is a display of Your sovereign grace. Your love has not only conquered sin, it has conquered my heart. I am eternally grateful. Amen.

Justified through the blood

For reading & meditation – Romans 5:1–11

'Since we have now been justified by his blood, how much more shall we be saved ... through him!' (v.9)

Justification is an act of God whereby a sinner, through faith in the innocent sufferings of Christ at Calvary, is counted by God as perfectly righteous. In other words, they stand in the presence of God as if they had never sinned. And what is the basis for this amazing fact? This: 'For God sent Christ Jesus to take the punishment for our sins and to end all God's anger against us. He used Christ's blood and our faith as the means of saving us from his wrath' (Rom. 3:25, TLB). In justifying us through the blood of Calvary, God wraps His completeness around our incompleteness and covers our nakedness with the royal robes of heaven. Because we are 'accepted in the Beloved', as Paul puts it in Ephesians 1:6 (NKJV), God treats us as if we had never sinned.

The book of Romans revolves on four pivots, all involving the word 'therefore'. As one wag said, 'When you see the word "therefore", you must ask yourself what it is there for!' These four pivots are found in Romans 2:1, 5:1, 8:1 and 12:1. Romans 2:1 is the 'therefore' of condemnation, Romans 5:1 is the 'therefore' of justification,

Romans 8:1 is the 'therefore' of sanctification and Romans 12:1 is the 'therefore' of consecration. Each 'therefore' has great meaning, but none more so than the 'therefore' of justification. In simple terms, it means that God looks at every repentant sinner through the blood of His Son, and sees that sinner as He sees Jesus – as perfect.

FURTHER STUDY

Gal. 2:1–21;

Titus 3:7;

1 Cor. 6:11

1. How does Paul describe the outworking of justification?
2. What does that mean for you today?

Prayer

Blessed Lord Jesus, how can I thank You enough for Your shed blood that makes me acceptable and perfect in the sight of Your Father. Help me to accept myself as You accept me, for I dare not reject what You have accepted. Amen.

Holy Communion

For reading & meditation – 1 Corinthians 11:17–34

'... *if people do not recognize the meaning of the Lord's body when they eat ... and drink ... they bring judgment on themselves* ...' (v.29, GNB)

The Communion service has three main purposes. Firstly, it focuses our attention on the past: 'Do this in remembrance of me.' The physical emblems of broken bread and poured-out wine remind us of the eternal significance of our Lord's offering of Himself for us. If we are not conscious of that thought when we take Communion, then we are missing the first part of its meaning. As I said earlier, the father or leader of a family recounted at the Passover Feast the story of Israel's deliverance from Egypt. And similarly, in my view, we should remind ourselves at the Communion table of the fact that Christ is Our Passover, sacrificed for us, and that we have been delivered from a bondage far greater than the bondage of God's people in Egypt.

Secondly, Holy Communion focuses our attention on the present: 'A man ought to examine himself' (v.28). It was the custom in Israel for the head of the home to make sure that no leaven (representing Egypt and its bondage) was hidden somewhere in the house when the Passover was eaten. Nothing that was on the other side of the Passover, so to speak, could be allowed to contaminate the feast (1 Cor. 5:6–7). We, too, are told to purge out the 'old leaven'.

Finally, the Communion focuses our attention on the future: 'Do this until He comes again.' One day, perhaps soon, we shall no longer need to use physical emblems to remind us of Christ's sacrifice – we shall see Him face to face.

FURTHER STUDY

Psa. 139:17–24;
51:6;
Lam. 3:40;
Matt. 7:5;
2 Cor. 13:5

1. How did David pray?
2. How should we pray?

Prayer

O Father, I thank You for reminding me of the seriousness and solemnity of the feast of Communion. May I receive from it, and through it, all that You have put into it. In Jesus' name. Amen.

Redeemed!

For reading & meditation – Galatians 3:1–14

'Christ redeemed us from the curse of the law ...' (v.13)

The word redemption means to purchase, to buy back or to loose. A story from the American Civil War might help us to see the truth underlying the word. A band of raiders known as the Quantrill Raiders used to sweep down upon the communities in the state of Kansas, rob them of their goods and ride away before help could be organised. After a while, however, the citizens of some of the towns organised themselves into groups and set out to find the raiders. Soon they captured some of the men, and brought them back to the town to be judged and sentenced by the courts. After the trial, sentence was given – death by a firing squad. As the group faced their executioners, a young man rushed out of the crowd and shouted, 'Wait! Wait!' He pointed to a man about to be shot and said, 'Let that man go; he has a wife and four children. I am guilty also, and I will take his place.' It was a strange appeal, but it was granted. The volunteer took the man's place, and soon fell dead before the firing squad. Later, when the volunteer was buried, the redeemed man went to his grave, and wrote on the headstone the words: 'He died for me.'

FURTHER STUDY

Rom. 3:1–24;
Eph. 4:30;
1 Cor. 1:30;
Col. 1:14

1. What comes by the law?
2. What comes through Christ?

Now, look again at Calvary. If anyone should have paid the penalty for your sin, it ought to have been you. But Christ took your place. He redeemed you. His death means you are free from the debt of sin. In your imagination, write in letters clear and bold over that cross: 'He died for me.'

Prayer

Blessed Jesus, the wonder of Your blood-bought redemption sends me to my knees in humble gratitude. If I can remain silent about this and vocal about other things, then all my values are twisted. Amen.

No forgiveness without atonement

For reading & meditation – Ephesians 1:3–14

'In him we have redemption through his blood ...' (v.7)

There are many people in today's Church who believe the cross to be unnecessary. Many of them base their thinking on the story of the prodigal son, and claim that all a person need do in order to find forgiveness is simply to ask for it, irrespective of the cross. One exponent of this theory puts it like this: 'There was no talk of atonement in the story of the prodigal son. No one had to bear punishment before the son was forgiven. The father met his son's penitence with a free pardon. And that is the way God deals with us.' What nonsense! It is quite improper to base our understanding of the gospel on the story of the prodigal son. It presents a part of the gospel, of course, but not the whole. The relationship between a human father and his son can never be a perfect parallel of the relationship between a sinner and a holy God. Sin is an offence to a holy God, and there is no way He can lightly toss it aside and say, 'Well, if you say you are sorry, then we can forget it.'

The tenor of the Christian gospel, as expressed throughout the New Testament, is that, in the cross and through the shedding of His blood, Christ has met and dealt with sin, suffering its evil so that we might go free. People who talk of God forgiving sin without an atonement have little or no conception of what sin really is. Sin is the most heinous, the most vile, the most obnoxious thing in the universe; so terrible that only Christ's death can atone for it.

FURTHER STUDY

1 John 1:1–10;
Prov. 20:9;
Isa. 53:6

1. How can we deceive ourselves?
2. What is the result of walking in the light?

Prayer

Blessed Lord Jesus, I am so thankful that in You sin and evil met their match. You didn't toss sin lightly aside, but grappled with it on a cross. And because You broke its hold on my nature, I can be free! Amen.

All barriers down

For reading & meditation – Ephesians 2:1–22

'But now in Christ Jesus you … have been brought near through the blood of Christ.' (v.13)

T he theme of this great chapter is alienation. Paul, a Jew, writes to the Gentile converts in Ephesus, reminding them that although they were once alienated from the commonwealth of Israel, now, through the blood of Christ, they are part of a new humanity where divisions no longer exist, and where the redeemed are 'all one in Christ Jesus' (Gal. 3:28). We must remember that in the first century, the division between Jew and Gentile was at its deepest. A saying was coined at that time which went like this: 'God loves only Israel … and the Gentiles were created by God to be fuel for the fires of hell.'

This alienation was symbolised also by the 'wall of partition' which was part of Herod's Temple. Gentiles were only allowed on the outer edge of the great Temple, where they could look up and view it, but they were not allowed to approach it. They were cut off by a surrounding wall, a one and a half metre stone barricade, on which signs in Greek and Hebrew said, 'Trespassers will be executed'.

How refreshing it must have been to the Gentiles, treated like dogs by the orthodox Jews, to be told that, through the blood of the Lord Jesus Christ, they were near to God, and had immediate access to the Father. The death of Christ on the cross made it possible, not only for men and women to be brought nearer to God, but to be brought nearer to each other. In Christ all partitions are down – spiritual, political and physical.

FURTHER STUDY

Acts 10:1–11:1; 13:48

1. How did Peter feel about the Gentiles?
2. What happened when Peter went to the Gentiles?

Prayer

O Father, I see that the nearer I come to You, the closer I am to my brothers and sisters. May it be also that the closer I come to my brothers and sisters, the closer I am to You. Amen.

A clean conscience

For reading & meditation – Hebrews 9:11–28

'How much more, then, will the blood of Christ … cleanse our consciences …' (v.14)

The word conscience comes from 'con', meaning 'in conjunction with' and 'science', meaning 'knowledge'. The meaning of the word, therefore, is 'knowledge held in conjunction with another'. At conversion, the conscience is cleansed from 'acts that lead to death, so that we may serve the living God!' Our consciences are made sensitive, in Jesus, to God's moral values. A new conscience is produced to guide the new Christian into new relationships with new sets of values.

Most of us have trouble with our consciences. We begin life with a downward pull that causes us to stray, and yet all the time our consciences quietly insist that we should seek to bring our lives in line with God's required standards. It is this conflict, between what we know to be right and our inability to reach up to it, that accounts for so much inner disharmony. Yet how wonderful it is when the blood of Christ touches our consciences and removes the root of our frustration – sin – enabling us to start all over again, but this time with an added power that helps us reach the standard which God has set. There is no power in the world that can cleanse the conscience apart from the blood of Christ. Psychiatry and psychology can do wonderful things with the human conscience, but they cannot cleanse it. This is God's prerogative, and His alone. How wonderful that we don't have to drag the ball and chain of past guilts into our daily living. We have been cleansed. Hallelujah!

FURTHER STUDY

John 8:1–11;
2 Cor. 1:12;
Heb. 13:8;
1 Tim. 3:9

1. What was the testimony of Paul?
2. What is the function of conscience?

Prayer

Lord Jesus, what You have cleansed, help me not to call unclean. Help me not to dig up what You have buried or remember what You have forgotten. Today I go on my way rejoicing – rejoicing in Your blessed, blessed forgiveness. Amen.

He brought me through

For reading & meditation – Hebrews 10:1–25

'Therefore ... having boldness to enter the Holy Place by the blood of Jesus.' (v.19, NKJV)

There are many who believe that the design of the tabernacle, with its outer and inner courts, is a reflection of heaven itself. God has a holy of holies, they say, where no one enters other than the members of the Trinity.

The writer to the Hebrews seems to be saying something similar here, for he talks about Christ not entering a sanctuary made with hands to appear before God for us (Heb. 9:24). In this 'greater and more perfect tabernacle' (9:11), Christ's bloodstained body bears witness to His completed mission, and by His presence the heavenly things themselves are purified (9:23). Why it was necessary that the heavenly things should be cleansed is not explained. Some believe that, because sin originated in heaven, with the fall of Lucifer, the scene of his conspiracy needed purification by the blood of the cross. However, this is only supposition. We shall have to wait until we arrive in heaven to know the final answer to that. What we do know with certainty is the fact that Christ's blood brings us not merely into the outer court of God's presence. It gives us access into the immediate presence of God.

A minister tells of how a soldier on a battlefield went through shellfire to bring back a wounded comrade. The rescuer was fatally wounded, but before he died, he kept repeating, 'I brought him through.' Look again at the blood of Christ. See the clear pathway it has made into the presence of God. He brought us through!

FURTHER STUDY

John 10:1–18;
Psa. 24:3–4;
Rom. 5:2;
Eph. 2:18; 3:12

1. What does Christ declare Himself to be?
2. Why do we come boldly into God's presence?

Prayer

O Father, just to stand in Your outer court would be bliss, but to have access into Your immediate presence through the blood of Jesus is a mystery I will never resolve. You brought me through. Amen.

'A streak of blood'

For reading & meditation – Hebrews 13:1–21

*'... who through the blood of the eternal covenant brought
back from the dead our Lord Jesus ...' (v.20)*

No book of the New Testament focuses on blood as does the epistle to the Hebrews. It is the clearest and most systematic exposition of the meaning and power of Christ's blood in the whole of the Bible. The writer, in the text before us today, is actually deliberating on the fact of the resurrection, but even so he brings in the subject of blood. James Stewart says of this verse: 'You can't help noticing that this magnificent verse has a streak of blood across it.' Listen to it again: 'The God of peace, who through the blood of the eternal covenant brought back from the dead our Lord Jesus.' There was no road to the power and glory of resurrection life except by way of the cross. Good Friday must precede Easter Sunday. This is a principle we must all face – we must go down with Christ into death before we can rise with Him into resurrection life. Does this mean that we can earn our own salvation by our suffering and sacrifice? No. Salvation is a free gift. Remember the great words of William Cowper: 'The dearest idol I have known, Whate'er that idol be, Help me to tear it from Thy throne, And worship only Thee.'

'Help me to tear it from Thy throne,' – this verse, too, has a streak of blood. When we tear things off the throne of our hearts, and permit Christ alone to rule, then we begin to realise the demands of discipleship. That is the Good Friday sacrifice, and beyond it, the power of a new Easter, the mystery of life emerging out of death.

FURTHER STUDY

Heb. 8:1–13;
Isa. 54:10; 55:3;
Rom. 11:27

1. What was the problem with the old covenant?
2. What was different about the new covenant?

Prayer

O God, now that I am in You, teach me the spirit of the cross, and help me see that before every Easter Sunday there is always a Good Friday. For Jesus' sake. Amen.

God thought it

For reading & meditation – 1 Peter 1:1–12

'… who have been chosen … for obedience to Jesus Christ and
sprinkling by his blood …' (v.2)

The apostle Peter makes reference to the blood of Christ on only
two occasions in his epistles. Here, in the first reference, Peter
introduces us to the Trinity, and points out that the major concern
of the Godhead is to bring sinful men and women into an obedient
relationship with God.

When man fell in the Garden of Eden, he fell into ruin, and
since the Fall, he has been existing on a level which is far beneath
his potential. Man was made for the will of God, and outside it he
is miserable. C.S. Lewis said, 'No one will ever find true happiness
except in relation to abiding in the will of God.' But how can we
sinners obey the will of God when there is some strange power
within us that tempts us to go the way of self-will? Ah, that is one
reason why Christ shed His precious blood. Knowing that the root
of sin is self-will and self-centredness, our Lord allowed His blood to
be shed on Calvary so that it could free us from the entanglements
of self-will, and enable us to give our wills back to God for them to
function in the way they were originally designed. No human being
can have greater fulfilment than in doing the will
of God.

Now picture it with me. Because God knew
that we could only be fully happy as we obeyed
His will, and that, because of sin, our wills did
not want to obey Him, He enlisted the aid of the
whole Trinity, who have concentrated on making
it possible for sinful human beings to once again
delight to obey a holy God.

FURTHER STUDY

Eph. 5:1–27;
John 17:17;
1 Cor. 1:30;
2 Tim. 2:21

1. What does
sanctification mean?
2. What is the result?

Prayer

O Father, I see that the task of redemption was so great it involved the whole
Trinity. God thought it, Christ bought it, the Holy Spirit wrought it, and though
the devil fought it – thank God, I've got it. Amen.

The precious blood

For reading & meditation – 1 Peter 1:18–25

'... the precious blood of Christ ...' (v.19)

I would think that to all Christians the most moving term in the whole of the New Testament is without doubt this – the precious blood of Christ. Preachers continually expound on the theme of why Christ's blood is precious, but let me focus on the one reason which I think is often missed. Christ's blood is precious because it represents the emptying of His own life, so that He could give us abundant life.

During the days of National Service in the late 1950s, I was conscripted, not into the Army, but into the mines. I had not been there very long when I witnessed a fatal accident. One day, without warning, a huge stone slipped from the roof and crushed a friend of mine to death. I remember the feeling of helplessness that came over me as, unable to lift the stone off his body and unable to get help, I watched his life flow out with the blood that poured from his open wounds.

For centuries we Christians have looked upon the streaming blood that flowed from Calvary, and have sung with deep appreciation: 'What can wash away my stain? Nothing but the blood of Jesus.' Is it any wonder why so many believers refer time and time again to the precious blood of Christ? Does anything speak in such clear terms of self-giving and self-sacrifice? The greatest expression of God's love is seen, not in the creation (visible as it is), but in the self-sacrifice of Calvary's cross, and in the blood that flows out from Christ's wounded hands and feet.

FURTHER STUDY

Eph. 1:1–23; 2:13;
Rom. 5:9;
1 Pet. 1:2

1. List some aspects of our spiritual heritage.
2. How have these been obtained?

Prayer

O Father, as I gaze upon Your self-giving that lies at the heart of this great mystery of the cross, may the wonder of Your love generate love in me. For Jesus' sake. Amen.

Walking in the light

For reading & meditation – 1 John 1:1–10

'But if we walk in the light, as he is in the light … the blood of Jesus … purifies us from all sin.' (v.7)

Many years ago some leading men in society were asked what they considered was the most hope-less word in the English language. One answered, 'Atheism'. Another, 'Unloved'. Another, 'Lost'. They were then asked what they thought was the most hope-full word, and on this they all agreed – 'But.'

How thrilling this word 'but' is in today's text. It leads us from a condition of gloom – walking in darkness – to a condition of gladness – walking in the light. The word 'but' is not only the most hope-full word in the English language; it is the most hope-full word in the whole of Scripture. We are walking in a condition of darkness … but! We are out of the will of God … but!

Living in a condition of gladness rather than gloom depends on one thing – 'if we walk in the light, as he is in the light'. We have only to be willing and He does the rest. We supply the willingness and He supplies the power. To have fellowship with God and with each other, we don't have to be good or mature or acceptable. When we take the steps towards being willing to do what God asks, then all the resources of the Godhead are at our disposal. We must remember, however, that it is only as we are 'walking the light' that the blood of Christ cleanses us from sin. It is a conditional statement and one which many Christians miss. Terry Fulham puts it most effectively when he says: 'The blood of Christ does not cleanse in the dark. There is no cleansing unless one is in the light.'

FURTHER STUDY

Eph. 4:1–32;
2 Cor. 5:7;
Gal. 5:16;
1 John 2:6

1. What did Paul urge the Ephesians to do?
2. List some qualities of the new nature.

Prayer

Blessed Lord Jesus, I cannot walk in the light unless You take my hand. I give it to You – now. I can only give one thing – my complete willingness. Give me now Your power. For Your own dear name's sake. Amen.

'By water and blood'

For reading & meditation – 1 John 5:1–12

'This is the one who came by water and blood – Jesus Christ ...' (v.6)

T his verse, as most Bible commentators agree, is one of the most perplexing in the New Testament. At first glance it seems to be saying that salvation comes, not only by blood, but by water also, and without a firm faith in both of these elements, one cannot be saved.

One explanation is that it refers to the water which flowed from the pierced side of Christ on the cross. Another is that it alludes to the baptism of John, and the whole sacrament of water baptism. The true meaning (so I believe) can only be deduced when we consider the background. The Early Church was invaded by a number of errorists, one of whom was named Cerinthus. He believed that Jesus was merely a human being and that the divine 'Christ' descended on Jesus at His baptism in the Jordan, then left Him as He was about to be put to death on the cross. He claimed therefore, that Christ came 'through water' but not 'through blood'. This meant, as you can see, that to him and his followers, the incarnation, crucifixion and resurrection lost their true meaning.

With this in mind, John's words take on a much wider perspective, and can be seen to be a categorical statement of the deity of Christ as it relates to the whole of His human existence before His baptism and after His crucifixion. The water, the symbol of our Lord's dedication, and the blood, the symbol of His atoning death, interpreted by the Spirit's testimony, contain the full scope and significance of the gospel.

FURTHER STUDY
Rom. 6:1–23;
John 3:5;
Acts 2:38;
Gal. 3:27;
Col. 2:12

1. How are baptism and death linked?
2. How does this relate to Christ's shed blood?

Prayer

O Father, I am reminded yet again that the stain of sin was so deep within me that only Your shed blood could wash it away. My gratitude just can't be put into words. Amen

'Loved ... then washed'

For reading & meditation – Revelation 1:1–8

'... To Him who loved us, and washed us from our sins in His own blood.' (v.5, NKJV)

He loves us, then He washes us. Humanly speaking, one would think that it ought to be the other way round. First, He washes us, then He loves us. But not so. Doesn't this convey the whole wealth and wonder of the Christian gospel? Christ does not love us because He has washed us, He has washed us because He loves us.

What would you have said about the father in the story of the prodigal son if he had said to the wandering boy upon his return: 'Get yourself a good bath, spruce yourself up, get the smell of the swine off you ... and then I will love you'? You would murmur something about him having no real love for his wayward son – and you would be right. True love is unconditional – it loves because it can't help loving.

The most solemn, the most glorious and the most moving truth in this universe is that God did not wait until we were washed before He loved us. He loved us even while we were yet sinners (Rom. 5:8). The actual Greek indicates that this can be translated as 'while we were yet sinning'. Of course, the question can be raised: If God loved us before we were washed, why wash us at all? Ah, sin always takes its toll and someone must pay. How could the debt which sin piled up against us be removed? Well, you know the answer – the debt was met in Jesus. God loved us so much that He allowed the blood of Christ to be shed so that our guilt was atoned for and our debt of sin fully paid.

FURTHER STUDY

Eph. 2:1–10;
1 John 3:1;
Rom. 5:8;
John 15:13

1. List six characteristics of our unregenerate state.
2. Why was God able to love us?

Prayer

Father, how can I ever begin to understand a love like this, that loved me even when I was wayward. Deepen my understanding of the fact that You did not love me because Jesus died for me, but Jesus died for me because You loved me. Thank You, dear Lord. Amen.

Hymns ancient and modern

For reading & meditation – Revelation 5:1–14

'And they sang a new song …' (v.9)

There are many songs in the Scriptures. One of the most famous is in Exodus 15 where, following their deliverance from Egypt and the crossing of the Red Sea, the people of Israel burst into rapturous rejoicing and praise: 'Sing to the LORD, for he is highly exalted. The horse and its rider he has hurled into the sea' (Exod. 15:21). This song has a special place in the life of the nation of Israel, and is known as 'the song of Moses'.

The deliverance of the people of Israel from Egypt's bondage was such a momentous event that they sing about it, not only on earth, but also in heaven (Rev. 15:3). Heaven, however, has hymns which are ancient and modern, for our text tells us that in eternity there will be a new song. And what is this new song, which seems to overshadow all other songs? Well, the passage tells us. It is a song about the blood of Christ: 'You are worthy … because you were slain, and with your blood you purchased men for God from every tribe and language and people and nation' (v.9).

The song of Moses focused on the deliverance of hundreds of thousands of people from Egypt, and their entrance into a new land. The new song will focus on the march, not of hundreds of thousands, but of multiplied millions, drawn from every nation under heaven, who have been delivered from a bondage far greater than Israel's bondage, and given entrance to the glories of heaven itself. What a song! What a Saviour!

FURTHER STUDY

Psa. 33:1–22; 40:3;
144:9; 149:1;
Rev. 14:1–3

1. What does the psalmist encourage us to do?
2. Sing your own new song to the Lord today.

Prayer

O Jesus, my Lord, I do not deserve to sing. I sing through Your redeeming grace. And when I shall join with others in singing that new song in glory, I know it will be a sound that will be the most wonderful sound in all eternity. I can hardly wait. Amen.

A twofold theme

For reading & meditation – Revelation 15:1–4

'and sang the song of Moses the servant of God and the song of the Lamb …' (v.3)

The songs of Moses and of the Lamb are brought together, and seemingly given equal prominence. Does this mean that in eternity the Exodus from Egypt will have equal honour with the exodus which Christ effected by His death on Calvary? I think not. The merging of these two themes is, I believe, God's way of highlighting the work of Christ, by comparing it with the ministry of Moses. There were two great accomplishments in Moses' life: one was leading his people out of Egypt, and the other was conveying to them the Law of God which he had received on Mount Sinai.

Let us concentrate for a moment on the giving of the Law. If men and women are to be saved from their sin, then the first step is to show them that they are sinners. This the Law did – it laid down a standard against which men and women were judged. It was a rule of measurement that enabled humanity to see its deficiencies. When the Law was given, then men saw that they needed a Saviour, for without divine strength, they were doomed to failure.

In singing the song of Moses in heaven, we will not be saying that we give him equal honour with Christ, but simply recognising that he played a vital part in preparing the way for the Saviour. In Jesus, the Law, which Moses majestically announced, has been fulfilled. It is not a club held over us; it is a law written in our hearts. We love to fulfil it, because we love Him. We are grateful for Moses, but we adore the Lamb.

FURTHER STUDY

2 Cor. 3:1–18;
Jer. 31:31;
Heb. 10:16–18;
Rom. 7:22

1. What letter do non-Christians read?
2. What is the veil that is taken away?

Prayer

Gracious Father, I see that when I sing the song of Moses and the Lamb, I am expressing the greatest truth in the whole of creation. Let the wonder of it grow in my heart and mind day by day. Amen.

The Lamb on the throne

For reading & meditation – Revelation 5:1–7

'... I saw a Lamb that seemed to have been slaughtered ...'
(v.6, Phillips)

At the heart of the eternal throne is 'a Lamb that seemed to have been slaughtered'. I have said before that the Old Testament saints had several visions of the throne of God and also of the Lamb of God, but not once were they ever seen together. Take Isaiah's prophecy, for example. In chapter 6, he sees a vision of the throne, and in chapter 53, he sees a vision of the Lamb, but they are separate and distinct. In this vision of the future, however, John sees the Lamb, not separate from the throne, but in the centre of it. This (in my view) is God's way of showing the universe that He has been propitiated; and by virtue of the blood of His own Son shed on the cross, redeemed sinners can approach His throne in the utmost confidence.

What marvellous news! God's anger against sin has been appeased by the death of His Son. Your salvation and mine are eternally secure. God will not go back on His word. And, just in case a doubt should arise concerning the security of our salvation, God, as He did in the days of Noah, beautifies the scene with a glorious rainbow (Rev. 4:3). In Noah's day, the rainbow was divine confirmation of the fact that God would never again flood the world. He pledged His word and confirmed it with a rainbow. If any doubt arises in your heart concerning the validity and power of Christ's atonement, then gaze long at that rainbow-encircled throne, and be assured of this – God will never go back on His word.

FURTHER STUDY

1 Cor. 15:1–11;
John 10:11;
12:23–25;
Rom. 5:6

1. What was the principle of Jesus' life?
2. How does this apply to us?

Prayer

Blessed Saviour, how could I have known eternal love unless I had seen it in You, and in the blood that You shed for me on Calvary's cross. Thank You, Lord Jesus. Thank You. Amen.

The crowning worthiness

For reading & meditation – Revelation 7:9–17

'For the Lamb at the centre of the throne will be their shepherd ...' (v.17)

The crowning worthiness heaven puts upon Christ is due to Calvary. All His attributes, all His beauty, all His qualities are concentrated upon those wounds. The place for a lamb is upon an altar, but, by reason of the perfect atonement the Son of God presented on the cross, the Lamb is now on the throne. The wounds are still upon Him. It is, as it were, a fresh death, a frozen time-frame in God's camera which will be shown throughout all eternity. God can never forget it, the angels can never forget it, and the redeemed will never want to forget it. 'Eternal wounds,' says one theologian, 'are the pledge of an eternal pardon.' The man who knows the incarnate God, slain for human sin, stands at the innermost core of truth and knows heaven's final secret.

Our Saviour was slain prospectively from the foundation of the world. He was slain typically in the thousands of sacrifices that were part of the ancient temple worship. He was slain actually by a few Gentiles when they hammered Him to the cross. He is slain retrospectively by those who ignore His cross, and regard the death of Christ as unnecessary. The blood alone purchases the sinner for God. The redeemed in heaven do not sing, 'Our tears and our struggles, our labours and our righteousness brought us here'. No, they sing: 'Worthy is the Lamb'. They glory in Him who for them wrought righteousness, fulfilling the claims of God's holy law on the cross.

FURTHER STUDY

1 Cor. 6:11–20;
7:23;

Acts 20:28;

Eph. 1:14;

Rom. 3:24

1. With what are we purchased?
2. What does redemption mean?'

Prayer

O Father, as I contemplate the worship of heaven, I can hardly wait to join it. Until that day dawns and the shadows flee away, make my life a paean of praise in honour of the Lamb right here on earth. Amen.

'Worthy is the Lamb'

For reading & meditation – Revelation 5:6–14

'… Worthy is the Lamb, who was slain, to receive power …
and honour and glory and praise!' (v.12)

This passage tells us that the hosts of heaven, which cannot be numbered, forever commemorate and rejoice in the Saviour's accomplishments on Calvary. They find nothing so worthy of their praise, nothing so deserving of their worship, nothing so fitting an object of adoration as the Lamb who was slain. 'All the splendours of heaven,' says F.J. Huegel, 'are eclipsed by the matchless splendour of the cross.'

At the beginning of these studies you will remember we said that the Old Testament could be summarised by a pointed question: 'Where is the Lamb?' The New Testament really provides the answer to that question: 'Behold, the Lamb of God who takes away the sin of the world!' But here in the book of Revelation, time passes into eternity and the song of the future is contained in these thrilling words: 'Worthy is the Lamb.'

Those three statements tell you what life is all about. Heaven, as Norman Grubb points out, is heaven because the Lamb is there and has His rightful position there, while hell is hell because there is no Lamb there. The fire is there, and the wood – but no Lamb. There are only those who have turned from the cross, and, by wilful rejection, have spurned the Saviour's love. The words of Scripture put the position so clearly that there is no mistaking it: 'how shall we escape … if we ignore such a great salvation' (Heb. 2:3). If you have not yet committed your life to the Saviour, do it, I beg you, today.

FURTHER STUDY
Luke 9:28–36;
Matt. 16:27; 19:28;
John 17:5;
Rev. 21:23

1. How did Peter,
John and James see
Jesus' glory?
2. How can we see
His glory?

Prayer

Lord Jesus Christ, I see that to choose You is to choose life – Life with a capital 'L'. To refuse You is to refuse Life. It means I choose death. I surrender to You now – all I have and all I am. Receive me – a lost sinner. In Jesus' name. Amen.

By the blood we conquer

For reading & meditation – Revelation 12:1–12

'They overcame him by the blood of the Lamb ...' (v.11)

My purpose at the moment is not to expound this passage, but to focus on this intriguing text, which shows that Christ's blood not only cleanses – it conquers too. Many Christians live frustrated and defeated lives because they fail to appropriate the qualities in Christ's blood which, when applied, help them live victoriously. The blood of Christ can not only cleanse us from sin – it can keep us from sin. If we really appreciated this fact, then we might not have to spend as much time asking for cleansing from sin, because we would have discovered how to have victory over sin.

Take, for example, the area of troublesome or evil thoughts. It is true that evil thoughts, in themselves, are not sin, but when they keep coming into our minds, we can find ourselves focusing on them to such an extent that eventually they lead us into sin. If you are plagued with wrong thoughts, have you tried putting your mind under the blood of Christ? Let me explain: before each day begins, come in prayer before the Lord, and claim the power of His blood over your thought life. Take, by faith, the virtue of His blood, and trust Him to give you victory in this area. It might sound strange, to put your mind under the power of His blood, but thousands of Christians do it every day and find victory. We must use all the weapons available to us in our Christian walk and warfare – the grace of God, the power of the Spirit and the blood of Christ – by these we conquer.

FURTHER STUDY

Rom. 8:31–39;

Psa. 44:5;

Luke 10:19;

1 John 5:4

1. What does it mean to be 'more than a conqueror'?
2. What overcomes the world?

Prayer

Gracious heavenly Father, teach me how to bring my whole being under the protection and power of the blood of Christ so that I experience, not only its cleansing, but its conquering and overcoming power. For Your own name's sake. Amen.

A cosmic event

For reading & meditation – Revelation 13:1–9

'… *the Lamb that was slain from the creation of the world.*'
(v.8)

A lthough we have been tracing the trail of blood from Genesis to
Revelation, we see from this verse that the trail does not begin
in Genesis but in eternity past – from the foundation of the world.
The death of Christ was not just conceived in the mind of God in
eternity but was enacted there.

This text is telling us that the death of Christ on the cross was a
cosmic event. It is something that really happened in eternity before
it happened in time. It was lifted up in time – on Calvary – that we
might see something that is really timeless. The fact that Christ was
'the Lamb slain from the foundation of the world' gives His death
a cosmic validity. Had it merely taken place in time, then it would
have been extraneous to the universe and not inherent in it. The
outer cross on that rugged hill outside Jerusalem is an event through
which I see an inner cross that lies at the heart of God. It shows me
that at the very centre of the universe, there pulsates the power of
redeeming love.

How could we have ever known that there was an unseen cross
upon the heart of God were it not for this verse?
How could we know it except He show us – show
us by an outer cross that there is an inner cross on
His heart? Let this thought infiltrate every part of
your spiritual being – no greater discovery can be
made, or will ever be made, that at the heart of our
God lies the power of redeeming love.

FURTHER STUDY
John 1:1–18;
1 Cor. 2:7;
2 Tim. 1:9;
Titus 1:2

1. What is eternity?
2. How does the cross
   relate to eternity?

Prayer

Blessed Lord Jesus, You are the One through whom I see right into the heart of
God. And what I see there sets my whole being on fire. I see love, anticipating,
sacrificing, saving. And I am grateful more than words can convey. Amen.

'A robe dipped in blood'

For reading & meditation – Revelation 19:11–21

'He is dressed in a robe dipped in blood ...' (v.13)

Here our Saviour is seen, not as a weak and helpless being, dying upon a cross, but as a conqueror and a mighty King. Christ, the glorious Head of the Church, is seen sitting on a white horse, the emblem of justice and holiness. He has many crowns upon His head for He is the King of kings and Lord of lords. His name, we are told, is the Word of God, and He is dressed in a robe which is stained with blood.

The phrase: 'He is dressed in a robe dipped in blood' is, in my view, one of the most important statements of the Bible. Here we are left in no doubt as to the quality of the power which finally overcomes sin and evil. It is a power which once demonstrated its moral integrity on the cross. No one on earth, in hell or in heaven, will be able to stand up and accuse God of being unjust in the way He deals with the world in those end times, for the power that took Christ to the cross is the same power that wields the sword that smites the nations.

What is at the heart of final power in the universe? Different people have answered; justice, law, indifference, favouritism, nihilism (nothingness). But as the curtain descends on the final scene of time, the whole universe will see that God rules by the power of His self-sacrificing love. The Almighty has earned the right to rule and judge sinners, for He has died Himself to save them. And the 'robe dipped in blood' is everlasting proof that absolute power is in the hands of absolute love.

FURTHER STUDY

1 Cor. 15:12–58;
1 Tim. 6:15;
Rev. 1:5; 19:16

1. What is the last enemy that Christ has conquered?
2. What does this mean for the believer?

Prayer

O Father, help me to understand that it is Your love that leads You to have such intolerance towards sin. May Your love, shed abroad in my heart, lead me to that same position. For Jesus' sake. Amen.

The Lamb's book of life

For reading & meditation – Revelation 21:22–27

*'Nothing impure will ever enter it … but only those whose
names are written in the Lamb's book of life.' (v.27)*

'There are just two books in the universe,' says a famous writer,
'and every person's name is in one or the other. The Lamb's book
of life and the self's book of death.' He went on to explain by saying,
'Those who make themselves God, who are centred in themselves as
God, who refuse to surrender themselves and insist on working out
from themselves as God – their names are written in the self's book
of death.' On such people a verdict has already been pronounced:
'Whosoever will save his life shall lose it' (Matt. 16:25, KJV). The
other group are those who are humble enough to receive salvation as
a gift, who recognise the self-giving of God at Calvary and who say:
'Nothing in my hands I bring, Simply to Thy Cross I cling.' Their
names are written in the Lamb's book of life. They will live forever
for they come under the law: 'Whosoever will lose his life … shall
find it.' They live now and they will live eternally. The other group
die now – and will die eternally.

The Lamb's book of life! That book is now open for examination.
Your name is there if you are in Christ. But you are only in Christ if
you have surrendered your self to Christ. You are
out of Christ if the self is on the throne of your
life, no matter how religious you may be. If self
is on the throne then you are registered in the
book of death. Everything in Christ comes under
the law of life – it is written in the Lamb's book
of life.

FURTHER STUDY

Dan. 12:1–13;

Rev. 3:5; 20:12,15;
22:19

1. Who will be
delivered from the
time of trouble?
2. How will God use
the book of life?

Prayer

O Father, I am so glad that salvation is a gift, and not a reward for great spiritual
achievement. And because I trust the blood that was shed for me on Calvary, I
know that my name has been transferred from the book of death to the book
of life. Amen.

'The Redeemer's scars'

For reading & meditation – Revelation 22:1–5

'… *The throne of God and of the Lamb will be in the city* …'
(v.3)

The term 'Lamb', as we have seen, when used in Revelation refers to a slain Lamb. In the Old Testament, the throne of God and the Lamb of God were never seen together. It is only when we reach Revelation that we see the Lamb at the heart of the throne. How intriguing, therefore, to find that, as John describes the future, he refers not just to the throne of God but to the throne of God and of the Lamb.

Is this the way the throne of God will be described in the future? Yes, I believe so. Eternity will be lived out in the light of the fact that heaven is what it is because Jesus is what He is. Were it not for the Lamb and the blood He shed on Calvary, then heaven would be emptied of its inhabitants, and God's throne become a symbol of darkness and judgment. In eternity, we shall worship the Lamb 'looking as if it had been slain' (Rev. 5:6), sing constantly of His triumph and His victory upon the cross, and observe forever the marks of His suffering.

Mrs Penn Lewis says of this: 'Christ's death on the Cross generated moral forces which will be in operation in eternity.' His blood not only cleanses from sin but constitutes a bulwark against sin. If some soul in the halls of the blessed should ever feel moved to turn away from God and centre upon 'self'– one glance at the Redeemer's scars will be sufficient to order all things within to the perfect order of heaven.

FURTHER STUDY

Isa. 6:1–13; 66:1;
Psa. 45:6; 103:19

1. What did Isaiah experience?
2. What effect did it have on him?

Prayer

Father, I see so clearly that though sin first broke out in heaven before it ever broke out on earth, it will never reoccur in eternity. Not only has earth been redeemed by Your blood but heaven has been forever secured by it. Amen.

The final word

For reading & meditation – Hebrews 9:11–28

*'... without the shedding of blood there is no forgiveness of
sins.' (v.22, RSV)*

In tracing the trail of blood that runs from Genesis to Revelation,
one overwhelming conviction remains – the blood may be left out
of some modern hymn books and pulpits, but it has pride of place
in the Scriptures. We must expect that a gospel of blood will be an
offence to the world. Some react to it in ignorance, not knowing its
true meaning, but many find the blood offensive because it denies
them the opportunity to earn or merit their own salvation.

There is a legend which tells of a rich man seeking entry into
heaven. As he approached the gate, an angel asked him for the
password. The finely-dressed man thought for a moment and said,
'Money?' The angel shook his head. 'Try again,' he said. The rich
man thought for a moment: 'Good works?' 'No, not that,' said the
angel. He tried again: 'Charity?' 'No, not even that.' Just then an old
woman approached the gate, her body bowed through years of toil.
'What is the password?' said the angel. Without hesitating, the old
woman lifted up her hands and began to sing: 'The blood, the blood
is all my plea. Hallelujah! It cleanseth me. Hallelujah! It cleanseth
me.' Immediately, the gates swung open and, as the
dear soul entered into heaven, the choirs took up
the refrain: 'Hallelujah! The blood is all my plea.' I
shall allow James Grey to have the last word: 'I am
redeemed, but not with silver, I am bought, but
not with gold. Bought with a price – the blood of
Jesus, Precious price of love untold.'

FURTHER STUDY

Heb. 7:1–28; 8:6;
12:24;

1 Tim. 2:5

*1. What is the
characteristic of
Christ's priesthood?
2. What is a
mediator?*

Prayer

Thank You, blessed Lord Jesus. Thank You! Amen.

The Divine Gardener

Meet the Vine-dresser

For reading & meditation – John 15:1–8

'He lops off every branch that doesn't produce ... he prunes ...
branches that bear fruit for ... larger crops.' (v.2, TLB)

O ur heavenly Father – the Divine Gardener – goes about the task
of pruning our lives in order to make them more fruitful and
productive. There is no way to spiritual fruitfulness except through
careful and relentless pruning. Conversion may be described as
being grafted to Jesus Christ, the Vine, whereby His divine life begins
to flow in us and through us. We are made partakers of the divine
nature. The pruning process – cutting away the things that hinder or
prevent our growth – provides for a continuous conversion in which
we are converted from the irrelevant to the relevant, from being just
busy to being fruitful. The Divine Gardener knows that it is possible
to have the most luxuriant growth with no fruit. The useless non
fruit-bearing growth – the suckers that take life but give no fruit
– must be cut away.

In Japan, land is so scarce compared with the population, that
everything must be cultivated to the maximum. In a hotel room in
Tokyo some years ago, I saw an apple that was twice the size of
an ordinary one. I said to myself, 'This isn't an apple, it's a whole
tree!' How do the Japanese achieve such amazing
results? Mainly in two ways – fertilisation and
pruning. And especially pruning. Every useless
branch and every bit of unproductive growth is cut
away so that everything is prepared for maximum
fruitfulness. This is how it must be with us. If we
are not able to give up, then we will not be able
to give out.

FURTHER STUDY
John 20:1–15; 18:1;
19:41

1. What was the
significance of
gardens in Christ's
life?
2. What did Mary
suppose?

Prayer

Loving Father, I am setting out on a journey today that I sense will carry many
challenges. Show me the difference between the useless and the useful, and help
me say 'Yes' to the pruning process. For Jesus' sake. Amen.

Your life in His hands

For reading & meditation – Psalm 103:1–22

'As a father has compassion on his children, so the LORD has compassion on those who fear him.' (v.13)

It is vital that we see the pruning process in positive terms, for a negative attitude can greatly hinder the purposes of the Divine Gardener. Some years ago, when counselling a woman I said, 'God's shears are at work in your life, cutting, pruning and shaping your being for greater fruitfulness. Look at the 'V' shape of God's shears and interpret it as 'V' for victory.' She said nothing for a while, and then remarked, 'You may see the 'V' shape of God's shears as representing 'V' for victory. I see it rather as 'V' for victim.' While I could not agree with the woman's attitude, I could certainly understand it, for usually it's not very pleasant to be pruned. Further counselling, I'm glad to say, helped this woman to see that God was not treating her like a 'victim' – but as someone who was the subject of His infinite love and care.

This insight is most crucial, for if we have any doubts about the intentions of the Almighty, when He puts us through the pruning process, then we hinder His purposes, and cause the whole issue to become unproductive. The shears, or knife, which cut away at the non-fruit-bearing growth are held in the hands, not of an angel, nor, for that matter, an archangel, but in the hands of our loving heavenly Father. 'I am the true vine,' said Jesus, 'and my Father is the gardener.' Note the word 'Father'. Whatever needs to be done in your life, you are in good hands! Your Father is the Gardener.

FURTHER STUDY

Rom. 8:1–15;

Isa. 64:8;

Matt. 7:11

1. How did Jesus illustrate the Father's care?

2. What is our response?

Prayer

O Father, I am so thankful for this truth – that my life is in Your hands. Have Your way with me, dear Lord, and prune from me everything that hinders me from being my best for You. In Jesus' name I pray. Amen.

Let there be no doubt

For reading & meditation – Ephesians 2:1–10

'But God is so rich in mercy; he loved us so much.'
(v.4, TLB)

A fter a lifetime of counselling and helping people with their problems, I have come to the conclusion that one of the biggest difficulties Christians have is in relation to their concept of God. Time and time again I have gently asked those who are going through the 'vale of sorrow' the question: How do you see God? What goes on in your emotions when His name is mentioned or comes to mind? And the answer has come so consistently, and so often, that it is beyond coincidence. They have said such things as this: I see God as distant, unfeeling, uncommunicative, inconsiderate, harsh, confrontational, and so on. This is why, whenever I am asked what I consider to be the biggest single problem Christians face. I usually reply – their view of God.

If you hold any doubts or any misconceptions about God, then this will have all kinds of repercussions in your life. A wrong view of God, for example, leads to distrust of Him. If you are not quite sure of the Almighty's purposes and intentions in your life, and you doubt His sincerity or love, then you will hardly be able to trust Him when He takes the pruning shears in His hands and snips away at the things you consider to be harmless and unimportant. We must make sure that our view of God is based, not on the opinions of men, nor on our own understanding, but on the revelation of Him that is contained in the Word of God.

FURTHER STUDY
1 John 3:1–11;
Jer. 31:3;
Rom. 5:8
1. How has God
demonstrated
His love?
2. What is our
great hope?

Prayer

O God, I begin to see that my view of You is crucial to the way I will respond to You when You pursue the pruning process in my life. Help me to see You as You really are – with no mists between. For Jesus' sake. Amen.

What is God like?

For reading & meditation – 1 John 4:1–15

*'In this act we see what real love is: it is not our love for God,
but his love for us ...' (v.10, TLB)*

S ome people base their view of God on the mental images of Him which flow through their minds. However, no man or woman has the resources within themselves to discover, unaided, the true and living God. Job asks: 'Who by searching can find out God?' (11: 7). The answer is plain – no one! For what we find in our upward search for God is not God, but the projection of our thoughts into the heavens. We create God in the image of our imagination – and it is not a true image. If God could have been discovered by human searching, then the philosophers would have found Him. But have they? No. Through philosophy, they have come out with a God who is other than the God of the Bible.

Someone has facetiously described philosophy as 'a blind man in a dark room looking for a black cat that isn't there'. There is much truth in that jibe. Philosophical reasoning has searched in a dark universe for a philosophical God who isn't there. The God of the Bible can only be discovered by revelation. No one could ever imagine that the God of the universe would step out of heaven, come right down to earth, live in a human body and die on a cross to redeem us. A love like that just doesn't exist – not in the category of philosophy. But seeing is believing. The Creator, knowing that we could never come to Him, came to us, and, through the revelation of the Bible, gives us the truth, about Himself. And the truth is: He is not just omnipotent power but eternal Love.

FURTHER STUDY

John 15:9–27;
16:27; 13:1

1. Where did Jesus find His security?
2. How did He demonstrate the Father's love?

Prayer

O God, help me, I pray, not to rely on my own understanding in building a picture of You in my mind. Take me deeper into the Scriptures and show me what You are really like. Then I know my heart will be kept in perfect peace. Amen.

Your God is too small

For reading & meditation – Luke 11:1–13

'If you then … know how to give good gifts to your children, how much more will your Father in heaven give …' (v.13)

How can we trust God if we are not convinced of the nobility of His character? We saw yesterday that some try to build up a picture of God by projecting their thoughts into the heavens. They create God in the image of their imagination, but it is not a true image. Some people's image of God, as I have said before, is determined by their early relationships with their parents. J.B. Phillips, in *Your God is too Small*, says that our concept of God is invariably founded upon a child's idea of his father. If he is fortunate enough to have had a kind, indulgent and considerate father, then, when he becomes a Christian, he tends to project that same image on to God. But if the child has a stern, punitive parent, of whom he lives in dread, the chances are that His Father in heaven will appear to him as a fearful being. Some outgrow such a misconception, and are able to differentiate between the early 'fearful' idea and the later mature conception. But many don't. They carry a 'parental hangover' into their Christian life and endure rather than enjoy it because they are never quite sure that God has their highest interests at heart.

I wonder, am I speaking today to someone who pictures God as tyrannical, judgmental, punitive, or just plain disinterested? Ask yourself: where did I get this picture of the Almighty? Not from the Scriptures. Decide now to leave behind all misconceptions, and discover the true God – the God of the Bible.

FURTHER STUDY

Isa. 40:11–31;
Job. 26:12;
Psa. 62:11

1. What is Isaiah's question?
2. What is his answer?

Prayer

O Father, my heart aches to know You as You really are. Today I leave behind my misconceptions, and reach out to You for a new revelation of Yourself. Grant it, in Jesus' name. Amen.

The best photograph

For reading & meditation – John 1:1–18

'Nobody has ever seen God, but God has been unfolded by ...
the only Son ...' (v.18, Moffatt)

Today we ask ourselves: how does the Bible convey to us a clear picture of God's heart and character? Well, it is not just the Book, wonderful though it is, but what the Book says about God's self-revelation in the Person of His Son. You see, if God gave us a book containing the most intimate details of His heart, it would never have enabled us to know Him as He really is. We may catch glimpses of Him in the words He utters, but the only way God can be seen as He really is, is in the incarnate life of His Son. There was, and is, no other way for God to reveal Himself, in understandable terms, except through a human life. He has to show His character where your character and mine are wrought out, namely in the stream of human history. So Jesus makes 'known' the character of God in the only possible way His character can be made known, namely through another character – His own.

One great theologian said, 'Apart from Jesus we know little or nothing about God the Father. You see God in the face of Jesus Christ, or you do not see Him.' And I would add that if you haven't seen God in the face of Jesus Christ, then you have not seen the Father. You have seen something else. The whole emphasis of the New Testament is this – the Father is seen only in the face of the Son. So if you want to know what God is really like, take a look at Jesus. 'Jesus,' as one little boy said, 'is the best photograph God ever had taken.' He is!

FURTHER STUDY

Matt. 17:1–13;
12:18;

Mark 1:11

1. How did the Father express His love?
2. What does 'beloved' mean?

Prayer

Blessed Lord Jesus, what a comfort it is to know that I see the Father in You – in what You are, in what You say, in what You do. Looking at You I see right into the heart of God – and what I see is so beautiful. Amen.

My Father – the Gardener

For reading & meditation – John 18:1–14

'… Shall I not drink the cup the Father has given me?' (v.11)

If I were to undergo some major surgery, I think I would want to be assured that the surgeon not only possessed the required skills and experience but also had my highest interests at heart. Jesus, knowing the fears and uncertainties that linger in the human heart, went to great lengths to assure us that God's care for us runs down to the tiniest and most insignificant details. On one occasion, He took up the most extravagant metaphor He could find: 'the very hairs of your head are all numbered' (Matt. 10:30). Jesus' own untroubled spirit arose, I believe, from the fact that He had complete confidence that His Father's purposes were loving, wise and good. We see this in the last testing hours of His life. After His agony in the Garden of Gethsemane, when He is arrested, He declares, 'Shall I not drink the cup the Father has given me?' The cup which He had been given to drink was full of bitterness, but He found solace in the fact that the cup was in His Father's hands. And so, my friend, must you.

In the weeks that follow we shall look at the ways in which the Divine Gardener goes about the task of pruning us for greater effectiveness and fruitfulness. There will be times when you will be tempted to wonder whether God knows what He is doing. When you are, then I urge you to reflect on what we have considered this week, that the pruning shears are in the hands of One who loves you with an everlasting love. Remember – your Father is the Gardener.

FURTHER STUDY
John 10:14–38; 14:10; 17:11,22
1. What was Jesus' testimony?
2. Why was Jesus able to lay down His life?

Prayer

O God, how foolish I am to needlessly burden myself with unnecessary worries and cares. You will never permit me to go through anything that is not for my highest good. Help me to always remember this. Amen.

Pruning through the Word

For reading & meditation – Hebrews 4:12–16

'… the word of God is living and active. Sharper than any double-edged sword …' (v.12)

W e turn now to examine some of the methods God uses to prune us for greater effectiveness and fruitfulness. God prunes through His Word. Have you ever found yourself reading the Scriptures when suddenly a verse seems to leap out at you, fasten itself to your conscience and plead with you to put something right in your life that you know to be wrong? That was God at work, pruning your life through His Word. This is why it is vitally important that we expose ourselves, daily if possible, to the power and authority of the Word of God. Incidentally, I hope you do more than just read the verse at the top of this page, I hope you read the whole passage, for divine authority rests, not on what I say, but on what God says. *Every Day with Jesus* is useful as a spiritual primer, but it must always be regarded as secondary, never as a substitute for first-hand contact with the Word of God.

Some time ago, I went through a difficult patch of criticism, most of it based on twisted meanings and things taken out of context. And then, one morning, I turned to the Scriptures, looking for some comfort, and I read this: 'And the LORD restored Job's losses when he prayed for his friends' (Job 42:10), Who were Job's friends? The people who criticised him and condemned him. The Spirit whispered to my heart, 'If you pray for your critics, I will set you free.' I did, and instantly my heavy heart was filled with perfect peace.

FURTHER STUDY

Psa. 119:1–16;
John 15:3; 17:17

1. List five things the psalmist says about God's Word.
2. What does God's Word do?

Prayer

O God, I begin to see that one of the reasons why I lack Christlikeness is because I do not sufficiently expose myself to Your Word. Help me to remedy this, beginning today. For Jesus' sake. Amen.

God's best method

For reading & meditation – 2 Timothy 3:10–17

*'All Scripture is … useful for teaching, rebuking, correcting
and training in righteousness.' (v.16)*

In order for the Divine Gardener to prune us through the Word,
we must soak ourselves in that Word. As Emily Dickinson put it:
'He ate and drank the precious words, His spirit grew robust . . . He
danced along the dingy days, And this bequest of wings, Was but a
book. What liberty, A loosened spirit brings!'

Indeed, what 'liberty' it brings if we expose ourselves to the Book,
and give God the opportunity He desires to prune away the suckers
that take life, but give no fruit. I believe that the chief method by
which God desires to prune our lives is through His Word contained
in the Scriptures. The Bible is eminently suitable for this, because it
is both searching and sensitive.

What happens to those Christians who give just a few minutes
now and again to the reading of the Scriptures? I will tell you. God
may have to find some means, other than His Word, to prune and
purify their lives. He may have to engineer a set of difficulties or
trials in order to prune His servant. I am convinced that sometimes
Christians pass through perplexities and trials which might not have
come about had they taken time to let God speak
to them through His Word. And such trials, I must
stress, are not the result of God being peeved
because we haven't read His book, but because He
is committed to producing in us the image of His
Son. And if we ignore His Word – His chief means
of pruning – then what else can He do but take up
the next best means possible?

FURTHER STUDY

Rom. 15:1–13;
Eph. 5:26;
1 Pet. 1:22

1. What do the
Scriptures bring?
2. Why were they
written?

Prayer

O God, I see that I live precariously when I ignore or skimp the reading of Your
Word. Help me spend more time in the Bible, and then perhaps I might spend
less time struggling with life's perplexities. In Jesus' name. Amen.

Am I in bondage?

For reading & meditation – Romans 8:1–17

'For you did not receive the spirit of bondage again to fear ...'
(v.15, NKJV)

J ust recently I had lunch with a man who once worked for an
organisation that produced Bible reading notes. It was expected
of him, during his term of employment, to read the notes faithfully
every day. When he left the organisation, he told me that being
released from the pressure of having to read the notes every day
was like being freed from a prison sentence. This man, I might add,
is a deeply spiritual person. I have known many Christians who
read the Bible daily, not to feed from the Word, but to meet some
neurotic need for self-discipline. One such person said to me, 'If
I don't open my Bible at a certain time and read the exact number
of verses stated in my Bible reading guide, I feel I am a failure as a
Christian.' That person, although he didn't realise it, was struggling
with a psychological problem, not a spiritual one. He was unable to
cope with the feelings that arose within him when he fell below his
own standards.

My own view is this – it is of immense spiritual benefit to spend
some time daily in the Bible, but we must be careful not to allow
ourselves to get into bondage over it and think
that if we miss out on reading a portion of the
Scriptures each day, God might push us under
a bus. Try to read the Word of God daily, but if
for some reason, such as tiredness, sickness or a
period of unusual pressure, you are not able to do
so, don't be too hard on yourself, but return to a
regular schedule as soon as you can.

FURTHER STUDY

Acts 17:1–12;

Deut. 17:19;

Isa. 34:16

1. What did the
Bereans do?
2. What was the
result?

Prayer

Father, while I see the importance of spending time daily in Your Word, help
me not to get into bondage over it. Teach me spiritual balance. In Jesus' name.
Amen.

The greatest need

For reading & meditation – John 5:31–47

'*… search the Scriptures …*' (v.39, NKJV)

T he goal in every Christian life ought to be that of spending some time every day in the Bible. None who seek to be conformed to the image of Christ can afford to neglect the Book. This doesn't mean, of course, that only reason we ought to read the Bible is so that God can have an opportunity to knock us into shape. I doubt whether I would be motivated to open the Scriptures daily if I thought that every time I did so God would reprimand me. Of course, if my life was way out of line, then God would be justified in doing this, but normally God's way of ministering to us is to mix His blessings and speak through His Word right into the area of our current need. One day our greatest need might be for comfort; and so He says: 'My grace is sufficient for you' (2 Cor. 12:9). Or it might be counsel. Then He says: 'This is the way; walk in it' (Isa. 30:21). When our greatest need is reproof, then, of course, He speaks with the same authority and love.

Because our needs are so varied, that is why we should spend time with the Bible and not with substitutes. 'Promise boxes' or booklets that contain selected verses dealing only with comfort, may be useful, but they must never become the whole meal. If God is to develop our lives through Scripture, then we must take care to read as much of it as possible. As far as the Bible is concerned, God can develop most those who read it most.

FURTHER STUDY

Matt. 22:23–46;
Deut. 4:10; 11:19

1. What was Jesus' judgment of the Sadducees?
2. Which was the most important O.T. commandment?

Prayer

O God, You who are always reaching out after me in love and awakening me, help me to see that the more I give my mind to You in the reading of Your Word, the more You are able to give Your mind to me. Thank You, Father. Amen.

Clean through the Word

For reading & meditation – Ephesians 5:21–33

'… cleansing her by the washing with water through the word.' (v.26)

After Jesus had been with His disciples for nearly three years, during which time they had watched Him and caught His ideas and His spirit, He turned to them and said: 'You are already clean because of the word I have spoken to you' (John 15:3). What was this 'Word' that made them clean? Why did He use 'Word' instead of 'words'? The reason could be that His words gathered themselves into such a living body of truth and insight, into such unity and oneness, that they were no longer words – they were 'the Word'. Over the period of time Christ spent with His disciples, His 'Word' had been at work in their lives, cleansing, purifying and pruning.

Jesus cleansed their ideas about God. He got them to see that the Almighty was not an autocratic, irresponsible despot but a Father and a Friend. He not only cleansed their ideas about God, but He cleansed their ideas about the kingdom of God. The kingdom of God was, to the Jewish mind, a setting up of a power base from which God would rule with strength and force. Jesus showed them that the rule of God would not be by the force of might, but by the force of love.

FURTHER STUDY

John 1:1–14; 6:36;
Luke 21:33

1. What does Scripture say about the living Word?
2. How does this relate to His spoken word?

He also cleansed their ideas about prayer. When they first came to Him, they obviously thought of prayer as getting something out of God, but they came to see that it was God getting something out of them. Through His Word, Jesus cleansed their total conception of life. And as we heed His Word, the same thing will happen to us.

Prayer

O God, help me to absorb that 'Word' into every part of my being so that my attitudes, my ideas, my concepts, my relationships may be completely cleansed. For Jesus' sake. Amen.

Further cleansing

For reading & meditation – James 1:19–27

'… *the implanted word, which is able to save your souls.*'
(v.21, NKJV)

J esus cleansed through the 'Word' which He spoke to His disciples. He cleansed false thinking about the family. He cleansed it from polygamy on the one side and polyandry on the other, and took His disciples back to the original purpose of God in the Garden of Eden – of one man and one woman in equal partnership until parted by death (Matt. 19:5–6). He cleansed the idea of greatness. It was no longer to be seen as the possession of wealth or as having power over the lives of men. The greatest of all was to be the servant of all (Matt. 23:11).

He cleansed religion. Jesus made Himself the definition of religion. He said, 'I am the way and the truth and the life. No-one comes to the Father except through me' (John 14:6). To be religious, in the true sense of the word, is to be one of Christ's committed followers. His definition forever cleanses the mind from unworthy and lesser conceptions. When we have looked into the face of Jesus Christ, we can no longer think of religion except in terms of His wondrous life.

But Jesus went further and cleansed love. He found it as lust and left it as love. The love of which He spoke can be between those of the same sex, as well as those of the opposite sex, between the married or unmarried – and it is without lust (John 15:12–13). What a cleansing!

FURTHER STUDY

Matt. 23:13–39;
6:2–5,16; 12:2

1. What is
Pharisaism?
2. How did Jesus
respond to it?

Prayer

O God I am so grateful for the breadth of this cleansing, and for its depth. May this cleansing take place in me day by day as I expose myself to Your 'Word'. In Jesus' name I pray. Amen.

Steps in reading the Word

For reading & meditation – Psalm 119:9–24

'Open my eyes that I may see wonderful things in your law.' (v.18)

What steps do we take to get the best out of our daily reading of the Scriptures? Firstly, relax. You are receptive only when you are relaxed. Nothing can be inscribed on a tense conscious mind. Secondly, recall. Ask these questions as you read a passage: Who is writing? What is the purpose? How does it apply to me? How shall I put it into practice? When do I begin? Thirdly, rehearse. If you find a verse or a thought from the Word that speaks to your condition roll it over in your mind. Do as Spurgeon once suggested to his students. Take a choice portion of God's Word as you would a sweet – put it on the tip of your spiritual tongue and suck every precious drop of flavour from it!

Fourth, retain. Commit a verse to memory. Fifth, rejoice. In reading the Word remember that the purpose of the Bible is to take you by the hand and lead you to the Word, which is Christ. So as you read, look for Him, and when you find Him – rejoice. Sixth, realign. A quaint Negro preacher used to pray, 'Prop us up, Lord, on our leaning side.' The problems of life often cause us to get out of alignment with God's purpose for our existence, so as you read God's Word keep realigning your life with His life. Seventh, release. When something grips you from the Word, pass it on to someone that very day. The repetition will help you retain it and might also lighten the path of the other person.

FURTHER STUDY

2 Tim. 2:1–15;
John 14:26; 16:13

1. What was Paul's exhortation to Timothy?
2. How does the Holy Spirit help us?

Prayer

O God, help me to have so much of Your Word hidden in my heart, that it will determine all my conduct and character. For Your own dear name's sake. Amen.

The blessed Paraclete

For reading & meditation – John 16:1–15

'... he will convince the world of its sin, and of the availability of God's goodness ...' (v.8, TLB)

God also prunes us through the Holy Spirit. The Holy Spirit is referred to in various terms in the New Testament, one of which is the term 'paraclete'. The word 'paraclete' comes from two simple Greek words: *para*, which means 'alongside' and *kaleo*, which means 'to call' or 'to summon'. Can you see the picture? The Holy Spirit is the one who comes alongside us to help us in time of need, not least to plead and remonstrate with us whenever we are tempted to sin. One hymnist, when contemplating this aspect of the Holy Spirit's work, put it like this: 'O plead the truth and make reply to every argument of sin.'

The arguments of sin? What does that mean? One argument that sin advances is that moral violations don't really matter. Its voice cries out in the soul, 'It isn't important – let yourself off lightly.' But sin does matter. The Bible says plainly that 'the wages of sin is death' (Rom. 6:23). Where would you and I be right now in our Christian life if the blessed Paraclete had not come alongside us the moment we were seduced by sin, and 'pleaded the truth' with authority and conviction? He came and showed us that the first thing to do was to recognise the sin as sin, to repent of the wrong we had done, claim forgiveness from God, and hate the evil for the loathsome thing it was. I say again: if in the moment of overwhelming temptation He had left us without a word – where would we be?

FURTHER STUDY

Rom. 8:1–16;

Ezek. 36:27;

John 14:16–17;

Gal. 5:16–18

1. What is the law of the Spirit of life in Christ Jesus?
2. What are we able to do through the Spirit?

Prayer

O Father, I dread to think what my position would be today were it not for that gentle but clear voice of Your Holy Spirit, pleading the truth and making reply to every argument of sin. I am so thankful. Amen.

Don't minimise, don't rationalise

For reading & meditation – 2 Samuel 12:1–14

'Then David said to Nathan, "I have sinned against the LORD" …' (v.13)

One of the arguments of sin is that of minimisation – 'moral mishaps are not important'. But sin does matter, and the Spirit says so – loud and clear. Today we consider another 'argument' which sin advances – that of rationalisation. To rationalise something is to make excuses for it, and sin is an expert at attempting to justify itself. Look at how it worked in the life of David, then you might be more ready to spot it in your own soul. David wanted the wife of one of his officers. While the officer was away on active service with his army, David seduced the woman. Then, fearing the consequences, he 'arranged' the death of her husband, adding the sin of murder to that of adultery and lust (2 Sam. 11).

How did David 'the man after God's own heart' ever get into such a situation? He did it by rationalising. A sinful thought entered his mind, and instead of blasting it with prayer, he fed his imagination upon it. Once the sinful thought was entertained, it proceeded to upset his moral compass. He made excuses for his immorality, and, as far as the death of Uriah was concerned, persuaded himself that gallant soldiers do fall to their death on the field of battle. He was, however, a victim of the arguments of sin. He rationalised his problem, and made excuses for himself. His mind became so blunted against reality, that God had to use Nathan's barbed parable to get through to him.

FURTHER STUDY

1 Cor. 5:1–8;
Songs 2:15;
Eccl. 10:1;
Gal. 5:19–26

1. What are some 'little foxes' that may spoil our vine?
2. What is the result of living in the Spirit?

Prayer

O Father, whenever sin rises up in the courtroom of my soul to argue its case and plead its cause, be there, I pray, in the power of Your Spirit to make reply to every argument of sin. In Jesus' name, I ask it. Amen.

'The Ten Commandments shine'

For reading & meditation – Psalm 119:89–104

'Your word, O Lord, is eternal; it stands firm in the heavens.' (v.89)

So far we have looked at two of the arguments of sin. First, that sin doesn't really matter and is unimportant, and second, that it can be easily justified. A third argument of sin is that morality varies from one generation to another. Have you heard the phrase, 'Oh, that's old-fashioned and Victorian'? It's usually used to dismiss a moral quality or value by implying that it belongs to a former age. Well, customs may come and go, but not, I assure you, the edicts of the eternal God. When we are dealing with morality, we are not dealing with something like the shape of a woman's hat, or the style of her clothes, but with the requirements of a just and holy Creator. When God established the Ten Commandments in ancient times, He didn't just give them to the nation of Israel: they were given to the whole of humanity. They were meant to be the basis of all morality for all people at all times. One poet put it like this: 'Engraved as in eternal brass, The Ten Commandments shine: Nor can the powers of darkness raze, Those everlasting lines.'

Time makes no difference to the moral counsels of God. His edicts apply to the Negro as well as to the Eskimo; in the West and the East; for kings and citizens alike. People's perceptions may change, but not the decrees of God. How grateful we ought to be that the Holy Spirit rises up at appropriate times in our hearts to help us see sin for the loathsome thing it is.

FURTHER STUDY
2 Cor. 3:1–18;
Rom. 2:15;
Heb. 10:15–16
1. What are we to be?
2. What brings the
Word to life?

Prayer

Father, how desperately I need the ministry of Your Spirit in my heart and life, for I gather self-defensive arguments around me like a magnet. It is only when Your Spirit lives in me that sin will die in me. So live on – mightily. For Jesus' sake. Amen.

Using the right name

For reading & meditation – Romans 8:1–11

*'… those who follow after the Holy Spirit find themselves
doing those things that please God.' (v.5, TLB)*

Another way by which sin seeks to enter our lives, and get past our guard, is through the use of euphemisms – calling a deadly or serious issue by a less offensive name. It calls a lie a 'fib', and stealing, 'scrounging'. It calls living a loose sexual life, 'love'. It calls the avoiding of responsibility, 'being smart'. It calls drunkenness, 'alcoholism'. It calls practising homosexuals, 'male lovers'.

A minister tells of a joint meeting of doctors, psychiatrists and ministers he once attended to think through ways in which the various professions could work together. There was a great deal of talk about pre-marital and extra-marital sexual relationships. One old rural parson was confused by the terms, and couldn't keep up with the conversation. Finally he said, 'Pre-marital and extra-marital sexual relationships? Do you mean fornication and adultery?' Those plain, but biblical, words came like a bombshell to that highly trained and sophisticated group of men.

We live in an age, which, as you well know, likes to gloss things over with less challenging names, and that is one way in which society greases the path to sin. The Holy Spirit, however, works in the hearts of those who are His, encouraging them to see sin for the ugly thing it is, and to stubbornly refuse to change the labels. A deadly thing is not made innocuous by a less distasteful name. Leukaemia is still leukaemia even when you call it 'a problem in the blood'.

FURTHER STUDY

1 Thess. 4:1–12;
2:4 ;

Prov. 16:7;

Heb. 11:5

1. What is the result
of pleasing God?
2. Are you a men-
pleaser or a God-
pleaser?

Prayer

O God my Father, illuminate my whole being by Your Holy Spirit, and help me see through every argument of sin. Give me, not only clear insight, but the courage to call things by their rightful name. For Jesus' sake, I pray. Amen.

'Everybody does it'

For reading & meditation – 1 Corinthians 10:1–13

'... *You can trust God to keep the temptation from becoming so strong that you can't stand up against it* ...' (v.13, TLB)

I recently came across a report of a certain denomination in Scandinavia, where the young people were engaged in a great deal of sexual permissiveness. Some of the leaders of the denomination argued that the clear principles of Scripture ought to be expounded so that the young people might have some moral guidelines. Others said, 'Well, most young people sleep around these days – it's part of the modern lifestyle – so let's not try to stamp it out, but encourage them to be faithful to one partner, and not to become promiscuous in their love-making.' Despite some objections, the matter was finally put to the vote and carried.

How sad that a so-called Christian denomination can settle a moral issue such as this by popular vote rather than by the clear standards of Scripture. Oh how desperately we need the cleansing flow of the Holy Spirit to flood our lives and reinforce our moral convictions. In Christ's name, I plead with you today, don't fall for the argument that says 'everybody does it'.

I am not unmindful of the struggles and temptations of the flesh, neither am I unaware of the strong forces that surge within us, clamouring for expression; but I have to be faithful to Scripture, and say with equal emphasis that all the resources of heaven are engaged against sin. It is false reasoning to excuse sin on the grounds that everybody does it. God promises a way of escape.

> **FURTHER STUDY**
>
> Rom. 1:1–32;
>
> Isa. 53:6;
>
> Judg. 21:25
>
> 1. What was the start of man's downward course?
>
> 2. What was the result?

Prayer

Father, You know that I do not sail calm seas. I am driven by tempests of emotion and strong desires. Yet, in every storm, You promise a way of escape – a harbour into which I can run. Help me, whenever I am tempted, to look for it and head towards it. Amen.

Is sin necessary?

For reading & meditation – Romans 13:8–14

'… do not think about how to gratify the desires of the sinful nature.' (v.14)

In Wales, many years ago, a minister preached a sermon which produced a strong reaction. 'Sin is necessary,' he said, 'for without it how would we know about the riches and the forgiveness of God? The more we sin, the more we can be forgiven, and the more opportunity we can give God for demonstrating His attributes.' Later, it was discovered that the man had been involved in a secret extra-marital affair.

It has always intrigued me how the mind sometimes works to justify sin, and to twist the plain statements of the Word of God. Our spiritual fathers had a simple technique for showing people that sin isn't necessary. They would say, to those who argued that we must sin, 'Can you live without sin for a minute? Yes? Can you live without sin for five minutes? Yes? Can you live without sin for an hour?' You see how their simple logic worked? They didn't say that a redeemed Christian was not able to sin: they just insisted that he was able not to sin.

Make no mistake about it – sin is avoidable. I know that in some mysterious way, beyond our human fathoming, God can use sin, but that doesn't make it necessary. In an age when some sections of the Church appear to have gone 'soft' on sin, I find myself wishing that another John Wesley would rise up and encourage us to 'claim a perfect cure', and reaffirm the message of New Testament holiness. God not only raises the standard to great heights, He also provides the power by which we can attain it.

FURTHER STUDY

Rom. 6:1–23;
Gal. 5:24;
Col. 3:3;
1 Pet. 2:24

1. What does Paul say about grace and sin?
2. How does he equate this with fruitfulness?

Prayer

Father, I need You to corner my soul. Don't let me wriggle and slip past Your redemptions. Help me to take my medicine, however bitter to the taste of self it may be. For I would be whole, with no part sick. In Your name. Amen.

Where would we have been?

For reading & meditation – John 14:1–21

'Someone else … to be with you always. I mean the Spirit …
(vv.16–17, Phillips)

Where would you and I have been but for the blessed Paraclete? If, at our first encounter with sin; if, as soon as we were seduced in our hearts by desire; if, when our vagrant nature clamoured for sinful expression; if He had left us without a word … where would we have been? How grateful we ought to be that the Divine Gardener has given us the Holy Spirit to be always present in our lives, so that when evil desires begin to plead the arguments of sin, there is another voice that rises in the court of our soul, pleading for holy things.

Some years ago at the Sheffield Quarter Sessions a case was held up because a judge complained that he could not 'see' a barrister in court. The barrister was there, but he was not wearing his wig and gown. According to English law, the judge can only see an advocate when he is properly attired. There was a prisoner in the dock, and a barrister ready to plead his cause, but his plea could not be given because, according to the courts, he was 'invisible'. There was no one to plead for the prisoner. No one to say, 'He has learned his lesson, he will not fall so easily again.'

I am bold enough to say that in the lives of those of you who belong to Jesus Christ, the Holy Spirit will always be visible. He is always ready to stand up in the courtroom of your soul to plead the truth and make reply to every argument of sin. So take heart – He is always there.

FURTHER STUDY

Gal. 4:1–7;

Neh. 9:20;

1 Cor. 2:13

1. What does the Holy Spirit do within us?
2. What are we then able to do?

Prayer

O God, what a relief it is to know that You don't abandon me to the forces of sin that rise up within me. You are always there, protesting, refuting and pleading the cause of truth and righteousness. My gratitude just won't go into words. Amen.

The good or the best

For reading & meditation – Acts 9:10–19

'Immediately, something like scales fell from Saul's eyes ...'
(v.18)

This week we shall look at how God prunes our lives through prayer. One of my favourite definitions of prayer is the one used by Kagawa, the Japanese Christian leader, who said that 'prayer is revision'. He went on to explain what he meant in these impressive words: 'A revised version of your life is published every time you pray, really pray. For in the silence before Him, you bring more and more areas of your life under His control, more and more powers are put at His disposal, more and more channels of receptivity are opened up and more and more alignments of our wills are made to the will of God.'

One of the reasons why God calls us to prayer is because He knows that much of our lives become overgrown with suckers that sap our strength, bear no fruit themselves and keep us from bearing fruit. Suckers (like many of the things that clutter our lives) are not bad in themselves: they simply draw from us the strength that should go into fruit-bearing. How many of us, I wonder, are busy doing nothing! We rush here and there, but achieve little. When we get down before God in prayer, and take time to listen to what He has to say to us, He brings the important to the centre of consciousness and pushes the unimportant to the edge. Therefore, in prayer, that is listening prayer, God prunes our purposes and our persons.

FURTHER STUDY

Luke 18:1–14;
1 Chron. 16:11;
Eph. 6:18;
Psa. 91:15

1. What was Jesus teaching about prayer?
2. How do we develop perseverance?

Prayer

O God my Father, I want to be at my best, but I am weighed down with a lot of useless activities. Help me discern between what is good and what is best. For Jesus' sake. Amen.

The eternally worthwhile

For reading & meditation – 2 Corinthians 3:7–18

'... *And as the Spirit of the Lord works within us, we become
more and more like him.' (v.18, TLB)*

T he Divine Gardener brings the important to the centre of
consciousness and pushes the unimportant to the edge. I once
saw a cartoon of a girl who had got out of her car to ask a policeman,
'Can you tell me where I want to go?' She was going, but didn't know
where. A man who had attended a Christian conference asked, as
others were preparing to leave: 'Is there anyone going anywhere in
a car?' Most people understood what he meant, but they laughed
because it struck home. Many live without any clear plan for their
life which results in a lot of running around in circles, getting
nowhere.

One artist kept a supply of coloured stones. Whenever he
felt that his sense of colour became jaded, he would take out the
stones and, as he put it, 'wash his eyes in the colours of nature'.
The colours clarified his sense of colour. 'One look at Jesus,' said a
famous preacher, 'and I am gripped with a sense of the worthwhile,
and every time I come out of His presence, I feel as if I want to
throw something away.' Many years ago, a Sunday school teacher,
working in the slum district of London, tried
to get the children to wash their faces. They
wouldn't respond until a child with a clean face
and clothes was brought to them. Then they went
off, one by one, and washed their faces. How do
you feel when you come before the Lord in prayer,
and look into His face? When I do, I realise that
I must wash my own – and not only my face, but
my heart and my life.

FURTHER STUDY
Isa. 6:1–8;
Jer. 29:13;
James 5:16;
Psa. 51:6
1. How was Isaiah 'pruned' when he saw the Lord?
2. What does God require in the inner parts?

Prayer

Lord Jesus, I look into Your face, hear Your voice, and I feel as if I want to throw
something away. I want to empty my hands to grasp the whole of You. I want
the eternally worthwhile. Amen.

Our Father's business

For reading & meditation – Luke 2:41–52

'Did you not know that I must be about my Father's business?'
(v.49, NKJV)

People often say to me, 'How are you able to keep on constantly writing *Every Day with Jesus*, preparing the seminars, the rallies, and the other things in which you are involved?' I have one simple answer – prayer. I do not wish to present myself as an expert in prayer but I have found that the more I pray, the more effectively and quickly I can accomplish my tasks. Those who say they are too busy to pray are fooling themselves. If they prayed, then God would come to them and help them prune their lives for greater fruitfulness and effectiveness.

Permit me to share with you some of the things I have learned through prayer in relation to the best use of time. (1) In prayer, God prunes our lives so that we achieve His highest purposes. Many of us live lives that are overgrown and cluttered up with the unimportant. We are busy doing nothing. The more we pray, the more God is able to separate the irrelevant from the relevant, and show us the things upon which we ought to concentrate. Just before Jesus suffered upon the cross, He said, 'Father, I have finished the work you gave me to do' (John 17:4, GNB). There were many things Jesus could have done, which would have been helpful and beneficial to the people of His day, but because He had a list of priorities, which had been worked out in prayer, He kept to them, and achieved, not just a good purpose, but God's purpose. And the result? Mission accomplished.

FURTHER STUDY

John 17:1–26;
2 Chron. 7:14;
James 5:16

1. What did Jesus focus on in His prayer life?
2. What sanctifies us?

Prayer

O God, my life is cluttered with so much that is irrelevant and unimportant, give me the courage to say to You – 'Cut'. Prune, dear Vinedresser, prune. In Jesus' name. Amen.

Don't be a people-pleaser

For reading & meditation – 1 John 2:7–17

'... he who does the will of God abides for ever.' (v.17, RSV)

We must not view God as a strict schoolmaster, bending over us and demanding that we make use of every minute of our time. We need time to relax, unwind, and forget our responsibilities. Jesus enjoyed such times. 'Come with me,' He once said to His disciples, 'and get some rest' (Mark 6:31). I have found that the more I pray, the more effectively and quickly I can fulfil my tasks – therefore, the more time I have for relaxation. Prayer helps us to see clearly the things God wants us to do, and we have all the time we need to perform His tasks.

Another thing I have learned through prayer is how to use the two letters of the alphabet – N and O – 'No'! In the early years of my life, I was a people-pleaser. I tended to take on more tasks than were good for me, because I hated to disappoint anyone. Prayer pruned me of the desire to please people, and gave me an overwhelming desire to please God. Now, whenever I am asked to speak at a certain meeting or conference, I take the matter to the Lord. If He gives me permission, I say 'Yes', but if I do not get His mind on the matter, then I say 'No'. Once I used to accept every invitation, and I almost broke down under what someone has called the 'burden of busyness'.

Do you find it easy to say 'No'? Thousands of Christians are unable to do so. If you are one of those people who can't say 'No', then you need to ask yourself: who has my first allegiance – God, or others?

FURTHER STUDY

Heb. 4:1–16;
Isa. 28:12, 30:15;
Matt. 11:29

1. What is more important than physical rest?
2. How does this affect our lives?

Prayer

Lord Jesus, I know I must surrender myself to the discipline of something – to the discipline of the pressures around me, or to the discipline of Your will and purposes. If I do the first, I shall pass away. If I do the second, I shall abide forever. Amen.

Using spare minutes

For reading & meditation – Colossians 4:2–6

'… make the best possible use of your time.'
(v.5, Phillips)

The pruning process of prayer helps us realise the importance of spare minutes. Talk to anyone who is involved in doing great work for God (or, for that matter, anyone involved in the running of a successful business), and you will probably find that the person is a 'minute-minder'. Productive people know how to use those spare minutes that invariably crop up in even the busiest days. This explains why busy people, given additional jobs, get them done.

Proper use of idle moments reveals a positive outlook on life. Those who use spare minutes to turn over critical thoughts, or rehash lost battles, come out with unhealthy attitudes, but the person who converts spare minutes into constructive thinking will make a mark on the world. Strauss wrote one of his famous waltzes on the back of a menu while waiting for his meal in a Viennese restaurant. Harriet Beecher Stowe gripped a pencil between her teeth while kneading dough, so that, in between times, she could write snatches of *Uncle Tom's Cabin*. George Muller used to pray while he shaved every morning. What does your mind do when it has nothing to do? The answer to that will determine the kind of person you are. Some people allow their minds to dwell upon all kinds of fantasies, old arguments or past failures. One cathedral has a beautiful stained-glass window made up of all the unused spare fragments of glass from all the other windows. What do you do with all your spare minutes?

FURTHER STUDY

Eph. 5:1–18;

Psa. 90:12;

James 4:14

1. How does time relate to being filled with the Spirit?
2. To what does James liken life?

Prayer

O Father, I want so much for my life to be geared to Your highest purposes. Teach me how to utilise the spare minutes of every day, and make them count for You and Your purposes. For Jesus' sake. Amen.

'Eternity is in it'

For reading & meditation – Ephesians 5:8–20

'Live life, then, with a due sense of responsibility ... Make the best use of your time ... '(vv.15–16, Phillips)

The fourth lesson God wants to teach us in this respect is the value of time. We must not become obsessive about it, but our lives will be lived with greater effectiveness for God if we learn to value the minutes, the hours and the days the Almighty gives us. This resolve must become an integral part of our daily thinking: 'Time is valuable. I dedicate myself to spending my time as wisely as possible to the glory of God.'

The Christian who wants to make the best use of his time must have a keen awareness of its value. Time should be regarded with great importance, for it is God-given. Though others may have more talents, we all have the same amount of time. God gives it to all, equally. Time cannot be bought, no matter how rich you are. And no matter how poor, you won't receive less. The Archbishop of Canterbury has no more time than you and I. Every one of us has 60 minutes to the hour, 24 hours to the day and seven days per week. However, perhaps the greatest reason why time should not be wasted is because it is irrevocable. I noticed this advert in a newspaper: 'Lost, yesterday, somewhere between sunrise and sunset, two golden hours, each set with sixty diamond minutes. No reward, they are gone forever.' Someone has said: 'Yesterday is a cancelled cheque. Tomorrow is a promissory note. Today is the only cash you have. Spend it wisely.'

FURTHER STUDY
1 Pet. 1:1–17;
Psa. 39:5;
1 Chron. 29:15
1. How are we to treat time?
2. To what are we likened?

Prayer

O God my Father, I am so thankful that You have given me all the time I need to do Your work while I am here on earth. Help me to be a good steward of it – for Your own dear name's sake. Amen.

Budgeting each day

For reading & meditation – 2 Corinthians 5:11–21

'... that those who live should no longer live for themselves,
but for him ...' (v.15)

T he best way to use money is by budgeting. It is the same with
time. 'When you budget your time,' says Dr Edward Hakes,
an expert on time-management, 'you discover that you don't have
to "buy" everything ... you "buy" with time only those activities
worth "buying". Without some attempt to budget, you waste time,
and "buy" activities not worth the expenditure.' Just as we have a
financial budget, so we should have a time budget for the tasks of
the immediate future. I know that I would never get done what has
to be done were it not for a daily budget of my time.

A motto I saw on someone's desk, although humorous, has
a good deal of sense. 'Think! Maybe you can dodge some work!'
It's not just funny – it's true. Thinking is the greatest time-saving
activity. A few minutes at the start of each day, prayerfully and
carefully planning the programme for the day ahead, is the most
productive way I know of getting the best out of each day. One
needs to know what is important, what is less important and what is
trivial. The most difficult decisions should be made in the morning
while the mind is fresh. Some advocate making
out a schedule the night before. This way one can
start right the next morning. If we plan each day
with God, then we won't need to spend so much
time fretfully re-examining our decisions. After
all, time is not ours, but His.

FURTHER STUDY

Rom. 14:1–12;
6:11;

Luke 20:38;

Gal. 2:19

1. How are we to live
each day?
2. How will God
hold us accountable?

Prayer

O Father, just as You pruned the days of Jesus while He was here on earth,
prune my life also. May all the clamouring voices that bid for my attention be
silenced at Your command. For Jesus' sake. Amen.

The ministries of the Church

For reading & meditation – Ephesians 4:1–13

'… to others he has given the gift of being able to preach …'
(v.11, TLB)

G od prunes us through the Church. The ministries that function in Christ's Church are designed, not only for our encouragement and edification, but for our spiritual correction as well. Looking back over my life, I am filled with gratitude to God for the way He has prodded me into usefulness, not only through His Word or directly by His Spirit, but also through the ministries which He has placed in His Body, the Church. Take first the ministry of teaching and preaching. How many times have you listened to a preacher or Christian teacher and realised that what he was saying was a direct word from God to yourself? I remember as a youth walking into a church in Merthyr Tydfil where Idris Davies was preaching. I was somewhat cold in my heart toward the Lord at that time, but as soon as he began to speak, I sensed that this was God's message direct to my heart. I tried to get out of my seat, but I felt as if invisible cords bound me to it. I wriggled, I squirmed, I resisted, I argued, but God's Word penetrated to the depth of my heart like a rapier. That night I surrendered, not just a part, but the whole of my being to Jesus Christ. When I spoke to others later, they seemed to regard the sermon as nothing out of the ordinary, but for me it was like receiving a telegram direct from heaven. I said to a friend of mine on the way out, 'I've had my insides sand-papered here today.' God prunes through preaching.

FURTHER STUDY

Acts 8:1–13;

Mark. 16:15;

1 Cor. 1:21;

2 Cor. 4:5

1. What was Christ's commission to the disciples?
2. What happened when Philip went to Samaria?

Prayer

O God, I am so thankful for the times You have pruned me through the words of a preacher or teacher. Sometimes it takes a human voice to make me conscious of the divine voice. I am deeply grateful. Amen.

The small fellowship group

For reading & meditation – Acts 2:42–47

'They devoted themselves ... to the fellowship ...' (v.42)

For many years I lived without a disciplined group correction. My life was overgrown with a lot of useless things. However, when I joined a disciplined group, the pruning process began. Every Christian needs to be involved in a small group of loving, caring believers, where the true 'koinonia' can be developed. Koinonia is the Greek word for fellowship: the kind of fellowship which functions under the constraint of love and truth. Notice I say love and truth. Some Christians are good at speaking the truth, but bad at loving. Others are good at loving, but hesitate to speak the truth, or the whole truth. How impoverished we are in the 21st-century Church because we do not cultivate such groups. There are notable exceptions, of course, but they are few and far between.

In one group to which I belonged, a person said very gently and lovingly, 'I notice that whenever someone has a problem, you seem to want to come right in with the answer. Is it possible that perhaps sometimes God might want to use someone else to give an answer?' I was corrected – and in this case by someone who had not been a Christian for more than a year. Following that group encounter, I have learned to hold back, to see whether someone else might have the answer, before sharing my own thoughts or views on an issue. It was a necessary pruning. The small fellowship group, if properly constructed and supervised, is one of the most effective pruning processes in the world.

FURTHER STUDY

Matt. 20:1–28;

Eph. 4:15;

Phil. 1:3–5

1. What emerged in the disciples' small group?
2. What did Jesus do?

Prayer

Dear Father, I am so thankful for the fellowship of those who are faced toward the Light and are striving to walk in it. Help Your Church to experience a closer fellowship than ever and help me to be a part of it – a giver as well as a getter. Amen.

'Touching elbows on Sundays'

For reading & meditation – 1 John 4:7–21

'Dear friends, since God so loved us, we also ought to love one another.' (v.11)

While the Church is one of the greatest agencies for perfecting us and making us more like Christ, it often lacks the elements of what the early Christians called the *koinonia*, the fellowship. The Church is often simply a group of individuals touching elbows on Sundays, and then relapsing into their isolated individualism for the rest of the week. While there are notable exceptions to this, generally speaking the Church of today lacks real fellowship.

Many churchgoers meet in small groups to explore modern forms of spirituality and 'togetherness' which are not necessarily Christian. I think it sad (and possibly dangerous) when people have to join such groups because their own church does not cultivate the true koinonia. Fortunately there are signs that the Church is recognising the need for small fellowship groups, not just groups for prayer or Bible study, but groups where people are free to enjoy companionship and share their deepest needs.

'I'm afraid to be a part of a group where people share on a deep level,' said one woman to a friend of mine. When he asked why, she replied, 'I'm not afraid of sharing myself, but I am afraid of criticism.' However, as you know, there is a world of difference between destructive and constructive criticism. Christian criticism is always constructive – or else it isn't Christian. The woman eventually joined a sharing group, and is growing by leaps and bounds.

FURTHER STUDY

1 Thess. 3:1–13;
John 13:3; 15:12

1. What was Christ's new commandment?
2. What will be the result of our fulfilling this commandment?

Prayer

O Father, You who always seek to bring things to the surface, not to shame us, but to save us, give us grace to follow You all the way – through exposure to experience. For Jesus' sake. Amen.

The gift of counselling

'... let us mind our service ... the speaker his words of counsel ...' (vv.7–8, Moffatt)

It goes without saying that the ministries in the Church function in other ways besides correction, but as this is the aspect we are discussing, we shall look at them from that point of view. Another ministry God uses to prune us is that of personal counselling. There are those in every community of God's people who are gifted by Him for the work of individual counselling. If you find yourself motivated to search out answers for people's problems, and long to help them unravel their spiritual and psychological difficulties, the chances are it is because the gift is working within you.

Here again, I feel the Church is failing in its mission because it doesn't seem able to help its members discover and develop their basic spiritual gifts. One of the greatest needs in the Church at this time is for its leaders (pastors, elders, deacons) to show people how to discover and exercise their basic gifts. If this were done, then I am convinced that there would be many who would discover within them the gift of counselling and, with guidance and instruction, could use that gift to restore struggling and bound Christians to fuller and more productive lives. If Christians were to unwrap their gifts, particularly the gift of counselling, and, with God's help, assist struggling believers toward greater fruitfulness and effectiveness, then we would convey to the world, not just by our lips, but also by our lives, that Christ is truly all-sufficient.

FURTHER STUDY

John 4:1–30;

Isa. 9:6;

Gal. 6:1

1. Why did Jesus 'need' to go through Samaria?

2. List other people with whom Jesus had a personal encounter.

Prayer

O God, I see so clearly the plan You have for Your Church. Yet many gifts lie unexplored and unused. I pray that You will root out unemployment, thaw out the frozen assets, and release Your people into productivity. In Jesus' name. Amen.

The great 'because'

For reading & meditation – 1 Corinthians 11:17–34

*'A man ought to examine himself before he eats of the bread
and drinks of the cup.' (v.28)*

The Communion service has many wonderful aspects, not the least being that of self-examination. Why does God, speaking through the apostle Paul, command us to examine ourselves before we take the bread and wine? Where better? It is at the foot of the cross that we discover the mainspring of all Christian action. Some press on to perfection and self-improvement out of a desire to earn God's approval. They long to hear the words, 'Well done, good and faithful servant.' Sometimes there is a tinge of self-centredness in such a desire. We like to feel that we have done something to *deserve* His love.

I have said often that the mainspring of any Christian action, be it caring, evangelism or self-discipline, should not be on the basis of attempting to earn His love, but on the basis that we are already loved. In bidding us come to the Communion Table to examine ourselves, God wants us to see how much He loves us so that love, not fear, can be the challenge that brings about change. You see, if you try to love God without first realising how much He loves you, then all attempts at self-improvement and self-discipline will be mechanical. In the light of His love for us at Calvary, as vividly dramatised through the bread and the wine, we are fortified to let go of all that is unlike Him, and to let Him love us into greater Christlikeness. John captured the thought most effectively when he said, 'We love *because* … (1 John 4:19, italics added).

FURTHER STUDY
1 Cor. 10:1–17;
Matt. 26:26–29;
Heb. 9:22
1. What does the bread represent?
2. What does the wine represent?

Prayer

Gracious Father, as I ponder the meaning of the bread and wine, and consider how great is Your love for me, I feel like releasing everything in my life that is incompatible with that love. You are the great 'because' of my existence. I am so grateful. Amen.

Grasping the nettle

For reading & meditation – Revelation 3:14–22

'So, because you are lukewarm ... I am about to spit you out of my mouth.' (v.16)

Today we consider the matter of church discipline. A minister wrote, 'I have in my church a member who is involved in a serious moral sin. He does not try to hide it. What can I do? If I make an issue of it, I know I will split my church.' The problem of church discipline is a thorny one, but it is one the Church must take up, nevertheless. God is eager and ready to forgive anyone who is repentant and willing to give up their sin, but when sinful behaviour continues in the life of a Christian, then the Church must obey the Word of Christ and institute disciplinary action. People fear that discipline will divide and destroy the Church. Actually the opposite is true. Wise biblical discipline will unite the Church, revive its spirit and produce solid growth. My words might sound strong, and, in some quarters, may be resisted, but those churches who refuse to institute proper disciplinary measures are in danger of having Christ withdraw His presence from them.

Can Christ leave a local church? He left the Laodicean church. Outwardly they got along so well without Him, they never even missed Him. They had forgotten their dependence and their loyalty to Him. So He delivered the church over to judgment. Disgusted, He spat them out of His mouth. There is no eternal security for a local church. The Lord doesn't have to come just because we invoke His name. He knows when He is no longer in charge, and when He sees it to be so, He leaves.

FURTHER STUDY

Matt. 18:1–17;
5:21–25; 7:1–5

*1. What should we
do if a fellow believer
sins against us?
2. What must we
do first?*

Prayer

O God, You are probing deep. But keep drilling, for You must strike the hard resistances if You are to strike the clear living water of Your presence and power within me. Cleanse Your Church that it may become a cleansing agent. For Jesus' sake. Amen.

Discipline – or die

For reading & meditation – 2 Cor. 2:5–11; Gal. 6:1

'… if someone is caught in a sin, you who are spiritual should restore him gently …' (Gal. 6:1)

C hurch discipline has two principal purposes. First, it preserves the character of the Church. Second, it saves the soul of the offender. (1 Cor. 5:5). Discipline saves a believer by restoring him to obedience. Obedience, believe me, is the only place of safety for a Christian. Salvation has been described as 'escaping from the kingdom of Satan, and finding protection under the gracious rule of Christ'. Disobedience, here, means much more than a temporary lapse – it means a continued, wilful persistence in sin.

Where do we start? Exactly what sins call for discipline? Do we discipline people who, as we say, have to get married? Or what about people who get caught exceeding the speed limit? Or, again, what about someone who has been convicted of crime? The issue is not what sin a Christian has committed, but whether he has repented. Is he walking with God now? Discipline aims to produce repentance and restore fellowship. Under the guidance of the Holy Spirit, the Church must give whatever discipline is required to accomplish these objectives.

In many years of pastoral ministry, only once, on behalf of a church, did I excommunicate a member. He went out bitter and rebellious, but within two years he came back changed and repentant. In an acceptance meeting, he said, 'I'm glad you loved me enough to take that final action.' When a church fails to discipline, it loses its soul. That is why the Church must discipline – or die.

FURTHER STUDY

Heb. 12:1–14;
Deut. 8:5;
Psa. 94:12;
Prov. 3:11

1. Why does the Lord discipline us?
2. What does it produce?

Prayer

My Father and my God, I realise we are touching on deep and vital issues in Your Body, the Church. Help us all to face the challenge, and be willing to be pruned so that we, in turn, may prune. For Your own name's sake. Amen.

God's hammer and chisel

For reading & meditation – Romans 13:1–7

'Everyone must submit ... to ... authorities, for there is no authority except that which God has established ...' (v.1)

The Divine Gardener prunes our lives for greater fruitfulness through the authorities He places over us. I'm amazed at the number of Christians I meet who fail to see that the principle of authority is not something thought up by autocratically-minded individuals, who delight in lording it over others, but is something which the Creator established when He designed the universe.

The wave of anti-authority sweeping the world at the moment is yet another evidence of mankind's stubborn refusal to bring their lives in line with the design which God has set for them. This general attitude of anti-authority is, I fear, in danger of infiltrating the ranks of those who are followers of the Lord Jesus Christ.

Some time ago I had occasion to speak to a Christian who told me that he was thinking of changing his job because he couldn't stand the personality of the man who was over him. I said, 'Have you considered that God may want to use the irritating characteristics of your boss as a kind of hammer and chisel to chip away at the rough spots in your personality?' He admitted that he had never considered it in that way, but he promised to give the matter some further thought. He wrote to me later to say that the concept of seeing his boss as God's hammer and chisel transformed his attitudes towards God, towards his work and towards himself. God prunes though many things, not the least the authority He places over us.

FURTHER STUDY

Eph. 5:22–6:1;
4:11–13;

Col. 3:22-25;

Titus 3:1

1. What four
authority structures
does God place
us in?
2. How are we to
respond to them?

Prayer

O Father, help me to understand that the authority You put over me, although sometimes irksome and irritating, is Your way of pruning me for greater usefulness and effectiveness in Your service. For Jesus' sake. Amen.

The first rebel

For reading & meditation – Isaiah 14:12–27

'I will … rival the Most High!' (v.14, Moffatt)

Satan's influence in human affairs includes his strategy to persuade men that the violation of divine principles is in their best interest. There is good reason to believe that Satan seeks to bring about deception in the area of authority more than in any other. His very spirit of rebellion, as today's reading shows us, was the cause of his own downfall, and he attempts today to deceive even God's children with plausible arguments that are opposed to God's order and design.

A careful examination of Scripture shows that the principle of authority comes into operation at all stages of our development. We first begin to understand authority through the disciplines of home and family life (Eph. 6:1–4). Later, we come in contact with it when we start school, and later still when we take up employment (Col. 3:22–25). God has established in society a structure of authority by which men and women can live peaceably and in harmony with one another (Rom. 13:1–2). Once we become Christians, we become members of the Christian Church, where there is also a clear line of authority (Eph. 4:11–12). Almost every day of our lives we find ourselves in situations and circumstances which bring us directly under someone's authority, and unless we see that God wants to use this authority to bring His purposes to pass in our lives, then we will miss out on one of life's greatest character-building processes.

FURTHER STUDY

Matt. 23.1–12;

Luke 2:51–52;

Acts 7:51

1. What did Jesus teach about submission?
2. How did He exemplify this?

Prayer

Gracious God and Father, You have written Your principles into the very warp and woof of life. Behind every principle is a purpose. Help me to discover what You want me to know concerning this important principle of authority. Amen.

'Lift your gaze higher'

For reading & meditation – Philippians 2:1–13

'For God is at work within you, helping you want to obey him …' (v.13, TLB)

O ne of the most freeing insights of Scripture is the fact that God is the highest authority in the universe, and works through all lesser authorities to prune our lives and develop our effectiveness. It is 'freeing' because, once we discover it and grasp it, we have the insight we need to cope with any pressure that is put on us by those who are in authority over us. We know, as Jesus said to Pilate, 'You would have no power over me if it were not given to you from above' (John 19:11).

Are you under pressure at the moment from the authority over you at work, at school, at home, or at church? Is it hard to take? Then instead of focusing on the authority that is immediately over you, lift your gaze higher to the highest authority of all – God. Ask yourself: is God allowing this pressure because He sees in me a character deficiency which He wants to correct? Is He permitting, or even influencing, the person who is over me to come down upon me more heavily than usual because He wants to bring about important changes in me?

FURTHER STUDY

1 Pet. 3:1–22;
Eph. 1:18–23;
1 Cor. 8:6

1. What things are subject to Christ?
2. How is His lordship represented?

Once we see that the hand of God may be at work, and expressed through the attitudes and actions of those in authority over us, we begin to learn something of how such pressure can, in the Almighty's purposes, work for good in our lives. The most important thing we can discover, when under pressure from authority, is not how to get away from it, but to ask God what lesson He may be trying to teach us in the circumstances.

Prayer

O Father, You are teaching me Your ways, which are written, not only in Your Word, but also in me. I am designed by You, from infancy, to develop by a right response to authority. Teach me more about this vital and important principle. Amen.

Building up respect

For reading & meditation – Colossians 3:12–25

*'Whatever your task is, put your whole heart and soul into it,
as into work ... for the Lord ...' (v.23, Phillips)*

Whenever I mention the subject of a right Christian attitude to authority in any meeting where questions are invited, someone usually asks: 'The person over me is unfair, inconsistent and undeserving of respect. How can I obey someone I cannot respect?' My answer is this: A person in authority over us may have many character deficiencies. He may have a bad temper, use obscene language, be subject to moodiness, shout, rave or become abusive, but these deficiencies must not stop us from adopting an attitude of respect for the person's position, even if we find it difficult to respect that individual's personality. You see, when you respect a person's position of authority, you are respecting God, for it was He who ordained authority in this universe. Once you see this, then you have in your hands the key to the development of the right attitude towards authority. It is more important for you to recognise that God is working through even the deficiencies of the one above you, to bring about improvements in your character, than it is for that person to act more kindly and considerately towards you.

Our Christian growth is often hindered by wrong attitudes, and suffers more from a wrong attitude toward authority than any other thing. One of the first lessons we must learn, therefore, is to respond as God wants us to respond, irrespective of whether the authority over us improves or not.

FURTHER STUDY

Acts 23:1–7;

Eph. 6:7;

1 Pet. 2:17

1. How did Paul respond to authority?
2. What was his admonition?

Prayer

Father, the more I study Your Word, the more I am impressed with the rightness of things as laid down in the Scriptures. I know what the right attitude to authority should be, but it is often difficult to put into practice. Help me please. Amen.

All are under authority

For reading & meditation – Romans 14:1–8

'We are not our own bosses to live or die as we ourselves might choose.' (v.7, TLB)

Everyone is under authority (or should be), and the person who is a law unto himself is in an extremely dangerous position – morally and spiritually. In the family, the child comes under the authority of its parents, the wife under the authority of her husband, and the husband under the authority of God. In the Church, God expects us to be under the authority of those whom He calls to leadership positions. In society, we are expected to be under the authority of the laws of the land, enforced by the police and the magistrates.

One of the most salutary lessons I learned, concerning my role in society, happened many years ago. I was driving on my way to preach at a Christian conference, and I exceeded the speed limit. In the rear mirror I saw a police car come up behind me with its lights flashing, and I prayed, rather petulantly, 'Lord, You know I'm on my way to preach, and I'm already late. Why didn't You make these people go in a different direction?' The Lord answered me in words that rang out loud and clear in my mind. He said, 'Who do you think sent them?' Believe me, ever since then I have looked upon law-enforcers in an entirely new light. Those involved in law enforcement may not realise it, but they are not only the representatives of Government, but also the representatives of God. In the home, in the Church and in society, we must recognise that all legitimate authority is derived from God's authority.

FURTHER STUDY

Acts 16:1–40;

Matt. 6:10;

James 4:7

1. What are we able to do when we submit to God?
2. What was the result of Paul's submission to the Holy Spirit?

Prayer

O God, You whose will is wrought into the natural order, and who, by that very order, is discipling me to lawful, orderly living, help me to accept Your discipline, and rejoice in it; for Your discipline is my freedom, and Your law, my liberty. Amen.

Meekness is not weakness

For reading & meditation – Matthew 5:1–12

'Blessed are the meek, for they will inherit the earth.' (v.5)

I s it ever right to stand up and resist authority? Francis Schaeffer raised a storm amongst evangelicals in America by advocating that Christians be less passive towards governments who pass laws that are blatantly anti-scriptural (such as abortion on demand), and he encouraged believers to resist the State by whatever means necessary – even civil disobedience.

There can be little doubt, when we examine the Scriptures, that God requires Christians to develop a spirit of obedience. He wants us to recognise that He is the One who designed the lines of authority, and He encourages us, not merely to abide by them, but to delight in them. Once we have cultivated a truly obedient spirit, and show, both to God and others, that we have conquered the innate rebellion that is endemic to the human heart, then we are in a position of great strength if we find it necessary, on scriptural grounds, to resist the authority over us.

You see, then our resistance will be seen for what it is – a genuine attempt to stand up for righteousness, rather than personal pique at what is happening to us. A wife who says that she must resist her husband's authority because he places unscriptural demands upon her, or an employee who refuses to obey a directive from an employer because it will place him in an unbiblical position, would make their case more powerful if they showed that, in matters where obedience was possible, they had passed the test.

> **FURTHER STUDY**
>
> James 1:1–21;
> Luke 6:29;
> Gal. 5:22–23;
> 1 Pet. 3:4
>
> 1. What is of great price?
> 2. What are we to receive with meekness?

Prayer

O God, I want so much to possess a spirit of obedience, for I see that this is the way to true power. The more willing I am to obey, the more powerfully You can use my resistance whenever that is necessary. Thank You, Father. Amen.

How to disobey

For reading & meditation – Daniel 1:1–20

'... *God gave them learning and skill ... and wisdom; and
Daniel had understanding ...* (v.17, RSV)

While obedience to authority is a divine requirement, there are
times when it is right and proper to resist. What criterion can
we adopt to help us know when to obey and when to resist? This:
we obey the authority over us with as much enthusiasm as we can
generate until we are asked to do something that violates the clear
standards of Scripture.

We ought to know exactly how to proceed when asked by
someone in authority over us to do something that is dishonest,
immoral or unscriptural. We should ask ourselves: Is my Christian
testimony not clear enough, so that the one in authority over
me finds it easy to make such a request? Next, we should try to
understand what is going on in the mind of the person who is giving
the instruction. Maybe the person has moral values that differ from
yours. Be sensitive to this. An explanation of your own moral code,
rather than an open confrontation might be more helpful at this
point.

Ask God to help you to be respectful to the person concerned,
even though you have to disobey. A Christian
teenager, who was requested by his father to tell
a lie, said, 'Dad, if I did that it would destroy all
the character you have tried to develop in me.'
His father never asked him to lie after that. Daniel
was given wisdom when he resisted the king's
invitation to eat the meat that had been offered to
idols. That same wisdom is available to you.

FURTHER STUDY

Acts 5:1–33;
James 1:25;
John 14:23

1. What was Peter's
and the apostles'
response to those in
authority?
2. How do we show
our love for Christ?

Prayer

O God, how can I stop thanking You for the way You teach me to walk through
this world in wisdom. Your ways are so right. Everything within me says so.
Help me to be a truly wise person. For Your own dear name's sake. Amen.

'Making even Satan serve'

For reading & meditation – John 14:25–31

'... He has no hold on me, but the world must learn that I love the Father ...' (vv.30–31)

This week we consider how God uses the attacks of Satan to advance our progress and develop our spiritual effectiveness. Moffatt translates the text before us today like this: 'His (Satan's) coming will only serve to let the world see that I love the Father and that I am acting as the Father ordered.' Our Lord made even Satan serve! And when the Master has control of your life, He can do the same for you, and turn the attacks of Satan to your spiritual advantage.

The secret of Jesus' power, to turn Satan's coming to advantage, is contained in the words: 'The Prince of this world is coming. He has no hold on me' (Moffatt). There was nothing in our Lord's personality through which Satan could gain an advantage – no sin, no self-pity, no bitterness, no self-centredness. So Christ was able to turn the efforts of Satan towards positive ends.

The same, of course, cannot be said of us, for we are sinners, albeit saved sinners, with much sinfulness and self-centredness still resident in our natures. Despite this difficulty, however, God, Christ and the Holy Spirit are working hand in hand to help us overcome our sinful nature; and such is the skill and wisdom of the Trinity that they can use even the attacks of Satan to further those purposes. Do you feel as if you are being attacked by Satan at this moment? Then take heart for God will help you bear it (1 Cor. 10: 13). As you draw close to God, He will make even the attacks of Satan serve.

FURTHER STUDY

Eph. 6:10–18;
John 8:44; 14:6;
2 Cor. 11:3,14; 2:11

1. What has God given us to withstand Satan?
2. How has He exposed Satan's devices?

Prayer

O Father, help me to drop my anchor into the depths of this reassuring and encouraging revelation, that when I am in You, then everything serves, even Satan's coming. I am so thankful. Amen.

Paul's thorn in the flesh

For reading & meditation – 2 Corinthians 12:1–10

*'… there was given me a thorn in my flesh, a messenger of
Satan, to torment me.' (v.7)*

God can make even the attacks of Satan serve. Today we
examine this principle in the life of the apostle Paul. Some
Christians believe Paul's 'thorn in the flesh' to be a sickness, such as
recurring malaria or failing eyesight. The phrase, or a similar phrase,
however, is used several times in the Scriptures, and always refers
to personalities, never to things or conditions (Num. 33:55; Josh.
23:13; 2 Sam. 23:6). These statements refer to people who were
going to be extremely hurtful to the nation of Israel.

It is most likely that Paul would have used it in the same way.
This argument is greatly strengthened by what he says: 'There was
given me a thorn in my flesh, a messenger of Satan, to torment me.'
The word 'messenger', here translated from the Greek 'aggelos',
always denotes a person, never an object. Paul's 'thorn in the flesh'
(so I believe) was an evil Spirit specially commissioned by Satan
to harass the apostle in his work and bring about his downfall and
defeat.

Three times, Paul prayed that this 'messenger of Satan' might
be removed, but God permitted him to stay, and
continue to harass the apostle. Why? Because
the Almighty, who saw things from an eternal
perspective, knew that Paul would be a greater
servant, and a more effective witness, with the
harassment than he would be without it. God
matched the challenge, however, with a special
supply of His unfailing grace, and in this way
made Satan's coming serve.

FURTHER STUDY

Matt. 13:18–43;

John 8:44;

1 Pet. 5:8

1. What did Jesus
reveal about the way
Satan works?

2. What did Jesus
say about Satan?

Prayer

My Father and my God, I know that at times Satan will seek to attack my life,
too. However, help me to see, not the problem, but the possibilities. You make
even his coming serve. Thank You, Father. Amen.

Satan – on a leash

For reading & meditation – Job 1:1–22

'Have you not put a hedge around him and his household and everything he has? ...' (v.10)

I believe that Job was singled out by God to become a classic example of unconditional faith in God, and that today's Christians should not walk around wondering if at any moment God is going to allow Satan to invade their lives with all kinds of disasters and catastrophes. Job had a 'hedge' around him. What does it mean – a 'hedge'? God, I believe, has established a boundary of spiritual protection around every human life, for if not, Satan's power, being what it is, would eliminate every child born into the world. The Almighty God, protective of the life He creates, ensures that Satan does not have an open door into the human personality. If this were not so, there would be much greater chaos in human affairs than there is.

Some people may, through dabbling with the occult, or by consulting Satan in seances, break open that hedge. Then, of course, unless they repent and turn to Christ, they openly expose themselves to Satan and his power. In Job's case, God took away the protective hedge from around His servant so that Satan could enter his life in a way not normally permitted, and inflict upon him the full extent of his strategies. Job, of course, came through victoriously, proving that it was possible for a man to serve God because he loved Him, and not for personal advantage. We need to keep in mind that Satan's attacks come under the strict supervision of the Almighty, and He permits only that which accords with His eternal purposes.

FURTHER STUDY

Luke 21:1–19;
2 Chron. 16:9;
Psa. 34:7; 91:4

1. What did Jesus promise during times of great trial?
2. How can we endure these trials?

Prayer

O Father, I'm so relieved to know that Satan's attacks upon me are seen and supervised by You. Help me to be free of anything that will give him an advantage in my life so that all his efforts can be made to contribute. This I ask in Jesus' name. Amen.

Satan has his uses

For reading & meditation – Luke 4:1–14

'Jesus, full of the Holy Spirit … was led by the Spirit in the desert … returned … in the power of the Spirit …' (vv.1,14)

T he question is often asked: why does God permit the devil to have such power? Why, for that matter, didn't God eliminate Lucifer as soon as he had sinned, and thus spare the universe from a good deal of chaos and suffering?

We can never fully answer that question because, quite simply, we are unable to see into the divine mind. However, I have no doubt myself that the answer is partly because God, knowing the end from the beginning, knew that He could turn all Satan's efforts to advantage; and this, at the end of the day, would justify the Almighty's decision. This answer, I know, does little for those who point out the terrible suffering that Satan's rebellion has brought into the universe, but I believe that even that, when viewed from the divine standpoint in eternity, will be seen as necessary to God's overall purposes.

Satan, therefore, has his uses. Although it is not in the nature of God to tempt, He allowed Satan to try to take advantage of Jesus after His 40-day fast in the wilderness, and so attempt to bring about His downfall. But watch what happens. Christ, in His weakened condition, triumphs over the devil's repeated temptations, and comes out of the wilderness in the 'power of the Spirit'. Notice, He went in full of the Holy Spirit (v.1), and came out in the power of the Spirit (v.14). What did Satan's attacks succeed in doing? They helped to turn mere fullness to power.

FURTHER STUDY

James 1:1–12;
1 Cor. 10:13;
Heb. 2:18

1. How does the Lord use temptation?
2. Why are we able to bear it?

Prayer

Father, I think I am beginning to see what You are trying to show me – every battle with Satan which I come through makes the next one easier. Glory! Amen.

Outgrowing temptation

For reading & meditation – Revelation 3:7–13

'… I also will keep thee from the hour of temptation …'
(v.10, KJV)

When we stay close to Christ, then our own battles with the devil will have the same effect as His – our spiritual tissues become hardened in the struggle. One of Wales' greatest theologians, Dr Cynddylan Jones, used to say that two things happen as we face Satan's attacks in the strength and power of Jesus Christ: (1) Our temptations move on to a higher plane, and (2) we outgrow many of them. When you examine the temptations of Jesus, you find that they were on a very high plane indeed. He did not struggle with lust and passion, but with the more subtle questions of how to bring in the kingdom. 'It is a compliment,' says Cynddylan Jones, 'when we are tempted on that level. It shows that we are growing spiritually.' Here temptations become less gross and more subtle. The battle with things like spiritual pride takes the place of the battle with lust, greed, dishonesty and lies. Then there comes a time, through experience and conflict, when you outgrow many temptations of Satan.

A man I know, who held an important position in local government in Cardiff, was imprisoned for accepting a bribe. While in prison, he was converted, and when he came out, he worked his way back to a responsible position in society. He now has the respect of hundreds of people. He told me once, 'I say this humbly, and in dependence on God, but I don't think I could ever again be tempted by bribery. My character automatically spurns it.'

FURTHER STUDY
Dan. 1:1–21;
2 Pet. 2:9;
Prov. 1:10
1. What was the key to Daniel's resisting temptation?
2. What was the result?

Prayer

O Father, how I long to reach that level where I outgrow most of my temptations. I have a long way to go, but I know that every battle I win by Your strength and power brings me closer to that time. I am filled with anticipation. Amen.

There's victory in Jesus

For reading & meditation – 1 Corinthians 15:35–58

'... thanks be to God! He gives us the victory through our Lord Jesus Christ.' (v.57)

I have talked with many Christians over the years, some of whom have now gone on to glory, and have noticed that those who appear to be immune from temptation, reveal, in private conversation, that their immunity was won through a series of spiritual battles. I know in my own life that temptations, which would at one time have shaken me to the very foundation of my being, now have little impact upon me. This is not true of all temptations, but it is true of most. I have, as one writer put it, 'Got into the habit of experiencing victory.' I say this, of course, in utter dependency on the Holy Spirit, for I am fully conscious that in this life we never achieve full immunity from temptation. However, I find that, more and more, the unconscious effort takes over the functions of the conscious effort. To my delight and amazement, I find I am becoming fixed in goodness. Habit is now working for me where once it worked against me.

Those of you reading these lines who are struggling with some strong and fierce temptations – take heart. God is permitting you to be engaged in a battle with Satan which will not deprive you but deepen you. In His strength and power, you will emerge from this conflict with a refinement and a poise that you never thought possible. The battle will serve to show you that it is 'Not by might, nor by power, but by my Spirit, says the LORD' (Zech. 4:6). You will rejoice, not in what you can do, but in what He can do within you.

FURTHER STUDY

Rom. 8:32–39;

John 16:33;

Rev. 2:17;

1 John 5:4

1. What is the victory that overcomes the world?
2. What does it mean to be 'more than a conqueror'?

Prayer

My Father, I see so clearly that my battles with Satan wean me from self-dependency to God-dependency. If this is the outcome – then I face every temptation with confidence. Thank You, Father. Amen.

'Time to pull out all the stops'

For reading & meditation – 2 Corinthians 6:1–10

'... always "going through it" yet never "going under". We know
sorrow, yet our joy...inextinguishable...' (v.9, Phillips)

When we keep close to the Lord, and absorb the unfailing grace
He provides for us, then Satan's attacks serve only to develop
our resistance to temptation, and help wean us from self-dependency
to God-dependency. Some time ago, I came across a letter from a
missionary out in the jungle of New Guinea. It was written to his
friends at home. I don't know whether I would be able to write this
kind of letter, but it certainly catches the very spirit of the Christian
faith in relation to this matter of Satanic attacks. He wrote:

'It's great to be in the thick of the fight, to draw the devil's
heaviest guns, to have him blast away at you with discouragement,
slander, and so on. He doesn't waste time on a lukewarm bunch.
He hits good and hard when a fellow is hitting him. You can always
measure the weight of your blow by the one you get back. When
you're on your back, when some of your converts backslide, when
you learn that your most promising enquirers are only fooling,
when your mail gets held up, and some don't bother to answer your
letters, is that the time to put on mourning? No sir. That's the time to
pull out all the stops and shout Hallelujah.'

I doubt whether, as I said earlier, if I was in
that missionary's shoes, I would write such a letter,
but he holds out to us the radiant possibility that
when we see even Satan's attacks from God's point
of view, it can turn an attitude of defeat into an
attitude of victory.

FURTHER STUDY
1 Cor. 1:19–31;
Psa. 8:2;
2 Cor. 12:9;
Heb. 11:32–34
1. When is God able
to demonstrate His
strength?
2. What is the
testimony of those
whose faith is
in God?

Prayer

O God, I think I'll have to change my vocabulary because I'm certainly changing
my attitudes. The things I have called stumbling blocks I'm now seeing as
stepping stones. Amen.

Not everything – 'in' everything

For reading & meditation – Romans 8:28–39

'And we know that in all things God works for the good of those who love him …' (v.28)

God also prunes through perplexing events and difficult situations which He allows to come into our lives. Some of these events and situations may have evil ingredients in them, but it must be clearly understood that although God sometimes uses evil, He does not purpose it or design it. The only reason God permitted evil in His universe was because He knew He could outwit it and turn it to good.

The verse before us today may give the impression that God is responsible for everything that happens to us, but a closer examination of that text shows differently. One of the best translations of this verse is given at the top of this page, 'And we know that in all things God works for the good of those who love him'.

The wording is crucial. To say that all things work together for good is not the same as saying we know that in all things God works for the good of those who love him. All things do not necessarily work together for good: they may work for evil. To say that in all things God works for the good endows those 'things' with purpose –

a purpose for good to those who love Him. Things by themselves have no purpose unless we and God put a purpose in them. The 'things' may not be good, and may not of themselves work together for good, but 'in' those things God places His purpose, and makes them contribute to His ends. He turns the evil into good if we co-operate with Him and love Him.

FURTHER STUDY

2 Cor. 4:1–18;

Psa. 41:3;

Isa. 43:2

1. What did Paul say about trouble and perplexity?
2. What was happening to his 'inward man'?

Prayer

O God, what a gospel this is – even if the worst should happen to me, we can turn it into the best. I say 'we', for I can't do it without You, and You won't do it without me. I am in a co-operative partnership. Thank You, Father. Amen.

It's not what happens

For reading & meditation – 1 John 4:7–21

'There is no fear in love. But perfect love drives out fear …'
(v.18)

Many times, when Christians quote Romans 8:28, they recite the first part of the verse, but for some reason seem reluctant to complete it. They say, 'All things work together for good', but that is only half of the matter. The other part of the verse says, 'to those who love him, who have been called according to his purpose.' The verse needs to be completed in order to be fully understood. God is able to use everything that happens to us and make it contribute to His, and our, good, but only when we love Him and co-operate with Him.

Why is our love and co-operation so necessary for God to further His purposes through the difficult events and situations that arise from time to time in our lives? The answer is found in a statement I have used hundreds of times in these notes since I started writing them in 1965, and I make no apology for using it again. It contains a most powerful and life-changing truth: it is not so much what happens to us, but how we view it that is important. In other words, our inner attitudes determine the final results. God's ability to make a difficult or unpleasant situation work for good is limited by our capacity to love Him and co-operate with Him. If we love Him, we will trust Him, and if we trust Him, then we will rest assured that nothing that happens to us can successfully work against us. To triumph in adversity means that God is doing His part and you are doing yours.

FURTHER STUDY

2 Cor. 11: 21–30;
12:5–11;
Phil. 4:11

1. List some of Paul's
trials.
2. What was his
inner attitude?

Prayer

O Father, burn this thought into the depth of my being, that it is not what happens to me, but how I view it and what I do with it that determines the results. Help me to see all my problems from the same viewpoint as Yourself. For Jesus' sake. Amen.

The vital difference

For reading & meditation – 2 Corinthians 4:1–18

'… We get knocked down, but we get up again and keep going.' (v.9, TLB)

We need to realise that, although we are Christians, we are not exempt from the ordinary problems and difficulties that afflict humanity. If we insist that we ought to be exempt, then, when adversity strikes, we will go down like ninepins. If we say such things as, 'Why should this happen to me? I'm a Christian. God should treat me better,' then we take the first step towards depression and disillusionment.

Someone might say, 'What difference, then, does it make in being a Christian?' A Christian has (if he wishes to embrace it) a perspective on life that assures him that whatever happens can be used. Unfortunately, not all Christians see it in these terms, and instead of being sweetened by life's situations, they are soured by them. Paul the apostle had the following perspective. He said: 'If I am in distress, it is in the interests of your comfort' (2 Cor. 1:6, Moffatt). He made his distress contribute to other people's comfort. The distress was a pruning that made him more fruitful. A Sunday school teacher drew up a list of qualities that were characteristic

FURTHER STUDY

Rom. 5:1–11;
John 14:1;
1 Pet. 4:12–13

1. What was Paul's attitude to tribulation?
2. How did he see God using it?

of Christians. She listed such things as love, forgiveness, gentleness, honesty, and so on. A little boy put up his hand and said, 'Miss, you've missed out the most important.' 'What is that?' she asked. 'Please miss, the way to take things on the chin.' He was right! When life hits a Christian on the chin, it tilts his face upward to look on the face of God.

Prayer

Gracious Master, I want to walk amidst adversity with my head up. But I can't do that unless I have the right perspective. So teach me more, dear Father. In Jesus' name. Amen.

'Pagans waste their pains'

For reading & meditation – Jeremiah 51:45–58

'… and pagans waste their pains.' (v.58, Moffatt)

I n the passage before us today, the prophet pronounces doom on
the city of Babylon. The city, say the historians, was at this time
one of the wonders of the ancient world. With its hanging gardens, its
peacocks, its exquisite buildings and extravagant lifestyle, Babylon
was the envy of the surrounding nations. Yet, when God decided to
judge the city and bring about its destruction, there was nothing, or
no one, that could save her.

The Moffatt translation of the verse before us today says that
'pagans waste their pains'. What an interesting phrase. The real
thought here, of course, is that the pagans who built Babylon
laboured in vain, because by their denial of God and His cause, they
really got nowhere.

Pain, as we know, is nature's warning bell which draws our
attention to something wrong. If we see it as such we can profit
from it, but if we ignore it, then we must accept the consequences.
Ignoring pain is 'wasting' pain. I am speaking now not so much of
physical pain as of the pain which unpleasant events and situations
set up in the personality. How does a Christian
deal with these pains? Instead of 'wasting' them,
he uses them, sets them to music and makes them
sing. He is like the apple trees which, for some
reason, when slashed produce finer and bigger
apples. They are, as one horticulturalist put it,
'slashed into fruitfulness'.

FURTHER STUDY
Acts 16:19–40;
Psa. 30:5; 34:19–20
1. How did Paul and Silas respond to adversity?
2. What was the outcome?

Prayer

O Father, help me not to waste any of the pains which the difficult situations
of life might set up in my personality. If life slashes me, then let it slash me into
greater fruitfulness. For Jesus' sake. Amen.

Events make us

For reading & meditation – Psalm 119:65–72

'The punishment you gave me was the best thing that could have happened to me …' (v.71, TLB)

We ended yesterday by making reference to the apple trees which, when slashed on the trunk, yield bigger and better apples. 'For some reason,' said a horticulturalist, 'the trees bear better fruit when slashed and wounded in this way. So we slash them into added fruitfulness.'

Are you, at this moment, a victim of someone's bitter and sarcastic tongue? It hurts, doesn't it? One can retaliate, of course, but recrimination is no way forward: it only increases the bitterness. Here's a better way – if you can do it: let the tongue-lashing slash you into fruitfulness. See the rebuff as an opportunity to smooth out the rough edges in your soul. The wound, strangely enough, brings healing.

Let no one think that what I am advocating is easy. No one likes to be treated with sarcasm and contempt. But the nearer we get to the spirit of Jesus Christ, and the more closely we inspect the principles of Scripture, the more we discover that there is a better way than retaliation – the way of making events make us.

FURTHER STUDY

Prov. 3:1–13; 27:6;
Deut. 8:5;
Rev. 3:19

1. What does discipline demonstrate?
2. Why are a friend's wounds faithful?

We may feel the pain, but instead of 'wasting' it, we accept it, and let it become a discipline for us – a discipline that makes us better in character and conduct. In other words, we take the pain and, with God's help, build a purpose into it. Pain that has no purpose in it is fruitless, it simply ends in suffering – and no more.

But pain which has a purpose – or into which a purpose is built – contributes to the growth of the personality, and, in the end, greater spiritual fruitfulness.

Prayer

O God, help me to grasp this, for then I shall realise that I need not be afraid of anything, for I can use everything that comes, be it good, bad or indifferent. Thank You, Father. Amen.

'Stung into beauty'

For reading & meditation – Romans 5:1–11

'... we glory in tribulations also: knowing that tribulation worketh patience.' (v.3, KJV)

I am told that the bird's eye maple wood is made by the sting of insects. The sting is transformed by the tree into a beautiful wood that adorns many a home. The tree is stung into beauty. Let me share with you how to turn your 'stings' into maple wood, and thus adorn God's world with the beauty of your character. Say to yourself, 'God loves me and will allow nothing in my life that does not work for good. These 'stings' can make me bitter or make me better. I will throw myself on His grace and absorb His strength and allow Him to turn each 'sting' into greater character development.'

Look again at the text at the top of the page: 'tribulation worketh patience'. Anyone can be patient when there is no tribulation. Patience, true patience, like gold, is developed in the furnace of affliction. Socrates, though not a Christian, was said to be an extremely patient man. He had a violent and nagging wife who one day, after giving him a tongue lashing, threw a bucket of water over him. The sage quietly replied, 'After the storm, the rain.' The 'rain' watered the plants of patience growing in the garden of his heart. If a man who was not a Christian and had no access to the grace of God could do that, then how much more you and I can do who profess to have a personal relationship with the Almighty. It was said of John Wesley that a nagging wife contributed as much to his achievements as anything. He learned how to make the 'stings' make him. And how!

FURTHER STUDY
Dan. 3:13–30;
Isa. 48:10;
1 Pet. 1:7;
Job 23:10
1. What happened to the Hebrew boys in the furnace?
2. What does God achieve through our trials?

Prayer

O Father, help me to turn every sting I receive into stimulation, every irritation into irradiation, and every sorrow into a song. For Jesus' sake. Amen.

God and man – invincible

For reading & meditation – Luke 6:1–12

*'But they were furious and began to discuss with one another
what they might do to Jesus.' (v.11)*

Opposition may harm us or help us. The Living Bible puts verse
11 like this: 'At this, the enemies of Jesus were wild with rage,
and began to plot his murder.' How did Jesus react to that most
difficult situation? A few days later, we are told, He decided to
spend the whole night in prayer. What His thoughts were during
that night of prayer, we can only conjecture, but I can't help feeling
that, although He knew that He was destined to die at Jerusalem,
it must have been borne home to Him that night in an even more
powerful way. He saw clearly that the opposition to His ministry
would eventually culminate in His death. So before that happened,
He decided that this would be the moment in which He would
choose the men who would continue His ministry. When day broke,
He promptly proceeded to select the Twelve, the men who would
carry His message to the world when His own mission had been
fulfilled.

Here is a perfect example of what happens when God works
in someone whom He loves and who loves Him. Such was Christ's
love for His Father that He had absolute trust
in the Father's will. He knew that God loved
Him so much that He would allow nothing in
His life unless it furthered the purposes of their
partnership. And in the same way God wants to
set up a similar partnership in your life and mine.
He pleads for our absolute confidence and trust,
so that whatever happens we know that out of it
will come a purpose that is wise and good.

FURTHER STUDY

Isa. 53:1–12;
Luke 22:35–53;
Matt. 27:11–14

1. How did Jesus
respond to adversity?
2. Why did it please
the Lord to bruise
him?

Prayer

Father, now that I have this sacred secret in my hands, I realise that I am
invulnerable and invincible. Things may shake me, but they will not shatter me,
for I am a partner with You. And Your cause never fails. Amen.

Divinely ordained failure

For reading & meditation – Philippians 1:12–26

'Now I want you to know … that what has happened to me
has really served to advance the gospel.' (v.12)

The last method of pruning we shall study together is the way
God uses circumstances of deprivation and loss to further His
purposes in our lives. Some of our failures are due to the fact that we
didn't try hard enough, didn't study hard enough, or didn't properly
count the cost. Some failures, no doubt, are due to our physical
condition – lack of energy, sickness, and so on. There are, indeed,
many reasons for failure.

However, there are some failures which are deliberately
engineered in heaven. They are brought about in the purposes of
God for a very good reason. God may arrange for us to fail in a
secondary thing that we might succeed in a primary thing. Many
people are ruined by secondary successes. They become tangled up
in them, and never get to the worthwhile things.

I am sure that God prevented me from achieving the success
in engineering that I had set my eyes upon when I was a youth. I
left college with good results, and was chosen from many applicants
for an apprenticeship in a first-class engineering firm. But after a
few years, the targets I had set for myself were
not being achieved. I knew I could do it, but
somehow things eluded me. One day I woke
up and concluded that God wanted me to be an
evangelist, not an engineer. My conclusion was
right. I might have been crippled by a secondary
success. At first I found it difficult to countenance
the failure of my youthful ambitions, but now I
am thankful for God's preventative grace.

FURTHER STUDY

Phil. 3:1–21;
Mark 8:35;
John 12:24

1. What did Paul
count as loss for
Christ?
2. What did he say
about the past?

Prayer

O God, I realise that some of my failures are due to deficiencies in me while
others are brought about by Your divine hand. Give me the wisdom to discern
the difference. For Jesus' sake. Amen.

Cramped finances

For reading & meditation – Colossians 3:1–17

'… seek those things which are above … Set your affection on things above, not on things on the earth.' (vv.1–2, KJV)

Today we look at another condition of deprivation or loss – cramped financial circumstances. Are you in a financial hole at the moment? It could be due, of course, to bad money management, inadequate budgeting, unemployment, sickness, or a dozen other things. But there are times when God takes a hand in our affairs, and gently squeezes us financially in order to get our attention more firmly fixed on Him.

Today I received a letter from a friend who said that he was going through a difficult time financially. He then said something which I asked his permission to share with you. He said: 'Whenever I permit my spiritual affections to wander, God knows how to bring me to heel: He dries up the flow of my finances. Then it's not long before I am back at His feet, and pouring out my heart to Him in prayer.'

I know many other Christians who have told me that one sure way for God to bring them into line is by bringing them into cramped financial circumstances. If you are having financial difficulties at this time (and keep in mind there could be other reasons than the one I have just mentioned), then reflect for a moment on your spiritual progress. Is God trying to get your attention in the only way He can – by drying up your finances? God doesn't delight in impoverishing us, but if we move towards being independent of Him, then low finances soon change our position.

FURTHER STUDY

Matt. 6:25–34;
1 Cor. 9:24;
Phil. 1:27;
Col. 1:29

1. What was Jesus' promise?
2. What does Paul equate with spiritual achievement?

Prayer

Lord, help me to see that Your will is always my highest interest. You are not seeking to impoverish me but enrich me. Help me to accept Your disciplines as evidences of Your love, not Your judgment. For Jesus' sake. Amen.

Enforced inactivity

For reading & meditation – Galatians 1:11–24

'… I went immediately into Arabia … Then after three years I went up to Jerusalem … (vv.17–18)

Some inactivity is due to indisposition or other reasons, but what I am talking about here is the inactivity that comes because God has seemingly shut us up for a period of silence, where we appear to have no definite task to do for Him. Sometimes our lives are so full of unprofitable activity that God has to put us on His 'unemployment list' so that we have time to listen to what He has to say to us. The temporary periods of being laid aside, of finding yourself without a task to do for Him, are sometimes part of His pruning purposes. If you are in such a condition at this moment, then it is important that you come before the Lord to find the reasons for this enforced inactivity. If it is due to an obvious cause, such as I have described earlier, then just rest in the fact that He is with you in the situation. But if it is due to some deficiency in you which God is trying, lovingly and gently, to prune from your life or character, then you need to ask Him to help you identify it.

Many of us become involved in endless activity in the church, and take up every task given to us because it provides us with an escape route from our primary responsibilities. And what are they? Daily contact with God through prayer and the reading of His Word. If you don't have time for that, then you are far busier than God wants you to be. Sometimes we won't stop being active because we are afraid of what God might say to us when we come in silence before Him.

Prayer

O Father, make me patient under restriction, and help me learn the lessons You are teaching me, so that I may be all the richer when I am released. For Jesus' sake. Amen.

When God removes your crutches

For reading & meditation – Hebrews 12:1–13

'... strengthen your feeble arms and weak knees ... the lame may not be disabled, but rather healed.' (vv.12–13)

I heard recently of a Christian woman who could not walk without crutches. One day she slipped on the stairs and fell to the bottom, her crutches remaining halfway up the stairs. She lay there for a long time, calling for help, but no one came. Eventually she said to herself, 'This is ridiculous. I can't stay here all day.' She pulled herself up and began to walk. And she has been walking ever since! The fall and the loss of those crutches was the best thing that could have happened to her.

There are many things in your life and mine, as we have been seeing, upon which we tend to lean heavily: success, money, friends, family, position. They may not be wrong, but they become crutches which weaken our moral fibre. We depend upon them too much. Then something happens, and they are taken away. At first we are stunned and crushed. Our crutches are gone – what's left? Why, our feet and our backbone, and the grace of God!

A friend of mine, a medical doctor, through no fault of his own, lost his practice, his possessions, everything. When a friend tried to console him, he said, 'Don't worry, the shaking has done me good. Christ has been on the margin of my life too long. Now He will be the centre.' He set out with his family to another country, and he is doing a marvellous and wonderful work for God. The old routine broke up, and he started a new routine – a wider one! Do not weep over lost crutches. God is not punishing you, but pruning you.

FURTHER STUDY

John 5:1–16;

Amos 6:1;

Psa. 123:4

1. Why did Jesus ask, 'Do you want to get well'?

2. What was Jesus challenging?

Prayer

O Father, how foolish I have been to think of troubles as Your punishments when really they are Your prunings. When my crutches are taken away, help me not to whimper and whine, but stand on my feet and walk – right into a wider ministry. Amen.

My Father, the Gardener

For reading & meditation – John 15:1–8

'I am the true vine and my Father is the gardener.' (v.1)

Effectiveness and fruitfulness in the Christian life doesn't just happen: they come and continue as a result of careful planning. And in the planning there must be pruning. There is no way that we can be effective disciples of Christ except through relentless pruning – the cutting away of non fruit-bearing suckers that sap our energies, but bear no fruit. Our Father, the Gardener, knows that it is possible to have luxuriant growth with no fruit, and so the useless non-fruit-bearing growth must be cut away. Life, as we said at the beginning of our studies, depends as much upon elimination as it does upon assimilation. It is only when we are willing to give up, that we are able to give out.

With many of us, much of our lives are overgrown with useless things. God has many pruning knives, and with some of us, He may have to use them all. When He prunes however, He does so with the utmost tenderness and care, and He will not permit anything to happen to us unless it accords with the purposes which He planned for us before the world began. So be open to Him in the days that lie ahead, for He needs your consent and co-operation if He is to do a perfect and complete job. Let Him prune you from mistakes to mastery, from despair to delight and from blunders to beauty. And when the pruning process feels painful, remember that the knife is in good and reliable hands. Your Father is the Gardener.

FURTHER STUDY

Psa. 1:1–6;
Rom. 7:14;
Col. 1:10;
John 12:24

1. What is the characteristic of the godly man?
2. How much fruit are you bearing?

Prayer

O Father, into Your hands I commend my spirit. Now You have me – all of me – to do with what You will. Any knife You use will be acceptable to me if it makes me a more acceptable person. Thank You, dear Father. In Jesus' name. Amen.

The Letters
of James
and John

My brother and my 'Lord'

For reading & meditation – James 1:1

'James, a servant of God and of the Lord Jesus Christ …' (v.1)

We begin today a series of verse by verse studies on the epistles of two of the greatest men in the New Testament – James and John. Unlike our usual approach, where a theme is developed over a variety of different Bible passages, we will move verse by verse through these two exciting books.

My reason for choosing these two epistles at this particular time is because there seems to be a sense of destiny on my spirit, that God wants to speak to many of you in a special and direct way through these books.

We begin by focusing on the opening verse of James' epistle: 'James, a servant of God and of the Lord Jesus Christ'. James, who was the brother of our Lord, introduces himself not as a family member, but as Christ's willing and obedient servant. We do not know when James actually became a committed follower of Christ, but we can imagine some of the difficulties he might have faced in coming to such a decision. Brothers usually see each other in a different light from those on the outside of a family. What, I wonder, did James feel when Jesus left home to become an itinerant preacher? How did he view the stories of His miracles? Whatever doubts he might have had were all dissolved at Christ's resurrection. Jesus proves conclusively that He is God by coming back from the dead.

The scripture says significantly: 'Then he appeared to James' (1 Cor. 15:7). Never again will James refer to his brother simply as 'Jesus'. From now on He is to be much greater than a brother. He is to be 'Lord'.

FURTHER STUDY

John 13:1–17;

Psa. 2:11;

Eph. 6:7–8;

Heb. 12:28–29

1. What did Jesus teach about servanthood?
2. How did He demonstrate it?

Prayer

Lord Jesus, how clearly Your deity must have been seen by James in order for him to acknowledge You, not as his brother, but as his Lord. Help me also to see Your deity in such clear terms, and to crown You continually as the Lord of my life. Amen.

'A berry in the mouth'

For reading & meditation – James 1:2–4

'Consider it pure joy, my brothers, whenever you face trials of many kinds.' (v.2)

J.B. Phillips paraphrases James', words as follows: 'When all kinds of trials and temptations crowd into your lives … welcome them as friends!' Some Christians have asked: is James really serious? Surely the time to rejoice is when problems are on their way out, not on their way in! Not so, says James: when problems crowd into your lives, treat them as you would a long-lost friend – rejoice. James has a good rationale for making this statement: 'Realise that they (trials) come to test your faith and to produce in you the quality of endurance' (v.3, Phillips).

One of the greatest discoveries I have made in my Christian life (and I am sure you are discovering it, too) is that God has a brilliant and wonderful way of disguising opportunities, so that they look like problems. If we learn this secret, we know how to live. If we don't, then we fumble this business of living. No one can face trials and temptations heroically unless they see some meaning in them.

In Africa there is a berry which, when held in the mouth, sweetens the taste of everything that is eaten. The Christian who takes these words of James, and lives by them, has something like that – he has the power to transform difficulties into opportunities. The power to use everything is the 'berry' that sweetens the biggest calamity. Are trials and problems crowding into your life at this moment? Then don't let them make you bitter – let them make you better.

FURTHER STUDY

Acts 16:19–40;
1 Pet. 1:6–7;
Job 23:10;
Isa. 48:10

1. How did Paul respond to his difficult situation?
2. What was the result?

Prayer

O God, my Father, I see that when problems come I need not whine or complain. I can make music out of misery, a song out of sorrow and achievement out of every accident. I am so thankful. Amen.

Help – what do I do?

For reading & meditation – James 1:5–8

'If any of you lacks wisdom, he should ask God … and it will be given to him.' (v.5)

What, then, is wisdom? 'Wisdom,' said one great man, 'is the right application of knowledge.' Knowledge is the gaining of information, but wisdom is the ability to put that knowledge to best effect. In the age in which we live, man has wrested a good deal of information from the heart of the universe, but he lacks the wisdom to put it to good use. 'Man,' said someone, 'shows off his knowledge by flying faster than sound, but shows his lack of wisdom by going in the wrong direction.' The wisdom God uses in dealing with the problems of the universe is available to you and me – just for the asking. But how do we obtain it? It's simple – pray in faith. Ah, so easy to say, so hard to do. But really praying in faith is simple. Perhaps that's why we stumble so much over it.

Time and time again, when counselling people over their problems, I have enquired: 'Have you prayed about this? Have you asked God to help you unravel the problem?' And I am simply staggered at the number of times people have said, 'No'. Praying in faith means giving God the problem and leaving it with Him. If you let your mind flit backwards and forwards between His greatness and your own inadequacy, you will end up in hopeless confusion, tossed like a wave in the wind. The man who came to Jesus cried: 'Help me overcome my unbelief!' (Mark 9:24). When he admitted he needed faith, Christ helped him with his problem. He will do the same for you – today.

FURTHER STUDY

Prov. 3:1–35;
Job. 28:28;
Matt. 7:24;
Luke 21:15

1. What are some of the characteristics of wisdom?
2. What is Jesus' promise to believers?

Prayer

Father, I see my problem. I try to struggle through my difficulties and work them out myself. But now I ask for Your help, Your wisdom and Your faith. Show me how to give You my problems – and not take them back. For Jesus' sake. Amen.

Problems are custom-made

For reading & meditation – James 1:9–12

'Blessed is the man who perseveres under trial … he will receive the crown of life that God has promised …' (v.12)

A re you poor – lacking in money, in talents, in looks, in opportunities? Then don't let these things get you down – you are the child of a King. You belong to the Ruler of the universe who loves and adores you and longs to bless you. Are you rich, talented and live a life full of opportunities? Then don't cling to these things too tightly. Money can be lost, talent can be snatched away, circumstances can change for the worse. Rejoice in the thing you cannot lose – your relationship with God.

No matter whether you are rich or poor, you will face problems. Indeed, they are custom-made for you. A man said to me once, 'Why can't my life be like Bryan's? He never seems to have any problems.' I happened to know that Bryan was in the middle of some deep and depressing problems. Almost everyone has problems, but with some they don't show. We must learn that there is more to problems than meets the eye. 'A Christian', said someone, 'is like a tea bag: he's not much good until he has been through some hot water.' Trials, says James, returning to his previous theme, come to test our faith. If you could see the complete picture of your life, there would be no room for faith. But then you would be like a bird in a cage who is bereft of any opportunity to spread its wings and soar into the highest heavens. God keeps just enough from you to give your faith an opportunity to soar!

FURTHER STUDY

Matt. 19:16–30;
Psa. 62:10;
Mark 4:18–19;
1 Tim. 6:9

1. What did Jesus teach about the danger of material possessions?
2. How did He respond to His disciples' perplexity?

Prayer

O God, when I am in the midst of circumstances and surroundings I cannot change, let me learn the secret of making them into a whetstone on which my spirit will be sharpened. For Jesus' sake I ask it. Amen.

Who is to blame?

For reading & meditation – James 1:13–15

*'When tempted, no-one should say, "God is tempting me."
For God ... does [not] tempt anyone.' (v.13)*

Some Christians blame God whenever they fall into temptation. This attitude of blame-shifting, and an unwillingness to accept responsibility, has been in the world since the Garden of Eden. Remember what Adam said when God confronted him over the question of his sin? He faced it like a man – and blamed it on his wife! 'The woman you put here with me – she gave me some fruit from the tree' (Gen. 3:12). A refusal to accept responsibility is an immature response to life.

Anna Russell puts into rhyme the conclusions of a man who went to a non-Christian psychiatrist because he had killed his cat and blackened his wife's eyes. The psychiatrist told him that the reason he did this was because of the various things that had happened to him. 'You are not to blame,' said the psychiatrist. 'Others have made you the way you are.' Anna Russell says this was the man's conclusion: 'I'm so glad that I have learned, the lesson he has taught, that everything I do that's wrong, is someone else's fault.'

It's time we Christians stopped blaming God for our difficulties and faced up to the fact that it is not what happens to us that is important but how we respond to it. Our responses are our own responsibility.

You may not be responsible for what happens, but you are responsible for the way you respond to what happens. And until you and I learn this, we will remain immature personalities, and fail to grow up.

FURTHER STUDY

Eph. 6:10–18;
1 Cor. 10:13;
Heb. 2:18;
2 Pet. 2:9

1. What is the best way to withstand temptation?
2. How does God help us in the hour of temptation?

Prayer

O Father, help me not to become a blame-shifter – blaming You and others for my problems. Show me how to respond to life with understanding and maturity. In Jesus' name. Amen.

'If only'

For reading & meditation – James 1:13–15

'... *each one is tempted when, by his own evil desire, he is dragged away and enticed.*' (v.14)

W e must stop blaming God for our difficulties and our problems. There is a natural tendency in us all to blame someone else, and ultimately God, for our being confronted with temptation to sin, but every Christian must accept the responsibility for any evil they commit. It is no good saying: 'If only I had not met that person ... If only I had gone to a different school ... If only I had had different parents ... If only I had not got married.' These are just excuses.

James explains that the source of man's temptation to do evil is not in God, but in man himself. The lust within man tends to involve him in compromising situations. Temptation would be helpless if there were nothing in us to which it could appeal: it has to strike an answering chord. The progression of evil is described here in three stages. First, there is the lust (or the desire), then there is the yielding, then there is death. Shakespeare, in his play *Macbeth,* illustrates these three stages very clearly. Lady Macbeth set her goal to become Queen of Scotland. But between her and this goal stood her husband's kinsman. So great was her desire to be Queen that she plotted the man's murder, and got her husband to carry it out. There was just one problem – she had to live with herself afterwards First, there was the desire – the lust for power. Lust resulted in sin, and sin gave birth to death. Her story is, in one way, the story of every human being who yields to the lust of the flesh.

FURTHER STUDY

Gal. 5:1–26;
1 John 2:16;
Titus 2:12;
Matt. 5:28

1. What is Paul's admonition to the Galatian church?
2. How can we overcome the lust of the flesh?

Prayer

O God, I know I cannot stop tempting thoughts from entering my heart, but I can stop them taking root. Help me to overcome every evil thought, by turning swiftly away from it, towards You. For Jesus' sake. Amen.

'It was a happy day for him'

For reading & meditation – James 1:16–18

'He chose to give us birth …' (v.18)

Through all the changes in this mad, mad world, God remains steadfast, unchanging and completely reliable. His gifts are designed for our greatest good. However, the greatest thing God does for us is to make us His children. Listen to how the Living Bible puts verse 18: 'And it was a happy day for him when he gave us our new lives, through the truth of his Word, and we became, as it were, the first children in his new family.'

Did you notice those words, 'it was a happy day for him'? For Him? Yes, difficult as it may be to grasp, especially for those with a low opinion of themselves, God was actually overjoyed when you surrendered your life to Him. We usually think of this the other way around – it was a happy day for us when we accepted Him – but here James is telling us that it was also a happy day for Him.

This statement brings into focus the way God really feels about us. Some Christians think that when they gave their lives to God, the Almighty, rather begrudgingly and half-heartedly, gave them shelter in His fold. The picture they carry in their hearts of God is that of a Creator who has to accept us into heaven because of the death of His Son upon the cross. I was in a group once where a lady was asked: how do you see God? She replied, 'God is someone who puts up with me because of the sacrifice of His Son.' God doesn't just 'put up' with you. It was 'a happy day for him' when you trusted in His Son. Yes – you are loved.

FURTHER STUDY

John 3:1–21;
1:12–13;

Luke 15:7;

2 Cor. 5:17

1. Write down your definition of 'born again'.
2. What makes the angels rejoice?

Prayer

O God help me to see myself as You see me, and love myself as You love me. Then and only then, can I have a proper estimate of my worth. Amen.

'Mirror, mirror on the wall'

For reading & meditation – James 1:19–25

'… is like a man who looks at his face in a mirror and … immediately forgets what he looks like.' (vv.23–24)

James gives us six practical commands which are then illustrated throughout the rest of the chapter. These commands are simply stated: 'be quick to listen, slow to speak and slow to become angry … get rid of all moral filth and the evil that is so prevalent, and humbly accept the word … Do what it says' (vv.19-22).

Let's examine these one by one. (1) Be quick to listen: Are your ears open to what God says to you in His Word? The problem often isn't that God doesn't speak, but that they are not listening. (2) Be slow to speak: Far too many speak, not because they have something to say, but just because the want to say something. (3) Be slow to become angry: anger is a choice, no matter how people argue against it. You can choose to be angry, and you can choose not to be angry. (4) Get rid of all moral filth: The person who listens to God, who thinks before he speaks and who chooses not to be angry, will have little difficulty in setting aside those sins and vices that destroy his effectiveness for Christ. (5) Accept the word: This means opening yourself to it, reading it, studying it and, above all, believing it.

FURTHER STUDY

Matt. 7:7–29;
Prov. 8:34;
Eccl. 5:1;
Luke 8:15

1. To what did Jesus liken those who did His sayings?
2. To what did Jesus liken those who did not do His sayings?

(6) Do what it says: If you hear truth and don't put it into practice, then you are self-deceived. You are like a man who looks in a mirror, and then goes away forgetting what he looked like. If you don't attend to the imperfections you see while you look in a mirror, it's hardly likely that you will attend to them later.

Prayer

Lord, I get the point. If I don't put things right as soon as You point them out to me, then my time spent in Your Word is of no profit. Help me develop a deep sense of immediacy in my daily walk with You. For Jesus' sake. Amen.

Taming the tongue

For reading & meditation – James 1:26–27

*'If anyone … does not keep a tight rein on his tongue, he
deceives himself and his religion is worthless.' (v.26)*

'Each of us,' says one writer, 'has an enemy that is always with
us. Just when we think we are the victor, we experience new
defeats. We are able to defeat some enemies, but never this one. And
what is this enemy? – our tongue.' Many Christians have told me,
pointing at their tongue, 'This is really my trouble. If I could control
my tongue, life would be a lot easier and happier.' But we will never
be able to control the tongue until we control our spirit, because the
tongue will always reveal the true thoughts of our inner being. 'For
out of the abundance of the heart,' said Jesus, 'the mouth speaks'
(Matt. 12:34, RSV).

Here are six ways to help you tame the tongue. Check each
scripture out, apply it in your life, and, with God's help you can
be a tongue-tamer. (1) Dedicate your heart and your tongue to
the Lord daily (Rom. 12:1). (2) Assume responsibility for every
word you speak (Matt. 5:21–22). (3) Ask those around you what
offensive words you use (Prov. 17:10). (4) Learn how to use words
that encourage, edify, comfort and inspire (Heb. 10:24–25). (5) Ask
a person's forgiveness every time you offend them
with wrong words (Matt. 5:23–24). (6) Urge your
friends to tell you when you offend them by your
words (Prov. 27:6). If you follow this prescription,
I promise you that it will transform you from
being a tongue-lasher to a tongue-tamer.

FURTHER STUDY

Col. 4:1–6;
Job. 6:25;
Prov. 16:24; 25:11

1. How should we
always speak?
2. How can our
conversation be
'seasoned with salt'?

Prayer

Father, I see that without Your help, no man can tame the tongue. I bring the
inner depths of my being to You for cleansing. You work on my heart – I will
work on my tongue. In Jesus' name I ask it. Amen.

Are you a snob?

For reading & meditation – James 2:1–5

'… *as believers in our glorious Lord Jesus Christ, don't show favouritism.*' (v.1)

James begins this second chapter with an important instruction for those who believe in Jesus as their Lord and Master: don't be a snob. One of the responsibilities that evolves from the Christian faith is relating properly to other people. And people, as you know, can present us with some difficult problems. A missionary wrote home to his church, after having been on the mission field for some time, and said: 'The work here is great – except for the people.'

Here James presents a dramatic vignette of first-century Church life. Into a church service comes a man of great wealth, and he finds himself seated next to a poor man – perhaps a slave. Someone bustles around trying to find the rich man a better seat, but such favouritism, says James, is evil and judgmental. God chooses poor men, he goes on to say, whose only wealth is their faith. So everybody who has Christ is rich: Christianity has given us one common denominator – Christ. The sin of favouritism is prevalent in the Church today, only now it is not so obvious as it once was. Let's ask ourselves, right now, this pointed and personal question: Am I part of a clique in my church or fellowship? Do people see you as someone who accepts some but rejects others? Someone defined a clique as 'where the popular people gather to reassure each other that they really are'.

Don't be a snob is James' message to us today. Don't even be a snob about snobs. It doesn't pay.

FURTHER STUDY

Matt. 5:33–48;
19:21;

Lev. 19:15;

1 Tim. 5:21;

Acts 10:34–35

1. What did Jesus
relate being perfect
to?
2. How do we often
display the attitude
of the publicans?

Prayer

Lord Jesus Christ, as You probed the Early Church, probe the Church of today also. Probe me. Drain to the last poisonous drop any snobbery or cliquishness in me. For Your own dear name's sake. Amen.

Let's call sin – sin

For reading & meditation – James 2:6–13

*'But if you show favouritism, you sin and are …
law-breakers.' (v.9)*

T he apostle is not saying here that it is sinful to be wealthy. The rich
man who came to the same church service was not condemned
because of his wealth. The sin of giving greater respect to the rich
man was committed by the person who made the discrimination.
James speaks directly to this person, and accuses him of favouritism.
He says: 'You have insulted the poor' (v.6).

The apostle then adds: 'Is it not the rich who are exploiting
you? Are they not the ones who are dragging you into court?' This
question referred to the custom in those days of what was termed
'summary arrest'. A wealthy man, meeting on the street a poor man
who owed him money, could seize him and drag him into a court
of law, demanding that his debt be paid. If the poor man could not
pay it, he was liable to be thrown into a debtor's prison, where he
remained until his debt could be paid.

James then asks: 'Are they not the ones who are slandering
the noble name of him to whom you belong?' (v.7). In raising
this question, James was not implying that a wealthy person was
inherently evil because of his wealth, but, if he
employed the practice of 'summary arrest', he
was failing to consider a person's human rights.
The whole point and purpose of this passage is
to show that snobbery is sin, just as adultery and
murder are. The God who said that you must not
steal, lie, murder, cheat, or be unfaithful to your
wife, also said that you must not be a snob.

FURTHER STUDY
Luke 10:25–37;
Psa. 82:3;
Prov. 21:1; 19:17
1. What was Jesus
teaching in this
parable?
2. Do you have any
prejudices?

Prayer

O God, save me from the central wrong of thinking of big sins and little sins.
All sin is abhorrent to You. Help me to see all deviations from You in that same
light. For Jesus' sake. Amen.

Don't just stand there

For reading & meditation – James 2:14–26

'... Faith that doesn't show itself by good works is no faith at all – it is dead and useless.' (v.17, TLB)

This section of James' epistle is what led Martin Luther to refer to it as the 'epistle of straw'. Luther thought that James was contradicting Paul's theology in Romans, where the great apostle talks of being justified by faith, but really there is no contradiction between Paul and James – just a different viewpoint.

James is saying: what good is it if those who profess to be Christians do not help their brothers and sisters who are in need? Such people, says James, are demonstrating by their actions that they have no faith. If they did, then their faith would show itself in some fruit. The man who claims to have faith in God, but is blind and deaf to the needs of others, only demonstrates that nothing has really happened to him in his heart.

James would be the first to agree with Paul that we are saved by faith, and by faith alone, but where faith is present, then good works will follow. We are not saved by good works, we are saved to do good works (Eph. 2:8–10). James is so eager for us to understand this truth that he illustrates it from the lives of Abraham the patriarch and Rahab the prostitute. Abraham demonstrated his faith in God by his obedience, and so did Rahab. James chose these two extremes to let us know that nobody is exempt. 'Don't just stand there – do something' applies to all Christians – at all times.

FURTHER STUDY

Heb. 10:1–24;
Matt. 5:16;
1 Tim. 6:18–19;
1 Pet. 2:12

1. How can we 'spur one another on'?
2. By what good works are you demonstrating your faith to others?

Prayer

Father, help me to get my values straight, and to realise that when I say I have faith, but do nothing about it, I am just a bundle of contradictions. Straighten me out, Lord – now. Amen.

That tongue again

For reading & meditation – James 3:1–5

*'... take ships as an example. Although they are so large ...
they are steered by a very small rudder ...' (v.4)*

I believe that these words are being read by members of many different churches, who need, more than anything, to understand how to tame the tongue. Someone has said, 'When the Church puts into practice the teaching of James 3:1-12 then most of its problems will disappear.'

James begins by warning us that no one should aspire to become a teacher for purely selfish reasons. If we want to teach just to gain the admiration and applause of people, then we dig a pit for ourselves into which we will eventually fall. In order to be effective in teaching, one must be willing to pay the price of long hours of prayer, study, perseverance, isolation from others, and, above all, to illustrate one's teaching by one's own lifestyle.

James then swings into a detailed and vivid exposition of the need to control our tongue. But the tongue is so small. How can it cause so much trouble? James answers by saying that we control the movements of a horse by a bit that is extremely small. Ships, too, for all their size, are controlled by a very small rudder. What the bit is to the horse and the rudder is to the ship, so the tongue is to the personality of a Christian. If we permit God to use our tongue as a horseman uses the bit, or a pilot the rudder of a ship, then our lives will move in the direction the Almighty decides. But if not, then we face the greatest tragedy of all – spiritual downfall or spiritual shipwreck.

FURTHER STUDY

1 Cor. 5:1–13;
Prov. 6:10–11;
Eccl. 10:1;
Songs 2:15

1. Why are the little things so important?
2. What is leaven a type of?

Prayer

Gracious heavenly Father, I come to You once again with this tongue of mine. Help me to work with You to make it responsive to Your perfect will. For Jesus' sake. Amen .

The tinder tongue

For reading & meditation – James 3:5–6

'… *Consider what a great forest is set on fire by a small spark.*' (v.5)

The tongue, used carelessly, is like a spark that sets a forest on fire. Small and insignificant though a spark may be, it can cause total devastation, turning the loveliest of forests into a charred mass. Consider some of the ways in which the tongue can cause trouble. It can do it by exaggeration. You know the kind of thing I mean: 'You *always* do that, and you know very well I don't like it.' Always? You really mean *sometimes*. It can also do it by leaving out some of the facts. A ship's captain occasionally entered in his log the phrase: 'The first mate was sober today.' He left out the fact that the first mate was sober every day! The first mate was fired.

The tongue can also cause trouble by a deliberate lie. 'The pastor's car was outside her house for hours.' This one came up in the case of a pastor friend of mine whose reputation was torn to shreds by a woman who knew that he left his car outside one house, while he made several other calls in the same street. The tongue can cause trouble by the use of waspish words. This is often done under the guise of: 'I speak the truth, even though it hurts.' But isn't it true also that such people can like the hurt they cause?

Like a forest fire, the devastation that can be caused by a tongue that is not under control can be far-reaching. But this 'tinderbox' does not only do its damage to other people: it can make our own lives 'a blazing hell'. You cannot hurt others without hurting yourself.

FURTHER STUDY

Acts 5:1–11;

Psa. 34:13;

Prov. 13:3;

1 Pet. 3:10

1. What was the sin of Ananias and Sapphira?
2. Check your tongue today in the four areas mentioned above.

Prayer

O God, You have me cornered. I wriggle and squirm, but there is too much truth in what You are saying for me to ignore it. Help me to take my medicine, however bitter it may taste. In Jesus' name I ask it. Amen.

It can be conquered

For reading & meditation – James 3:7–12

'Can both fresh water and salt water flow from the same spring?' (v.11)

James tells us in this passage that though man has successfully tamed almost every living creature, he has not come to the place where he can tame the tongue. How many of us, I wonder, have had the experience of making a statement which we have lived to regret?

The tongue can be the most hypocritical thing in the world. It can be used to bless God and curse men. A man can go into church on Sunday and use his tongue to praise God, and then on Monday employ that same tongue in cursing one of his workmates who has upset him! Just as it is absurd to expect a fountain to produce both salt and fresh water at the same time, and just as it is absurd for a fig tree to bear olives – so it is equally absurd for a believer to use his tongue to bless God at one moment, and the next moment curse his fellow men.

It is true, as James says, that no man can tame the tongue. God, however, can tame it. When a person surrenders to the Holy Spirit, God gives them the ability to control their tongue. Christians, who are honestly concerned about controlling their tongue, will not try to achieve this in their own strength, but will ask God's help to make an unequivocal surrender. When they falter, they will at once confess it and receive the forgiveness of God. Such a Christian will eventually come to the place where they will be able to bridle their tongue, and, as a consequence, they will become more mature in the faith.

FURTHER STUDY

Titus 1:1–18;

Matt. 7:3;

Rom. 2:1,23

1. In what way are we often hypocritical?
2. Decide how you will encourage and bless others with your words today.

Prayer

My Father and my God, I don't want to live out an absurdity, like a fountain gushing with salt water and fresh water. I want to live abundantly – sending out only love. Help me, my Father. For Jesus' sake. Amen.

Devilish wisdom

For reading & meditation – James 3:13–16

'Such "wisdom" does not come down from heaven but is earthly, unspiritual, of the devil.' (v.15)

James explains that there are two types of wisdom available to people – one is earthly, the other heavenly. Earthly wisdom approaches life from a humanistic standpoint, and ignores the Creator. This results in bitter envy, strife, confusion and every evil work. If you don't believe that, then just open today's newspaper. I can almost guarantee that in your paper today will be reports about one or more of the following – conflict, murder, theft, divorce, child-abuse, rape, mugging, and such other things. We are living in one of the most enlightened periods of history, but just look at what wisdom without God is producing – a baby aborted every few minutes, marriages that fall apart, open homosexual relationships, increasing crime statistics, and economic instability.

Human wisdom, says James, comes from the lower nature, even from the devil himself. I doubt whether our non-Christian friends would appreciate us telling them that some of the laws that are passed (like the 1967 Abortion Act, for example) were inspired by the devil, but there is no doubt in my own mind that he is the source. Two major causes of chaos are listed – envy (jealousy) and selfish ambition. Where these two things are present, then no society, or, for that matter, no church, can enjoy security and peace. 'For where you have envy and selfish ambition, there you find disorder and every evil practice' (v.16).

FURTHER STUDY

Col. 2:1–23;

Isa. 11:2;

Matt. 13:54;

Luke 2:40

1. Where are the treasures of wisdom to be found?
2. What must we be careful not to be deceived by?

Prayer

Loving heavenly Father, help me not to look at the sins of others with wide-open eyes, and then turn a blind eye upon my own sins and weaknesses. If there is envy and selfish ambition in my heart, then root it out – today. In Jesus' name. Amen.

Divine wisdom

For reading & meditation – James 3:17–18

'But the wisdom that is from above is first pure, then peaceable, gentle …' (v.17, KJV)

D ivine wisdom has eight distinguishing characteristics which the apostle delineates, and I shall list them here as they appear in the King James Version. It is pure. The wisdom of the world is often impure. A doctor told a lady I know to go out and experience sex with someone other than her husband. His advice was bad because it was impure. Heavenly wisdom is always based on purity. It is peaceable. Some people have the right answers, but the wrong attitude. A Christian, in whom God's wisdom flows, will have a serenity about them that marks them out as being 'in' the world, but not 'of' it. It is gentle and easy to be entreated. Gentleness means to be kind and tender. God's wisdom replaces the harshness and hardness of our basic human nature with qualities that make us approachable, warm, understanding and kind.

It is full of mercy and good fruits. This means being uncritical, forgiving, putting yourself in the other person's place. It also involves, not only telling a person what to do, but helping them to do it. It is without partiality. To be impartial is exceedingly difficult. Our own feelings so easily affect our judgment. But spiritual wisdom does not take sides – except against evil. It is without hypocrisy. The world is full of people advising others to do what they cannot do themselves. But the policy of 'do as I say and not as I do' does not come from God. Wisdom that is from above is without hypocrisy.

FURTHER STUDY
1 Kings 3:1–28;
Job 28:12, 16;
Prov. 3:13–14;
8:10–11;
Eccl. 7:19

1. What was a characteristic of Solomon?
2. What did he ask God for?

Prayer

My Father and my God, I want this wisdom that comes from above to dwell in me, and dwell in me deeply. Make me truly wise, so that I may bring glory to Your name. For Jesus' sake. Amen.

Church fights!

For reading & meditation – James 4:1–2

'What causes fights and quarrels among you? Don't they come from your desires that battle within you?' (v.1)

The Early Church, like some 21st-century churches, had its share of internal dissension, and James, speaking on behalf of his Lord and Master, Jesus Christ, takes them to task over it. He makes an earnest plea for them to examine themselves in the light of God's Word. If we don't have time for an occasional 'check up', then we live carelessly, foolishly and irresponsibly.

What causes Christians to fight? James identifies the basic cause as inordinate desire: 'You want something but don't get it' (v.2). This problem is as old as the human race and originated in the Garden of Eden. 'And when the woman saw that the tree was good for food … and a tree to be desired … she took of the fruit' (Gen. 3:6, KJV). Many of our desires, of course, are legitimate. It is not wrong to desire health, food, education, and so on. Where trouble begins is when we desire something – whatever it is – more than we desire the will of God.

If, in every Christian's heart, this thing called 'desire' could be controlled, then we would wipe out overnight the basic cause of church discord and disharmony. Is your church going through a problem like this at the moment? If it is I guarantee that the roots of the problem can be located in the fact that someone wants something too soon, too much or in the wrong way, or at the expense of someone else. If James were writing these notes, I suppose he might add – is that someone you?

FURTHER STUDY

Col. 3:1–17;

Psa. 37:4; 73:25;

Isa. 26:9;

1 Pet. 2:2–3

1. Where should our affections be set?
2. What is Paul's admonition about quarrelling?

Prayer

Father, now You are digging deep. But keep going, I pray, for I need some straight talking. And when You strike hard resistances, don't give up, for I want a heart that is true and clean. For Jesus' sake. Amen.

'A bottomless pit'

For reading & meditation – James 4:1–3

'When you ask, you do not receive, because you ask with wrong motives …' (v.3)

Because of our inordinate desires, we scheme and covet – and kill. Does this mean that there were Christians in the Early Church who murdered one another? No – at least not in the physical sense. The killing to which James refers is that which John describes thus: 'Anyone who hates his brother is a murderer' (1 John 3:15). That's one text that is rarely expounded in our churches. I wonder why?

Another problem that arises from inordinate desire is envy. 'You kill and covet.' Any Christian who is motivated by envy will inevitably be contentious and hostile in their attitude towards others. They will make trouble wherever they are. But James gives a further reason for internal wrangling in the body of Christ – the neglect of one's prayer life. 'You do not have, because you do not ask God.' The quickest way to get out of fellowship with other Christians is to get out of fellowship with God, and the quickest way to get out of fellowship with God is to neglect to pray.

However, it is not only neglect of prayer that James identifies, but prayer requests that are made with wrong motives – 'you want only what will give *you* pleasure' (v.3, TLB). If what we want in life is based on comparisons, envy and greed, we will never be satisfied, no matter what or how much we get. There will always be someone else to envy, something else to possess, some other objective to be gained. This kind of desire is like a bottomless pit – it can never be filled up.

FURTHER STUDY
Luke 12:1–21;
Jer. 6:13;
Ezek. 33:31;
Col. 3:5
1. What does a covetous man focus his life on?
2. How did Jesus illustrate the folly of this?

Prayer

O God, I come to You for freedom. I do not want to be in bondage to inordinate desire – a slave to my passions. Cut deep into my life this very hour, and set me free. For Your own dear name's sake. Amen.

'Give all and take all'

For reading & meditation – James 4:4–6

'... That is why Scripture says: "God opposes the proud, but gives grace to the humble."' (v.6)

Notice the strong language James uses in addressing those who are the source of trouble in the Church. He calls them 'you adulterous people'. He is speaking here of spiritual adultery – no lesser a sin than physical adultery. The Living Bible says: 'You are like an unfaithful wife who loves her husband's enemies.' What condemnation! The only justification for such strong language must be that Christians, who allow worldly desires to dominate them, need to be shocked out of their complacency. But, however shocking the language, the reality is worse, for anyone who deliberately adopts a worldly attitude, and cultivates rather than curbs illegitimate desire, is an enemy of the Almighty.

God, however, never asks us to obey His commands without supplying us with the strength and power we need to live up to them. James puts it like this: 'He gives us more grace'. Whenever we find ourselves struggling with a problem that is too big for us to handle, then, once we humble ourselves enough to ask for God's help, immediately an endless supply of grace becomes available to

FURTHER STUDY
Luke 14:1–11;
Prov. 29:23;
Psa. 138:6;
1 Pet. 5:5
1. What is the
reward of the
humble?
2. What is the
reproach of the
proud?

us. A little boy from an impoverished home, was taken to hospital. On his first night, just before going to sleep, he was given a glass of milk. He eyed it for a moment, and then asked timidly: 'How much can I drink?' 'You can drink all of it,' said the nurse. 'There's plenty more where that came from.' So it is with God's grace. Take what you need – there's more where that comes from!

Prayer

O God, it seems too good to be true – that all Your grace and power are at my disposal. In all honesty and humility, I confess my need of Your help, and I open my being now to absorb all the grace I need. I give all and I take all. Thank You, Father. Amen.

A seven-point sermon

For reading & meditation – James 4:7–12

*'Submit yourselves, then, to God. Resist the devil, and he will
flee from you!' (v.7)*

James gives seven practical commands, which, if obeyed, will keep
us in fellowship with God, and in fellowship with one another.
The first one is – submit yourselves to God. This means placing your
life completely under God's control: letting Jesus be your Saviour
and Lord. An African Christian says, 'Being submitted to God is like
a needle and a thread. He is the needle and I am the thread. He goes
first, and I follow wherever he leads.'

The second command is – resist the devil. And how does one
do that? The same way that Jesus did when He was tempted in the
wilderness – not with human arguments, but with the Word of
God. Memorise some appropriate Bible verses, and keep them in
readiness to use against Satan whenever he attacks you. The third
command is – draw near to God. This means spending time with
Him in personal prayer, praise, worship and meditation in His Word.
And not just occasionally but *daily*, whenever possible. The fourth
command is – cleanse and purify yourself. This involves confession
of any known sin, putting right any wrongs, and making sure that
every Scriptural violation has been corrected. It
means also a definite decision is taken to keep
one's conversation free from obscenities, smutty
jokes and suggestive stories. Don't wait for some
miracle to be performed that will get rid of these
from your life without you doing anything about
them. Throw your will into it, and, I promise you,
God will throw in His power.

FURTHER STUDY
Heb. 7:1–28;
10:19–22;
Psa. 73:28; 145:18
1. What is the 'better
   hope' by which we
   draw near to God?
2. In what ways does
   the Lord draw near
   to us?

Prayer

O Father, thank You for challenging me like this. For too long I have waited
for You to have Your will in my deliverance, but I see I must have a will in it
too. In Your name I break with every impurity in my life for Your honour and
glory. Amen.

Cutting deeper still

For reading & meditation – James 4:8–12

'Grieve, mourn and wail. Change your laughter to mourning and your joy to gloom.' (v.9)

Today we consider the remaining three commands to maintain fellowship. J.B. Phillips translates verse 9 thus: 'You should be deeply sorry, you should be grieved, you should even be in tears.' How sad that in today's Church repentance rarely affects our emotions. It has become so matter-of-fact. If we saw our sin as it really is – not just as the breaking of God's laws, but as the breaking of His *heart* – then perhaps we might put more feeling and meaning into our acts of repentance.

James' next piece of advice is this: 'Humble yourselves before the Lord, and he will lift you up.' To humble ourselves is to deliberately trample on our pride and self-centredness, and take any action that breaks the vicious circle of egocentricity that is at the core of our personality. James' final word is: 'Brothers, do not slander one another.' This is probably one of the most explosive and most damaging problems that can arise in any church – one member slandering another. Blaise Pascal once said, 'It's a fact that if all men knew what others say about them, there would not be four friends in the world.' The Christian who speaks evil of another Christian is guilty of two sins. Firstly, he breaks the law of Matthew 22:37–40 – loving God and loving one's neighbour. Secondly, he breaks the principle of Matthew 18:15–17 – talking about another instead of talking to him. What a change there would be in the Church if every Christian obeyed these two commands.

FURTHER STUDY

Psa. 51:1–19;
34:18;

Acts 3:19;

2 Cor. 7: 10

1. What does the word 'repentance' mean?
2. How did David display this?

Prayer

O God, help me to stand before You with an open heart and an open mind. Search my heart to see if there be any wicked way in me. I want to rise, from this moment, to a life of wholeness and obedience. Help me, dear Lord. For Jesus' sake. Amen.

Christian atheist

For reading & meditation – James 4:13–17

'Why, you do not even know what will happen tomorrow …'
(v.14)

S ome Christians live their lives as if God had nothing to do with them. Such people are, as someone described them, Christian atheists. They are atheists because they leave God out of their planning, but they are Christian because once they have mapped out the way ahead, they invite Him to bless it. Then when He doesn't go along with their plans, they become despondent and accuse God of being disinterested in their welfare. It never seems to occur to them that perhaps the reason for their failure is that they are out of line with God's will for their lives, and what they want to do is not His perfect plan for them.

It is important to remember that James is not against Christians making plans, but against them making plans – without God. The phrase, 'How do you know what is going to happen tomorrow?' (v.14,TLB) shouldn't cause us to go around in a pall of gloom, and close our eyes to the weeks, months and years ahead. James' point is that we should go about joyfully and confidently making short- and long-term plans but thinking all the time, 'Lord, however long You want me to live on this earth, show me Your will so that I can plan my life in accordance with Your divine design.' When you make your plans contingent upon God's will for your life, then you automatically stop getting frustrated over the obstacles in your path. A 'closed door' is no longer a devastating situation. Instead you say excitedly to yourself: 'I wonder what the Lord is up to now!'

FURTHER STUDY

Matt. 6:19–34;
2 Tim. 1:12;
Luke 12:7;
1 Pet. 5:7

1. What was Paul's testimony to Timothy?
2. What should be our response to worldly concerns?

Prayer

O God, help me to plan my life with You as my forethought, not as my afterthought. For I cannot live on what I surmise, I must live on Your summons; not on a guess but on a goal – Your goal. I await Your bidding and Your blessing. Amen.

Money – servant or master?

For reading & meditation – James 5:1–6

'Now listen, you rich people, weep and wail because of the misery that is coming upon you.' (v.1)

Some people spell the word 'God' in a strange way: they spell it m-o-n-e-y. They worship before the shrine of accumulated wealth. They conduct devotions before the financial pages of the daily newspaper. Security, for them, is measured in terms of wealth. These are the people to whom James refers. He is not denouncing all rich men and women indiscriminately. He is talking about the ungodly rich. We cannot help but be impressed with the social passion James displays here. If a politician made a speech like this today, then I don't doubt but that it would be on the front pages of every newspaper the next day! This is how the Living Bible puts it: 'listen! Hear the cries of the field workers whom you have cheated of their pay. Their cries have reached the ears of the Lord of Hosts' (v.4). Strong language – but James is quite right, of course. Indeed every Christian ought to share his concern, and adopt the same attitude toward the amassing of dishonest and selfish gain – no matter what political party they belong to.

The warning James gives to the ungodly rich, who have built up their riches in a dishonest manner, is a roundabout way of alerting Christians to the pitfalls of materialism. Keep in mind that money is a good servant but a terrible master. If it gets on top, and you get under it, then it means that your life is decided by a thing. If money is your god, then your enfeebled personality is the price you pay for the worship of that god.

FURTHER STUDY

Acts 8:1–25;

Deut. 8:11–14;

Eccl. 5:10;

1 Tim. 6:9–10

1. How did Simon misunderstand the use of money?
2. How did Peter respond?

Prayer

Father, I live in an acquisitive society where worth is judged by wealth. As a Christian, I know my judgments must be different. Help me decide all matters relating to money in a Christian way – no matter how strange that might seem to others. In Jesus' name. Amen.

Waiting for His coming

For reading & meditation – James 5:7–8

'You too, be patient and stand firm, because the Lord's coming is near.' (v.8)

This last section focuses on the practical preparation every believer ought to make as they look forward to the Lord's return. All over the world at this moment there is a strong feeling, amongst Christians of all denominations, that we are very near to the second coming of Jesus Christ. Some feel otherwise, of course, but honesty compels me to admit that I share the view that Christ's coming is close at hand. How then ought we to be living in the light of this stupendous fact? James proceeds to tell us. First, he says – be patient. Those interested in Greek will be intrigued to know that the word here is *makrothumasata*, which means 'waiting with patient expectation'. Be like the farmer, says James, who, having sown the seed, waits patiently for the autumn and spring rains. He knows they will come and banks his whole existence on the fact. That is how we must wait for Christ's return, patiently and expectantly – knowing that in due time He will come again from heaven.

Secondly, says James – stand firm. How applicable is this phrase to the contemporary Christian scene? Almost daily I get letters from people telling me they are on the point of giving up their faith because of the unnerving and distressing times through which we are passing. I can understand their consternation and despair, but the word James gave to the people of his day is also God's Word for this hour: stand firm.

FURTHER STUDY
1 Thess. 5:4–5;
Phil. 4:5;
Heb. 10:37;
Rev. 3:11

1. What is the believer's great hope?
2. What is Paul's admonition to the Thessalonians concerning the Lord's return?

Prayer

O God, help me to remain calm and confident amid the flux and flow of this confused age. May I be like a sturdy oak tree – firm, solid and immovable. For Jesus' sake. Amen.

Get rid of grudges

For reading & meditation – James 5:9–10

'Don't grumble against each other, brothers ...' (v.9)

We are to get rid of all grudges and grumbling. The Christian is to refrain from complaining against, and criticising, fellow believers, as he looks forward to, and prepares for, the coming of the Lord. Someone said of James, 'He certainly knows how to make you squirm. Just when you think you have everything squared, he comes up with one more point. If you did not know that God was speaking to you in love, and for your own good, it would be easy to say – "All this man wants to do is hurt."'

The King James Version, instead of using the word 'grumble', uses the word 'grudge'. I think it captures the force of what James is saying much better. Do you have a grudge against anyone at this moment? Well, let me share a simple fact with you: a grudge has to be nourished if it is to be kept alive. If you stop feeding it by going over and over in your mind the hurts that someone has caused you, it will soon wither and die. One of the reasons why we dislike giving up our grudges is because it helps to excuse our own bad behaviour. We reason subconsciously: if he can do that to me, then I have an excuse for the way I act and behave. It is a rationalisation. Decide now to hand over to God every grudge in your heart. Let Him uproot them – every one. See the force of James' argument – The Lord is coming! Are you still at each other's throats when the Lord is at the door? Kill that grudge now – or else, believe me, it will kill you.

FURTHER STUDY

Luke 17:1–10;

Matt. 5:23–25;
18:21–22;

Mark 11:25;

Eph. 4:32;

Col. 3:13

1. How can we overcome grudges?
2. How many times should we forgive?

Prayer

O God, what a fool I am to live with a grudge when I can live with grace. My subconscious mind plays tricks on me, so reach down and uproot even those grudges of which I am not conscious. In Jesus' name. Amen.

No double talk

For reading & meditation – James 5:11–12

'… do not swear – not by heaven or by earth … Let your "Yes" be yes, and your "No", no …' (v.12)

It's almost impossible to think of Job without the word 'patience' popping into our mind. Job had his moments of doubt and disillusionment, of course, but the overall testimony of his life was one of victory and triumph. He sank, but rose again. He doubted, but yet struggled through to faith. To be 'patient' doesn't mean that we live our lives like Stoics, with no negative feelings, no moments of despondency or doubt. It means that we have an inner quality that accepts the negative feelings and doubts, even weeps over them if necessary, but then sweeps them aside to take hold of God's lifeline of faith.

James continues this section, in which he has been showing us how to live in the light of Christ's coming, with the command: 'Do not swear – not by heaven or by earth.' This verse is similar to the words of Jesus in the Sermon on the Mount – Matthew 5:34–37. The meaning of these statements is quite simple – Christians should be so open and honest that their words need not be backed up by an oath. 'Your yes should be a plain yes, and your no a plain no, and then you cannot go wrong in the matter' (Phillips). I heard someone say of a politician, 'If he tells you his word is his bond – take his bond.' It would be sad if that remark was said, and said justifiably, of a Christian. Those whose word is not their bond are not living in the light of Christ's return.

FURTHER STUDY

Luke 21:1–19;
Heb. 10:36;
Rom. 12:12;
Psa. 40:1

1. What characteristic do we need for the end times?
2. How does this help us to 'possess our souls'(Luke 21:19, NKJV)?

Prayer

O Father, make me a steadfast and reliable person – one whose word is as good as his bond. Work so powerfully in me that I shall be a surprise – even to myself. For Jesus' sake. Amen.

Stop worrying – and pray

For reading & meditation – James 5:13–14

'Is any one of you in trouble? He should pray ...' (v.13)

James' next command is this: 'Is any one of you in trouble? He should pray.' How strange that when we get into difficulties, often the last thing we think of doing is to pray! We seem to have a built-in complex that says, 'I can get out of this by myself – so why pray?' One wag put it like this: 'Why pray – when you can worry!'

In using the word 'trouble' in this passage, James is no doubt thinking of the things he had already written about: persecution, injustices, fears, misunderstandings, and so on. We are to meet these things head-on – by prayer. As Jesus illustrated in His parable, "Men ought always to pray, and not to faint" (Luke 18:1, KJV). It is pray or faint – literally that. Those who pray do not faint, and those who faint do not pray. So it's pray, or be a prey – a prey to fears, futilities, problems, and ineffectiveness.

We are to be prayerful, too, not only when facing the general stream of troubles that come our way, but also when facing sickness. Does this mean that we are to ignore the help of physicians? No, of course not. Doctors, nurses, and all of those who work in the medical profession are, whether they realise it or not, part of God's Providential Medical Service to help humanity overcome sickness and disease. Prayer marshals the healing power that emanates from God, and makes it flow, either naturally or supernaturally, into the spirit, soul and body of the person who is sick. Prayer speeds up the process of healing.

FURTHER STUDY

John 15:1–17;
16:24;

Matt. 7:7; 26:41;

1 John 5:14–15

1. What is the key to answered prayer?
2. Why can we pray with confidence?

Prayer

Father, what fools we are to try and face our problems and our sicknesses in our own strength, and make no recourse to prayer. Today I bring all my difficulties to You – physical and spiritual – and ask for or Your delivering and healing touch. Amen.

Who's a spiritual giant?

For reading & meditation – James 5:15–18

'... confess your sins to each other and pray for each other so that you may be healed ...' (v.16)

J ames reminds us that whenever we are sick we should call for the elders of the church, let them anoint us with oil, and pray over us in the name of the Lord for healing. Although this is practised in many churches, it is quite staggering how many Christians ignore this biblical command. Notice the words: 'He should call'. It is quite clear from this that the person who is sick is to be the one who initiates the action: he has to call. There is always a higher degree of faith and expectation in the heart of someone who asks for prayer for healing, generally speaking, than in those who wait to be approached. Confession of sin needs to be made, too, so that the spirit is cleansed and made whole.

Why the use of oil? Oil is a symbol of the Holy Spirit (Acts 10:38). Don't take it to mean, as do so many, that the oil has to be drunk. Why the 'elders'? Elders should be people of faith, appointed by the Holy Spirit, and able to guard and feed the flock of God (Acts 20:28). When the elders pray and anoint a sick person with oil, they should draw together the faith of the whole church, focusing it in believing intercession on the person who is sick.

God's promise is that such faith will be rewarded: 'prayer offered in faith will make the sick person well'. And if you think that this type of ministry is only for the spiritual giants, James reminds us that Elijah was just an ordinary person like you and me. A spiritual giant is anybody – plus God.

FURTHER STUDY

Matt. 8:1–17;
17:20–21; 21:22;
Acts 16:25–26

1. What was a characteristic of Jesus' ministry?
2. What did Jesus say about the centurion's faith?

Prayer

O God, forgive us that we allow sickness and disease when You have shown us the way to deliverance and healing. Impress upon Your Church worldwide the benefits of obeying Your instructions and commands, and heal us of our sicknesses. Amen.

In conclusion ...

For reading & meditation – James 5:19–20

'... that person who brings him back to God will have saved a wandering soul from death ...' (v.20, TLB)

James ends by drawing attention to the fact that the main business in which Christians should be engaged, as they wait for and look toward the Lord's second coming, is in helping those who have been spiritually hurt and injured, encouraging them back on to the Christian path. Ethel Barrett, in her commentary on the book of James, says that we have to wait until these two final verses to see precisely what motivated James in writing this epistle. He is really saying that if a Christian friend stumbles, through unbelief or despondency, they will never be brought back by criticism, or by an attitude of self-righteousness. Your effectiveness at restoring them will depend on how efficiently God's principles are working in your own life. In other words, you will bring them back by living out the great moral, social and spiritual truths that are contained in this letter.

As we part company with James, don't take the view, I beg you, that now you have gone through James' letter verse by verse, you need not refer to it again. If there is one epistle that ought to be read every six months as a kind of routine spiritual check-up, it is this. In its 108 verses, there are 60 commands. As I have been writing this, I have put a tick against the ones I have kept and a cross against the ones that need working on. And, believe me, my heart is ashamed: so this final prayer is very much my own.

FURTHER STUDY

Matt. 25:31–40;
Gal. 6:1;
Acts 20:35;
Rom. 15:1;
1 Cor. 9:22

1. List the 60 commands found in the book of James.
2. Following Selwyn's example, put either a tick or a cross beside each one.

Prayer

O God, the more I look into the mirror of Your Word, the more unlike You I appear to be. But as I wait and watch, another face appears – the face of Jesus. Transform me more and more into His perfect image, I pray. Amen.

Jesus – Incarnate God

For reading & meditation – 1 John 1:1–4

*'... which we have seen with our eyes, which we have looked
at and our hands have touched ...' (v.1)*

Westcott, a scholar and a Bible expositor, describes the first
epistle of John as 'the capstone of divine revelation ... the
point at which the highest hope for mankind is proclaimed'. You will
discover that here the cream of divine unfolding rises to the surface,
and we are presented with some of the greatest and most exciting
truths of Holy Scripture.

John begins his epistle by focusing our attention on a Person
– Jesus. It was not mere chance that made John begin there, for the
Church, at the time John penned these words, was plagued with
an invasion of errorists who called themselves Gnostics – a Greek
word meaning 'Knowing Ones'. They said that you didn't need to
go through Jesus to God: if you had the key – mysterious passwords
and formulae – you could know God immediately. They also claimed
that the spirit was good, but the flesh was evil. 'Man's spirit,' they
said, 'is a divine being imprisoned, contrary to its nature, in the
body: a divine seed sown in hostile matter.'

The idea of Christ becoming incarnate in a body of flesh was
repugnant to them. They saw Jesus, not as God
becoming man, but as a revealer of the secrets of
Gnosticism. Here, to counteract the erroneous
views of the 'Knowing Ones', John begins his
epistle with the ringing assertion that Christ's
incarnation was not a fantasy, but a fact. We
touched and handled the very Son of God,
affirms the apostle. The Christian faith offers us
redemption where we are – in the flesh.

FURTHER STUDY
John 1:1–18;
Heb. 10:20;
1 Pet. 4:1;
Gal. 4:4
1. How do we know
Christ came in
the flesh?
2. Why is this
important to us?

Prayer

O Father, I am so grateful that You have shown us Yourself in a way that we can
comprehend and understand – in flesh and blood. Thank You for coming in at
such a lowly door. Amen.

The centre of our faith

For reading & meditation – 1 John 1:2

'The life appeared; we have seen it and testify to it …' (v.2)

The Gnostics believed that the spirit was good and matter was evil. The question of good and evil is not a question of spirit and matter: it is a question of the will. The seat of evil is in the will, not in matter. The attempt to place evil in matter was an attempt to evade responsibility. Matter, of course, has been affected by evil, but essentially evil is in the will.

In order that we might see that God did become flesh, John piles statement upon statement, 'That which was from the beginning, which we have heard, which we have seen with our eyes, which we have looked at, and our hands have touched …' In these simple but telling words John nails down the fact that the Word actually did become flesh. John saw the vast importance of this – and so must you and I. Our salvation hinges on accepting Jesus, not merely as a moral teacher or a great prophet, but as Incarnate God.

John comes right to the heart of the whole matter in the words, 'for the life was manifested' (KJV). In Jesus, the life of God became tangible and visible. Make no mistake about it, the centre of the Christian faith is the incarnation – God becoming flesh. The controversy over the nature of Christ rages now as it did then. Modern theologians try to explain away the incarnation. But wherever there has been a dimmed emphasis on Jesus, there has been decay: wherever there has been a rediscovered or a renewed emphasis upon Jesus, there has been revival.

FURTHER STUDY

Phil. 2:1–11;
1 Tim. 2:5;
Isa. 7:14; 9:6

1. How was Jesus' humanity manifested?
2. Why did God take on human flesh?

Prayer

Blessed Lord Jesus, I look into Your face and I know I am looking into the face of the Eternal God. In You the Eternal becomes approachable, understandable, comprehensible. I am so grateful. Amen.

No bypassing Jesus

For reading & meditation – 1 John 1:3

'We proclaim to you what we have seen and heard, so that you also may have fellowship with us ...' (v.3)

In this epistle we do not really come face to face with God until the second and third verses. The initial presentation is all about Jesus. In John's day, as well as in ours, if we don't get our starting point right then the finishing point will not be right. And the starting point of the Christian faith is – Jesus.

One writer puts it this way, 'You cannot say God until you have said Jesus, for Jesus puts the character content into God.' Can you see what he means? He is saying that God cannot be comprehended until we see Him in the face of Jesus. We will know the Father only as we relate to the Son. That's the starting point, and if we don't get this straight, we will finish up where the Gnostics finished up – trying to get to God by finely-spun theories and formulae.

When we do get to God in this epistle, however, He is presented with absolute clarity and certainty: 'And our fellowship is with the Father, and with his Son Jesus Christ.' John is emphasising, of course, that you cannot get to the Father without first knowing the Son, and you cannot say 'Father' until you have first come to the Son. Some are tempted to do what the Gnostics did – to bypass Jesus and turn to something that seems more intellectual, more modern, more in keeping with the times and more fashionable. They end where the Gnostics ended – in oblivion. 'I am the way, the truth, and the life,' said Jesus. If you bypass Him, you bypass Life.

FURTHER STUDY
Heb. 1:1–14;
Luke 1:31;
Rom. 8:3;
1 Tim. 3:16;
Isa. 9:6–7

1. How does the writer of Hebrews reveal Christ?
2. What does Isaiah declare about Jesus?

Prayer

Loving heavenly Father, I turn from the vagaries of self-knowledge to the vitalities of Jesus-knowledge. I know that when I know Him, I really know. And I know that I know. Amen.

Joy that is full

For reading & meditation – 1 John 1:4

'We write this to make our joy complete.' (v.4)

John reveals here the underlying purpose of his epistle – that our joy maybe complete. Joy is a mark of spiritual maturity and comes about in direct proportion to how deeply we relate to God and to His Son, Jesus Christ. When we get rid of inner conflicts and wrong attitudes to life, we will almost automatically burst into joy. Someone said, 'Where there is no joy there is no Christianity, and where there is Christianity there is joy.'

Why then do so many Christians appear to have such little joy? I have pondered this problem for many years now, and I have come to this conclusion – many Christians lack joy because they allow things to happen to them rather than through them. John gives us the clue to this, I believe, when he says: 'We write this to make our joy complete.'

John is testifying here to the joy of creative sharing. He is saying that as we share with others the staggering news that God has come in the Person of His Son, so our joy is made complete. Joy comes in only to flow out, and in the flowing it is increased. C.S. Lewis once said, 'Only that joy abides which is a creative joy.' Can you see it? Joy that is kept to ourselves is immature and precarious. It will not and cannot abide. I heard about a Christian man some time ago, who, on the verge of suicide himself, met a girl who was also feeling suicidal. He talked her out of her deeply depressed state and led her to Christ, with the result sadness lifted and he became a new man.

FURTHER STUDY

John 15:1–11;
17:13;

Isa. 61:10;

1 Pet. 1:8

1. What is the key to maintaining our joy?
2. How does spiritual joy differ from natural happiness?

Prayer

Father, how I need to take hold of this truth – that joy must not only flow into me, but flow through me. Deepen my understanding of the fact that when joy is creatively outgoing to others, it will always be incoming. Amen.

Jesus – the light of the world

For reading & meditation – 1 John 1:5

'... *God is light; in him there is no darkness at all.*' (v.5)

John's epistle presents the gospel is as it always should be – Jesus first and then God Himself, for it is only in Jesus that we see what God is really like. Having made that clear, John now bursts out with this: 'God is light, and in him is no darkness at all.' No one could make a statement like that unless he had seen God in the face of Jesus. You could not say that, for example, if you looked up at God simply through the face of nature, for there are dark spots in nature that throw a shadow on the character of God. You could not say it either if you looked up at God through the pages of the Old Testament, for there God often appears to be full of vengeance and recrimination. But when we look into the face of Jesus Christ, the God we see there is light with 'no darkness at all'.

Two little sisters were out playing when a cloud passed over the face of the sun. One said to the other, 'That mean old God again, always spoiling our fun.' Their mother heard them and told their father what they had said. 'Where did they get such an idea?' he enquired. The mother confessed that when the girls did anything wrong, she made them say their prayers as a punishment. Prayers as punishment! The mother was unconscious of her part in forming that idea of God. Is the point becoming clear? Turn your face away from Jesus, and you turn towards the darkness – casting a shadow on your understanding of God. But when you see God in the face of Jesus then 'God is light' – light on everything.

FURTHER STUDY
John 8:12–30;
2 Cor. 4:6;
Eph. 5:14;
Rev. 21:23
1. What did Jesus
declare about
Himself?
2. Why is there no
darkness in heaven?

Prayer

O Father, there are many who, not seeing the face of Jesus, have misjudged You and misunderstood Your purposes. I am so glad that to me Your Son is truly the 'light of the world'. Amen.

Moral and spiritual – one

For reading & meditation – 1 John 1:6

'If we claim to have fellowship with him yet walk in the darkness, we lie and do not live by the truth.' (v.6)

John skilfully pulls the mat from beneath the feet of those who claimed they could live in fellowship with God and be unaffected by the morality or immorality of their relationships. The Gnostics alleged that they could live as they liked on the material level, providing they concentrated on developing qualities on the spiritual level. John announces that morality is rooted in the nature of God, and you cannot be in fellowship with Him without being moral. Morality is not merely God's will – it is God's nature. Many think that God arbitrarily decides certain things to be right and certain things to be wrong, and then issues commands accordingly. Nothing is further from the truth. God's laws are a transcript of His own character. We see revealed in Jesus a God who does everything He commands us to do. He obeys His own laws of right and wrong, and does so because they are inherently right. This makes the universe of morality one and indivisible – for God and man.

Sin, then, is serious – serious to God, to the universe and to you. And morality is serious – serious to God, serious to the universe and serious to you. It matters how we act. It affects everything, everywhere. The universe has a moral head, and a moral head after the pattern of the highest moral standard ever known – Jesus. To say that we have fellowship with Him and walk in darkness (moral disorder) is to live a lie. And a lie, 'has short legs – it won't take you very far'.

FURTHER STUDY

Eph. 2:1–22;
Phil. 3:18;
1 Pet. 4:3–4;
2 Pet. 2:10;
Jude 18

1. How did Paul make this distinction clear?
2. Why is the 'but' now so important?

Prayer

Father, I see so clearly that I cannot cultivate spirituality and engage in moral sin at one and the same time. I must make my choice. By Your grace I choose light – spiritual light and moral light. Amen.

His light, approachable light

For reading & meditation – 1 John 1:7

*'But if we walk in the light, as he is in the light, we have
fellowship with one another ...' (v.7)*

John is now ready to take us on to the next stage – a twofold
fellowship. Dr E. Stanley Jones said, 'Maturity is a capacity for
fellowship. You are mature to the degree, and only to the degree,
that you can fellowship with God and with others.' Sin, you see, is not
merely the breaking of a law: it is the breaking of a fellowship. The
moment one sins there is a sense of estrangement, of orphanhood, of
loneliness. On the other hand, when one is redeemed from sin, there
is a sense of fellowship with God and with others.

How do we go about making this important verse a reality?
What does it mean to 'walk in the light, as he is in the light'? To have
fellowship with God and man you don't have to be perfect, but you
have to be willing to be perfect. You have only to be willing – and
He does the rest. You supply the willingness and He supplies the
power. The reason why many Christians struggle in trying to give up
their bad habits is because, deep down, they are not really willing to
give them up. I promise you, be willing to break with all that keeps
you back from a vital and joyous fellowship with Jesus Christ, and
the power of God will sweep into your being and
break the stranglehold of sin. There is one more
thought to consider: how is Jesus 'in the light'? Is
He in a blinding light that cannot be approached?
On the contrary – He is in the light that lights a
sinner out of the darkness without blinding him
in the process.

FURTHER STUDY

Eph. 5:1–16; 4:1;
Rom. 6:4;
Gal. 5:16

1. Can light and
darkness live
together?
2. What will light
always do?

Prayer

Father, I am so grateful for the 'light' that doesn't blind me into goodness, but
beckons me into it. I give You my willingness: in exchange, give me Your power.
Set me free from every crippling habit and sin. Amen.

Freedom from sin

For reading & meditation – 1 John 1:8–10

'If we confess our sins, he is faithful and just and will forgive us our sins and purify us …' (v.9)

Long and fierce debates have taken place about the exact meaning of this passage. Some believe it to mean that as long as we are in this life we must accept the fact that we will fall into sin, and any denial of that fact, they say, is not only foolhardy but the height of self-deception.

Such an interpretation, however, is not exactly what John is saying here. The apostle is writing to combat the error of the Gnostics who believed that sin exists only in the flesh and has no reality in the realm of the spirit. The Gnostics lived 'in the spirit', and were unaffected by their contact with matter, which alone was evil. They denied that they had any sin from which they needed to be cleansed. The apostle wrote these words to combat this erroneous view, and states quite plainly and firmly that the human spirit is stained by sin, and that its only purification lies in the application of the blood of God's Son.

Another view of this verse is that John is writing to show us that while we can be cleansed from sin, it cannot be entirely eradicated, and we must learn to live with the fact that sin is a lifelong characteristic of the human condition. But surely, when John says Christ cleanses us from 'all' sin and 'all' unrighteousness, he means exactly that– a full cleansing. If this is not so, then John is involved in a hopeless contradiction. Make no mistake about it, as far as sin is concerned, through the power of Christ's blood we can be free – really free.

FURTHER STUDY

Psa. 32:1–11;
103:2–3;
Acts 5:31;
Eph. 1:7

1. What happened when David didn't confess his sin?
2. What was the result of his confession?

Prayer

Blessed Lord Jesus, Your nail-pierced hand has passed over my life, and I am clean – clean in You. And, as I confess my sin, Your continual cleansing keeps me clean. I am redeemed, I am being redeemed, and one day will be forever redeemed. Amen

My advocate – not my adversary

For reading & meditation – 1 John 2:1

'... if anybody does sin, we have one who speaks to the Father in our defence – Jesus Christ ...' (v.1)

God's great purpose for our lives is first to free us from the penalty of sin (at conversion), then go on to destroy the power of sin in our daily experience. Now John says, 'I write this to you so that you will not sin' (v.1). As far as sin is concerned, John is absolute. He does not say, 'I write this to you so that you may sin less.' No, it is clear-cut and absolute: 'I write this to you so that you will not sin.'

There are many ways in which the human mind goes about handling sin. One way is to do what the Gnostics did – relegate it only to material things. Another way is to deny its existence – as do many modern philosophers. Still another way is to say that sin is an integral part of human nature and thus inevitable. A fourth way is to condemn it, but resign yourself to it. The right way to deal with sin, however, is to acknowledge it as an intrusion, confess any participation in it, and ask for Christ's perfect cleansing and forgiveness.

The apostle goes on to say that if we sin, we are not left in that sense of awful loneliness and estrangement which sin inevitably produces, for we have one who speaks to the Father in our defence. And what does He say to the Father? The same words that He has always spoken – the language of love. He says, 'Father, forgive them, for they do not know what they are doing.' Does this mean that Christ excuses our sins? No, for the Saviour cannot condone sin. It is rather grace stretching the truth at love's demand.

FURTHER STUDY

Heb. 9:1–28; 8:6;
1 Tim. 2:5;
Isa. 53:12

1. Why was the OT priesthood inadequate?
2. What is the 'new covenant' of which Jesus is mediator?

Prayer

Lord Jesus, I am so grateful that when I sin I am not given the 'stand-in-the-corner' treatment. You are not against me for my sin, but for me against my sin: my advocate, not my adversary. Thank You, dear Lord. Amen.

The divine self-sacrifice

For reading & meditation – 1 John 2:2

'He is the atoning sacrifice for our sins, and not only for ours but also for the sins of the whole world.' (v.2)

John brings us face to face with the cross. The Gnostics saw salvation as being the result of their own self-effort – an attainment. John saw it as an expression of divine love – an obtainment. This question divides all religions into just two types – one sees salvation as the work of man, the other as the gift of God. There are no other types: all fall into one category or the other.

The question which John faced in those far-off days is still around today. Does man strive to reach God by human self-effort or does God come down to man? Do we go to Him or does He come to us? The sharpness of this statement cannot be blunted by saying it is both. It cannot be both, for one begins with man and the other begins with God. Since the starting point is different, the finishing point will be different. Every religion in the world, with the exception of the Christian religion, is basically man's search for God – Jesus is God's search for man.

Since the world began, man, feeling the estrangement between himself and God, has tried various ways to get back into fellowship with God. He has offered sacrifices, given of his possessions and endeavoured to perform righteous deeds. All these are man's attempts to bridge the gulf between himself and the Deity. However, we cannot climb to God on any of these ladders – God must come to us. The Word must become flesh and bear our sins in His body. And the Good News is this – Jesus, God incarnate, did it!

FURTHER STUDY

Heb. 10:1–39;
Rom. 3:25;
Matt. 26:28;
Luke 3:3;
Acts 2:38

1. Why is Jesus' sacrifice unique?
2. What does this produce within us?

Prayer

Father, I am conscious that right now I am looking into the heart of the deepest mystery in the universe – Your sacrifice for me on that cruel tree. Help me to see it – really see it – for then I see everything. Amen.

Doctrine – tested by its fruit

For reading & meditation – 1 John 2:3–6

*'… This is how we know we are in him: Whoever claims to
live in him must walk as Jesus did.' (vv.5–6)*

The Gnostics claimed to have a knowledge of God outside of
Jesus Christ, and they believed that this knowledge was enough
to bring them salvation. John refutes this assumption by stating that
the test of knowing God is a willingness to obey His commandments:
'We know that we have come to know him if we obey his commands'
(v.3).

The Gnostics had fallen for the temptation of the Garden of
Eden – the temptation to make themselves 'as God' through special
knowledge. 'For God knows that when you eat of it [the tree of
knowledge] your eyes will be opened, and you will be like God'
(Gen. 3:5). Adam fell for it and lost Paradise. Jesus came to restore
what was lost through a knowledge of Himself. When we surrender
to Him, and live in obedience to His Word, then, and only then,
do we know God. If we say we know God, but fail to do what He
commands then we are liars and the truth is not in us. For John,
knowledge of God came directly from his contact with Jesus Christ,
and was validated by his obedience and upright living.

Those who claim to have a knowledge of God,
but have experienced no cleansing from sin, no re-
orientation of the will, no setting of the affections
in the direction of the moral excellence, perfectly
revealed in the Lord Jesus Christ, have no true
understanding of God. Their so-called knowledge
is a sham, an attempt at self-exaltation, and a
futile stirring of the emotions, 'Whoever claims to
live in him must walk as Jesus did.'

FURTHER STUDY

Rom. 1:18–32;

Isa. 14:12–15;

2 Tim. 3:5

1. What was 'the
morning star's
cardinal error?
2. What danger can
we fall into?

Prayer

Father, save me, I pray, from the error that emphasises knowledge of God
without obedience. Hold before me constantly the fact that although I am not
saved by good works, I am saved to do good works. For Jesus' sake. Amen.

The old and the new

For reading & meditation – 1 John 2:7–8

'… I am not writing you a new command but an old one,
which you have had since the beginning …' (v.7)

The central theme of John's epistle is the supremacy of love. The phrase, 'an old one,' (command) 'which you have had since the beginning', refers to the First Commandment: '… Love the LORD your God with all your heart, and with all your soul. and with all your strength' (Deut. 6:5).

Love for God was the foundation on which the Ten Commandments were constructed. It was embodied in the very elements of God's principles for human life from the beginning. But then John adds a fascinating phrase: 'Yet I am writing you a new command; its truth is seen in him and you …' (v.8). Was John thinking here of the statement of Jesus in John 13:34, 'A new command I give you: love one another. As I have loved you, so you must love one another'? I think so.

That last phrase of Jesus, 'As I have loved you', lifted the commandment from the Old Testament to the New, from law to grace. The mystery of love would never really have been understood by this world unless Jesus had come and demonstrated it by His words, by His deeds and by His death. The word would have been barren had not Jesus filled it with the content of the purest and highest love this world has ever seen. 'Love one another as I have loved you' is the high watermark in the history of mankind. Jesus made it clear what love really is by putting into the word the content of His own character. Such was the revelation that it required a new word to express it – agape – sacrificial, unconditional love.

FURTHER STUDY

1 Cor. 13:1–13;
John 15:9,13;
Rom. 5:8

1. List the characteristics of God's love.
2. What is the greatest expression of love?

Prayer

Blessed Lord Jesus, I look into Your face and at once I know the meaning of love. All other definitions fade into insignificance. You are the word of love become flesh. Thank You, dear Lord. Amen.

Darkness – the penalty for hate

For reading & meditation – 1 John 2:9–11

'Anyone who claims to be in the light but hates his brother is still in the darkness.' (v.9)

This passage returns to the clash between profession of faith and conduct. We have seen this clash presented previously in terms of truth and falsehood, light and darkness: now it is love and hate. The one who hates his brother, says John, is still in the darkness. No work of grace is yet manifest in him. The person who cherishes hate incurs the penalty of spiritual blindness. He chooses the darkness and the darkness penetrates his whole being.

Professor Henry Drummond tells of the fish found in the Mammoth Cave, Kentucky, whose eyes had completely shrivelled. As no natural light entered the cave, nature, with her strange logic, said, 'There is no light – so there is no need for eyes.'

It seems to be a law of the universe that unused powers atrophy. New Zealand is the home of more flightless birds than any other country – the kiwi, the kakapo, the penguin and the weka rail. These birds had wings but lost them through neglecting to use them. Scholars say that they neglected using them because food was always abundant, and there was no danger near – New Zealand has no predatory wild animals or dangerous reptiles – so they had no necessity to fly. And no necessity, became in time, no ability. So it is with the mind, the heart and the spirit of man. Worse than the loss of sight or flight is the loss of the ability to see spiritually. When we allow hate to enter our hearts, and fail to live by the law of love, we drink deep of a poison which blinds and kills.

FURTHER STUDY
John 3:14–36;
Job 22:28;
Psa. 112:4;
Prov. 4:18
1. To whom is light promised?
2. How did Jesus demonstrate this?

Prayer

O God, I don't want to stumble around in the darkness, making myself and those I live with miserable and unhappy. Help me to remove every trace of bitterness and hatred from my heart this day, and walk in the light – the light of love. Amen.

Love – at home with all ages

For reading & meditation – 1 John 2:12–14

'I write to you, dear children … I write to you, fathers … I write to you, young men …' (vv.12–13)

John was probably over ninety years of age when he wrote these words, but he retains a positive and constructive interest in the age levels of those to whom he is writing. He was neither suffering from a hardening of the arteries, nor a hardening of the attitudes.

It is a sign that you are maturing in love when, like John, you can take an interest in people of all ages. It is a sign of immaturity when you can be at home with only one age group – your own. John was interested in 'the children', in 'the young men' and in 'the fathers'. And his interest was not in judging them or in setting one generation in judgment over another, but in commending and approving them. John believed in people, and this comes across in almost every verse of his writings.

It is quite staggering what happens to people when we make it clear to them that we believe in them. Jesus once said to Simon Peter, 'You are a reed … but you shall be a rock' (John 1:42 – direct translation from the Greek). When we take positive steps towards people, and give them the impression that we truly believe in them, we will begin to see some amazing changes in their attitudes and behaviour. When we adopt negative attitudes toward people, we tend to produce negative results. A schoolteacher said to her class of small children, 'I'm going to leave the room for a few minutes. Now don't put paper in your ears while I am gone.' Guess how many had paper in their ears when she returned!

FURTHER STUDY

Titus 2:1–15;
1 Tim. 3:1–16;
1 Cor. 7:1–40

1. How did Paul instruct the various age groups?
2. What is Paul's admonition to the young?

Prayer

O Father, help me to look with creative eyes upon all ages – the young, the middle-aged and the old. And help me to approach people positively – to see and appeal to the good in them. For Jesus' sake. Amen.

Our relationship to the world

For reading & meditation – 1 John 2:15–17

'Do not love the world or anything in the world …' (v.15)

John focuses once again on one of his sharp contrasts – this time between the Church and the world. What does he mean when he tells us not to love the world or anything in the world? Does he mean the world of John 3:16, which 'God so loved'? No, the world John is speaking of here is the world whose life is organised apart from God. It refers to the basic philosophies of men which are in direct opposition to the divine will and are under the leadership of Satan, the prince of this world (John 14:30).

One writer says: 'I never saw the "world" – the real world, God's world – until I had renounced the dominance of the false "world", and accepted a world organised around God. I never saw the sky, the trees – everything – as I did the morning after I was converted. Every bush was aflame with God.'

John goes on to detail for us the characteristics of worldliness – 'the lust of the flesh', 'the lust of the eyes', and 'the pride of life'. The 'lust of the flesh' is the desire for unlawful indulgence. The 'lust of the eyes' is the desire for sensuality. The 'pride of life' is the desire for possessions – acquisitiveness. All these, says John, are passing away. They are in the very act of dying. They are transient – a moribund sham. He whose life is organised around the will of God, however, will not pass away. He has hold of a value system which has the stamp of eternity upon it.

FURTHER STUDY

Matt. 13:18–30;
16:26;

Luke 21:34;

Col. 3:2;

Rom. 12:2

1. How did Jesus spell out the danger of worldly cares?
2. What was Paul's admonition?

Prayer

Gracious Father, as I stand centre stage in this drama of life, help me to remember what I have learned from Your script, and not to take my cue from those who stand in the wings. For Jesus' sake. Amen.

The divine anointing

For reading & meditation – 1 John 2:18–29

'As for you, the anointing you received from him remains in you ... his anointing teaches you about all things ...' (v.27)

John warns his readers against the antichrist and anti-Christian doctrines. It seems that some 'antichrists' were actually nominal members of the Church, but, of course, they were never truly part of it. How could they be, accepting as they did, a 'lie'? We must never forget, as Dr Dodd put it, that 'the supreme enemy of Christ's redeeming work is radically false belief'. The quaint old notion that it does not matter what a man believes as long as he leads a decent life is not biblically tenable. The conflict between Christ and anti-Christian doctrines is fought out in the battlefield of the mind (2 Cor. 10:3–5). From this position, however, John turns with an expression of confidence in his reader: 'But you have an anointing from the Holy One, and all of you know the truth' (v.20).

The Gnostics taught that the understanding of God came through a superior mental intuition which was self-developed. Not so, says John, it is not something that comes up from within, but something that comes down from above – an 'anointing'. When we become Christians, God does not leave us to muddle through on our own. He abides with us and becomes our constant Teacher and Guide. We need not worry about falling prey to teachers who might lead us astray. God dwells with us and in us to sharpen our sensitivity to truth, and give us that inner witness which helps us to know when we are in danger of being led astray by false teachers and errorists.

FURTHER STUDY

John 16:1–16;
14:16–17; 15:26;
Acts 13:2; 16:6

1. What is one of the titles given by Jesus to the Holy Spirit?
2. What was the strength of the Early Church?

Prayer

O Father, how wise and wonderful are Your ways. I am thankful that I need not worry about being at the mercy of men's words. You dwell in me to be my Teacher, my Witness and my Guide. All glory and honour be to Your wonderful name. Amen.

Love made us His sons

For reading & meditation – 1 John 3:1

'… that we should be called children of God …' (v.1)

The term 'son of God' or 'sons of God' is sometimes used in the Bible to refer to a being, or beings, who are direct creations of God. The angels, for example, being direct creations of the Almighty, are referred to as 'sons of God' in Job 1:6. In Luke 3:38, the writer traces the lineage of Christ all the way back to Adam. As he traces name after name, he refers to each one as the son of his father, but when he comes to Adam, he states, 'the son of Adam, the son of God'. Adam, being the direct creation of God, and not coming through a human parent, has this high and honoured distinction.

Adam, when he was created, was made, so I believe, to love and be loved. Dr Karl Menninger, a psychiatrist, tells in his book, *Love Against Hate*, how he stumbled on to this revelation when he saw that man's greatest need, his greatest urge, was the urge to love and to be loved. He found, through trial and error, what the Bible has taught for centuries, that without love human life becomes disrupted – spiritually, emotionally, mentally and physically.

Because of Adam's sin, every single human being comes into the world crying out to be loved. That deep need for love cannot be fully met in an earthly relationship. God must take us again into His own hands, and breathe into us His own eternal love. Listen! In Christ, He does just that! We step out of His creative hands just as dramatically as did the first Adam – a fresh and creative act of the Almighty God.

FURTHER STUDY

Gal. 4:1–7;

John 1:12;

Rom. 8:14–15;

Phil. 2:15;

2 Cor. 6:18

1. How have we been made sons and daughters of God?
2. What do you understand by the word 'adoption'?

Prayer

O Father, this makes me feel like throwing my hat in the air. I am not just a descendant listed on my family tree. I am a direct creation of the living God. Hallelujah!

Where are we heading?

For reading & meditation – 1 John 3:2–10

'… we know that when he appears, we shall be like him …'
(v.2)

What is to be the final goal of humanity? Some believe the human race will evolve into a species of super-beings: others believe it will blow itself to pieces with the nuclear bomb. Scripture is quite clear on the subject. All who reject God's offer of everlasting life through His Son will be condemned to a lost eternity, but those who receive that offer of eternal life will be given the citizenship of heaven.

Wonderful though that prospect may be to those who are redeemed, there is a greater prospect still. It is this – we are going to be transformed into the glorious image of our Lord and Saviour Jesus Christ. Both John and Paul spoke of the ultimate goal of redeemed humanity. John said, 'We shall be like him', and Paul said, 'For from the very beginning God decided that those who came to him … should become like his Son' (Rom. 8:29, TLB).

One of the greatest assurances we can have in life is that of knowing exactly where we are heading. Until that is clear we will be like the Texan of whom it was said that 'he mounted his horse and went off in all directions!' Christians can be certain where they are heading – 'into His likeness'. To paraphrase the words of Coleridge: 'Beyond that which is found in Jesus of Nazareth, the human race has not and never will progress. He is the absolute Ultimate in character for God and man.' Now we know where we are heading, we need not be at the mercy of the problems of this world.

FURTHER STUDY

1 Cor. 15:35–58;
13:12;

1 Thess. 4:16–17

1. What is the believer's hope?
2. What is the mystery Paul reveals?

Prayer

Lord Jesus, this open-to-all possibility of being transformed into Your likeness is the most breathtaking and nerve-tingling one I know. My past may not be anything to boast about, but my future most certainly is. Hallelujah!

We do what God does

For reading & meditation – 1 John 3:11–16

*'This is how we know what love is: Jesus Christ laid down his
life ... And we ought to lay down our lives ...' (v.16)*

We come today to a verse that has been described as 'the pivotal point around which the whole of John's epistle revolves'. There are two John 3:16s in the New Testament. One is found in the Gospel of John: the other here in John's epistle. Both have the same theme.

In the Gospel of John the message of God's love for the world is spelt out in words that are breathtakingly beautiful: 'For God so loved the world that he gave his one and only Son, that whoever believes in him shall not perish but have eternal life'. It is no wonder that Christians of all ages have fastened on this verse as the greatest in all literature.

In the epistle of John the same theme continues, but with a difference: 'Jesus Christ laid down his life for us. And we ought to lay down our lives for our brothers.' How strange that the Christian Church has taken to the first John 3:16, but not so much to the second. The latter, in my experience, is seldom quoted. Why? Perhaps for the reason that in the first one God does everything – we have only to believe. In the second, God does His part – He laid down His life for us – but then it bids us to do our part – 'We ought to lay down our lives for our brothers'. That last part isn't quite so popular, is it? We have popularised the one and neglected the other. What God does in Christ, we should carry out through Christ. He laid down His life; we should be willing to lay down ours also.

FURTHER STUDY

2 Cor. 8:1–24;
1 Cor. 10:24;
Phil. 2:4;
Rom. 12:10

1. What does Paul say is a test for love?
2. How did he illustrate this?

Prayer

Lord Jesus, Your patience and love, when faced with our inconsistencies, are amazing. How can You bear with us? But bear with us more, and maybe we shall yet take Your Way in all our ways. Amen.

The little is in the big

For reading & meditation – 1 John 3:17

'… if someone … has money … and sees a brother in need, and won't help him – how can God's love be within him?' (v.17, TLB)

Just as Christ laid down His life for us, so we should lay down our lives for our brothers. When we look at the next verse in this chapter, however, we find that John does not lay down any dramatic application of this principle. We would expect him to point to some aspect of martyrdom, but instead he says: 'If anyone has material possessions and sees his brother in need but has no pity on him, how can the love of God be in him?'

One commentator says: 'This sounds like an anticlimax – from martyrdom to material goods.' But this is true to the incarnation. In the incarnation, ideas and principles take flesh, take shoes and walk. The Word becomes flesh. And that 'becoming flesh' was undramatic – a baby in a manger, a carpenter at a bench, sleeping on the hillsides, and so on. The outer shell, so to speak, of the incarnation was ordinary, but Christ put into that outer shell an extraordinary spirit. Every little thing Jesus did became big, because He did it in a big, wholehearted way. So here John is saying, in effect, 'Don't always look for a big demonstration of your love by dramatic means and methods, but demonstrate your love by little acts of kindness – meeting your brother's need, sharing your material goods.'

Many Christians refuse to do anything because they can't do everything. Because they can't set the world on fire, they refuse to light a candle. Love is doing the little thing at hand, thus opening the way for the bigger in the future.

FURTHER STUDY

Acts 20:17–35;

Prov. 25:21;

Eccl. 11:1;

Isa. 58:7;

Luke 12:33

1. What were Paul's final words in his charge to the Ephesian elders?
2. How can we demonstrate God's love?

Prayer

Precious Lord Jesus, You who showed that the way to the big lies through the little, help me to learn that lesson this very day. Teach me to do every little thing in a big way. For Your own dear name's sake. Amen.

False condemnation

For reading & meditation – 1 John 3:18–20

'… we set our hearts at rest … whenever our hearts condemn us. For God is greater than our hearts …' (vv.19–20)

God is less hard on us than we are on ourselves. We would have expected the opposite: God accusing us when our own heart was excusing us. In order to understand these verses we must recognise that there are two kinds of guilt – false guilt and real guilt. Our hearts may condemn us of both kinds. Thousands of Christians suffer from inner condemnation, not because they have violated a moral principle, but because they suffer from an oversensitive conscience. Their extreme sensitive conscience brings them into a condemnation that does not come down from God, but comes up from within themselves.

A nurse felt miserable and unhappy because she had fallen asleep when on night duty. She confessed this to her superior and received a stern reprimand. For weeks after this she felt a deep sense of condemnation, even though the matter had been dealt with by her superiors, so she sought the help of a Christian counsellor. The counsellor showed her that her guilt was a morbid guilt, false and useless. He said, 'Real guilt is when you violate one of God's principles. When that happens, confess it, and God immediately takes it away. False guilt is when you violate one of your own principles, and because of your overly strict conscience, you come down upon yourself with a disproportionate amount of condemnation.' Get clear in your mind the difference between false guilt and real guilt or else you will carry around with you a ball and chain that will paralyse you.

FURTHER STUDY

John 8:1–11;
Luke 6:37;
John 3:18; 5:24;
Rom. 8:1

1. What condemns us?
2. How can we be freed?

Prayer

Loving heavenly Father, train my conscience so that it is free from the morbid, the trivial and the marginal. I want a conscience that approves what You approve and condemns what You condemn. In Jesus' name. Amen.

God – 'on the inside'

For reading & meditation – 1 John 3:21–24

'... this is how we know that he lives in us: we know it by the Spirit he gave us.' (v.24)

The Holy Spirit comes to a Christian, not simply to inspire him, but to indwell him. It was not always so. In Old Testament times, the Holy Spirit came upon men to endue them with special power for specific purposes – then He would depart and return to heaven. This is why the Old Testament prophets longed for the day when the Spirit would dwell with men, not to fulfil a temporary purpose, but to abide permanently. That day has come. Since Christ's victory at Calvary, and the subsequent outpouring of the Holy Spirit at Pentecost, the Spirit is here to reside – and preside. As we obey the commands of our Lord Jesus Christ, the Spirit witnesses to our hearts that He lives in us.

How precious and reassuring is this glorious truth. We could never live effectively unless we knew that the Holy Spirit indwelt us. A God outside us is wonderful, but a God inside us is almost too good to be true. However, it's too good not to be true! God outside us is an Old Testament experience. God inside us is a New Testament experience.

FURTHER STUDY

Rom. 8:1–17;
Ezek. 36:27;
John 14:16–17;
1 Cor. 3:16

1. What is 'the law of the Spirit of life in Christ Jesus'?
2. What does the Spirit bear witness to?

Those of you who may not have had the same experience of the Holy Spirit that you read about in books or hear about in the testimonies of certain dynamic individuals, always remember that when you became a Christian, the Holy Spirit entered into you. He dwells in you now. You need to experience a greater flow of His power, of course, and so do I, but, while seeking for more, never forget what you already have – God 'on the inside'.

Prayer

Thank You, loving heavenly Father, for giving me this word today. In my desire for more of You, I sometimes forget how much I already possess. Help me to live in the full realisation of all that I now have in You. Amen.

Discerning counterfeits

For reading & meditation – 1 John 4:1–6

'… do not believe every spirit, but test the spirits to see whether they are from God …' (v.1)

Some false prophets tried to reinterpret Christianity in a way that would be more acceptable to the world. To this end they stripped the message of the offending cross, and reduced the Person of Christ to the level of a human being. John, therefore, lays down this clear guideline on how to judge these errorists: 'This is how you can recognise the Spirit of God: every spirit that acknowledges that Jesus Christ has come in the flesh is from God, but every spirit that does not acknowledge Jesus is not from God' (vv.2–3).

Every Christian must realise that there are spiritual influences loose in the world which do not emanate from God. A minister who speaks from a pulpit and attacks the deity of our Lord Jesus Christ, although he may appear to be highly respectable, intelligent and even angelic, is, at that moment, albeit unconsciously, the voice and expression of dark and sinister spiritual forces working in his personality. You may have listened to such a person in recent weeks or months. Let us not quibble about this, for there is such a thing as misguided charity and tolerance toward false prophets.

The basis of testing those in error is quite simple; it is the issue of the full deity of our Lord Jesus Christ. If a person will not confess that Jesus is God's eternal Son, the Word made flesh, then whoever he is, or whatever theological degrees he may hold, he is not speaking as a Christian.

> **FURTHER STUDY**
> Jude 1–25;
> Eph. 4:14;
> 2 Cor. 11:3;
> 2 Tim. 3:13
>
> 1. What are we to contend for?
> 2. What three things does Jude exhort us to do?

Prayer

Loving heavenly Father, thank You for showing me the way to discern between truth and error. While I must never cease to love, help me to be firm and resolute in my rejection of false doctrine, and to guard Your truth with a godly jealousy. Amen.

'Love builds up'

The Gnostics had thirty-six steps which they had to climb before they could come into union with God. Their motto was this: 'the more we know, the closer we will get to God.' But Gnosticism was egocentric – an attempt to find God through the mind and self-effort. John counters this by stating firmly and categorically that we get to know God, not through the efforts of the mind, but through love. Paul underlines this very same point when writing to the Corinthians: 'We know that we all possess knowledge. Knowledge puffs up, but love builds up. The man who thinks he knows something does not yet know as he ought to know. But the man who loves God is known by God' (1 Cor. 8:1–2).

How sad that so many people miss this point. A famous astronomer said that he had been trying to find God for years by looking through his telescope, but, of course, he had never found Him. If he had stopped trying to discover Him with the mind, and had got down on his knees, and sought to experience God in his heart, he would most certainly have found Him. There was a good deal of wisdom in the statement of the Christian astronomer who said, 'God is found not through a telescope, but through a tear.'

This is not to say that reason and intellect are unimportant. They most certainly are not. What I am saying is that God cannot be discovered by reason alone. A woman said, speaking of her love for the Lord, 'To know Him is to love Him, and to love Him is to know Him.' I agree!

FURTHER STUDY

Eph. 2:1–22;

Deut. 7:8;

Jer. 31:3;

Rom. 5:8

1. What is God's love rich in?

2. How do we know this?

Prayer

O God, I see so clearly that the more I love You, the more I will know You. Deepen Your love in me so that my awareness and understanding of You will grow greater, day after day after day. For Jesus' sake. Amen.

'They've got it!'

For reading & meditation – 1 John 4:13–16

'... God is love ...' (v.16)

'**G**od is love.' This is the high watermark of divine revelation. One writer says, 'I can imagine that all heaven bent over as John neared the writing of this phrase, "God is love", and as he finally penned it, heaven broke out in rapturous applause saying: "They've got it! They've got it! At long last, they have seen it. They see that God is love."'

It would be wrong to say that the idea of God's love was not known before this, but what men and women did not see was the fact that God is more than the author of loving acts: He is love, by very nature. This phrase says more than just that God has love, or even that He is loving. It says that the mainspring of His personality is love. Take love out of an angel – a devil remains. Take love out of a human being – a sinner remains. Take love out of God – nothing remains. For God is love.

Why was man so long in reaching this conclusion? The answer is simple. Man could not see this until he had looked into the face of Jesus. It is only in Him that the nature of God is fully revealed. It took the most loving of apostles, at the very last period of his life, to put the finishing touches on the whole process of revelation. The most momentous hour of the long march towards understanding God had come. From henceforth the human race would start with this as their initial focus – God is love. God loves you. He really does. The Incarnate Jesus is the proof!

FURTHER STUDY
Matt. 1:1–2:23;
Gal. 4:4–5;
Isa. 9:6;
Luke 1:31

1. How does the name 'Jesus' reveal God's love?
2. Write down the ways God's love has been revealed in your own life.

Prayer

O Father, what a priceless gift You gave me when You sent Your Son into this world for my redemption. I am so grateful. And when I ponder the fact that You are more than loving – You ARE love – I tingle on the inside. Thank You, dear Father. Amen.

Love that casts out fear

For reading & meditation – 1 John 4:17–18

'There is no fear in love. But perfect love drives out fear ...'
(v.18)

Do you have a problem with fear? Here John gives you the remedy – perfect love. Someone asked the dean of a girls' college: 'What is the basic problem of these girls?' And the dean replied: 'Fear.' The visitor was surprised, and asked the dean to comment further on the situation. 'These poor things are afraid of so much,' she said, 'afraid of failure, afraid of what others think of them, afraid of the future – just afraid. They seldom show it because they have pushed their fears into their subconscious, and there they fester. These subconscious fears create a climate of anxiety. The girls scarcely know why they are afraid, but they are – basically afraid.'

The root cause of fear is an absence of love. When Adam, because of sin, became separated from God and the awareness of His love, the first thing he said was: 'I was afraid' (Gen. 3:10). When love flows out, fear flows in. I assure you that if, at this moment, you had a vivid awareness of how much God loved you, every fear would vanish from your personality. And why? Because once your personality detects the presence of its Creator, then it responds to it with faith and not with fear. So you see the answer to your problem of fear lies, not in self-centred efforts to conquer it, but in focusing on the fact that God loves you, and has control of all the situations and circumstances of your life. The more you focus on that fact, the more His love will flow in, and the more fear will flow out.

FURTHER STUDY

2 Tim. 1:1–10;

Psa. 118:6;

Prov. 3:24;

Isa. 12:2;

2 Cor. 4:13–14

1. What was Paul's word to Timothy?
2. What kind of spirit has God given to us?

Prayer

O God, open my eyes that I might see, really see, just how much You love me. For then, when fear knocks at my door, love will answer and say, 'There is no one here.' In Jesus' name I pray. Amen.

Loved into love

For reading & meditation – 1 John 4:19–21

'We love because he first loved us.' (v.19)

John sees with crystal clearness that the love that flows in the heart of a Christian is initiated in heaven. We love Him because He first loved us. God started it. Time and time again, when counselling Christians, who think that love for Christ is something they manufacture, I have to say to them, 'Your love for Him is not the fruit of labour, but a response to His love for you.'

There are some believers who struggle along in their Christian experience desperately trying to create deeper feelings of love for God within their hearts. They say such things as: 'My problem is that I don't love the Lord enough. How can I come to love Him more?' Then I have to say: 'No, that isn't really your problem. Your problem is that you can't really see how much God loves you.'

Once we see how much God loves us, then we step off the treadmill of trying to manufacture love for Him, and relax in the knowledge that any love we have for Him will be the result of His love pouring into us. This takes the strain out of Christian living, and is, in my judgment, one of the most vital issues in the whole of Christian experience. So look to the cross. The love of God finds its most burning expression there. Sit before it. Meditate on it. God only knows the love of God, and only God can reveal it. In gazing at the Cross, and I mean gazing, not glancing, you will find that the scales will fall from your eyes, and, seeing His love, your own love will flame in response.

FURTHER STUDY

Eph. 3:1–21; 5:2;
John 16:27;
1 Pet. 1:8

1. What was Paul's desire for the Ephesians?
2. What was Paul's affirmation?

Prayer

O loving Father, thank You for showing me this blessed and vital secret. Kindle Your love in me as I stand before Your cross, and love me into love so that I may go out and love others into love. For Jesus' sake. Amen.

It's no burden to love

For reading & meditation – 1 John 5:1–5

'... *And his commands are not burdensome* ...' (v. 3)

G od places upon us the greatest responsibility: 'You must love the Lord your God with all your heart, with all your soul and with all your mind.' And notice it says: 'with all your heart'. God is not content with a portion of our heart, but insists on having it all. Nothing could be more demanding, more sweeping and more exacting than this. Yet John quietly and decisively says: 'His commands are not burdensome.'

Is there some contradiction here? No, for, quite simply, this is what it means. When God commands us to love, He is only commanding us to function in the way our personalities were designed to do from the very beginning. So what He commands, our nature commends. The deepest need of our being is to love. God's commandment and our deepest need fit together like a hand in a glove. They are made for each other, since He who made the command made our beings also.

It is not burdensome for an aeroplane to fly – that is what it is made to do. It is not burdensome for a bird to sing – that is its chief delight. A command telling two young people about to be married to love each other would not be a burden – it would be bliss. When God commands us to love, His voice finds an answering echo in the deepest regions of our heart. When we fulfil the command, we fulfil ourselves. No wonder, then, that John states so categorically: 'His commands are not burdensome.' The burden God lays upon us is the same kind of burden that wings are to a bird!

FURTHER STUDY

Matt. 11:20–30;
John 14:23; 15:9;
2 Cor. 5:14

1. What is the picture that Christ gives us?
2. How does God's love 'compel' us?

Prayer

Gracious, loving and heavenly Father, just as the eye is made for light and the ear is made for sound, so is my heart made for love – Your love. Let Your love flow in me, through me, and out from me, this day and every day. For Jesus' sake. Amen.

One in will – one in power

For reading & meditation – 1 John 5:6–15

*'This is the confidence we have in approaching God … if we
ask anything according to his will, he hears us.' (v.14)*

John tells us that the main purpose for his writing this epistle was
to help those who had entered into eternal life know that they
possessed it. Does this mean that we can have eternal life and yet
not be aware of its deep significance? Yes. In my time I have met
thousands of men and women who have surrendered their lives to
Jesus Christ, but have no positive assurance that they truly belong to
Him. They are not able to say, in the words of the well-known hymn,
'Blessed assurance! Jesus is mine!'

In the preceding chapters, John has made clear how to obtain
and maintain spiritual assurance. We must confess that Jesus Christ
is God come in the flesh, break with all known sin, and 'walk in the
light as He is in the light'. If we do this, then spiritual assurance will
follow just as day follows night. And this assurance means that we
can approach God through prayer, and, providing our prayers are
in accordance with His will, we can depend on getting a positive
answer.

A lady said to me recently, 'I have been praying for something
for months and I haven't had it. God doesn't keep
His word.' I found that she was expecting God to
answer her prayer, but was not willing to bring
some important matters in her life into line with
the will of God. We pray with our lives as well as
with our lips, and when our lives correspond to
what our lips say, then heaven stands ready and
alert to give us what we ask. God hears you, not
just what you say.

FURTHER STUDY
Luke 18:1–14;
Matt. 7:7–11;
John 14:13; 15:7;
16:24;
James 4:3
1. What was Jesus
teaching in the first
parable?
2. Why do we
sometimes not
receive?

Prayer

O God, cause Your words to penetrate my inner being so that I might realise
that when I am prepared to do Your will, You are prepared to do my will, and
that when we are one in will, we shall be one in power. For Jesus' sake. Amen.

'Sin that leads to death'

For reading & meditation – 1 John 5:16–20

'... There is a sin that leads to death ...' (v.16)

W hat does it mean – a sin that leads to death? In the main there are three views. One school of thought says that it is a sin which quite literally has physical death as its consequence (compare 1 Cor. 11:30 and 1 Cor. 5:5). Another school of thought says that the 'sin that leads to death' is that of apostasy – the total denial of Christ and the renunciation of the faith. This raises the question: Can a Christian who has been truly born of God apostasise?

If your answer to that question is 'Yes' then this is the interpretation that will no doubt satisfy you. A further school of thought claims that the 'sin that leads to death' is blasphemy against the Holy Spirit. This is a wilful, stubborn and unwavering belief that attributes to the work of the Holy Spirit a satanic source.

My own view is that John is referring here to those in the Church who appeared to be 'brothers' but in fact were false prophets because they systematically denied the deity of Christ and His eternal relationship to the Father. Since they rejected the Son, they forfeited life (v.12) and their sin, therefore, was described by John as 'a sin that leads to death'. John could not ask his flock to intercede for those who plotted such cynical ruin for the Church. By their obstinacy and wilfulness, sinning against light and their own conscience, they have, says John, put themselves beyond the reach of prayer. A solemn thought.

FURTHER STUDY

Luke 22:1–48;

Matt. 27:3–5

2 Pet. 2:1–3

1. What motivated Judas and what was the result?
2. How does Peter instruct us to guard against false teachers?

Prayer

O Father, guard Your Church from being invaded by false teachers, and let such a holy fear descend upon us that, like the Church after Pentecost, every believer will be living a life of total commitment to you. For Jesus' sake. Amen.

John's last great word

For reading & meditation – 1 John 5:21

'Dear children, keep yourselves from idols.' (v.21)

J ohn ends this great exposition of love with some of the strangest words: 'Dear children, keep yourselves from idols.' In this seemingly innocuous statement, he put his finger on one of the greatest problems in the Christian life – idols. We tend to think of idols as images or fetishes, objects that superstitious people believe have magical powers, but anything that constantly grips our attention, that obsesses us, and so excludes God from our lives – is an idol. The greatest hindrance to spiritual maturity, and a life in which God's love shines through, is to let something, or someone, occupy the centre of our existence – the part that is rightly God's. Self can be an idol. Money can be an idol. A minister can be an idol. A husband, wife, boyfriend, girlfriend, or any other human being, can be an idol. Some make an idol out of their denomination. 'An idol,' wrote a little boy in an essay, 'is something that does not work.'

An idol misrepresents God – Jesus represents God. He fulfils the desire which is at the root of all idolatry – namely the desire to worship. Jesus fulfils that need and makes God approachable and comprehensible. A little boy was afraid as he slept with his father in a strange room. Just before going to sleep, he said, 'Is your face towards me, Daddy?' Jesus gives God a face, and that face is towards us – always.

Let Jesus occupy the centre of your life, then what need have you for idols?

FURTHER STUDY

Rom. 1:1–32;

Acts 17:29;

Isa. 42:8;

Deut. 11:16

1. What is the danger of focusing on things?
2. Where should our focus be?

Prayer

O Father, sometimes I allow some idol to interpose itself between myself and You. Forgive me, and help me to tear every idol from the throne, and make You the centre of my loyalty and my love. In Jesus' name I pray. Amen.

The Cross in Modern Life

The challenge of the cross

For reading & meditation – Matthew 16:13–27

'Peter took him aside and began to rebuke him. "Never, Lord!"
he said. "This shall never happen to you!"' (v.22)

Our theme for the next two months centres on the life, death and
resurrection of our Lord Jesus Christ. It is my intention to draw
your thoughts towards the sacred hill called Calvary and invite you
to consider reverently the solemn events which culminated in the
crucifixion of our Lord Jesus Christ.

To set the scene for the theme I have chosen, we must ask
ourselves the question: what was it that brought about Christ's
grisly death on the cross? Notice I say 'what?' rather than 'who?' The
'who?' is important, but a much deeper meaning can be seen in the
cross when we ask 'what?' For the 'who?' embodies a 'what?'.

Eight embodied sins, at least, combined to crucify Jesus. The
probability is that just as Jesus lived out His life in the face of these
evils – so, too, do you. And the abundant life in you – just as it did
in Jesus – will meet its cross. That cross cannot be escaped. If it
is escaped then its sequel, the resurrection, is also escaped. If you
refuse to face up to opposition and take the line of least resistance,
you will become a recessive personality rather than a resurrected
one. The business of being a Christian in this
world is no easy task. It is not enough to possess
abundant life: that abundant life must be lived
out in the presence of those things that oppose it.
And when we meet these things, and meet them
unflinchingly, then this new life will crimson into
a cross. However – no cross, no resurrection.

FURTHER STUDY

1 Cor. 1:18–31;
Matt. 10:38;
John 10:10

1. What was the
message of Jesus to
His disciples?
2. What is the result?

Prayer

O God, my Father, like Simon Peter, something in my nature shrinks from the
thought of facing a cross. Yet Your Word is clear – no cross, no resurrection.
Deepen my understanding of this truth – and strengthen me to face it. In Jesus'
name. Amen.

Green-eyed envy

For reading & meditation – Mark 2:23–3:6

'Then the Pharisees went out and began to plot with the Herodians how they might kill Jesus.' (3:6)

We said yesterday that at least eight sins combined to crucify Jesus, and the probability is that, as Christ's followers, we, too, will have to live out our lives in the face of one or more of these embodied evils. And when we do, the life of God within us meets its cross.

For the next few days, we examine the first of these evils – envy. This is seen most clearly in the attitude of the Pharisees. 'The Pharisees went out and began to plot ... how they might kill Jesus.' The Pharisees were religious men. They ran the schools and the synagogues, and were the guardians of the moral law. But they were also envious and jealous of the growing influence of Jesus. People were turning away from them and crowding around Christ. So green-eyed envy reared its ugly head and slandered Him by twisting the meaning of His statements.

One of the ways in which envy expresses itself is to misinterpret the motives of others, to misrepresent what they say or do, even deliberately misquote them. 'Jesus,' said Dr Cynddylan Jones, a famous Welsh preacher, 'was crucified on misquotations.' Very often we, too, will be crucified on misquotations, twisted meanings and misrepresented motives. And what do we do then? Meet envy with resentment and anger? No – for you are a Christian. As Moffatt puts it in Leviticus 18:3, 'you must not rule your lives by theirs.' Jesus' way of meeting envy was to die for those who lied about Him – and He asks no less of you and me.

FURTHER STUDY

Gal. 5:16–26;

Prov. 14:30; 23:17;

Phil. 4:11

1. How did Paul combat envy?

2. Are you envious of anyone?

Prayer

Lord Jesus Christ, help me not to become angry, when confronted by envy, but to take the way of the cross. You died for those who envied You. I, too, must do that – or the equivalent of that. Help me, Lord Jesus. Amen.

Christ's note of authority

For reading & meditation – Matthew 7:13–29

'... the crowds were amazed at his teaching, because he taught as one who had authority ...' (vv.28–29)

Just as Jesus was crucified on a cross of misquotations, twisted meanings and misrepresented motives, we, who are His 21st-century disciples, must be prepared to face the same kind of injustice. Whether or not you have had some personal experience of what I am talking about, believe me, envy is at work still. It might be helpful if we pinpointed some of the reasons why the Pharisees envied Jesus, for the more clearly we understand envy, the more effectively we can deal with it. In the first place, they were angered by His note of authority. He didn't just say things: He announced them. The words He spoke came from God, and the common people noticed it immediately. They said, 'He teaches as one with authority and not as the scribes.'

Envy is often the cause of anger and it is not surprising, therefore, to find the Pharisees' statements about Jesus to be full of spite and spleen. Once you identify with Jesus and His note of authority, you, too, will become the victim of people's antagonisms. And who are those people? Not the worldly but the religious – those who go to church yet have little or no confidence in the authority of Scripture. Some of my greatest critics have been religious people who have said: 'How dare you speak with such authority on issues over which there is a wide difference of opinion.' My answer is this: 'Where the Bible speaks with authority – so do I.' If that is your position, too, then look out for opposition.

FURTHER STUDY
John 5:19–27;
Matt. 28:18;
Mark 1:27

1. From where did the authority of Jesus come?
2. What is the difference between authority and authoritarianism?

Prayer

Gracious Father, in a day when many of those who profess Your name are losing confidence in Your Word, sustain me, I pray, with a burning sense of its power and authority. And help me witness to it – in the face of all opposition. Amen.

When bigotry banishes love

For reading & meditation – Matthew 3:1–12

*'… do not think you can say to yourselves, "We have
Abraham as our father" …' (v.9)*

Today we look at another reason for the Pharisees' anger – our Lord's announcement that His mission was to all men. Jesus always conceded that His mission was to the Jews first, but He made it clear that it was not to them only. His message was to begin at Jerusalem and then encompass the whole world. No racial inferiorities are compatible with His teaching. He had time for the Samaritan woman and the Syrophoenician woman. The Pharisees saw in Him a threat to their bigotry, and interpreted His words and actions as a deprecation of their race.

The spirit of bigotry did not die with the Pharisees. It is with us still. Nowadays it exists in the form of denominationalism, snobbishness and racial prejudice. And those who, like Jesus, set their face against it will be crucified upon a cross. I am convinced that one of the greatest evils that must be rooted out of the Church is that of denominationalism. I am not saying that God wants to take people out of their denominations, but He does want to take the denomination out of them. Thankfully, thousands of Christians, while remaining loyal to their denominations, are beginning to see that the Church is bigger than just one group, and, in a spirit of true fellowship, are reaching out to those in other communions. If you are one of these then be on your guard. Bigotry was part of the evil that carried Christ to the cross. It will make you suffer too.

FURTHER STUDY

James 2:1–10;

Rom. 2:11;

Gal. 3:28

1. What does James say about bigotry?
2. What is the 'royal law'?

Prayer

O God, help me to resist, with all the force of my being, the bigotry that impoverishes Your Church and invalidates its claims. And if I suffer for so doing, then help me to see that every Good Friday is followed by an Easter Sunday. Amen.

'He mixes with sinners'

For reading & meditation – Luke 15:1–10

'But the Pharisees … muttered, "This man welcomes sinners, and eats with them."' (v.2)

The Pharisees were also angry because of the way in which Jesus contradicted some aspects of their puritanism. Notice I say some aspects of their puritanism, because there was much about them that was to be highly commended. Their fine moral behaviour and self-control would no doubt have earned the approval of Jesus.

One thing the Pharisees disapproved of in Jesus was His habit of mixing with tax collectors and sinners. When Matthew left his old ways to follow Christ, and gave a party for his friends, Jesus was there. When Zacchaeus, the most notorious tax collector in Jericho, entertained Jesus in his home, the Pharisees were deeply shocked. They said: 'He has gone to be the guest of a "sinner"' (Luke 19:7).

Christians who, like their Lord, go out of their way to mingle with sinners will often be criticised and condemned by those who have a Pharisaical spirit. The tendency to persecute is always a feature of Pharisaism. Circumstances may prevent it finding any fiercer expression than a barbed tongue, but the intolerance and the will to wound is there. Jesus was able to mingle with sinners because they sensed that, although He disapproved of their lifestyle, He loved them. If you, because of the ease with which you make friends with sinners, find yourself being condemned by your religious friends, then take heart: 'It is the way the Master went, Should not the servant tread it still?'

FURTHER STUDY

Luke 14:12–24;
7:34;

1 Tim. 1:15

1. What did Jesus teach in this parable?
2. What was Paul's estimate of himself?

Prayer

Father, no matter what it costs, help me to share Your love with those who do not know You, and to do it in a way that does not compromise my basic convictions. For Your own dear name's sake. Amen.

Tender – yet tough

For reading & meditation – Matthew 23:13–33

'You blind guides! You strain out a gnat but swallow a camel.'
(v.24)

T he Pharisees became angry with Jesus because He exposed them as hypocrites. Some people, those whose acquaintance with the Gospels is slight, believe that Jesus never denounced people. They should ponder the twenty-third chapter of Matthew. 'Christ did not just preach at the Pharisees,' said the late Dr W.E. Sangster, 'He lashed them.' He called them 'blind guides', 'fools', 'white-washed sepulchres', and warned them that they would not be able to escape the judgments of hell.

It is hardly surprising that the Pharisees became angry with Him. It is not in unredeemed human nature to like people who talk about us in that way. Although Jesus had the tenderest words for ordinary sinners, or people who made a mistake, His anger burned and blazed against those who were hypocrites.

Why did Jesus so condemn hypocrisy? Because hypocrites set true things in a false light. To lie, to steal, to cheat, to seduce – all these are obnoxious things, but to do them under the cloak of piety, and in the name of religion, is an abomination. The terrible paralysis which has fallen upon the Church here in the West is due, in no small part, to this malady. While we must be gentle with sinners and tolerant of those who make mistakes, we must not hesitate to denounce and expose those who use the Church for selfish ends. It is time that judgment began in the House of God. Remember, however, that when you confront hypocrisy, it will inevitably bring you to a cross.

FURTHER STUDY

Gal. 4:1–16;
1 Pet. 4:17;
2 Tim. 3:5

1. How did Paul deal with ritualism?
2. What is the main danger for the Church?

Prayer

O Father, I long so much to be like Jesus – tender in my attitudes to sinners, but tough with those who cloak their evil in piety, and set Your Church in a false light. Amen.

'A lie – a waning moon'

For reading & meditation – 1 Peter 2:13–25

'When they hurled their insults at him, he did not retaliate …'
(v.23)

To discover the deepest meaning of the life, death and resurrection of our Lord Jesus Christ, and its application to our lives, we must ask not who crucified Him, but what. Eight embodied sins combined to crucify Him, the first of which was anger mixed with envy. We, too, have to live out our lives in the presence of this evil, and when we do, then inevitably we meet with a cross. Perhaps at this very moment you know in a personal way something of what I have been talking about these last few days. Because of anger mixed with envy, you, too, have been crucified on a cross – a cross of misquotations, twisted meanings and misrepresented motives.

I heard recently of one Christian who told a story about another Christian, and when the truth of it was questioned and the falsehood pointed out, the one who told the story laughed it off by saying, 'Well, anyway, it made a good story.' It did, even if it did leave the reputation of another lying wounded and bleeding.

How are we to respond when crucified on a cross of deliberate falsehoods or misquotations? We do as Jesus did and face the cross, knowing that through it God will work to glorify His name and vindicate our honour. Jesus died for those who lied about Him and misquoted Him. Their lies perished. He lived on. The same thing will apply with you. 'A lie,' said someone, 'is a waning moon: the truth is a waxing moon. A lie goes out into the night: the truth goes out into the light.'

FURTHER STUDY

Matt. 18:21–35;
Prov. 16:7;
Luke 23:34

1. What did Jesus tell Peter?
2 How did Jesus demonstrate this?

Prayer

Blessed Lord Jesus, help me to respond to lies and falsehoods, not by stoutly defending myself and protesting my innocence, but by believing that, in Your eternal plan, my willingness to suffer will turn the evil into good. Amen.

The evil of expediency

For reading & meditation – John 11:45–54

'… it is expedient … that one man should die for the people, and not that the whole nation perish.' (v.50, NKJV)

The second of the embodied evils which combined to put Christ on the cross is expediency. It found expression in the actions of the Sadducees – aristocratic Jews who exercised the highest functions of the priesthood. Their head was the high priest himself – Caiaphas. In Jesus' time, politics and religion were not kept apart. The priests were not only the spiritual leaders of the people, they were the statesmen too. Unfortunately politics prevailed over spirituality, and the priesthood, especially in its upper echelons, was composed of men who were preoccupied with the conduct of the nation's affairs and were notoriously self-seeking.

How was it that the Sadducees came into conflict with Jesus? They saw Him as an agitator who could easily whip up an insurrection which would lead, in turn, to trouble with Rome. And trouble with Rome could interfere with their personal political ambitions. The Sadducees wanted Jesus out of the way because He was a threat to their self-interest.

You, too, if you are a follower of Jesus, will have to meet your chief priests. They will look at you, and when they see that the life you are living or something you plan to do for God is likely to conflict with their self-interest, they will nail you to a cross. What are you to do? Fight your opponents with their own weapons? That would be like fighting fire with fire. You do as Jesus did – maintain an unbroken spirit. And then nothing can conquer you – not even a cross.

FURTHER STUDY

Acts 19:21–41;

Matt. 27:3–4;

1 Cor. 10:24;

Phil. 2:4

1. Why was Paul persecuted at Ephesus?

2. What was Judas's motive for betraying Jesus?

Prayer

Gracious Father, whenever I am blocked by someone's self-interest, help me to remain calm and poised, knowing that when I maintain the right attitude, nothing can work successfully against me. Thank You, Father. Amen.

Our biggest asset

For reading & meditation – Proverbs 16:1–7

'When a man's ways are pleasing to the LORD, he makes even his enemies live at peace with him.' (v.7)

Caiaphas, the high priest, said, 'It is expedient for us that He should die.' He did not say, 'It is right!' He did not say, 'It is good!' He did not say, 'It is God's will!' He said, 'It is expedient *for us*.' In other words, 'It suits our purpose. It will make our position more secure. It fits in with our plans.'

If you had been there and had protested against the evil they were planning, Caiaphas would have no doubt argued that it was not a question of principle but of policy. He would have said, 'It is not a matter of right and wrong: it is a matter of expediency.' The voice of expediency is as much abroad in the world today as it was in the days of Jesus. It puts many a Christian upon a cross.

Some years ago, I counselled a man who told me a sad and depressing story. Mainly through his own efforts he had founded a successful company, and had brought to the board men who hitherto had achieved very little in life. While he was spending a few weeks' holiday out of the country, they found a loophole in the constitution that stated that a director could be removed from office if he was out of the country for more than five days. They acted at once, voted him out of office, and gained control of the company. He wanted to fight back and take them to court, but I said, 'Keep your Christian attitudes – they are your real asset.' He did – and went on to found a Christian organisation which became almost a household word.

FURTHER STUDY

1 Thess. 2:1–20;
John 8:29;
Matt. 3:17;
Heb. 11:5

1. What was Paul's objective?
2. What was Enoch's testimony?

Prayer

O Father, when I am blocked by another's self-interest, give me the power to accept it. Remind me that my Christian attitudes are always my biggest asset. And save me from developing 'acidosis of the soul'. In Jesus' name. Amen.

Keep your eye on the goal

For reading & meditation – Hebrews 12:1–11

'Let us fix our eyes on Jesus … who for the joy set before him endured the cross …' (v.2)

The Christian life has to be lived out in the face of evil and opposition. And one of those evils is that of expediency. We will want to get things done, say, for the sake of our families, our community, our workmates, or even our church, and someone's vested self-interest will block us.

Jesus was put to death by an adroit political move from the most unexpected source imaginable – the priests. One would expect it from the anti-religious. But the priests? The thing is almost beyond belief. Political moves can come from the least expected sources. They are made not only in the Houses of Parliament, but also in the House of God.

I wonder, am I speaking to some people today who are the victims of some political moves made against them by members of their own denominations? Vested self-interest was at stake, and because it was expedient for them, you were the one who was put on the cross. It hurts, doesn't it? But you have one thing open to you – you can suffer for your opponents as Jesus did for His. By 'suffering for', I

FURTHER STUDY

1 Pet. 2:11–25;
Matt. 10:22;
James 5:11

1. How should we react to unjust suffering?
2. Write out a definition of the word 'endurance'.

don't mean by adopting the attitude of 'grin and bear it', but by stretching out your arms towards the cross, as Jesus did towards His, and embracing its redemptive purpose. All spiritual suffering can be redemptive. The pain of being cast aside because of vested self-interest can be deeply wounding, but it can be endured, providing you see, as Jesus did, that the cross is but the prelude to a new dimension of God's purposes.

Prayer

O Lord, drive this truth deep into my heart, that when I am placed upon a cross, out of it will come what came to You – a resurrection. With that key – I can unlock anything. Thank You, Lord. Amen.

'Pawns of the Romans'

For reading & meditation – John 12:1–19

*'So the chief priests made plans to kill
Lazarus as well …' (v.10)*

I want to give you some background information about the
Sadducees so that you can understand a little more of their
thinking and motives. When Palestine became part of the Roman
Empire, the Romans used these governing priests rather like the
Nazis used Pétain and Laval during the years of the occupation
in France. Rome, of course, had its procurators over the Jewish
provinces, but the procurators were expected to work harmoniously
with the high-priestly party. The Sadducees were really the pawns
of the Romans. Their own comfort and safety depended, in part,
on their good relationship with Rome and its officers. Inevitably,
this led to them becoming more concerned with politics than with
religion.

Although the Pharisees came in conflict with Jesus early in His
ministry, the Sadducees were hardly aware of Him. But the day He
strode into the Temple and drove out the money-changers altered
all that. From then on, He was a marked man. Matters came to a
head after the raising of Lazarus. The event caused such a stir that
anything might have happened. Multitudes were
ready to take a sword and revolt. It was then that
the Sadducees, afraid of the political repercussions
a revolt might have, made up their minds to get rid
of Jesus. This was how they came into the picture
and how they started to march along the road that
led to Calvary. 'That was how … the deed was
done, Which shook the earth and veiled the sun.'

FURTHER STUDY

Acts 4:1–22;
Psa. 7:1;
Jer. 15:15

1. What upset the
religious people?
2. Did Peter and John
choose the way of
expediency?

Prayer

Gracious Father, as similar vested self-interests are in the world today, give me
the power to face them, and die for them, if necessary. For such evil is not
overcome in my own strength – but in Yours. Amen.

'Abundant living – in spite of'

For reading & meditation – Luke 24:13–32

'Did not the Christ have to suffer these things and then enter his glory?' (v.26)

T he thought engaging our attention at present is that the Christian life must be lived out in the presence of the same evils that put Christ on the cross, one of which is expediency. When self-interest stands across our path, we must meet it unflinchingly as did He.

E. Stanley Jones once said, 'Abundant living is sometimes on account of, but more often, in spite of.' Can you see what he means? We develop more in times of crisis than we do in times of ease. A cross can be painful and hard to bear, but it is one of the principles on which the universe is founded that when we suffer for doing the work and will of God, then every Good Friday will be followed by an Easter Sunday.

This does not mean that we must develop a stoical attitude to life, for this only cultivates a hard rather than a strong spirit. Jesus endured the cross because He saw beyond it to His Father's perfect purposes. You cannot bear a cross long unless you have the same attitude that Jesus had – of seeing beyond it to a higher and greater dimension. When you see that embracing the cross is not a defeat but a victory, then you are inwardly fortified to bear anything that God wants to allow. So if, at this moment, you are the victim of some evil strategy that is pushing you inch by inch towards a cross, then remember that if you go to the cross in the spirit of Jesus, you will rise in the spirit of Jesus. You will have resurrected life.

FURTHER STUDY

1 Pet. 5: 1–10;
Rom. 8:17;
James 5:10

1. What does God supply in times of trial?
2. What are four results of enduring trials?

Prayer

Lord Jesus, I begin to see Your secret. You went to the cross knowing that though life was speaking its cruellest word – evil – You would turn that word into God's most redemptive word – love. Give me power to do the same. In Your name I pray. Amen.

Was Jesus unassertive?

For reading & meditation – John 2:13–25

'So he made a whip ... and ... scattered the coins of the money-changers and overturned their tables.' (v.15)

An objection to the principle I am discussing is this: the attitude of accepting things rather than resisting them produces bland, unassertive individuals who finish up being steam-rollered by life. An army major in a seminar I once conducted said, 'I enjoyed everything you said, but I didn't like the word "surrender". I come from a background where that word is extremely unpopular.'

I said, 'When you surrender to God, you don't surrender to anything else.' He considered my answer for a moment, drew himself up to his full height, and said, 'Then that's OK.'

Was Jesus a bland, unassertive, spineless individual? Of course not! One has only to see Him at work in the Temple, overturning the tables of the money-changers, to know that at the right time and in the right circumstances He could be fiercely assertive. Yet in the Garden of Gethsemane, although 72,000 angels (twelve legions) were available to Him, He meekly surrendered to His captors.

There are times when it is right to resist and refuse to be pushed around, but there are other times when we must go to the cross, knowing that this is the way God wants us to take in this particular situation. I wish I could give you some guidelines to clearly differentiate between the two – but I can't. The wisdom to discern the difference comes from living close to God and absorbing the disposition and character of His Son.

FURTHER STUDY

Eph. 6:1–10;
Matt. 26:39;
Psa. 40:8

1. What should our attitude be?
2. What trap should we avoid?

Prayer

O my Father, give me wisdom, I pray, so that, like Jesus, I act rather than react to life. Fill my life with so much of Yourself that I know precisely what action to take in every situation – and why. In Jesus' name I ask it. Amen.

A classless society

For reading & meditation – Luke 18:18–30

'*... anyone who leaves home ... for the sake of the Kingdom of God will receive much more ...*' (vv.29–30, GNB)

The sin of expediency was committed by the Sadducees (the priests), and helped put Jesus on the cross.

You and I, living in a world that is soiled by sin, must face the fact that at times, perhaps even today, we, too, will become victims of the evil of expediency. People will use political moves against us simply because we stand in the way of their own self-interest. At such times life crimsons into a cross.

The point must be made also that wrong attitudes can be embodied in a class as well as a person. Men often think according to class interest instead of as people. In the UK we still talk of the working class, the middle class and the upper class. Sad to say, in recent years, many who have moved from the working class into the middle class then proceed to embody the class interest they deplored in others. Are you a victim of the class war? Do you feel looked down upon by others because life has cast you into the mould of what society considers a lower class? Are you conscious that expediency and self-interest in the minds of others has blocked your progress in this world? Then listen to me carefully. You can suffer, and die for, if necessary, the embodied class interests in others so that, here on earth, God can usher in a classless society. Believe me, that classless society is coming. Christ died for it – and so may you and I. And what is that classless society? It is the kingdom of God.

FURTHER STUDY

1 Tim. 5:1–21;
Lev. 19:15;
Job 13:10

1. What was Paul's exhortation to Timothy?
2. Do you have any prejudices?

Prayer

Gracious, loving heavenly Father, help me not only to witness to Your coming kingdom, but to die for it if necessary. In Jesus' name I pray. Amen.

The evil of betrayal

For reading & meditation – Matthew 26:14–25

'Jesus replied, "The one who has dipped his hand into the bowl with me will betray me."'(v.23)

Another of the embodied evils which put Christ on the cross was betrayal. There is a terrible sound to the word 'betrayal'. The opposite of this word is 'loyalty', and the more one regards loyalty, the more repulsive the word 'betrayal' becomes. People are not surprised when they are hurt and humiliated by their enemies, but no one expects to be humiliated by their friends. The Gospels do not specifically say that Jesus was hurt by the action of Judas, but our Lord, being human as well as divine, must have felt keenly the pain of being betrayed by one of His own followers. Yet in the face of all the hurt that betrayal can bring, He strode unswervingly towards the cross.

At some time, you, too, can expect to face the evil of betrayal – your Judas. Often those who dip their hand in the same dish will abandon you. When money, position or self-interest beckons, they fall away. It is not easy to remain unembittered when those who stood at your side and claimed to be your friends, turn away from you, and pass you by on the other side of the street.

How do we handle the pain of betrayal? We can do what Christ did in the beautiful story told by Dostoevsky. Christ came to preach in Spain but the Grand Inquisitor arrested Him, and said, 'Why did you come back? You left everything to the Church. You should never have returned.' Christ made no answer, but stepped up to the 90-year-old Inquisitor, kissed him on the cheek, and quietly slipped away.

FURTHER STUDY
Gen. 37:1–36;
45:5–8

1. Why was Joseph betrayed?
2. What was Joseph's conclusion and attitude?

Prayer

Lord Jesus, help me to do just that, or something similar to that, when I am called upon to face my Judas. And save me from betraying anyone else, lest Your burning kiss be left on my cheek. In Your name I ask it. Amen.

The low cost of unfaithfulness

For reading & meditation – Matthew 27:1–10

'... I have betrayed innocent blood ...' (v.4)

Sooner or later in this mixed-up world almost everyone has to face the pain of betrayal. It is not easy to remain calm and controlled when betrayed by someone you trusted and loved. There has been much discussion about the part Judas played in betraying Christ, and it might be helpful if we looked at the various views of theologians. Some say his part in Christ's death was a minor one. Mighty forces were bent on the arrest of Jesus, they say, and if the Son of God had no intention to resist their evil will, preferring to use their evil to promote His Father's purposes, then, even if Judas had not betrayed Him, the authorities would have had no difficulty in tracking Him down and crucifying Him.

This would make God the author of evil, and Judas merely a pawn in the hands of the Deity. Most certainly God worked through the action of Judas, but that was because God knew beforehand how Judas would decide, and prepared His strategy based on that foreknowledge. There is no doubt, in my mind at least, that Judas was a free agent in the matter, and this is why the Scripture sets

FURTHER STUDY

Luke 19:11–28;
1 Cor. 4:2;
Rev. 2:10

1. What was the master's response to the first two servants?
2. How did he deal with the third?

him in an evil light. The great perplexity to me is how a man who walked and talked with Jesus, saw Him perform the most amazing miracles, heard Him speak the most life-changing words, could do such a foul thing; and for so small a sum – thirty pieces of silver! In Old Testament times, it was the price of a slave. But then lowness is always a mark of a faithless friendship.

Prayer

Father, I ask one thing, not that I shall be preserved from being betrayed, but that I shall be preserved from betraying others. Help me to be loyal and true to all who put their trust in me. In Jesus' name I pray. Amen.

Sin is our responsibility

For reading & meditation – James 1:2–15

'… each one is tempted when, by his own evil desire, he is dragged away and enticed.' (v.14)

S ome argue that if Jesus knew beforehand that Judas was going to betray Him, and chose Him nevertheless, then the responsibility for what followed must be placed on Christ. By not choosing him, He could have avoided the pain of betrayal. The fact He chose him, knowing what he was going to do, puts the responsibility on Christ – not Judas.

One answer which is given to this, and one with which I do not entirely agree, is that our Lord's incarnation involved a lack of knowledge concerning certain things. There were things He said He didn't know, and occasions when He appeared to express surprise. He would have chosen Judas, therefore, with the same affection as He chose the others, and, being unaware of what he would do, placed him in a position of authority.

I believe that Jesus knew from the beginning of His ministry that Judas would betray Him, but foreknowledge is not foreordination. I know that the sun will rise tomorrow morning, but my knowing it will not make it rise. It is my belief that the knowledge that Jesus possessed, that Judas would betray Him, did not compel Judas to act in the way he did. When Judas committed his foul act of betrayal, he acted for reasons of his own, and with as much freedom as it is possible for a human being to have. Many people try to excuse their sin by claiming that foreknowledge means foreordination. However, there is no escape in taking that way. You are responsible for your sin – and I for mine.

FURTHER STUDY

Luke 12:41–48;
Rom.14:12;
Matt. 12:36

1. What did Jesus teach in this parable?
2. Do you take personal responsibility for your actions?

Prayer

O God, my gracious, heavenly Father, I want to live frankly and fully. Help me not to make excuses for my behaviour, but to admit that when I go wrong, it is no one else's fault but my own. In Jesus' name I ask it. Amen.

More theories . . .

For reading & meditation – Acts 1:15–26

'... from which Judas by transgression fell, that he might go to his own place.' (v.25, NKJV)

O ne view states that Judas was an honest patriot who had come to the conclusion that Jesus, by reason of His strong preaching, was in danger of upsetting the nation. He betrayed Him, therefore, out of love for Israel. What he did, say the advocates of this theory, may seem foul to us, but it was nothing more than the result of mistaken judgment. Yet another theory states that Judas wanted to see Christ demonstrate His divine power against the militarism of Rome, so he manoeuvred events in the expectation that Christ, after being apprehended, would exercise divine power to extricate Himself from their grasp. A similar theory to this, and one held by many, is that Judas, believing Jesus missed His chance of leading the people in an insurrection on Palm Sunday, tried to force Him into manifesting Himself as the King of Glory by arranging His arrest. He thought, so they say, that when he brought the soldiers to Gethsemane, Jesus would have been obliged to display His sovereignty, and take on the role of King of the Jews.

These views, and there are many others, run counter to the Scriptures. John says that he was a thief (John 12:6). Luke says: 'Then Satan entered Judas' (Luke 22:3). Jesus said: 'It would be better for him if he had not been born' (Matt. 26:24). The Bible places the responsibility for the betrayal of Christ fairly and squarely on the shoulders of Judas. He was a dishonest and scheming individual, fully aware of what he was doing.

FURTHER STUDY

Gen. 27:1–46;
32:24–28;

Prov. 27:6

1. What was Jacob's character like at first?
2. How did God change it?

Prayer

Father, I want to use this moment to ask, once again, that You will protect and preserve me from being either a betrayer of You – or a betrayer of anyone else. In Your name and for Your glory I pray. Amen.

Was there ever such a kiss?

For reading & meditation – Matthew 26:47–56

'… "The one I kiss is the man; arrest him."' (v.48)

Who was Judas? Of the twelve men Jesus chose to be with Him, eleven came from the north of Palestine and one from the south – Judas. He was a Judean: all the others were Galilean.

It is reasonable to suppose also that he was a man with a head for business, for he became the treasurer for the group. It appears that Judas was a covetous man, full of avarice. When Mary of Bethany brought spikenard, and anointed the feet of Jesus, Judas Iscariot rebelled against her action, saying, 'Why wasn't this perfume sold and the money given to the poor? It was worth a year's wages' (John 12:5). How pious that must have sounded – but, as John tells us, he didn't really care for the poor. He failed to see the inner attitude that prompted the action, and probably thought that the more money he had in the bag, the more he could pilfer.

After Palm Sunday, when Jesus began to tell the disciples plainly that He was not going to fulfil their hopes of becoming an earthly king, Judas, no doubt, became disillusioned, and decided to get as much as he could out of the situation. He went to the high priest and made a deal. It wasn't much, but it was better than nothing. Thirty pieces of silver! To earn it, he had to show the soldiers which one of the group to take. He went forward in the Garden of Gethsemane and kissed Him into their arms. Was ever the symbol of love so greatly prostituted? Oh, what agony that must have brought to the heart of Jesus.

FURTHER STUDY

Luke 12:1–21;
Exod. 20:17;
Eccl. 5:10;
1 Tim. 6:10

1. What was Jesus' warning?
2. What is a root of all kinds of evil?

Prayer

Blessed Lord Jesus, any betrayal I am called upon to suffer pales into insignificance by the side of Yours. But how comforting it is to know that You have felt every pain I feel – even the pain of betrayal. I am so thankful. Amen.

Could Judas have been forgiven?

For reading & meditation – Matthew 27:1–10

'When Judas … saw that Jesus was condemned , he was seized with remorse …' (v.3)

Judas showed remorse when he realised the enormity of his crime. As the chief priests were leaving the Hall of the Sanhedrin, Judas stopped them, still holding the money in his hands, and cried, 'I have sinned … for I have betrayed innocent blood' (v.4). He had played his part and they wanted nothing more to do with him. Overcome by remorse, he took a rope and went and hanged himself. It is sad that Judas's attitude, after realising the depth of his transgression, was merely one of remorse and not one of repentance.

The question is often debated in Bible colleges: if Judas had repented of his sin, and gone to Jesus to ask for forgiveness – would he have been forgiven? I believe he would. I cannot conceive, knowing as I do the depth of God's forgiveness in my own life, that if Judas had flung himself before Christ, and said, 'Lord Jesus, forgive me,' that he would have been refused. The One who prayed, 'Father, forgive them, for they do not know what they are doing' (Luke 23:34), and said to the dying thief, 'Today you will be with me in Paradise' (Luke 23:43), would have been no less forgiving to the man who had kissed Him into His captors' arms.

FURTHER STUDY

Acts 3:1–19;

Matt. 3:2;

Luke 13:2–3

1. What was the message of Jesus and the Early Church?
2. Why is this so important?

The crowning tragedy of Judas's life was that he stopped at remorse instead of repentance. Remorse says, 'I was a fool to do that.' Repentance says, 'I was a fool to do that – but O God, forgive me.' Remorse gets us nowhere. Repentance gets us everywhere.

Prayer

O my Father, I stand in awe as I consider the scope and wonder of Your forgiveness. Teach me how to cross that line between remorse and repentance. Then I know I shall be safe – eternally. Amen.

Love – not just a feeling

For reading & meditation – Romans 12:9–21

'… If your enemy is hungry, feed him …' (v.20)

How do we, as Christ's 21st-century disciples, deal with this evil of betrayal when it obstructs our path? We go on loving, no matter how hard or difficult it may be. Someone might say, 'How can I have loving feelings toward someone who has betrayed me?' God has a solution to that. He doesn't ask you to have loving feelings, but loving actions. The scripture does not say: 'If your enemy is hungry, try to have loving feelings toward him.' It says, 'If your enemy is hungry, feed him.' Love, in biblical terms, is more than a feeling, it is an action of the will – a will committed to doing what God asks, even though one does not feel like doing it.

It is at this point many Christians fall into bondage. They find themselves plagued with unloving feelings whenever they have been betrayed or let down, and they try to change their feelings – all to no avail. How many times have you asked God to change your feelings, and He hasn't answered your prayer? How many times have you tried, with all the strength at your disposal, to bring about a change in your feelings – but nothing has happened. You are going about it the wrong way. Commit your will to Christ, and say, 'Lord, I can't control my feelings, but I can control my will. And I will make my will do what You want it to do, despite what my feelings say.' I promise you, engage in loving actions toward someone who has betrayed you, and God will see to it that, in due time, loving feelings will follow.

FURTHER STUDY

1 Cor. 13:1–13;
Prov. 10:12;
1 John 2:9

1. List the actions of love in 1 Corinthians 13.
2. How much are you putting them into practice in your own life?

Prayer

O Father, I sense that this is an issue I haven't quite got straight yet. Help me to repeat to myself a hundred times today until I get it – really get it – I can't control my feelings, but I can control my will. In Jesus' name. Amen.

The cry of the crowd

For reading & meditation – Matthew 27:11–26

'... But they shouted all the louder, "Crucify him!"' (v.23)

A nother of the embodied evils which put Christ on the cross was the combined rejection by the multitude. Theologians have long discussed how much responsibility the multitude, who cried out, 'Crucify Him', had for Jesus' death. We know the parts the Pharisees, the priests and Judas played. But what was the part of the crowd who cried for His death? Were they as guilty as the rest? I believe they were.

Some scholars have suggested that the crowd were not as guilty as we might suppose. They say that the people who were there were just the sweepings of the slums of Jerusalem, priest-ridden and priest-paid. They were there because they had been told what to say. They were suborned. Therefore it is unjust to say that the crowd turned on Jesus. They were pressured to do it.

I cannot believe that the multitude was entirely composed of the sweepings of the streets. Undoubtedly, there were some there who could be placed in that category. However, I rather think it was a cross section of the community, the rich as well as the poor, the educated and the uneducated, the slum dweller and the street merchant, the religious and the irreligious. Together they rejected Him. They chose Barabbas – literally Bar-Abba, 'son of a father', and crucified Jesus, the true Bar-Abba, 'Son of the Father'. They chose a local patriotic rebel, and crucified the Creator of the universe. And for that they cannot avoid being charged with complicity in the crime of Calvary.

FURTHER STUDY

John 15:1–27;

Luke 6:11; 19:14;

John 7:7

1. Why did the world hate Jesus?
2. Why was He able to withstand it?

Prayer

O God, I am aware of the awful build-up that can take place in a crowd. When people come together, strange forces for good and evil are at work. Help me to stand against evil – even when a multitude are against me. In Jesus' name. Amen.

The power of the people

For reading & meditation – Mark 12:1–12

'... *But they were afraid of the crowd ...*' (v.12)

S ooner or later, we, too, have to face the problem of crowd rejection. However, before we consider how to meet this kind of opposition, let's look a little more deeply into the question we raised yesterday: how culpable were the crowd who cried out for the crucifixion of Jesus? Some would excuse them, saying they were suborned into it. The crowd themselves would probably have said, 'We had little to do with it: the priests really arranged His death.'

This question of what responsibility ordinary people have for the crimes committed by their rulers is not one of merely academic and biblical interest: it is one of the most burning issues of modern times. Just recently I saw a television programme which dealt with this same subject. A sociologist on the programme raised an interesting point. 'Ordinary people,' he said, 'wield tremendous power.'

Was this true of the people who lived in Jesus' day? I believe it was. Mark tells us that the priests would have ended Jesus' career sooner than they did except they feared the people. He tells us also that Pilate gave judgment against Jesus because he wanted to satisfy the crowd (Mark 15:15) – proof, incidentally, that the crowd who gathered in the early morning was a cross-section of the population and not just a rabble. Make no mistake about it – the people had power. And when they used it to deny and reject Jesus, they implicated themselves in the foulest deed the world has ever witnessed.

FURTHER STUDY

Acts 17:1–15;
21:30;

1 Cor. 14:33a

1. Who stirred up the crowd against Paul?
2. Why were they stirred up?

Prayer

Blessed Lord Jesus, help me not to fear when, because of my Christian convictions, a group are against me. Give me the poise and power which You displayed that day when You stood before the hostile crowd. For Your own honour and glory. Amen.

Crowd psychology

For reading & meditation – Acts 13:44–14:7

'There was a plot afoot among the Gentiles and Jews, together with their leaders, to ill-treat them …' (14:5)

We turn now to consider the question: when we meet with crowd pressure and opposition, what are we to do?

There are times in our lives – at work, at school, in the community – when we are confronted by crowd pressures that laugh us to scorn and attempt to sweep us aside. You must have had occasions in your life, as I have had in mine, when crowd pressure produces, in otherwise intelligent people, a temporary blackout that causes them to reject you. In the engineering shop where I worked in my teens, I remember being greatly unnerved by the fact that my workmates, who were quite cheerful and open when I spoke to them individually, became strangely hostile towards me whenever as at lunchtime, we all sat together as a group. They would say things then that they would never say when alone – hurtful, vile and sometimes venomous things. I could never understand this until, many years later, when I studied psychology, I learned about the strange pressures that can build up in a group.

Jesus faced this pressure – and so will you. What then can we do? We face it in the knowledge that the opposition we encounter may put us on a cross, but the suffering and pain we bear will give way to a glorious resurrection. I have been a victim of group pressures and I am better for it. God has turned the suffering to joy, and has used it to deepen my sensitivity to people and their needs. Believe me – He will do the same for you.

FURTHER STUDY

Acts 5:12–42;

Rom. 8:31;

Heb. 13:6

1. What was Peter's response to group pressure?
2. What was Gamaliel's advice to the council?

Prayer

O God, help me to do what You did when faced with the pressure of a hostile crowd – and go to the cross for them. I know that if I am willing to bear the cross, You will be willing to carry me through to resurrection. Amen.

First a cross – then resurrection

For reading & meditation – Romans 8:16–39

*'I consider that our present sufferings are not worth
comparing with the glory that will be revealed in us.'* (v.18)

How should we respond to a situation when a group or crowd
opposes us and is determined to bring about our downfall? The
option for a Christian is quite clear – we do as Jesus did. We accept
the suffering in the sure knowledge that God will work through it
towards a glorious resurrection.

Church history is replete with the stories of men and women
who, because they stood against the crowd, experienced considerable
suffering, yet lived to see their cause vindicated and accepted. Ever
heard of Martin Niemöller? He was a pastor in Germany prior to and
during part of the Second World War. When Hitler rose to power,
Martin Niemöller spoke out against some of the things the dictator
did, and, as you would expect, brought on himself a good deal of
suffering. But the greatest suffering he endured came not from Hitler
and his henchmen, but from his fellow Christians who counselled
him to turn a blind eye to these issues.

I heard Martin Niemöller speak in the little town of Merthyr
Tydfil, South Wales, shortly after the war, and he said, 'My greatest
suffering was not in Hitler's internment camp,
but when my fellow Christians, fearing that
what I said would have repercussions on them,
stood against me and demanded my silence.' He
stood against the crowd – both Christians and
non-Christians. And today there are thousands
in Germany who testify that his suffering and
example was the means of turning their hearts
towards Jesus Christ.

FURTHER STUDY
Heb. 11:1–28;
Acts 5:41;
Rom. 8:17
1. What is said of
Moses?
2. How did he resist
crowd pressure?

Prayer

O Father, again I ask, when the crowd stands against me and pressures me to
change my mind on what I know to be true, that You will give me the strength
to be able to suffer for my convictions. In Jesus' name. Amen.

Living on two levels

For reading & meditation – Psalm 41:1–13

*'In my integrity you uphold me and set me in your presence
for ever.' (v.12)*

Dr John Biegeleisen, a converted Jew and a professor in an American theological college, tells of having a tomato thrown at him while he was preaching. He says that he felt no resentment, no great upset – only pity. 'I have found,' he said, 'that it is possible to live on two levels at once – the outer level may be disturbed, but the inner level soon holds the outer one steady.'

Now there is, of course, a great difference between being hit in the face with a tomato, and being nailed to a cross, but the principle that John Biegeleisen spoke of was, I believe, the one that Jesus used as He faced His murderers. He lived on two levels at once, and the inner level held the outer one steady. The depths were occupied with God while the surface was occupied with man.

This is the secret of how not to be shattered and overcome by situations. It is possible, I believe, if we know how to live like this, to face anything that life brings. We may well be shaken – but not shattered. Like the old railway trains that used to scoop up water from the trough between the rails as they sped along, the inner depths are being renewed by contact with the resources of God. Jesus, because He was human as well as divine, would no doubt have been shaken on the surface by the bloodthirsty cries of the crowd: 'Crucify Him! Crucify Him!' but His inner life remained undisturbed. There He kept in constant fellowship with God and the depths were at peace.

FURTHER STUDY

Psa. 23:1–6; 4:8;
Luke 1:78–79

1. How did the psalmist overcome adversity?
2. What does the 'rising sun ... from heaven' bring us?

Prayer

O God, my Father, cleanse the depths of my being from all fears, resentments and tensions, so that in the crises of life, I may be able to be calm – no matter what happens on the surface. In Jesus' name I pray. Amen.

'Settled down in God'

For reading & meditation – Philippians 4:4–9

*'… the peace of God, which transcends all understanding, will
guard your hearts and your minds in Christ Jesus.' (v.7)*

If the depths of our being are cleansed from all fears, resentments
and tensions, then it is possible to face any opposition without
too much inner disturbance. We may be shaken, but we will not
be shattered. A lady wrote to me: 'You lift the standards so high, I
sometimes wonder whether you are living in the real world.' Some
years ago my wife suffered from the effects of pernicious anaemia.
From nine stone (126 lbs), she went down to six stone (84 lbs).
Eventually she was diagnosed with stomach cancer and after a
long illness the Lord took her. The circumstances in which I found
myself certainly shook me, but I had an unwanted opportunity to
test my own teaching. And it holds! Oh – how it holds! The outer
happenings have left their mark on me, but my real life is rooted
deep in Christ. There – and I say this honestly in the fear of God and
in the presence of my Lord Jesus Christ – the depths are at peace.

Yes, in the real world of problems and difficulties, it is possible
to face anything and know the inner peace which Jesus Himself
demonstrated, and which His followers have known down the ages.
If this is not so, then the words of our text today
are just a mockery. The peace of God which passes
all understanding (and misunderstanding too)
will 'keep' – or 'garrison' as one translation puts
it – the depths in tranquillity. We can 'settle down
in God' as the Quakers say – 'settled down' at the
depths. even though the surface is unsettled.

FURTHER STUDY

John 14:15–31;
Psa. 29:11;
Isa. 26:3

1. What did Jesus
promise His
disciples?
2. What did He warn
them to avoid?

Prayer

Father, I am so deeply grateful that You have provided for the depths – that they
can be held steady by Your power. The blows of life may shake me, but they
can't shatter me. I am 'settled down in God'. Thank You, Father. Amen.

At home – anywhere

For reading & meditation – Psalm 40:1–17

'Blessed is the man who makes the LORD his trust …' (v.4)

We can live on two levels at once – the surface tides may come and go, but the depths are held steady by the Spirit of God. But can we experience this inner security when the crowd is set against us and crying for our blood? Thank God – we can! A woman wrote, 'I am one of the leaders of a women's organisation, and just recently the committee voted to do something which I knew to be wrong and contrary to the Bible's teaching. I made my views clear, and instantly brought down on my head not only the wrath of the whole committee, but the large majority of the members. They wanted me to turn a blind eye, but I said, "No." The result is that I have been ostracised and treated as a persona non grata – one-time friends pass me on the street without a nod or a word. My only comfort has been my Bible and *Every Day with Jesus*. When my husband goes out in the morning, I get down before God and tune in to what He has to say to me. Outside the crowd clamour for my blood, but inside all is at peace.' She was living on two levels at once and the lower sweetened the upper level.

FURTHER STUDY

Psa. 18:1–50;

Psa. 31:3; 71:3;
91:2

1. What is the psalmist's testimony?
2. List the calamities that came upon him, and his statements about God.

Are you the victim of some group or crowd pressure that is causing you deep concern? Are you conscious that because of your Christian convictions, others stand against you? Then open the depths of your being to the Holy Spirit that He might come in on the lower level. When He takes over the depths then, believe me, you will never be afraid of what happens on the surface.

Prayer

O God, my Father, when You are at home in the depths of my being, then I am at home there too. And with You guiding the surface, I can be at home even there. With You, I am at home anywhere. Hallelujah!

Pilate – the Roman procurator

For reading & meditation – John 18:28–40

"What is truth?" Pilate asked ...' (v.38)

Another of the embodied evils which Christ faced on His way to the cross was the evil of moral cowardice and cynicism. This is represented by Pontius Pilate, the Roman procurator of Judea, who sentenced our Lord to death.

The main sources of information about Pontius Pilate are the Gospels and the writings of the Jewish historian, Josephus. These two sources provide a picture that is both interesting and arresting. His position in Judea was that of a sub-governor under the Governor who ruled over the whole of Syria. The position in itself, according to Josephus, was not a high one, but it was seen as a stepping-stone to bigger things. Pilate was a Roman. He belonged to a race that had conquered the world, and had no doubt the overbearing arrogance of a Roman victor. His greatest fault, however, in my view, was his moral cowardice and cynicism. It comes out in his famous question to Jesus: 'What is truth?'

Now just as Jesus, on His way to the cross, had to face His Pilate – moral cowardice and cynicism – so we, too, in this modern age will come up against the same evil. Jesus conquered Pilate by not being like him. He broke Pilate by letting him break His body, but not His spirit. That unbroken spirit broke Pilate, and the empire he represented. It will break anything that opposes it. The Roman Empire, with all its pomp and power, has sunk into the dust – Christ's kingdom lives on.

FURTHER STUDY
John 8:12–47; 14:6;
Eph. 4:21
1. What prompted
Pilate's question?
2. How would you
reply?

Prayer

Lord Jesus, I see so clearly that it wasn't You who was on trial that day – Pilate was. And when he wrote what he thought was Your doom, he unwittingly proclaimed Your eternal Kingship. What strategy! Amen.

Another look at Pilate

For reading & meditation – Luke 3:1–6

*'In the fifteenth year of the reign of Tiberius Caesar – when
Pontius Pilate was governor of Judea ...' (v.1)*

Before we look at what Scripture has to say about Pontius Pilate,
we shall dig a little more into his background, provided for us
by the historian, Josephus. Pilate came in conflict with the Jews as
soon as he had set foot in Judea. Judaism, as is well known, was
intolerant of idols, and the Jews would not allow the presence of any
idol in the vicinity of their holy Temple. One day Pilate, in a fit of
temper, commanded his soldiers to take some idols and leave them
at the doors of the Temple. When the Jews discovered this, their
anger was greatly aroused. Hundreds marched to Caesarea, where
the procurator normally lived, and demanded an interview. He kept
them waiting for six days, and then threatened them with death if
they persisted in questioning his orders. To his amazement, they
stretched themselves out on the ground, and declared that death
was better than seeing their laws and principles violated. Pilate had
to concede defeat. He promised it would not happen again – and let
them go.

He had other clashes with the Jews, and came to be regarded
by them in time as one of the cruellest and most

FURTHER STUDY

Dan. 5:1–31;

Psa. 36:2;

Gal. 6:3;

Matt. 23:12

1. How did God deal
with a ruler who
opposed Him?
2. How can a man
deceive himself?

arrogant of all the Roman rulers. But as C.S. Lewis
once said, 'We never see anyone in their true light
until we see them alongside Jesus.' And there, as
Pilate moves in the direct beams of the Light of the
World, the man is seen as he truly is – not only
arrogant, but a cynic and a moral coward.

Prayer

Father, how true it is that men are only fully seen when they are seen in Your
light. There all tinsel is swept away and reality is seen. Help me to stand forever
in that light. For Jesus' sake. Amen.

Pilate – on trial?

For reading & meditation – John 18:33–19:12

'Jesus answered, "You would have no power over me if it were not given to you from above…"' (19:11)

Pilate, like all other men, can only be seen in his true light when he appears in the same scene as Jesus. There, we are no longer deceived by the tinsel and titles of earth – we see him as he really is. How does Pilate stand up to the test when he comes into the presence of Jesus? Remember, in a sense, it was not Jesus on trial that day – but Pilate. He is seen first of all as conceited. He replies to a question which Jesus puts to him in this way: 'Do you think I am a Jew?' (v.35). It is obvious from this that Pilate regarded the imputation of being a Jew as the greatest insult anyone could have given him. He never really understood the Jews, and some say he never even tried. Doubtless, he would say it wasn't his business to understand, but to govern.

He was not only conceited, but as I have said, cynical also. 'What is truth?' he cynically enquires of Jesus. 'Cynicism', says one writer, 'is usually the product of a culture without real religion.' The word comes from the Greek *kuon* – dog. The picture is that of a snarling, fault-finding person, full of self-interest, who doesn't trust anyone but himself. A third characteristic comes to light as he stands in the presence of Jesus – he was annoyed. 'Do you refuse to speak to me?' he said. 'Don't you realise I have power either to free you or to crucify you?' (19:10). How sublimely different was Jesus. Noble, dignified, detached, loving – and superior. His character lives on – forever.

FURTHER STUDY

Col. 1:1–20;

Matt. 28:18;

John 10:18

1. How much power did Pilate have?
2. How did Christ show His true strength and character?

Prayer

Lord, I am so thankful that Your character is a character that lives on. Help me understand this and thank You for it. You are not just a character – You are Character – with a capital C. I am so thankful. Amen.

An epitaph long remembered

For reading & meditation – John 19:12–22

'Finally Pilate handed him over to them to be crucified …'
(v.16)

Pilate did attempt, albeit feebly, to bring about some form of justice. When they first brought Jesus to him, he refused to hear them unless they came up with a specific political charge (John 18:29). Then, when he had examined Christ and satisfied himself that He was innocent, he made his view clear to them (John 18:38). When Christ's accusers still pressed the charges they had made against Him, Pilate adroitly seized on one of their customs and offered Jesus as the prisoner who should be released at the feast. The Jews replied, 'If you let this man go, you are no friend of Caesar. Anyone who claims to be a king opposes Caesar' (v.12).

At that point their case was won. The selfish element in Pilate took over and so, firmly and deliberately, he condemned the innocent Son of God to death. After pronouncing sentence, he washed his hands in a bowl of water, saying, 'I am innocent of this man's blood' (Matt. 27:24). He washed his hands, but he could never wash the stain out of his soul. Perhaps he thought that was the end of his involvement in this sad affair. History records that he fell from power almost immediately after that and disappeared, as did his empire, from history. Disappeared? Not quite. His name rings out every Sunday in thousands of churches as Christians recite the creed: '…born of the Virgin Mary, suffered under Pontius Pilate, was crucified, dead any buried…' Was ever an epitaph and a judgment more prolonged?

FURTHER STUDY

Acts 24:1–27;

Psa. 82:2;

Luke 16:10

1. How was Paul's trial similar to Christ's?

2. In what way was Felix similar to Pilate?

Prayer

O God, I see so clearly that those who oppose You may seem to triumph for a while, but all such triumphs are short-lived. In You, I can put up with all temporary defeats because I am assured of long-term victory. I am so grateful. Amen.

Act – not react

For reading & meditation – 1 Timothy 6:6–16

*'… Christ Jesus, who while testifying before Pontius Pilate
made the good confession …' (v.13)*

Pilate's real sin was that he lacked moral integrity. He would not
be loyal to the highest he knew, when to be loyal interfered with
his self-interests. While testifying before Pontius Pilate, Jesus 'made
the good confession'. In other words He maintained a godly attitude.
No matter what Pilate did, Jesus would never allow Pilate's actions
to determine His.

There are really only two positions to take in life – we can
either act or react. When evil blocks our path, we can decide to let
it make us bitter – or make us better. There is a decision involved.
The decision might be made almost instantaneously, but there is a
moment – sometimes no more than a fraction of a second – when
the will is involved in making this vital decision: do I act – or react?
Unfortunately, many of us have had a lifetime of experience in
reacting to life's events, so that we respond negatively by flying off
the handle or sulking.

When Jesus stood before Pontius Pilate, He maintained 'the
good confession'. He acted, rather than reacted. He would not allow
Pilate's attitudes to influence His. He decided to
maintain His silence. It was not fear or timidity
that shut His lips. He decided to go on loving. He
decided to suffer the indignity. It was His decision
all the way. And that is victory! When facing your
own personal Pilate, remember that, and make up
your mind that, from now on, you will not allow
the actions of others to determine yours. You will
act and not react.

FURTHER STUDY

Isa. 53:1–12; 42:2;
Matt. 26:6–63;
27:14

1. How did Isaiah
portray Christ's
response?
2. How did Jesus
make His good
confession?

Prayer

Lord, help me, when faced with life's perplexities and problems, to act and not
to react. Make my will so strong that it instantly sides with truth in every conflict.
For Christ's sake I ask it. Amen.

I can do anything – for Him

For reading & meditation – Philippians 4:8–13

'I can do everything through him who gives me strength.'
(v.13)

Just as Jesus faced the embodied evil of cynicism and moral cowardice, so we, too, must be prepared to face a similar issue. You will set out to do something for God, and someone, in a position of power and authority, will block you and misjudge you because of self-interest and moral cowardice. What are you to do? Meet your opponent with his own weapons? Fight cynicism with cynicism? No, in a battle of beasts the bigger beast always wins. You do as Jesus did and keep 'the good confession'.

I am told that, in the Andes mountains, when two pack goats meet each other on a narrow ledge, where it is difficult to pass, one goat will instinctively kneel and let the other walk over him. There are times when we might have to kneel and let people walk over us. Notice, I say 'kneel' and not 'knuckle under'. Is there a difference? There most certainly is: in kneeling, you are bending low at the feet of Christ. In knuckling under, you are bending low at the feet of men. Kneeling is a spiritual action – you do it for His sake. Knuckling under is a human action – you do it for your own sake.

Nothing is impossible when it is done for Him. I cannot take criticism, but I can take it for Him. I cannot take defeat, but I can take it for Him. I cannot take setbacks, but I can take them for Him. I love the Moffatt translation of the verse before us today which says: 'In him who strengthens me, I am able for anything.' Anything? Yes 'as long as it is done for Him'.

FURTHER STUDY

Isa. 40:21–31;
41:10;
2 Cor. 9:8;
Eph. 3:16

1. What is Isaiah's exhortation?
2. What is his proclamation?

Prayer

Beautiful, strong Son of God, You are becoming more and more my treasure. More and more, I cannot think or love apart from You. And where my treasure is – there is my heart also. I am at rest – in You. Thank You, blessed Jesus. Amen.

Nothing can work against us

For reading & meditation – 2 Corinthians 13:1–10

'For we cannot do anything against the truth, but only for the truth.' (v.8)

T he way of Pilate is doomed – the way of Jesus goes on forever. When Pilate said, 'What I have written, I have written' (John 19:22), he was not bringing about Jesus' downfall, but contributing to God's eternal purposes. If we Christians could get hold of the idea that nothing can work successfully against us providing our lives are in harmony with the will and purposes of God – our everyday living would be transformed.

When I quoted the text at the top of this page to a Christian recently, he became greatly excited, and said, 'I never knew that was in the Bible.' But it is – and it is true. Nothing can work against the truth – only for it. Goethe in Faust said, 'I am part of that force which constantly seeks to do evil, yet none the less creates the good.' That statement could almost have come from the Bible. It certainly has the ring of truth in it. Evil has the smell of death upon it, for in its very nature it is doomed. It may seem to triumph for a while, as Lowell has put it in his memorable stanza:

'Truth forever on the scaffold, Wrong forever on the Throne, Yet that scaffold sways the future, And behind the dim unknown, Standeth God within the shadow, Keeping watch above His own.'

With the knowledge that the triumph of evil is only temporary, we can wait. The years and the centuries will speak against the hours.

FURTHER STUDY

Heb. 6:1–20;

Deut. 32:4;

Psa. 146:6;

Rom. 4:20–21

1. What is impossible for God to do?
2. What does this give us?

Prayer

Lord, in the light of this, I can put up with all opposition. What matters is not how things begin, but how they end. You have the last word in everything that comes into my life and I can wait. Amen.

'The King of the Jews'

For reading & meditation – Matthew 27:24–33

"'Hail, King of the Jews!" ...' (v.29)

Another of the evils which combined to crucify Christ was ridicule – or mockery. This was evidenced in the action of the soldiers who, having placed a crown of thorns upon His head, a scarlet robe on His back and a reed in His hand, stood back and mocked Him, saying, 'Hail, King of the Jews!' The Romans despised the Jews, so when they got hold of Jesus – 'the King of the Jews' – they made fun of the Jews by ridiculing their King. They were really pouring scorn on the whole nation – in Him. Jesus, however, took the scorn which was intended for the Jews and bore it, not only for the Jews, but for every other race as well.

What are we to do in the presence of ridicule and mockery? We can become embittered or sullen, or we can do what Jesus did – suffer for those who mocked Him. That possibility is always open. I wonder, am I talking to someone who, at this very moment, is the victim of ridicule and mockery? Then let me speak directly to your need. No one feels more deeply for you than Jesus. He knows precisely how you feel. The pitiable plight in which He found Himself at that moment when the Roman soldiers mocked Him and scoffed at Him makes Him kin to all those who feel that they are the victims of that selfsame evil. Thousands of Christians before you have taken courage from the thought that none knows more about the weight of scorn and ridicule than Jesus. Draw new strength from the fact that Jesus knows.

FURTHER STUDY

Matt. 13:45–58;

Phil. 2:7;

2 Cor. 8:9

1. How was Jesus mocked in His home town?
2. What was the result?

Prayer

O Lord Jesus, what a comfort it is to know that what I feel, You have felt too. You took scorn and ridicule as no man ever did, yet You emerged triumphant. Help me to do the same. Amen.

'Liberty for all – but me'

For reading & meditation – Galatians 3:23–4:7

'There is neither Jew nor Greek, slave nor free ... for you are all one in Christ Jesus.' (3:28)

W hy do mockery and ridicule come? What are some of the reasons for their presence in our lives? Some are ridiculed because they are members of another race. I suspect, myself, that there was a tinge of racial prejudice in the attitude of the Roman soldiers who ridiculed our Lord. I see something of it, too, in the words of Pilate, when he asked, rather sneeringly, 'Am I a Jew?'

Racial prejudice, despite all the laws that have been passed, is still with us. Laws do not change human nature. I meet many people, both here in Britain and in other parts of the world, who carry great hurt in their hearts due to being ridiculed and scoffed at simply because they are members of another race.

In the United States, I saw a television programme in which a black teacher was interviewed about the conditions in her school. She said that when the children in her school saluted the American flag and chanted the words, 'With liberty and justice for all,' some of the black children would say: 'With liberty and justice for all – but me.' The 'but me' was said under their breath. We must work to change these attitudes, of course, but there are some people so deeply entrenched in racial prejudice that they will never change. And when they scoff and ridicule you, because you are a member of another race, remember how Jesus silently took the racial insult of the Roman soldiers and emerged from that sea of hate, beyond race and beyond insult. He can help you to do the same.

FURTHER STUDY
John 4:1–30;
Prov. 22:2;
Rom. 10:12
1. How did Jesus demonstrate racial equality?
2. What is the key verse of this passage?

Prayer

O Jesus, when I cannot change things, help me to rise above them in the knowledge that my suffering is redemptive. You were a member of a despised race, yet through love, You rose above it. And by Your grace – so will I. Amen.

Where nobody suffers ...

For reading & meditation – 2 Corinthians 1:3–11

'... the more we share in Christ's immeasurable suffering the
more we ... give of his encouragement.' (v.5, Phillips)

Jesus took the racial prejudice of the Roman soldiers into His heart
and emerged from that sea of hate above race and above insult.
The cross, I believe, has done more to destroy racial prejudice than
anything the world has ever known. It is quite amazing how being
willing to suffer for one's beliefs has more power to bring about
change than any form of legislation.

In Formosa, many years ago, it used to be a custom among a
certain tribe to kill a man each year and lift up his head to their
ancestors. A Chinese magistrate, determined to stamp out head-
hunting, made little progress until one day he called in the chiefs
of the tribe and pleaded with them to bring the ancient custom to
an end. 'But our gods demand human blood,' they said. 'If we don't
placate them, then we ourselves will have to suffer.' Finally, the
chiefs agreed that they would bring the custom to an end only if
they could do so by cutting off one more head. 'All right,' said the
magistrate, 'just one more head – and you are to take it when and
where I appoint.'

FURTHER STUDY

Rom. 8:1–18;

Matt. 5:11;

2 Tim. 2:12;

1 Pet. 3:14

1. What is promised
to those who suffer
with Him?
2. To what should
we compare our
suffering?

Early one morning, on the day and in the place
agreed, the chiefs took up their positions to await
the arrival of the first unsuspecting traveller who
would come along. At last he came. They fired
an arrow into his heart, and the man had hardly
fallen before his head was severed and put in a
sack. Later, when the sack was opened – to their
great consternation and distress – out rolled the
head of the Chinese magistrate!

Prayer

O Father, I see so clearly that where nobody suffers – nobody cares! If change
can only come about through my own personal suffering, then help me face my
cross – as You faced Yours. For Your own dear name's sake. Amen.

'The marks of Jesus'

For reading & meditation – Galatians 6:1–18

'... I bear on my body the marks of Jesus.' (v.17)

The evil of ridicule and mockery can express itself in racial prejudice. Another way it expresses itself is through physical brutality. Roman soldiers 'twisted together a crown of thorns and set it on his head' (Matt. 27:29). What indescribable agony and suffering that must have caused!

Have you had to endure physical brutality because of your Christian commitment and your identification with Christ? I hesitated to write that last sentence, thinking that it would apply only to a small percentage of readers, but I have let it stand because I believe there are far more Christians than we realise who suffer physical brutality because of their faith. I have been amazed at the number of women who have told me recently that they have been beaten by their husbands because of their stand for Christ. Also I am bearing in mind that this will be read by Christians in countries where there is an atheistic or anti-Christian regime, who may perhaps have undergone some physical brutality because of their commitment to Christ.

We see from our reading today that the apostle Paul knew what it was to carry 'the marks of Jesus on his body'. Are you bruised, wounded or disfigured because of your Christian testimony? Then remember that Jesus comes very close to such a person. No one knows better than He the pain and hurt of physical brutality. Others may not be able to identify with your pain and hurt, but when 'other helpers fail and comforts flee' – there is always Jesus.

FURTHER STUDY

2 Cor. 11:24–33;
12:9–10; 6:4–5;
1 Pet. 2:24

1. What was the key for Paul?
2. What response did it produce in him?

Prayer

Father, I shudder at the thought of physical brutality, but if I ever have to suffer for my faith in this way, give me, I pray, an unending supply of Your strength and power. In Jesus' name I ask it. Amen.

'Not much of a preacher'

For reading & meditation – Acts 7:48–60

'While they were stoning him, Stephen prayed, "Lord Jesus, receive my spirit."' (v.59)

When Dr Kagawa, the famous Japanese Christian, read the story of Christ's crucifixion for the first time, he was overwhelmed with emotion. 'Is it true that cruel men persecuted and whipped and spat upon this man Jesus?' he asked. 'Yes, it is true,' he was told. 'And it is true that when Jesus was dying on the cross, He forgave them?' 'Yes, it is true.' Then Kagawa burst out in prayer, 'O God, make me like Christ.' And that became his life's prayer.

Kagawa knew what it was to be beaten for his faith and to suffer for Jesus. When he was in the United States on a preaching tour after the Second World War, someone who heard him preach said to a companion, 'He's not much of a preacher, is he?' 'No,' said his companion, 'but when you are hanging on a cross, you don't need to be.'

I have never been beaten for the sake of the gospel, and neither perhaps have you, but as the world becomes more and more anti-Christ, this is something we might have to face. Is Jesus able to succour us in times like this? He is! He will enable us to respond like

FURTHER STUDY

Acts 9:1–22;
Matt. 5:44;
1 Cor. 10:13;
Heb. 4:15–16

1. Who was Paul really persecuting?
2. What assurance can we take from this passage?

Stephen who 'knelt down and cried out in a loud voice, "Lord! Do not hold this sin against them!"' (v.60). Notice the phrase 'in a loud voice'. That loud voice drowned out the cries of his accusers and rang down the ages. The word of forgiveness became flesh in him as it did in Jesus. What worked for the Master worked also for the disciple.

Prayer

O Father, help me to realise that when I feel I am hanging on a cross, I don't need to say much. Things are being said – and said powerfully. I am so grateful for this truth. Help me not to just hold it, but to let it hold me. In Jesus' name. Amen.

Naked – the greatest indignity!

For reading & meditation – Matthew 27:27–31

'Then the governor's soldiers took Jesus ... and gathered the whole company of soldiers round him.' (v.27)

Another way in which the ridicule and mockery of the soldiers took their toll on Jesus was: 'They stripped him and put a scarlet robe on him' (v.28). Jesus is brought into the common hall, whereupon the group of soldiers gather around Him, strip Him of His clothes, and spit upon Him. For a few moments (we don't know how long) He stands before them – naked. What indignity! As we have considered the racial prejudice and the brutality of these soldiers this week, it seems to me that stripping Jesus of His clothes and making Him stand naked before them was the most cruel thing they could have done to Him. Those who survived the Jewish Holocaust said that their greatest indignity was not being beaten, but being stripped and forced to stand up before their captors – naked. Being forced to stand naked before the soldiers was an indignity that must have hurt Him deeply.

Indignity, according to the dictionary, is 'an affront; unmerited contemptuous treatment'. It is an action, simple in itself, and not necessarily brutal, designed to embarrass and cause great personal hurt. I wonder – have you suffered such an indignity as I am describing here? Then draw close to Jesus. He can teach you how to respond when men hurt you and humiliate you. There is no situation which, granted our willingness, He cannot work out for good. Millions down the ages have found it to be so. Like their Lord, they have learned how to deal with thorns. They wear them as a crown.

FURTHER STUDY

Acts 8:25–35;

Isa. 53:9;

Matt. 27:38;

Luke 2:7

1. In what ways was Jesus humiliated?
2. How did Jesus overcome humiliation?

Prayer

O God, You and I will have to work this out together. I am weak and shrink from all thought of indignity. But You are strong, so please – take the heavy end. This I ask in Jesus' name. Amen.

'Let evil die in me'

For reading & meditation – Romans 6:1–14

*'For we know that our old self was crucified with him …
that we should no longer be slaves to sin.' (v.6)*

T his is the last day in which we look at one of the evils Christ
faced – ridicule and mockery – and how to deal with it when it
comes our way. The message that is sounding out loud and clear is
this: when standing up to evil doesn't work, then as Christians we
have another option – we accept the suffering that evil brings and
bear it redemptively.

Let's be clear about this – bearing suffering redemptively does
not mean we adopt an attitude of resignation and say: 'Well, there's
nothing I can do, so I'll just have to sit back and take it.' That spirit,
believe me, will get you nowhere. It has in it the seeds of resentment
and animosity. There is a world of difference between that and what
I am talking about. Jesus was able to take the evils that were thrown
at Him and turn them to good because He had no animosity, no self-
pity, no hate, no resentment and no desire for revenge. When He
could not deal with evil by resisting it, He held it to Him and quelled
it in His mighty heart of love. The boomerang lost its momentum
because the venom which flew out at Him did not fly back again in
revenge.

FURTHER STUDY

James 3:1–18;

Heb. 12:15;

Eph. 4:31

1. Where do
resentment and
animosity come
from?

2. What do we need
to deal with them
effectively?

You see, evil, to be successful, needs soil into
which it can send its roots. Where there is no soil,
it withers away. 'The ruler of this world is coming',
said Jesus, 'and he has nothing in Me' (John 14:30,
NKJV). There was nowhere in Christ's nature
where evil could gain a foothold. Jesus conquered
Satan by not being like him. And so, my friend,
can you.

Prayer

O God, help me to live so that I triumph over every evil which comes my
way. Let all desire for vengeance, all desire to 'get even', die within me. For I
know that when the inner evil dies in me, then the outer evil cannot live in me.
Amen.

Peter's denial

For reading & meditation – Matthew 26:69–75

*'At that he began to curse and swear – "I tell you I don't know
the man!"…' (v.74, Phillips)*

The evil we consider this week is the one seen in the action of Peter, the disciple who denied Christ as He made His way to the cross – the evil of moral cowardice. In some ways the evil of Simon Peter's denial is akin to that of Judas's betrayal, but there is one important difference. Judas Iscariot's betrayal was premeditated and done with malice aforethought – Peter's denial was spontaneous and unpremeditated. I point this out, not to excuse Simon Peter's action, but to explain it. I sometimes wonder if Jesus was hurt more by Peter's moral cowardice than He was by Judas Iscariot's betrayal.

We are often hurt most by those we trust most, and there can be little doubt that Peter was one of Christ's most trusted disciples. When Jesus entered Jairus's house in order to raise his daughter from the dead, he selected three of His closest disciples to go with Him. And who were the three? Simon Peter, James and John. Simon Peter was also one of those chosen to witness the unveiling of Christ's glory on the Mount of Transfiguration. And he was selected again to witness the Master's sufferings in the Garden of Gethsemane. He was indeed a trusted disciple. How hurtful it must have been, then, for our Lord when, in all the accumulated pain of His passion. Simon Peter not only denies all knowledge of Him but reinforces his denial with an oath. As you may well have cause to know – nothing hurts quite like the denial of a friend.

FURTHER STUDY

Psa. 55:1–23; 41:9;
Zech. 13:6

1. How did David
respond when let
down by friends?
2. In what does he
put his confidence?

Prayer

O Father, if ever I have to face a moment when I am denied by someone whom I love and trust, help me to remember that Jesus faced that situation too. And the grace available to Him is available also to me. Help me to absorb it. In Jesus' name. Amen.

Saved by a look!

For reading & meditation – Matthew 26:57–75

'... *Peter followed Him ... to see the end.*' (v.58, NKJV)

I t is almost impossible to believe that Simon Peter, the one who appears so bold and confident in the pages of the Gospel, could deny His Lord three times and seal his denial with an oath. I wonder what made him do it? Was it disappointment that Christ had not turned the tables on His captors and overcome them by an act of divine power? Was it resentment that the Master had not forewarned him in clearer terms about what would happen? Or was it fear for his own physical safety? One thing is clear – Simon Peter saw the situation as being the termination of all his dreams. The Gospel writer captures Peter's mood in the cryptic words of our text for today – 'Peter followed Him ... to see the end.' But what Peter thought was the end turned out to be only the beginning – the beginning of a new hope for mankind.

What is significant in this whole story is not so much the moral cowardice which Peter expressed in this sad moment in his career – and I do not seek to minimise this – but the way in which Christ dealt with that evil. He saved him with a look! (Luke 22:61). What an expression of infinite tenderness and love must have been on Christ's face for it to have caused the 'Big Fisherman' to weep so bitterly. Though the pain of Peter's denial lay heavily on the heart of Jesus, He would not allow Peter's actions to determine His. And that is victory.

FURTHER STUDY

John 12:23–43;

Deut. 1:17;

Prov. 29:25;

Isa. 51:12

1. What was Peter's problem?
2. How did this problem affect the chief rulers?

Prayer

O Lord, help me to face the evil of denial and moral cowardice in the way You met it – by returning love for hate, kindness for injury and compassion for hurt. In Your name I ask it. Amen.

Pain produces a pearl

For reading & meditation – Revelation 21:9–27

'… each gate made of a single pearl.' (v.21)

The same evils which Christ met on His way to the cross will confront us as we seek to serve Him. And when they do, the divine life in us will crimson into a cross. The probability is that just as Jesus faced the evil of denial and moral cowardice so you, too, at one time or another, will be confronted by this selfsame thing. In fact, it may be that, at this moment, you are a victim of the very evil which I am describing here. Has someone whom you loved and trusted let you down by contradicting or refuting something you said or did? Have they, in an act of cowardly denial, backed down over some issue and left you in a difficult and invidious position? Then whatever you do – don't retaliate. Take the hurt to the Lord in prayer, and let Christ help you turn the pain into a pearl.

I have remarked before how intrigued I have always been with that verse in Revelation which describes the New Jerusalem as having gates of pearl. Pearl! Why pearl? Because a pearl, as you know, is a product of pain. A tiny irritant, such as a grain of sand or a microscopic parasite, sometimes gets inside the oyster, whereupon it exudes a precious secretion in order to heal the wound and save its life. The foreign irritant is covered, and thus a pearl is produced. The gates of pearl in the New Jerusalem symbolise the pain which Christ bore for us. And just as He made a pearl out of His pain, He will, by the same Spirit, enable you to make a pearl out of yours!

FURTHER STUDY

Rom. 8:13–27;

Rev. 21:4;

Job 42:10

1. In what way is the creation suffering pain?
2. How was Job's pain turned into a pearl?

Prayer

O Lord, thank You for reminding me that my pains, when covered by Your grace, become precious pearls. I rest not in the immediate – the pain itself, but in the ultimate – the pearl. Thank You, Father. Amen.

We profit from our pains

For reading & meditation – Romans 5:1–11

'… we know that suffering produces perseverance; perseverance, character; and character, hope.' (vv.3-4)

When John describes the New Jerusalem as having 'gates of pearl', this is a symbolic way of saying that the entrance to the city of God is through the wounds and suffering of Jesus. A pearl is a product, not of pleasure, but of pain. If there is no wound, there is no pearl. Remember that, those of you who are, at this moment, facing the repercussions of someone's moral cowardice and denial, or, for that matter, any other kind of evil. Pain is the possibility of greatness of soul, and the pearl symbolises triumph over it.

Now it goes without saying, I am sure, that the pain I am speaking of here is not physical pain, but spiritual and emotional pain – the pain of being misunderstood, of being the victim of someone's spite and spleen, of being let down by someone to whom you gave your confidence and in whom you deeply trusted. Most Christians clamour for the joys of the Christian life, and rightly so, but the things for which we do not clamour – the pains of life – these are the things which deepen and develop our character. 'There is a tragic element woven into the very fabric of our existence,' said one philosopher, 'and although we shrink from it, those who are wise receive it with joy saying, "If we do not have the pain – we cannot have the pearl."' The hymn writer put this truth most effectively when he wrote: 'So by my woes to be – Nearer, my God, to Thee, Nearer to Thee.'

FURTHER STUDY

Matt. 20:17–28;

Psa. 102:9;

John 18:11

1. What did Jesus say to those who wanted to be great?
2. Why could Jesus drink the cup of pain?

Prayer

Father, I am thankful that my pain becomes my servant when I am in You. It drives me to Your bosom. All things serve me when I serve You. I am so grateful. Amen.

The pain God uses

For reading & meditation – 2 Corinthians 7:1–11

'... the pain God is allowed to guide ends in a saving repentance never to be regretted ...' (v.10, Moffatt)

'If you are not willing to have the wound – you cannot have the pearl.' There is something in us that shrinks from the idea of suffering, but, mark what I say, for it is one of the most important aspects of the Christian life – unless we learn how to accept the pain of a Good Friday and stick with it until God turns it into an Easter morning, we are deprived of one of the greatest secrets in life.

In one church I pastored many years ago a woman told me of how a close friend of hers had landed her in serious financial trouble by being unwilling to confirm something she had told her many years previously. The case went to court and, in the witness box, the so-called friend not only denied all knowledge of what was said, but flatly contradicted it. It caused the woman great hurt and severe financial loss. It wasn't a wound; it was a gaping rent.

It was not until a month later that she was able to come to church, but when she walked in, we saw at once that a strange spiritual alchemy had been at work. She seemed possessed by an unearthly peace. The wound in her heart was being healed, and when I asked her to share with the church what God had done she said, 'I thought this blow would have made me a cynic, but through Christ's grace, it has become a stepping-stone to a new awareness of God and a new spiritual dimension in my life.' She joined the ranks of those who have learned their lesson from the mollusc and turned their pain into a pearl.

FURTHER STUDY

Isa. 53:1–12;
Luke 4:28–29;
Mark 6:3;
John 1:11

1. List the ways in which Christ suffered.
2. What was to come from this pain?

Prayer

O God, save me from drawing back when the turbulent seas of life drive an irritant into my shell. Help me to link my whole being to Yours so that Your grace might flow in and turn the irritant into an irradiation. In Jesus' name. Amen.

Abundant grace

For reading & meditation – 1 Peter 5:1–11

'And the God of all grace ... will himself restore you ...' (v.10)

I am often asked the question: why is it that the same trouble that turns one person sour, refines and sweetens another? The thing that is a stumbling-block to one person becomes a stepping-stone for another. Why? The answer, as I have been emphasising, is not in what happens to us but how we respond to it. How forgivable it would have been if Jesus, having been denied by Simon Peter, had turned upon him and said, 'Peter, you have been a great disappointment to me. Your thrice-repeated denial of me has disqualified you from being my disciple. I want nothing more to do with you.' You will look for such words in vain. He was hurt by what Peter did, but He did not allow Peter's action to freeze the love that flowed in His mighty heart.

If Christ had turned to Peter and had used such words as I have suggested above, then Peter would have been quick to defend himself with something like this: 'But Lord, you are to blame. You didn't warn me enough about this. You should have spelt it out more clearly. If you had, then I would have been better prepared.' Jesus, however, got behind Peter's defences without a word – just a look. And that response was a turning-point in the Big Fisherman's experience. If you can absorb the grace which Christ gives when you find yourself in the same situation of denial, then, believe me, that response can work for you also.

FURTHER STUDY

1 Pet. 1:1–12;
Psa. 66:10; 17:3;
Zech. 13:9

1. Why does God allow painful trials?
2. What are the qualities of gold, and what happens when it is heated?

Prayer

Blessed Lord Jesus, give me the grace to face denial – and die for it if necessary. Keep my soul from all bitterness, and help me to be as victorious in facing this problem as You were. Amen.

The central problem

For reading & meditation – Luke 9:18–27

'For whoever wants to save his life will lose it ...' (v.24)

Jesus calls us to do as He did – die for those who deny us. Christ cared little about what happened to Himself, but He cared deeply about what happened to others. Indeed the selflessness of His life was the whole reason for His death. His concern for others comes over in every detail of the events that moved through Maundy Thursday to Good Friday. In the high priest's palace, amid the abuse and raillery of the servants, He can turn to Simon Peter and save him with a look. In the Praetorium, His thought is so little of His sufferings that He can discuss with Pilate His mission to the world. On the way to the cross, He can turn to the women who weep for Him and say: 'Do not weep for me; weep for yourselves' (Luke 23:28).

A heart that is so occupied with a concern for others is secure against the greatest problem that afflicts the human race – selfishness and self-centredness. Take this thought on board your life at this moment as it can do more for you than anything else I have said – to be in touch with Christ is to be sensitised to unselfishness. He will deliver you from self-centredness and indifference to others. You will care so deeply what happens to others, even to those who hurt you and deny you, that you will be more concerned about them than you are about yourself. And when that happens, then believe me, you will know what victory is. The word 'Joy' in acrostic form spells out the message we all need to learn: J – Jesus first, O – Others next, Y – Yourself last.

FURTHER STUDY
John 15:1–16;
Prov. 17:17;
Eccl. 4:9–10
1. What is the
greatest expression of
love for a friend?
2. Would you
be willing to
demonstrate it?

Prayer

O Lord, what can I say? You are so skilful at throwing a dart right at my central problem – me. You wound me mortally to heal me vitally. So I accept: I surrender. Amen.

Those who ministered to Him

For reading & meditation – Matthew 25:31–40

'… whatever you did for one of the least of these brothers of mine, you did for me.' (v.40)

During the next few days I plan to divert a little from the theme that we are pursuing and consider an aspect of our Lord's last hours which is rarely discussed. Our focus has been on those who were cruel and unkind to our Master: now we shall focus on those who tried to help Him in His hour of grief, and who blessed Him with their sympathy. It is somewhat heartening to discover, amid the darkness and cruelty that surrounds the cross, that there were those who wanted to minister to Him.

I saw a television programme recently in which a mother who had lost her son in the Falklands War, sat and talked to the man who had cradled him in his arms while he died. It was obvious that she gained great comfort from the fact that in her son's last hours, there was someone with him who cared. 'Tell me every detail of his last moments,' she said. 'How did you hold him? Show me the position you were in …' and so on.

It might sound sloppy and sentimental to some, but I, too, find great comfort in the thought that in our Lord's last hours there were some, albeit only a few, who tried to mitigate His agony and bless Him with their sympathy and support. When the consummate weight of the world's wickedness – including your wickedness and mine – was laid upon the back of our Blessed Redeemer, how consoling it is to know that there were some who ministered to Him then.

FURTHER STUDY

Luke 10:25–37;
James 1:27;
Rom. 15:1

1. What was Jesus teaching in this parable?
2. Who is your neighbour?

Prayer

Father, I also find comfort in the thought that in the sombre setting of cruelty and violence that surrounded the cross, there were some who tried to help. I am so grateful for that. Amen.

That first Good Friday

For reading & meditation – Matthew 27:32

'… they met a man from Cyrene named Simon, and the soldiers forced him to carry Jesus' cross.' (v.32, GNB)

We look at the first of those who helped our Lord in His last few hours – Simon, the man who carried His cross. Tradition says that Simon of Cyrene became a Christian following that event. There is no clear evidence for this, of course, but I have often said that when I get to heaven, and have gazed for centuries on the face of my blessed Redeemer, one of the first persons I am going to look around for is Simon of Cyrene. If he is there, I intend to go up to him and say something I have been rehearsing for years: 'Thank you, Simon, for carrying my Saviour's cross.'

Some may object and say, 'But Simon was compelled to carry the cross. It was not done willingly. He was forced into it.' I know that. A man who was about to be crucified was supposed to carry his own cross to the place of execution, but Jesus, weak and exhausted by lack of sleep, a rushed trial, the lashings of the whip and the pain of the world's sin clawing at His heart, fell beneath the load. It was obvious He could not carry His cross, so the soldiers took a man out of the crowd and made him shoulder the burden.

I cannot help but feel that as Simon of Cyrene saw the piteous figure of Christ, struggling under the weight of the cross, and caught sight of the sorrow on His face, pity would have risen up in him which made him carry the cross gladly and not grudgingly. Conjecture? Well, maybe – but anyway he did carry our Saviour's cross. And I am grateful for that.

FURTHER STUDY

John 13:1–16;
Mark 10:43–44;
Gal. 6:2

1. What quality was Jesus displaying?
2. What did He instruct the disciples to do?

Prayer

O Lord Jesus, as I meditate on Your sufferings and Your pain, I am comforted to know that, to some extent at least, someone helped. Amen.

The weeping women

For reading & meditation – Luke 23:27–31

'A large number of people followed him, including women who mourned and wailed for him.' (v.27)

Today we look at the women who cried for Jesus. Theologians throughout time have been very critical of the women who stood in the Via Dolorosa and wept for our Lord as He went to His cross. One modern theologian says, 'Their tears were crocodile tears. They had no real sympathy. It was an outlet for their pent-up emotion. They were crying, not for Christ, but for themselves.' This was not our Lord's conclusion. He, who 'knew what was in man' sensed that the tears of the women were tears of real concern. 'Do not weep for me,' He said, 'weep for yourselves and for your children' (v.28).

Jesus accepted the fact that their tears were for Him – and so must we. Christ was not chiding them or reacting out of petulance and anger, as some claim, but demonstrating the security of a heart so occupied with love for others that He could pause in His own sufferings to warn them of the pain that would inevitably be theirs. But did their tears, even in some small way, console Him? We can only speculate. I know enough about my Lord to believe that He who wept at Lazarus's tomb, and knew the healing power of tears, would, in His walk to the cross, have found some solace in the action of these women.

Not everyone who stood and watched Him go to Calvary was there to scoff. Some came out of deep concern. It is the one bright spot in a setting of human failure.

FURTHER STUDY

Luke 6:17–36;

Psa. 30:5; 56:8

1. What is promised to those who weep?
2. When was the last time you wept for someone?

Prayer

Blessed Lord Jesus, I am so thankful that You manifested self-concern without a tincture of self-pity. Help me to do the same. For Your own dear name's sake. Amen.

The sympathetic soldier

For reading & meditation – Matthew 27:45–48

*'... one of them ... fetched a sponge, soaked it in vinegar ...
and held it up for him to drink.' (v.48, Phillips)*

Today we look at the soldier who moistened the lips of Jesus as He cried from the cross, 'I thirst.' Thirst, say those who have been forced to go without food and water for several days, is more terrible to bear than hunger. Picture the scene around the cross. Think of the heat, the noise, the dust – and the thirst. It is significant that the only physical torment Jesus expressed on the cross was in connection with thirst. 'I thirst,' He said. Have you ever been thirsty – really thirsty? Then you will know something of the agony that caused Jesus to utter those words.

Someone has pointed out that in the seven statements Jesus made from the cross, only one of them was in relation to Himself – and that was, 'I thirst.' What a terrible moment that must have been for Him. But, as He cried out in agony, one of the soldiers stepped forward and moistened His lips. How surprising!

Isn't it strange how, beneath a person's rough exterior, there is often a kind heart. The Bible doesn't say that mankind is incapable of doing kind and good things: it simply says that his goodness is insufficient to save him. The soldier's action does not absolve him from complicity in the death of Christ, but from where I stand now, surveying the agony that Jesus bore on Calvary, I cannot help but feel grateful to that soldier who relieved His thirst.

FURTHER STUDY
John 7:14–38;
Isa. 44:3; 55:1
1. What was Jesus'
announcement to the
crowd?
2. What is God's
promise?

Prayer

Lord Jesus, I am so grateful that though You had the power to come down from the cross, yet You bore its suffering and shame – just for me. Blessed be Your name forever. Amen.

The Jerusalem guild

For reading & meditation – Matthew 27:33–34

'… they offered Jesus wine to drink, mixed with gall …' (v.34)

A s we continue looking at the people who ministered to our Lord in his last hours, we come to a group of people who tried to ease His sufferings by offering Him some drugged wine. Crucifixion, as you know, was common in the days of Jesus, and because of the awful suffering that crucifixion caused, a few women in Jerusalem got together to form a benevolent guild. They concocted a special drink which contained a drug so that those who were crucified might have the edge taken off their agony. This was the drink they offered to Jesus. Our Lord refused it, of course, because if He was to redeem mankind then it was necessary for Him to plumb the depths of physical, mental and spiritual pain – and to experience that, He needed an unclouded mind.

I have no doubt, however, that our Lord, whose eye was always quick to detect an attitude of love and concern, would have judged their deed by its intention, and let it warm His heart. Remember how He chided Judas Iscariot for misunderstanding the motives of Mary of Bethany when she poured the costly perfume over His head? Jesus saw in her action a ministry of love and concern, and was greatly comforted by her extravagance. I think He must have felt something similar in that awful moment on the cross. He refused the drugged wine, but He would have seen the purpose behind the action – and that purpose would have comforted Him. If it did that for only a moment, I am grateful to those women for doing it.

FURTHER STUDY

Luke 7:31–50;

Prov. 31:20;

2 Kings 4:9–10;

Matt. 27:55

1. What did Jesus say to Simon?
2. What does this teach us?

Prayer

O Jesus, teach me how to look beyond life's events and see, as You did, the real intention of people's hearts. Give me an eye that is quick to detect true motives. For Your own name's sake. Amen.

His family and friends

For reading & meditation – John 19:25–27

*'Near the cross of Jesus stood his mother, his mother's sister,
Mary the wife of Clopas, and Mary Magdalene.' (v.25)*

Another group of people who tried to minister to Jesus as He hung upon the cross were His family and friends. His mother was there and so was John. And then – farther off – Mary Magdalene, Mary the mother of James, and others. There was little they could do, of course, but at least they could be with Him as He died. What more can you do when a loved one is dying?

I remember reading a newspaper report about a young man called Richard Aldridge, a 20-year-old university student, who was attacked and killed by a gang of hooligans after having been to watch his favourite football team. His father, Peter Aldridge, said that the thing that distressed him most was the fact that, while his son lay dying in hospital, 'he didn't know that we were there with him'.

The most frequent request of people about to die is to ask their relatives: 'Stay with me … stay with me.' They know there is little that their relatives can do, but just for them to be there is enough. Would it have comforted Jesus, when looking down from the cross, to have caught sight of His mother and His friends? I believe it would. They were saying, by their physical presence at the cross, 'We are powerless to ease Your suffering or to minister to Your pain, but whatever shame You are bearing, whatever agony You are carrying … as far as we are able … we want to share it too.' And I am deeply grateful to them for standing by Him and sharing, as deeply as they could, His grief and His pain.

FURTHER STUDY

Gal. 6:1–10;
Mark 10:43–44;
Luke 10:36–37
1. What are we to carry?
2. How can we achieve greatness?

Prayer

Lord Jesus, the more I survey Your agony on the cross, the more amazed I am at the love that led You to suffer there. Truly it is love without limit. I am eternally grateful. Amen.

'Christians ... people who care'

For reading & meditation – Matthew 27:36

'... they sat there and watched him.' (v.36, GNB)

We have been looking at the various evils which confronted Christ on His way to Calvary, and we have been saying that here in the twenty-first century, we have to live out our lives in the presence of these selfsame evils. Today we look at the eighth evil – the evil of indifference. I know of no crueller words in the whole of history than those which are before us today: 'they sat there and watched him'. Some among the crowd who gathered around Christ at the cross felt neither anger nor pity, but simply sat in stolid indifference and watched Him go through His agonies.

In some ways it is easier to meet opposition than indifference. A minister I talked to recently, who had suffered a nervous breakdown, told me that it had been caused by the indifference of his congregation. Now a nervous breakdown has much deeper roots than that, I know, but as he talked to me, I sensed that here was a man who could face the stoutest opposition – but indifference ... ah, that was another issue.

How should we act when faced with indifference? We do as Jesus did, and go on caring. One definition of a Christian I once heard struck a chord in my heart. It was this: 'A Christian is a person who cares for people who do not care.'

Love does not change, no matter the changes in the other person.

FURTHER STUDY

Luke 17:11–19;

Psa. 123:4;

Isa. 32:9

1. What attitude did the nine lepers display?
2. Are you indifferent to God's goodness?

Prayer

Blessed Lord Jesus, You who kept on caring even when the multitude sat in open-mouthed indifference and watched You dying on the cross – help me to care like that. In Your name. Amen.

He cared – that's enough

For reading & meditation – Matthew 5:38–48

'… Love your enemies and pray for those who persecute you.'
(v.44)

Yesterday we asked the question: how do we react when faced with the evil of indifference? The answer is, with God's help, to keep on caring. To allow others to determine our life and attitude is to become a mere reflection – the sum total of the attitudes of others. Perhaps we will have to do as one modern saint has suggested, 'Be so humble that you cannot be humiliated.'

Are you surrounded by indifference at the moment? Is everything you love being trampled upon with indifference? Are your words, your actions, and everything else you are trying to do in order to bring people to Christ, meeting with nothing but indifferent stares? What is important is not so much whether or not people respond, but that you do not lose your ability to care.

Years ago a highly-trained doctor gave up his practice in Europe and became a medical missionary. While attending typhus cases, he was himself stricken and ravaged by the disease. His efforts to help others were brought to a halt but, one day, after hearing that a woman would die in childbirth unless a Caesarian operation was performed, he asked his friends to carry him into the operating room. As he operated, his friends supported him on either side, and he saved the life of the woman and her baby. But the shock was too much for him – in two days he died. He cared. It is said that the woman whose life he saved didn't appear to care that he had given his life for her and her baby. He did – that is enough.

FURTHER STUDY

Matt. 22:1–14;
Amos 6:1;
James 4:17

1. How did those who were first invited respond?
2. How does James sum up indifference?

Prayer

O Father, when my love and concern is trampled into the dust by indifference, then help me quietly to go on and await Your process of resurrection. In Jesus' name I ask it. Amen.

'Love never fails'

For reading & meditation – 1 Corinthians 13:1–13

'Love never fails ...' (v.8)

It takes great courage and dedication to keep loving when we are up against a solid wall of indifference. But Jesus did – and in His strength, so can you. 'I can handle anything – but indifference,' writes a missionary. 'When people criticise me or contradict me or even get angry at me, I can respond to it with equanimity and poise. But when they say nothing but just sit and stare, then that, more than anything, makes my hackles rise.'

It's not hard to understand why people often find it easier to face opposition than indifference. Opposition brings out our fighting spirit. We have something to grapple with, something to focus on, and something against which we can measure ourselves. But indifference is another matter. It puts up no fight – it simply stands there, shows no feeling and refuses to budge.

The way to overcome indifference is found in first being willing to accept the pain it brings, then continuing to love and care in the strength which Christ gives. There is a cross waiting for all those who go on caring in the face of indifference. You will be hurt and deeply wounded – but if you go on caring, then even if your love does not meet with a response, you will be the better for it. Can you see what I am saying? If your love and care seem to do nothing for others, then most certainly they are doing something for you. 'Love never fails.' And it's true. If others don't respond to your love, you will still be the better for loving.

FURTHER STUDY

2 Cor. 5:1–15;
John 15:9;
Rom. 8:35–36

1. How does love 'compel' us?
2. What did this mean for Paul?

Prayer

O Father, imprint this truth in the depths of my spirit so that, from this time forward, I will never again doubt the power of love. It may fail to affect the one who receives, but it can never fail to affect the one who gives. Thank You, dear Father. Amen.

Life's greatest challenge

For reading & meditation – Philippians 2:1–13

'Your attitude should be the same as that of Christ Jesus.' (v.5)

How did Jesus overcome indifference? Not by adopting the same attitude, but by continuing to love and care.

Just imagine what would have happened if Jesus had met the indifference of the multitude with similar indifference. What, if looking down from the cross upon those who sat there stolid and indifferent, He had said: 'Are these the people for whom I am dying?' and then, calling upon divine power, had stepped down from the cross and walked away? One thing is certain – we would be eternally lost. Jesus, however, met the indifference of the multitude with care and consideration, and He bids those who are His followers to do the same.

The Moffatt translation of the verse before us today says: 'Treat one another with the same spirit as you experience in Christ Jesus.' How does Christ treat us? With love, with care and with consideration. The Amplified New Testament puts it this way – 'Let Him be your example in humility.' A little boy in Sunday School, when asked to give the meaning of humility, said, 'Letting people walk all over you'. Was he right? I believe in a way he was. But, you say, 'I believe in standing up for my rights and not letting others push me around.' Well, it is a good thing to stand up for your rights, but there are times when, for the sake of others, God will ask you to lay them down. And being sensitive to that issue is perhaps the greatest challenge in the Christian life.

FURTHER STUDY

Luke 14:25–35;

Matt. 16:24; 10:16;

Rom. 15:1

1. What did Jesus teach about self-denial?
2. What was Jesus' advice to the disciples?

Prayer

Lord Jesus, help me never to let other people's conduct and attitudes determine mine. Show me that I cannot lose by being loving, even though my love is not accepted or returned. Amen.

'It's tomorrow!'

For reading & meditation – Isaiah 25:1–9

'... The Sovereign LORD will wipe away the tears from all faces ...' (v.8)

We come now to consider Christ's crucifixion itself. We have to ask ourselves: is the cross God's last word? No! God's last word in human affairs is not the cross, but the resurrection – not defeat, but victory. A newspaper editor who was a Christian said to his team of journalists: 'On one side of my desk is a typewriter, and on the other is a Bible. I try to make the two sides of this desk speak the same thing. For I know if what I write in my editorials coincides with what is in that book, it will live on: if it doesn't – it will perish.' That, I think, sums up our Christian faith. Everything that is right has 'resurrection' stamped on it: everything that is wrong has 'death' stamped on it.

Brother Bashford, a great missionary, was asked why he lived out his life in obscurity in China when he could have been an influential bishop in the West. He replied simply, 'Because I believe in the resurrection.' He buried himself in China, knowing that obscurity was not the last word. And that 'resurrection' he believed in became a fact. His work lived on. A little boy, travelling for the first time by train, was whisked unexpectedly into a dark tunnel. When the train emerged into brilliant sunshine, he looked at his mother and said, 'It's tomorrow!' On Good Friday, Christ went into a dark tunnel, but on Easter Day He emerged victorious. This, then, is the message our hearts should echo when we think of the crucifixion. Look out for tomorrow!

FURTHER STUDY

Acts 2:14–40;
Rom. 4:25;
1 Cor. 15:3–4;
Eph. 1:19b–20

1. What was Peter's central theme?
2. What was the response?

Prayer

O God, how grateful I am that Easter Day, and not Good Friday, is the last word. I salute the dawning of this day with joy, for I have the dawn within me. Hallelujah!

Where it all ends

For reading & meditation – Revelation 5:1–14

'Then I saw a Lamb, looking as if it had been slain, standing in the centre of the throne ...' (v.6)

In a world where evil exists, a cross is inevitable. It has to happen. It is a law of life that where sin collides with love and righteousness, then a cross of pain is set up. All love has the stain of blood upon it.

You may think it would be more just for the guilty to bleed and not the innocent. But there is a justice that is higher than legal justice – it is the justice of love. The cross on which Jesus died may seem to many to be the depth of failure, but was God's way to victory It is a mystery which baffles human wisdom. No one except those whose hearts are illuminated by the Holy Spirit can comprehend it. Man's wisdom rises no higher than saying: return hate for hate and meet spite with spite. God's wisdom, however, takes an opposite line to that. It says: whenever you meet hate, respond to it with love, and whenever you meet evil, let it carry you to a cross. Everywhere that love meets sin and evil, love suffers. That is the meaning of the cross.

However, to see God's wisdom at its highest peak, we must look not only at the cross but at its aftermath – the resurrection. There God set His seal of approval on the fact that redemptive suffering is guaranteed a victory. Darkness and suffering may have to be faced for a while, but God's law of higher justice decrees that redemptive suffering will always lead to a throne. This is where Jesus ended, and when you follow in His footsteps, this is where you will end – on the throne!

> **FURTHER STUDY**
>
> Col. 1:1–23;
> Phil. 2:8;
> Heb. 12:2
>
> 1. What is ours through the blood of the cross?
> 2. Share the message of the cross with someone today.

Prayer

My Father and my God, I am so thankful that the last word is not with a cross, but with a throne. Hold this thought ever before me so that it might save me from all retreatism and defeatism. In Jesus' name I ask it. Amen.

Faith Thriving
Under
Persecution

'Another king – one Jesus'

For reading & meditation – Acts 17:1–9

'… *They are all defying Caesar's decrees, saying that there is another king, one called Jesus.' (v.7)*

We begin today a verse-by-verse study of Paul's letters to the Thessalonians. I have chosen Paul's letters to the Thessalonians because they, probably more than any other New Testament book, speak directly to the need of the Church at this present time. The apostle Paul arrived in Thessalonica during his second missionary journey, AD 52–53. The city, being the capital of Macedonia, was a thriving commercial and political centre in which Paul presented the claims of Jesus Christ and established a New Testament church. The ministry of Paul and his companions, Silas and Timothy, was cut short, however, when jealous Jews objected to them on the grounds that they were saying, 'There is another king, one called Jesus.' As a result of this, Paul and his companions were driven from the city and made their way to Corinth, from where the great apostle wrote these two inspired letters. Since Paul's departure, the Christians had faced great pressure and persecution because of their allegiance to Jesus, and his letters were written to nourish and strengthen their faith.

Is the hopelessness that is rife in this modern world getting to you? Are you under pressure because of your faith and commitment to Christ? If so, then be assured of this – to the degree that you assimilate the truth of these two letters, to that degree will you be able to stand unshaken amid a shaking world.

FURTHER STUDY

Psa. 42:1–11;
Col. 1:5;
Heb. 6:18;
1 Pet. 1:3

1. What was the psalmist's antidote for despair?
2. What did he base this on?

Prayer

O God, I am so grateful that Your Word, written close on 2,000 years ago, has the power to speak to my up-to-date needs. Make this study, not just an excursion, but an adventure. In Jesus' name. Amen.

Why the double emphasis?

For reading & meditation – 1 Thessalonians 1:1; John 14:6–14

'Paul, Silas and Timothy, To the church … in God the Father and the Lord Jesus Christ.' (1 Thess. 1:1)

Try to imagine the atmosphere that would be created in your church by the news that next Sunday morning a letter from the apostle Paul would be read out. Think how crowded the room would be, and how everyone would hang upon his every word. Be assured, as we said yesterday, that the words in this letter are as relevant today as they were when they were first written. Paul writes on behalf of all three members of the team who originally took the gospel to Thessalonica, and addresses the believers there as 'the church of the Thessalonians in God the Father and the Lord Jesus Christ'.

Notice the double emphasis Paul uses here: the church which is in God the Father and in the Lord Jesus Christ. In this greeting, Paul maintains an emphasis on both God and Christ. Paul often varied his greeting to the New Testament churches – sometimes calling them the 'church of God' (1 Cor. 1:2) or the 'saints … the faithful in Christ Jesus' (Eph. 1:1), but here the emphasis on both Christ and God is maintained. This is a truth that must not be overlooked, for, as someone said, 'God without Christ is a question mark; Christ without God is a question mark. The two together make an exclamation mark!' We must be careful not to lose sight of the fact that the Church belongs both to God and to Christ. When we belong to God, we belong to Christ, and when we belong to Christ, we belong to God. Together this must form the most exciting exclamation the world has ever known!

FURTHER STUDY

John 17:1–26;
Psa. 68:5;
Isa. 64:8;
Rom. 8:15

1. What characteristics of God does Paul emphasise?
2. How is this seen through Jesus' prayer?

Prayer

O God my Father, in You I see Christ, and in Christ I see God. The vision is so satisfying that I need go no further. This is it. I am eternally thankful. Amen.

You can count on it!

**For reading & meditation – 1 Thessalonians 1:1–10;
2 Corinthians 12:1–10**

'… Grace and peace to you.' (1 Thess. 1:1)

Paul continues with another double emphasis: 'Grace and peace
to you from God our Father and the Lord Jesus Christ' (NIV
footnote). Why this continued double emphasis? He is attempting
to show, so I believe, that the unity which exists between the Father
and the Son is the model on which the Church should base its life
and practice. Suppose God acted in one way and Christ acted in
another – what would be the result? It would produce a disturbance
that would reverberate from one end of the cosmos to the other. Our
eternal salvation and security depend on the fact that both Christ
and God, and, of course, the Holy Spirit, are in perfect unity, perfect
harmony and perfect agreement. Although the three members of
the Trinity have different names, functions and activities within the
Godhead, yet they co-exist in perfect harmony. And from that unity
flows grace and peace.

Just imagine what it would be like if there were no perfect unity
in the Trinity! Our prayer life would be the first thing to be sabotaged.
We would never be sure of their undivided willingness to give us what
we ask. Disunity in heaven would demoralise and
even destroy the Christian Church on earth. But
have no fear, grace and peace will continue to flow
into our lives with unfailing power because they
come from a source which knows no disunity or
disharmony. No matter what shortages there are
on earth, there will never be a shortage of grace
and peace. You can count on it!

FURTHER STUDY
Eph. 1:1–14;
2 Cor. 8:9;
2 Tim. 2:1;
1 Tim. 1:14
1. List some of the
'riches of God's
grace'.
2. Write out your
own definition
of grace.

Prayer

O God, I've been meagre and afraid – afraid my resources would run dry if I
used them. Help me to draw heavily upon Your resources and live by them. In
Jesus' name I ask it. Amen.

'A singing in men's blood'

For reading & meditation – 1 Thess. 1:2–3; 1 Cor. 13:1–13

'… your work produced by faith, your labour prompted by love … your endurance inspired by hope …' (1 Thess. 1:3)

I love the way J. B. Phillips translates this verse: 'for we never forget that your faith has meant solid achievement, your love has meant hard work, and the hope that you have in the Lord Jesus Christ means sheer dogged endurance.' It is an amazing fact that Paul, writing to different churches on the same subject, rarely repeated himself. Here, he picks out three things he had mentioned before (faith, hope, love) and presents them in a fresh and exciting way: 'work produced by faith', 'labour prompted by love' and 'endurance inspired by hope'. Notice that all three are to be found 'in our Lord Jesus Christ'.

Is it possible for non-Christians to have these three qualities? I think so. But they all lack something. Being 'in Christ', however, puts life into everything. It puts faith into our work, love into our labour, and hope into our endurance.

A missionary suggested to an official that the basis of a project he had started might be broadened to take in non-Christians. The official said: 'You Christians started this, so you had better keep it up. For what you begin you complete. Even when you get discouraged – you never quit.' And the reason why they never quit was because they were close to:

FURTHER STUDY

James 2:1–26;

Matt. 5:16;

1 Pet. 2:12;

Eph. 2:8–9

1. What is the balance between faith and works?
2. How are you demonstrating your faith with works?

> The pierced side of One,
> Who died upon an ancient hill,
> And left a singing in men's blood.

Prayer

O Father, You have put a song within my blood, too. And that song is one of being able to endure to the end. Help me to go through life singing this song – today and every day. For Your own dear name's sake. Amen.

How are we chosen?

For reading & meditation – 1 Thessalonians 1:4; John 15:18–22

'For we know, brothers loved by God, that he has chosen you.'
(1 Thess. 1:4)

This verse raises an issue which perplexes a great number of Christians and leads to much heated debate – the mystery of divine election. Permit me to share with you how I see this important issue. As I have said before, there are two rails running through Scripture – one is the sovereignty of God, the other, the freedom of the human will – and they run on parallel lines. If you try to run along one and ignore the other, then you will get derailed. There can be no doubt that God has the power to choose anyone He wishes to become His child – but will He use that power? No. None of God's attributes operate in a vacuum – He chooses in accordance with other aspects of His character. And one of those aspects is His respect for the freedom of the human will. God will not coerce or force anyone to become His child, but pursues them with love, compassion and, above all, a respect for their individual freedom of choice.

What, then, is the basis for God's choice? This. Long before we were born, God foresaw that we would respond to His offer of salvation in Christ, and on the basis of that foreknowledge, chose us and fitted us into Christ 'before the foundation of the world'. Notice, 'before the foundation of the world' and not 'from the foundation of the world'. God's purposes that began before the world was created, will continue after the world ends. We are saved, not merely for time, but for eternity.

FURTHER STUDY
1 Cor. 1:17–31;
Acts 22:14;
Eph. 1:4;
2 Thess. 2:13
1. What kind of people does God choose?
2. Why does He choose them?

Prayer

O Father, let this truth burn within me today – that I am a chosen child of God. And my destiny is written, not in the stars, but in the Son. Oh, glory! Amen.

Not just a word

For reading & meditation – 1 Thess. 1:5; 1 Cor. 2:1–4

*'because our gospel came to you not simply with words, but
also with power ...' (1 Thess. 1:5)*

Today the apostle tells us that his ministry among them was not based on good sermonising, but upon the energy and power of the Holy Spirit. The ministry that changes and challenges God's people is one that goes beyond good sermon construction – and one which only the Holy Spirit can accomplish. Far too many preachers are concerned with the mechanics of preaching, rather than the dynamics of it. Sermon construction is helpful and important, but there is much more to preaching than homiletical artistry and form.

Some time ago I listened to a preacher who showed great genius in the way he presented his message, but when it was all over I felt as if I was standing by a well which had run dry. There was a lot to captivate my mind, but little to feed my soul. If this sounds like carping criticism, let me hasten to add that there have been times in my own ministry when people might have said the same about me. While God does not ignore form and symmetry in a sermon, what gives it its cutting edge is the power and energy of the Holy Spirit.

I heard recently of a church whose minister had a mighty encounter with the Holy Spirit. One family said: 'Prior to this, our family would sit around the dinner table on Sundays and say, "What a wonderful preacher." Now we say, "What a wonderful Saviour."' Before the Spirit came upon their minister, they were only preacher-conscious. Now, however, they were Christ-conscious. The Spirit made the difference.

FURTHER STUDY

Psa. 119:1–48;

Matt. 7:28–29;

Jer. 5:14, 23:29;

Ezek. 37:7

1. How did the psalmist regard God's Word?
2. Why were the crowd amazed at Jesus' teaching?

Prayer

O God, I am so grateful for those whom You have called to preach and teach the Scriptures. Flood them with Your Spirit today – my own minister included – so that they might preach not just a word, but a word of power. Amen.

To the tune of 'suffering'

For reading & meditation – 1 Thessalonians 1:6; Acts 18:1–8

*'… in spite of severe suffering, you welcomed the message
with the joy given by the Holy Spirit.'* (1 Thess. 1:6)

Is it really possible to receive the word with JOY in spite of
suffering and persecution? Thank God – it is! I was intrigued
with Psalm 53 in the Moffatt translation which reads: 'From the
Choirmaster's collection "To the tune of Suffering"'. Many today,
as in Paul's day, live their lives to the 'tune of suffering' – that is the
dominant note. We need to keep in mind that the suffering they
endured was not physical sickness, but the suffering that came from
being persecuted, ridiculed and misunderstood.

The Christian faith does not promise exemption from suffering.
How could it, when at its heart is a cross? There, the purest heart
that ever beat writhed in an agony of unmerited suffering. How will
we cope with the suffering which persecution brings? The answer is
found in the very cross where Jesus took the worst thing that could
happen to Him – the crucifixion – and made it into the best thing
that could happen to the world – its redemption. When you can take
the worst and turn it into the best, then you are safe. You can stand
anything because you can use anything.

Did you notice, in today's second reading,
that when Paul was abused in the synagogue, he
went next door where some miraculous things
were happening? Even Crispus, the ruler of the
synagogue, believed! Paul used his opposition as
an opportunity. One door shut, another – a bigger
one – opened. This is victory! No wonder such a
message can be received with joy.

FURTHER STUDY

1 Pet. 2:1–25;

Acts 5:41;

Rom. 8:17;

1 Pet. 5: 10

*1. How did Jesus
respond to suffering?
2. How should we
respond to it?*

Prayer

O Father, help me, whenever I am under pressure, not to whine to be released,
but to ask for strength to turn the hell into a heaven and to make even sadness
sing. For Jesus' sake I pray. Amen.

'Crazy logic'

For reading & meditation – 1 Thessalonians 1:7–8; Acts 14:1–7

'And so you became a model to all the believers ...'
(1 Thess. 1:7)

Because the Christians at Thessalonica had a faith that could turn every opposition into opportunity, they were able, despite fierce persecution, to receive the message with joy. What was the result? This: 'The Lord's message rang out from you not only in Macedonia and Achaia – your faith in God has become known everywhere' (1 Thess. 1:8). The news of how these young Christians reacted to persecution was carried far and wide, and believers everywhere took courage from the fact that they had a faith that could withstand persecution.

Let this thought take root in your spirit: everything furthers the Christian – everything! The second passage we read states: '... the Jews who refused to believe ... poisoned their minds against the brothers. So Paul and Barnabas spent considerable time there speaking boldly for the Lord ...' (vv.2–3). This is what Halford Luccock calls 'crazy logic': 'The Jews ... poisoned their minds ... so Paul and Barnabas spent considerable time there ...' One would have thought it should have read: 'So they left', rather than they 'spent considerable time there'. Yesterday we read that Paul went next door when he was persecuted.

In both cases, staying where they were or going next door, the disciples were in command of the situation. They were flexible, and sensed how to get the best out of every situation. What a gospel! Sometimes we stay put and win: other times we move on and win. But either way, we win. This is victory. Incorrigible victory.

FURTHER STUDY

Acts 1:1–11;
Mark 16:15–16;
Matt. 24:14;
Rev. 14:6

1. What is the great commission?
2. How can we fulfil it?

Prayer

Gracious Father, let this thought dominate my mind from now on – that as the eagle rises against the wind, so I shall rise against all the resistances that life throws at me. Thank You, Father. Amen.

'To serve and wait'

For reading & meditation – 1 Thess. 1:9–10; Isa. 40:27–31

'… to serve the living and true God, and to wait for his Son from heaven …' (1 Thess. 1:9–10)

C hristians at Thessalonica had been converted from a life of idolatry to serve the true and living God. Now the apostle spells out for them the true Christian position – 'to serve and to wait'. Suppose he had used only the first of those words – 'to serve'. The Christians would have embarked upon so much activity that they would have become utterly exhausted. But what if he had just said 'wait'? They would have lapsed into apathy and indolence and, in no time, their spiritual experience would have dried up.

His advice to 'serve and wait' was inspired by the Holy Spirit, because it takes both these aspects to maintain spiritual balance. To serve without waiting produces Christians who are continually working, but have no time to enjoy and develop a rich relationship with the Lord. To wait without serving produces spiritual lethargy and lack of fruit.

When we serve and wait, however, we align ourselves with the heartbeat of the universe, and we absorb the provision of a loving God who has geared our lives to the principle of work and rest. Some Christians are good at working, but not very good at waiting. Others are good at waiting, but not very good at working. The balanced Christian looks at life from this two-fold perspective, knowing that there is a work to be done, but that the work to be done must be accomplished without stress. One poet wrote: 'To walk with God no strength is lost – walk on. To wait for God no time is lost – wait on.'

FURTHER STUDY

John 13:1–17;
Psa. 2:11;
Heb. 12:28;
Matt. 10:42

1. How did Jesus demonstrate the heart of a servant?
2. To what did He equate happiness?

Prayer

Heavenly Father, help me not to be geared to my inner drives that push me forward into ceaseless activity, but to the very heartbeat of the universe that knows when to work and when to wait. In Jesus' name I pray. Amen.

A trustee – greatly approved

For reading & meditation – 1 Thess. 2:1–4; 2 Cor. 5:16–21

'... we speak as men approved by God to be entrusted with the gospel ...' (1 Thess. 2:4)

In this section Paul reveals something of the power that motivated him in his life and witness for Jesus Christ. He says that no sooner was he set free from his bonds in Philippi than straight away he moved to Thessalonica to preach the gospel to the citizens there. It seemed that suffering and persecution sharpened rather than blunted the edge of his witness. However strongly the winds of adversity blew, they were, by the set of Paul's sail, made to contribute to his forward direction. One biographer, tracing Paul's great journeys across the ancient world says, 'Following Paul on his missionary journeys is like tracing the track of a bleeding hare across the snow. He left his blood in almost every place he visited.' A slightly exaggerated but nevertheless understandable statement.

What was it that moved Paul so deeply as to commit himself with such untiring devotion and dedication to the task of bringing Christ to the men and women of his day? It was this – 'we speak as men approved by God to be entrusted with the gospel'. Paul saw himself as a trustee of the riches of God in Christ. Nothing could compete with the honour and wonder of distributing those riches to the spiritually starving and hungry of his day. You may have heard of the missionary who was accompanied by a tourist as she worked among the poor in a large Indian city. 'I wouldn't do this for a million dollars,' said the tourist. 'Neither would I,' said the missionary. 'I do it for Christ.'

FURTHER STUDY

Acts 2:4–36;

Prov. 16:7;

Heb. 11:5; 13:16;

2 Tim. 2:15

1. What was Peter's testimony about Jesus?

2. What did Paul exhort Timothy to do?

Prayer

O Father, impress upon me the fact that I, too, am a trustee of the riches You have deposited in Christ. And help me never to do for gold what I wouldn't do for You. In Jesus' name. Amen.

'Tender loving care'

For reading & meditation – 1 Thess. 2:5–8; 2 Tim. 2:22–26

*'… we were gentle among you, like a mother caring for her
little children.' (1 Thess. 2:7)*

'**W**ords,' said the great writer Emerson, 'are like the tell-tale puffs
of smoke that hover over a volcano, letting you know there
is a fire burning beneath.' Our text today throbs with the passion
and intensity that burned in the heart of the great apostle toward
those whom he had won to Christ. The great longing of Paul's heart
for the converts at Thessalonica was that they might develop into
strong and healthy believers – and he applied himself to this end
with tender loving care. The Amplified Bible says: 'But we behaved
gently when we were among you, like a devoted mother nursing and
cherishing her own children.'

Many new Christians are being received into our churches as a
result of initiatives such as Alpha. The challenge facing us is this – will
we mother them or will we smother them? 'The Christian Church',
said someone, 'has many obstetricians, but few paediatricians.' He
meant that while we are good at bringing people into the Church,
we are not so good at helping them grow.

I regret to say this, but it will undoubtedly happen – some
new converts will suffer from stunted spiritual
development because they will be directed into
churches where the delicate needs of the newborn
are neither catered for nor understood. A sign I
saw in an Indian hospital read: 'Patients treated
here with tender love and care.' I almost wish a
sign similar to this could be hung outside all our
churches: 'New converts treated here with tender
love and care.'

FURTHER STUDY

Gal. 5:1–6:2;
Titus 3:2;
James 3:17

1. What does the
Holy Spirit produce?
2. List several
ways in which you
can demonstrate
gentleness.

Prayer

O Father, give me a sensitive and caring nature that can feel the slightest conflict
in the heart of a new Christian and nurse them through it. In Jesus' name I
pray. Amen.

Paul's 'motherly' care

For reading & meditation – 1 Thess. 2:9–10; Acts 20:33–35

*'Surely you remember, brothers, our toil and hardship; we
worked night and day … (1 Thess. 2:9)*

The care of converts is as demanding as that of nurturing a
newborn baby. A bottle of milk every few hours, washing lines
always full, broken or sleepless nights – the whole daily routine has
to be altered to suit the baby's needs. Most parents, however, gladly
give themselves to the task because their love for their offspring is all-
consuming. How ready are you to give up some of your routines for
the sake of the young converts who are coming into the Church?

When Dr Altizer, the founder of the 'God is Dead' movement,
was asked if he had helped anyone with his theories, he replied,
'I am not a counselling pastor; I am a theologian.' In his view,
theologians are not supposed to help people, they simply debate
abstractions about God and life. There is something wrong with a
theology that simply concerns itself with theories and is unwilling
to get alongside people and help them with their problems. Paul's
theology led him to great self-sacrifice; he even worked 'day and
night' so that his converts would not have to contribute to his keep.
There is no true spiritual caring without self-sacrifice and self-giving,
and unless we are prepared to face such things as
upset routines, disappointments, endless hours
of patient correction and training, the draining
of our own spiritual resources, agonising hours
of intercessory prayer, then what right have we
to call ourselves the followers of Jesus Christ. He
cared – so must we!

FURTHER STUDY

Luke 10:25–37;

Matt. 16:25;

1 Cor. 10:24;

Phil. 2:4

*1. How did Jesus
illustrate care and
concern?*
*2. Write out your
definition of
compassion.*

Prayer

Lord Jesus, You who cared so much that You stooped from the highest heights
to the lowest depths – help me to care like that. For Your own dear name's sake
I ask it. Amen.

Paul's fatherly care

For reading & meditation – 1 Thess. 2:11–12; Eph. 1:15–19

'For you know that we dealt with each of you as a father ...'
(1 Thess. 2:11)

Paul likened himself to a mother, nursing and cherishing her children. He also acted as a father nurturing his children. Great wisdom was needed in helping these young believers along the Christian path. They had to learn how to stand on their own feet, how to react when roughly treated, and how to discipline themselves for greater effectiveness. This kind of nurturing needed a fatherly touch. Within a family, a father's role is different from that of a mother. I know that modern-day society would argue with this view and claim that masculine and feminine roles are nothing more than cultural stereotypes. My belief is that these roles are clearly identified in scripture and are rooted in the act of creation. A child needs to see a clear model of masculinity and femininity if they are to develop properly, and where these roles are blurred or indistinct, all kinds of problems can occur.

Paul not only modelled the characteristics of a mother – gentleness and affection – but those of a father also – firmness mingled with encouragement. Notice, I say firmness mingled with encouragement. Some fathers are firm, but do not know how to encourage. Others encourage, but do not know how to be firm. Paul combined many characteristics in his personality – hence his success. In a church, as well as in a family, the characteristics of motherliness and fatherliness must be in evidence, for without them the scale is tipped toward deprivation and maladjustment.

FURTHER STUDY

2 Cor. 11:21b–12:19;

1 Cor. 4:16;

Phil. 3:17;

2 Thess. 3:9

1. List some of Paul's characteristics.
2. What did he boast about?

Prayer

O Father, make me a deeply sensitive and spiritual person, for I see that the more I am adjusted, the less new Christians will be maladjusted. This I ask in Jesus' name. Amen.

A Bible-believing community

For reading & meditation – 1 Thess. 2:13; 2 Tim. 3:10–17

'… you accepted it not as the word of men, but as it actually is, the word of God …' (1 Thess. 2:13)

'The Christian Church,' says a modern-day writer, 'must realise that it exists in this world under combat conditions. It is surrounded and outnumbered by a world that is continually seeking to bring it into a state of siege. Therefore, the Church needs enormous resources and energy to survive.' The church in Thessalonica was not just surviving – but thriving. Their strength and endurance, it seems, stemmed from one thing above all others – their unconditional acceptance of the Word of God. The Thessalonians recognised that Paul and his companions were not the authors of the good news, but the announcers of it; the truth originated in God.

What a transformation would take place if every church accepted the Bible in the same way as those Christians in Thessalonica. Many do, but there are growing numbers of churches which, on their own admission, are going through what they call 'a crisis of confidence in the Scriptures'. This simply means they do not believe the Bible to be the inerrant and authoritative Word of God. They ignore the bits they don't like, avoid the parts that are too demanding and question the reliability of some passages. Let's be clear about this – any church which is unsure that the Bible is the Word of God will soon lose its sense of mission and its spiritual drive. The church at Thessalonica was not disrupted by inner doubts or imprisoned in a cage of question marks. It was sure of God, and, therefore, sure of itself.

FURTHER STUDY

Col. 2:1–15;

Acts 17:11, 2:42;

Matt. 13:23

1. *What was Paul's desire for the Colossians?*
2. *What was the testimony of the Thessalonian church?*

Prayer

O Father, reinforce within me the conviction that the Bible is the Word of God. Help me to saturate my inner thinking with Your mind, until I cannot tell where my mind ends and where Yours begins. In Jesus' name. Amen.

No good unless taken

For reading & meditation – 1 Thess. 2:13; Col. 3:12–17

'… which is at work in you who believe.' (1 Thess. 2:13)

A church unsure of the Bible's authority will soon lose its spiritual drive and sense of mission. The churches who engage in enthusiastic evangelism are, almost without exception, churches who accept the Bible as the eternal, inerrant and authoritative Word of God. When we take the Bible seriously, then we take evangelism seriously. The one follows from the other as naturally as night follows day.

The final part of the verse we are focusing on tells us that because the Thessalonian Christians accepted the Word of God as authoritative, it was at work within them. 'God's Word', said someone, 'is never hot air; it is the steam which drives the turbine.' Once you let the Word of God come in, then, believe me, it will not remain stagnant but will be active in your mind, your soul and even your body.

A young man I know, who at one time loved the Bible and drank every day from its exhaustless depths, entered a liberal theological college where his view of Scripture as inerrant was challenged. Gradually he absorbed the view of his tutors, gave up his daily Quiet Time, and came to look at the Bible as nothing more than inspired literature. Within a year or two, he gave up all thought of the Christian ministry and instead took up another profession. I have known many follow a similar pattern. Our view of Scripture is crucial to the extent of our spiritual growth and energy. How can the Word work in us if it can't get into us?

FURTHER STUDY
2 Pet. 1:1–21;
2 Tim. 2:15; 3:16;
Deut. 6:6

1. What was Peter's testimony about the Scripture?
2. What was Paul's instruction to Timothy?

Prayer

O Father, forgive me that so often I complain that I lack spiritual energy when the real reason is that I have not taken my daily vitamins. Help me to realise that Your Word is like medicine – it will do me no good unless I take it in. Amen.

The importance of a name

For reading & meditation – 1 Thessalonians 2:14; John 21:15–17

'For you brothers, became imitators of God's churches …
which are in Christ Jesus …' (1 Thess. 2:14)

Paul now draws on another illustration from the family to describe his relationship to the converts at Thessalonica – brother. As an apostle and founder of the church at Thessalonica, Paul had a great responsibility toward his converts; he was both a nursing mother and an encouraging father. But there was a sense in which these young Christians were on the same level as him, and it is this he seeks to bring out in the word 'brother'.

It is important to see that although we do not all have equal roles in the Church of Jesus Christ, we all have the same status. The word 'brother' is used quite often in the New Testament. It occurs, for example, 21 times in these two letters to the Thessalonians, and it reminds us that 'in Christ' we are closely related to each other. As I have said before, there are no strangers in the Church of Jesus Christ – only brothers and sisters whom we haven't met yet.

We should be careful, however, about over-use of this term. It is right and proper to use it whenever we want to stress the intimate relationship or equal status that exists between members of the Body of Christ, but we should not use it as a substitute for a person's name. When someone calls me 'brother', I begin to wonder if they have either forgotten my name or have some reason for being displeased with me. Jesus addressed Simon by name. We deprive a person of something when we deprive them of their name.

FURTHER STUDY

Gen. 32:1–32;
Luke 10:20;
John 1:42;
Rev. 2:17; 3:12

1. What was the significance of Jacob's change of name?
2. What can we rejoice about?

Prayer

Father, help me to understand the deep importance of names and their effect upon our beings. If I am to be loving, then let me see it in the right terms. For Jesus' sake. Amen.

The north wind made the Vikings

For reading & meditation – 1 Thess. 2:14–16; Rom. 8:28–39

'You suffered from your own countrymen the same things those
churches suffered from the Jews ...' (1 Thess. 2:14)

The Christians at Thessalonica had received the Word of God with great eagerness and readiness. The proof was to be seen in many ways – God was at work in them and around them. It is not surprising, therefore, to discover that Satan takes some emergency action against the Christians in Thessalonica by stirring up a wave of hostility and persecution. We are not given precise details as to what form the persecution took, but we can deduce something of its force by these descriptive words: 'You suffered from your own countrymen the same things those churches suffered from the Jews, who killed the Lord Jesus and the prophets and also drove us out.'

How did the Christians at Thessalonica respond to this wave of hostility and persecution? They seemed to be thriving under it! This is because they had learned the secret of letting the wind of hostility and persecution drive them forward. An old European saying goes like this: 'The north wind made the Vikings.' And why? Because the Vikings made the north wind blow them where they wanted to go – and it toughened them up in the process. Philosophers have tried to explain why Christians thrive under persecution, but it is quite simple: they have the power to take everything that life throws at them, and turn it to good. A Christian is able to say: 'I cannot determine what happens to me, but I can determine what it will do to me. It will make me better and more productive.' And that is mastery!

FURTHER STUDY

Matt. 5:1–12;
Phil. 4: 11;
Acts 5:41;
1 Pet. 2:20

1. How should
we respond when
persecuted?
2. Why can we
respond like this?

Prayer

O Father, what an exciting faith You have given me! Every time I am jolted, providing I am in tune with You, all it does is jolt me forward. Help me stay in tune – then I know that everything is grist to my mill. Thank You, Father. Amen.

Satan – the hinderer

For reading & meditation – 1 Thessalonians 2:17–18;
Romans 16:17–20

'… *but Satan stopped us.*' (1 Thess. 2:18)

Forced to leave Thessalonica because of the fierce hostility against him, Paul's heart remains warm toward the Christians there. Christians are not just people who share a common interest; they enjoy a common life – eternal life given to them by Christ. And this bond quickly cements relationships in a way that is not found in any other section of society.

Paul's reference to Satan hindering his plans for a return visit is often viewed with surprise by some Christians. They say: 'If God is all-powerful, why does He allow Satan to hinder or prevent His purposes?' I puzzled over this question a good deal in my early days as a Christian, and one night I remember getting down on my knees and saying to the Lord, rather petulantly I am afraid, 'God, if You are so big, why do You let the devil get the better of You?' The answer that came was this: 'Satan is allowed to make only those moves which accord with My purposes. He thinks he is advancing his own plans, but all he succeeds in doing is advancing Mine.' That answer satisfied me then, and it satisfies me now.

FURTHER STUDY

Matt. 4:1–17;

Eph. 6:10–11;

James 4:7;

1 Pet. 5:8–9

1. How did Jesus deal with Satan?
2. What is the key to overcoming Satan?

Is Satan blocking your path at this moment and causing your plans to be frustrated? Then remember this – the devil is only permitted to go as far as the purposes of God allow, and if God foresees that He cannot work through that hindrance to further His purposes, then He will never allow it to happen in the first place. Everything serves the Christian – even Satan's hindrances!

Prayer

O Father, thank You for showing me Your overwhelming supremacy over Satan. His blocks become my blessings; his interruptions, my interpretations. Because I am in You then everything is under my feet! I am so grateful. Amen.

People – the best investment

For reading & meditation – 1 Thessalonians. 2:19–20;
Galatians 4:12–20

'Indeed, you are our glory and joy.' (1 Thess. 2:20)

During the short period of Paul's ministry in Thessalonica he received, as we saw, no financial support or material rewards for his ministry. He laboured night and day so that he would not have to take anything from those who listened to him.

Although Paul had no material rewards for his services at Thessalonica, he most certainly had some spiritual rewards. The converts who came to Christ under his ministry were worth more to him than a king's ransom, and he describes them here as 'our hope, our joy ... the crown in which we will glory'. The Amplified Bible puts it like this: '[you are] our victor's wreath of exultant triumph when we stand in the presence of our Lord Jesus Christ at His coming.' In verse 18, Paul looked back at his ministry in Thessalonica with a tinge of nostalgia, but now he looks forward to the day when all wrongs will be righted and all evil subdued.

Paul had fought many spiritual battles since the day he was converted to Christ on the Damascus road, but it seems the picture of the Christians at Thessalonica held pride of place in his gallery of memories. They were among his most prized campaign medals! He found great joy in reflecting on the fact that one day he would stand in the presence of His Master and proudly present the Thessalonian Christians as one of the fruits of his ministry. And the thought of this great, triumphant union seems to take out of the apostle's heart some of the pain of his present separation.

FURTHER STUDY

Luke 15:1–32;
Psa. 126:6;
John 4:36;
Acts 15:3

1. What was Jesus teaching in these three parables?
2. What took place in each of these parables?

Prayer

O Father, I see so clearly that the investments that outlast time are not those I make in stocks and shares, but those I make in people. Help me to invest in people, for Jesus' sake. Amen.

Deflected grace

For reading & meditation – 1 Thessalonians 3:1–2; Luke 8: 26–39

'So when we could stand it no longer, we thought it best to be left by ourselves … We sent Timothy …' (1 Thess. 3:1–2)

We now see something of the way in which God led the apostle Paul to overcome the hindrances of Satan. If Paul couldn't go himself, then he would do the next best thing – send Timothy. This is always the Christian position – if we are blocked in one direction, then we go in another. Nothing beats us if we have the right attitude of mind. One of the most difficult things to handle in life is the frustration of one's plans. This often throws everything into confusion, for everything might be geared to those plans. Paul, however, was an expert at handling frustration because he had learned the secret at the feet of His Master.

How did Jesus meet frustrating situations? The story of the demon-possessed man reveals His strategy. When Jesus healed him, the people came and saw the man 'sitting at Jesus' feet, dressed and in his right mind; and they were afraid' (Luke 8:35). They begged Jesus to leave. His presence had cost them too much. But was Jesus blocked by their ignorance and greed? No, He was not blocked, but diverted. His grace was deflected. It simply turned in another direction. So He embarked upon another phase of His ministry. He carried on and accomplished some of His greatest miracles as a result of that blocking – the frustration turned to fruitfulness. If He couldn't do this – He would do that! And I am bold to say that in His strength, so can you!

FURTHER STUDY

Acts 16:1–13;

Phil. 4:11;

1 Tim. 6:6;

Heb. 13:5

1. Was Paul frustrated at being unable to preach the gospel in Asia?
2. How did he respond?

Prayer

Gracious Father, thank You for showing me that I need not be deterred by a decisive blocking of my plans. If I cannot get through, I will find a way round. Give me a resilient spirit that bends, but is never broken. In Jesus' name. Amen.

Can you handle a crisis?

For reading & meditation – 1 Thess. 3:2–5; 2 Tim. 3:10–17

'… everyone who wants to live a godly life in Christ Jesus will be persecuted.' (2 Tim. 3:12)

Paul's decision to send Timothy to Thessalonica was not simply to ease his mind, but to strengthen the converts in the faith. It was a brotherly visit designed to encourage them to stand firm in the midst of their trials. Paul, of course, had prepared the converts to expect trials, and had assured them that suffering and persecution were to be expected.

One of the deficiencies of the Christian Church in modern times is its failure to prepare people to meet a crisis. There are notable exceptions, of course, but far too many churches fail in this respect. Why do so many Christians go under in times of crisis and difficulty? Mainly because they have not been prepared, by proper training and teaching, to anticipate problems and work out beforehand how to meet them. We are so busy answering questions people are not asking, that we fail to get down to the basic issues of the Christian life. Issues such as showing people how to handle crisis situations like severe disappointment, redundancy, bereavement, criticism, financial collapse, persecution, a broken marriage, and so on.

Sometimes I tremble inwardly as I sense that many Christians are unprepared for the great wave of persecution which, I believe, will one day come against the Christian Church in Britain. If there is one thing we should be praying for at this moment, it is that God will raise up teachers in our churches who will establish believers in the principles of how to act in a crisis.

FURTHER STUDY

Heb. 4:1–16;

Job 11:18;

Psa. 91:5, 112:7;

Prov. 3:24

1. What is the concern of the writer to the Hebrews?

2. Are you 'resting' in God?

Prayer

Father, I would add my prayers to those who will be reading these lines today, and ask that You will raise up more teachers to prepare Your Church for the crisis days that lie ahead. In Jesus' name I pray. Amen.

A word of encouragement

For reading & meditation – 1 Thess. 3:6–7; Isa. 41:7–16

'Therefore … in all our distress and persecution we were
encouraged about you because of your faith.' (1 Thess. 3:7)

Timothy's news of the Thessalonians could not have arrived at a better time as far as Paul was concerned, for he had not been unaffected by the trials and persecution which he himself had gone through. Paul, as you know, wrote this letter from Corinth where he faced many problems, so the news of the thriving community at Thessalonica would have been a great encouragement to him. Doubtless he would have said to himself: if God can do this at Thessalonica, He can do it at Corinth too! I wonder am I speaking to someone today who is discouraged by the lack of growth or spiritual development of their own local church or fellowship? Then I pause, led by the Spirit I believe, to give you this word:

Put not your trust in men, in finance, nor in the strategies of those who seem to have earthly wisdom. I will come as a refiner's fire and will purge away the dross so that only gold will remain. Even now, as I speak to you, the refining is going on. You see the dross, but I see the gold. You see the process, but I see the result. Remember, My child, that I am never in a hurry. My timing is not your timing. Things are happening that you are not able to see or measure. Be encouraged that I am at work behind the scenes, shaping, moulding, refining, delivering and preparing My children for the day of My power. In due time you will see that the waiting time proved transformative and that My answers are not a moment too soon, or too late, but right on time.

FURTHER STUDY

Isa. 43:1–21;

Exod 14:13;

Matt. 14:27, 10:30

1. Why are we not to fear?
2. What has God promised to do?

Prayer

Father, I am so grateful that You know the moments when I stand in need of great encouragement. Thank You for speaking to my heart today. Your words are always right on time. I am eternally grateful. Amen.

'I am if you are!'

For reading & meditation – 1 Thess. 3:8–10; 2 Tim. 4:9–18

'For now we really live, since you are standing firm in the Lord.' (1 Thess. 3:8)

Paul seems to be saying: 'When you live spiritually, I live, and when you die, I die.' Does this mean that Paul's happiness and security was rooted in the lives of his converts? Of course not. He is using an expression to illustrate how closely identified he was with the well-being of his converts. Paul's life was not dependent on the life of his converts: his security was in Christ. When they went up or down, he didn't go up or down. He was in Jesus Christ who is the same 'yesterday, today and forever' (Heb. 13:8). There is a difference between being alive in a convert and living through a convert, but it is this thought of being alive in his converts that the apostle is bringing out here.

As one who has been involved in a good deal of evangelism in different parts of the world, I have often felt that I was alive in the life of a convert, and that something within me died when they failed to grow. In some parts of Africa the reply to the question: Are you well? is this: I am if you are! It is a beautiful way of saying: 'My well-being depends on your well-being. If you are well, then so am I. If you are not, then I am not.' This is much deeper than sympathy, 'suffering with' – this is empathy, 'suffering in'. Paul explained, 'If one part suffers, every part suffers ... if one part is honoured, every part rejoices ...' (1 Cor. 12:26). We must have an empathy with those around us, even though it is limited. Final and unlimited empathy is with Him.

FURTHER STUDY

Eph. 1:15–23;
Rom. 12:15, 15:1;
Gal. 6:2

1. How did Paul demonstrate his care for the Ephesian believers?
2. What was his hope and prayer for them?

Prayer

Father, help me to understand that it is in You that I live and move and have my being – in others I just live and move. In Jesus' name. Amen.

Love that increases and abounds

For reading & meditation – 1 Thess. 3:11–12; 1 John 4:7–12

'May the Lord make your love increase and overflow for each
other and for everyone else …' (1 Thess. 3:12)

Paul expresses in these words his great longing for the converts at
Thessalonica that their love might not just remain static, but that
it might 'increase and overflow' not only for each other, but for all
people. The reason why this truth was part of the apostle's teaching
is, quite simply, that we become what we give out. If we give out
selfishness, for example, then we become the kind of people who
want something for ourselves out of everything we do. If we give out
criticism, then our whole nature becomes critical and we build
a critical atmosphere all around us. If we give out hate, then we
establish an aura of hate around us. But if, on the other hand, we give
out love, then we become more loving, and if we love in increasing
measure, we will get it back in the same abundant supply.

The Moffatt translation reads: 'The Lord make you increase and
excel in love … so as to strengthen your hearts.' There is room for
competition in Christianity – the competition is over who can excel
in love. This is a healthy competition, and the result not only benefits
others, but you as well! It contributes to our own life. The heart that

FURTHER STUDY

1 Cor. 13:1–13;
Matt. 22:39;
John 13:35,15:12

1. How do we
demonstrate love?
2. What is
the 'eleventh'
commandment?

loves is not a weakened heart – weakened by the
giving – it is strengthened by the very giving. The
giver and the receiver are both strengthened, for
love itself is strength. The more we excel in love
the more everyone benefits. We benefit by being
strengthened, and others benefit by being loved.

Prayer

Father, I am relieved that Your love never weakens. Help me not only to grow
in love but to overflow with it. This I ask in Christ's peerless and precious name.
Amen.

Unblamable holiness

For reading & meditation – 1 Thess. 3:13; Gal. 2:17–21

*'May he strengthen your hearts so that you will be blameless
and holy in the presence of our God ...' (1 Thess. 3:13)*

Today we discover another longing in Paul's heart: '... that He may ... establish your hearts faultlessly pure and unblamable in holiness' (Amplified Bible). How fitting that Paul should put love first and holiness next. Some Christians put it the other way round, and all this produces is a cold and legalistic type of Christianity. A man introduced his wife to a group of people in the church, and when they asked her what she did, her husband said, before she had time to reply, 'She's a wrestler.' The group were nonplussed. 'What do you mean?' they asked. 'Do you actually get into a wrestling ring and wrestle with other women?' 'Oh, no,' said the man, 'what I meant was, she's a "wrestling" Christian – she wrestles hard to be good.' During the conversation that followed, the woman shared with the group that she was so preoccupied with being good, she had no time for anything else. She was so busy trying to be holy that she had no time to love. That kind of Christianity is decidedly unattractive.

You will no doubt have heard St Augustine's famous statement: 'Love God and do as you like.' He meant, of course, that when you love God then your desire will be to please Him always and do what He wants. We rise to the level of holiness on the raft of love. Just as water reaches its highest level, which is never higher than the reservoir from which it flowed, so does God's love, overflowing in us, return to Him in pure love and unblamable holiness.

FURTHER STUDY

Heb. 12:1–29;
Exod. 15:11;
Lev. 11:45;
Psa. 99:9

1. What is the result of pursuing holiness?
2. What happens when we miss the grace of God?

Prayer

Father, this description of a wrestling Christian fits me. I try so hard, yet I see today that it is not trying but trusting that is the key. Help me take that key and with it open all the doors that hitherto have remained closed. Amen.

The divine stimulus

For reading & meditation – 1 Thess. 4:1; Phil. 3:7–14

'... we instructed you how to live ... Now we ... urge you in the Lord Jesus to do this more and more.' (1 Thess. 4:1)

Paul knew exactly how to bring the best out of people by first complimenting them for what they were, then pointing them to new horizons of Christian living. Listen again to this: 'How can we thank God enough for you? ... Now we ask you and urge you in the Lord Jesus to do this more and more.' Can you see what Paul is doing? He is patting them on the back with one hand and pointing his finger in the direction of new spiritual goals with the other. He is saying, 'The things you are now doing, continue to do more and more. You are doing fine, now stretch yourself to even higher realms.'

This is spiritual genius at work! If every Christian practised this art of stimulating others to higher things, what a transformation we would see in our churches! The Thessalonian converts were being subjected to a divine stimulus – and rightly. The life in Christ is a growing life, or it is not in Christ. As Christ is the eternally creative One, so He is eternally creating us anew. The continual cry of the growing Christian is 'more'. 'I've seen so much – I want to see more.'

FURTHER STUDY

1 Tim. 4:1–16;

Job 17:9;

Psa. 84:7, 92:12;

Heb. 10:24

1. How did Paul encourage Timothy?

2. What was his concern and exhortation?

This 'more and more' will stretch beyond the grave and forever, for the finite will forever approach the Infinite, and will be conscious of unending vistas yet to be explored. Will we continue to grow in heaven? Yes, inevitably so. In Christ we have taken hold of the inexhaustible, the unexplorable. We will be on the move and yet have rest. We have everything – and want more.

Prayer

O Father, the more I ponder on what You have done for me in Christ, the more I sense that I am satisfied – but with an unsatisfied satisfaction. I am content – yet want more. Amen.

Straight talking on sex

For reading & meditation – 1 Thess. 4:2–6; Rom. 6:11–14

*'It is God's will that you should be holy; that you should avoid
sexual immorality.' (1 Thess. 4:3)*

I n Paul's day Roman society was as permissive as the age in which
we are now living – probably more so. One commentator says of
those days: 'Wife-swapping, homosexual practices and prostitution
were all the rage. Such goings-on were not confined to a small way-
out group, but widely accepted in society.' Against this backdrop the
words of Paul are clear and incisive: 'God's plan is to make you holy,
and that means a clean cut with sexual immorality' (Phillips). God's
standards must be adhered to, no matter what others say.

So what does God have to say about this subject of sex? The
sexual drive, in itself, is a natural and normal appetite – as much a
normal part of us as eating or drinking. And the God who designed
us with a sex drive provided the power to use it correctly. Christians
must surrender their sex drive to God so that it comes under His
mastery and control. Sex must not be first – God must be first. If sex
climbs into the driver's seat and is allowed to guide your life, you
are in for a crash.

Surrender of the sex drive to God breaks its tyranny and its
power. Alexis Carrel says that the people who
do the greatest work in the world are strongly-
sexed people who subordinate sex to the ends for
which they live. In marriage, the sex drive must
be channelled into procreation and the giving of
pleasure to one's partner. Outside of marriage, the
sex drive must be sublimated and channelled into
creativity in the kingdom of God.

FURTHER STUDY
2 Tim. 2:1–26;
John 17:17;
Heb. 13:4
1. What does it mean
to be 'sanctified'?
2. What was Paul's
warning to Timothy?

Prayer

Gracious, loving and heavenly Father, I would be free from the bondage of sex
that can take control over my life. I would be bound to nothing – except You.
Help me, my Father. In Jesus' name. Amen.

Sexual expression – God's way

For reading & meditation – 1 Thess. 4:7–8; Col. 3:1–5

'For God did not call us to be impure, but to live a holy life.'
(1 Thess. 4:7)

A s in Paul's day, modern life seems to be heavily loaded on the side of sex. More and more advertisements use it to attract attention. With all this emphasis upon sex, one would have expected this age to have found sexual fulfilment. On the contrary, no age seems to have become more sexually dissatisfied and thwarted than this.

Every normal person has a sexual drive, and those who refuse to accept this land up with all kinds of complexes. Bring the fact of sex into the open in your thinking – look at it, but not for too long, and decide what you are going to do with it. Note: what you are going to do with it, not what it is going to do with you. Sex is a wonderful servant but a terrible master. Even married couples can find their lives dominated by sex unless the drive has been surrendered and dedicated to God.

Keep this thought always before you – both within marriage and outside marriage, the sex drive can be sublimated. This leaves an open door for those who, because they are unmarried, are denied the ordinary outlets of sexual expression. The sex urge is the creative urge. But physical creation is not its only creative area. It can function creatively on other levels of life, for instance, in the realm of the mind – creating new thoughts, new systems of thought, new mental attitudes and new spiritual movements. Creative drives blocked on one level can be released on another. This is not suppression, but divinely approved expression.

FURTHER STUDY

1 Pet. 4:1–11; 1:16;
Luke 1:74–75;
2 Pet. 3:11–14

1. How does the Holy Spirit enable us to be holy?
2. What is our responsibility?

Prayer

Gracious Father, I surrender today these turbulent urges within me. Still them with Your calm, direct them by Your will and lift them by Your redemption. We must work this problem out together, for apart from You I can do nothing. Amen.

Love – exposed, not imposed

For reading & meditation – 1 Thess. 4:9–10; John 15:9–17

'… you yourselves have been taught by God to love each other.' (1 Thess. 4:9)

Paul now returns to a theme which he has touched on several times before – the importance of love. Paul is undoubtedly trying to show that the full benefit of keeping Christ's commandments can only be realised when it is prompted by love. We have only to read again the classic passage in 1 Corinthians 13 to see that man's noblest actions take on their deepest significance when motivated by love.

How then do we receive that love by which every human value is heightened and transformed? Paul reminds them that this was not something that came through his instructions, but that they had been 'taught by God' to love one another. Taught by God! What a delightful phrase. But what does it mean? It means, I think, that when the Thessalonians received Christ into their lives, He set about the task of teaching them, not only to live for Him, but to love others as He had loved them.

The way in which God teaches His children to love is not by imposing a law from without but by exposing His love from within. True Christians do things – or omit to do things – not simply because there are rules governing those things, but because they have the will to love. It is a training that goes on within, not merely from without. A Christian is not compelled to love: he is impelled to love. We are trained by the One who not only loves but who created love. Who better as a teacher?

FURTHER STUDY

1 John 3:1–24;
1 Pet. 1:22;
1 John 2:10, 4:7

1. How do we perceive the love of God?
2. What ought we to do?

Prayer

Loving heavenly Father, Your words and my needs fit together as a hand fits into a glove. I am so glad that when I follow You, I am not following a code but a character, not the extraneous, but the intrinsic. Teach me more. Amen.

Down to earth

For reading & meditation – 1 Thess. 4:11–12; Col. 3:22–25

'Make it your ambition to lead a quiet life, to mind your own business and to work ...' (1 Thess. 4: 11)

It is evident from these words that some Christians in Paul's day were so obsessed with the idea that Christ was coming again that it wasn't worth getting involved in anything that was secular. They stood around like tourists in an airport lounge do today, chatting excitedly while waiting for the flight to be called. Paul's advice is to 'calm down'. Christians cannot escape the routines of life, however dull they may be, and they must work as if Christ was not coming back for a thousand years – yet live as if He might return today.

To the busybody, he says, quite bluntly – mind your own business. Christians sometimes pass on information about another, piously disguised as points for prayer. Confidences should never be paraded or dragged into the open without the permission of the one concerned. Paul has a word, too, for the layabouts – those who prefer to stay on the dole rather than work. Care, of course, must be taken to differentiate between those who are unemployed because of no fault of their own, and those who are just social parasites. We must be firm with those who are work-shy, who don't like getting their hands dirty, and let them know that indolence is something on which Christ frowns. 'The object of social welfare,' says one writer, 'is not to provide splints for lame ducks, but to give them an opportunity to get back into the swim.' It is.

FURTHER STUDY

Prov. 6:1–11;
Eccl. 9:10;
Eph. 4:28;
John 6:27

1. What should we learn from the ant?
2. Why is it important for us to work?

Prayer

Father, I see that Your Church establishes its reputation in this world by the way it deals with down-to-earth matters. Help me not to be work-shy, a clock-watcher or a cadger. In Jesus' name. Amen.

Death – God's anaesthetic

For reading & meditation – 1 Thess. 4:13–14; 1 Cor. 15:54–57

*'... we do not want you to be ignorant ... or to grieve like the
rest of men, who have no hope.' (1 Thess. 4:13)*

Pagan religion, from which the Thessalonian Christians had
turned, offered little hope beyond death. Paul now reveals that
death is not something to be afraid of, but something to be faced
with joy. How despairing life becomes for those who have no hope
beyond death. Schopenhauer, the German philosopher, spent half
his life brooding on the mystery of what happens after death, and he
grew more and more depressed as he tried to resolve the problem.
Bertrand Russell, a man with a keen and brilliant mind, also failed
to find any answers to the Great Beyond. His conclusion was this:
'We are an eddying speck of dust; a harassed driven leaf.' These men
walked in deepest darkness with little or no hope for the future.

Men and women outside of Christ live in an understandable
pessimism and gloom when it comes to this matter of life after
death. Christianity, however, bursts into this atmosphere of
despondency and despair with the glorious news that in Christ there
is life after death – eternal life! This confidence does not rest on
mere conjecture, or the 'voices' of mediums, but on solid historical
fact – the resurrection of the Lord Jesus Christ.
'We believe that Jesus died and rose again and so
we believe that God will bring with Jesus those
who have fallen asleep in him.' (4:14). So for the
Christian – what is death? Death is merely the
anaesthetic God uses to put us to sleep while He
changes our mortal bodies into immortal.

FURTHER STUDY
Rom. 5:1–21;
Job 19:25–26;
Heb. 9:27;
1 Cor. 15:6

1. What was the
result of one man's
disobedience?
2. What is the
result of one man's
obedience?

Prayer

Lord Jesus Christ, had You stalled at the last ditch, had You been beaten at the
barrier of death, then I would be stalled – eternally. But now I can go over the
barrier with You – into glory. I am eternally thankful. Amen.

Christ is coming – hallelujah!

For reading & meditation – 1 Thess. 4.15–18; 1 Cor. 15:50–53

'For the Lord himself will come down from heaven ... and the dead in Christ will rise first.' (1 Thess. 4:16)

We come now to the classic passage which portrays what will happen when Christ comes again. Firstly, says Paul, those who have died, believing in Christ, will be the first to rise to life! In other words, they will be first in the queue! Then those who are still alive will hear a tremendous noise, the shout of the archangel, and will be caught up in the air to be with the Lord. This sounds so incredible and fantastic that many Christians can't believe it. But it will happen – because God has said so.

I read that in the USA there is an airline, 'whose directors positively refuse to allow two Christian pilots to be jointly responsible for the flight of any one of their aircraft'. Why? Because they believe that if Christ returned, and the two pilots were caught up to be with the Lord, then an air disaster could result.

I must confess that the idea of Christians suddenly disappearing from the world, and the consequent chaos it would cause, led me, in the early days of my conversion, to reject this particular passage of Scripture. However, the more I have come to believe in the absolute inerrancy and authority of the Bible, the more I realise that God, being who He is, can be counted on to accomplish this amazing event with the minimum of chaos and disorder. Those who stumble over this passage need not fear for the consequences. We can safely leave those to the One who has the interests of all men at heart.

FURTHER STUDY

Luke 12:22–59;
21:27;

Acts 1:11;

Matt. 26:66

1. What was Jesus teaching in His parable about the servants?
2. How did Jesus reply to Peter's question?

Prayer

Father, there are many passages in Your Word that I struggle to comprehend, but help me to see that my first obligation is not to understand – but to stand. Some things are beyond my reason but not beyond my faith. I am thankful. Amen.

Be ready

For reading & meditation – 1 Thess. 5:1–2; Matt. 24:36–42

*'... you know very well that the day of the Lord will come like
a thief in the night.' (1 Thess. 5:2)*

The young converts at Thessalonica had a good grasp of the truths which appertain to Christ's second coming. They were fully prepared for the coming of Christ to take place at any time. Their early warning system was in good, working order – they were alert and ready. How different from the Church of this age. Which people are using terms such as 'the end of the world' or 'Armageddon' in our society? Not the Christians, generally speaking, but the politicians, the ecologists and the scientists. For some strange reason, Christians are silent on this vital and important issue. Perhaps we are trying so hard to get away from the sandwich-board image on which are displayed the words 'Prepare to meet thy God', that we have gone to the other extreme and are toning down this powerful and momentous truth.

Throughout the centuries the idea of a D-Day, when the final curtain would come down on the world, has been laughed at. But not any more! Nowadays, there is hardly a man or a woman on the face of the earth who does not realise that the end of the world is not just a remote possibility, but a real probability. Satan, I am afraid, has lulled many Christians into a false sense of security over this issue. We look back over history and think, because so many centuries have passed, there must be an equal amount of time left to come. We say, 'It couldn't happen to us.' Just like the housewife who after a shopping trip comes home to find her house burgled!

FURTHER STUDY

Matt. 24:1–35;

2 Pet. 3:10;

Luke 12:40;

Rev. 16:15

1. List the prevailing conditions at the return of Christ.
2. How many are being fulfilled today?

Prayer

Gracious Lord and Master, I see that this truth must be brought into clear focus in my thinking. Help me not only to see its tremendous importance but to live always in the light of the fact that You are coming soon. In Jesus' name I ask it. Amen.

Labour pains

For reading & meditation – 1 Thessalonians 5:3; Luke 21:8–19

'... *destruction will come on them suddenly, as labour pains on a pregnant woman ...*' (1 Thess. 5:3)

Today Paul likens Christ's return to a woman in labour. At the end of the nine-month period, as the moment of birth approaches, so the contractions begin. Sometimes these contractions are a false alarm and the mother-to-be may wonder, 'Are these the real thing? Will it happen today?' When the pains get more regular and intense, then there is a tremendous flurry of excitement. It's on the way! Call a taxi! Let the hospital know we are coming! Once in the labour ward, it is not long before the expected baby arrives. I say not long, although to the anxious father it may seem an eternity.

We must not take this analogy too far, however, because the illustration is not meant to be taken too literally. The return of Christ to this world is like the birth of a baby in the sense that once the signs start to appear, events quickly follow each other, and there is no stopping them. The question we must now ask ourselves is this: are the signs of world trouble and distress that we see around us evidence of Christ's near return – or are they 'false alarms'? I cannot be certain about this, of course, but I have a strong feeling that the increasing confusion and uncertainty we are witnessing all around us at the moment are the signs that His coming is near. I have said it before and I say it again – this present generation may well be the one that will witness the return of Jesus Christ to this world.

FURTHER STUDY

Matt. 25:1–13;
Mark 13:35;
Luke 12:35–36;
Rev. 19:7

1. What is the message of the parable of the virgins?
2. Why was there no oil in their lamps?

Prayer

Lord, I know I can't be certain about the precise time of Your coming, but help me to live in such a spirit of expectancy that I would not be surprised if it happened today. For Jesus' sake. Amen.

Stay awake and stay sober

For reading & meditation – 1 Thess. 5:4–7; Matt. 26:36–41

'You are all sons of the light and sons of the day. We do not belong to the night or … darkness.' (1 Thess. 5:5)

Paul's message, quite simply, is this: keep awake! If that was his word to the church at Thessalonica in the first century, what, I wonder, would he have to say to the millions of Christians in this century who are fast asleep? After all, the whole purpose of biblical prophecy is not that we might have a fixation about a certain date or even a certain period, but that we might be ready for that all-important event. The sleeping Church of this century needs to be woken up, and just as in a family, when the first person to awake, wakes up the rest, so those who are alert must rouse their brothers and sisters. Then together we must do all we can to tell the world. But Paul reminds us that it is not enough simply to keep awake; we need to stay sober. Is he speaking literally here? I think not. Elsewhere Paul talks about such things as drunkenness and overindulgence, but here he is illustrating the fact that it is not enough to be awake – we must also be alert.

I once read in a newspaper about a security guard who was so affected by drink that he allowed some thieves to get past him and rob the firm of thousands of pounds. He was not asleep – his senses were dulled and he was just not alert. Each one of us must ask ourselves: am I allowing anything into my life that threatens to deaden my spiritual alertness? If the answer is 'yes', then decide to rid yourself of it – without delay. We must await His coming with a steady gaze and a clear head.

FURTHER STUDY
Matt. 25:14–30;
Rev. 3:11;
1 Cor. 16:13;
Col. 4:2
1. What is the message of the parable of the talents?
2. What was the lazy servant's excuse?

Prayer

Father, I see it is not enough just to be awake. I must also be alert. Teach me how to be a disciple with a clear head and a steady gaze. For Jesus' sake I ask it. Amen.

Ready for anything

For reading & meditation – 1 Thess. 5:8–11; 1 Cor. 13:8–13

'... putting on faith and love as a breastplate, and the hope of salvation as a helmet.' (1 Thess. 5:8)

Paul shares the secret of being daytime Christians in night-time surroundings. And the secret is this – faith, hope and love. Notice the emphasis – faith and love. Time and again in his writings, Paul ties these two qualities closely together. They both have individual importance, of course, but to be fully effective they must function together. Someone has said, 'Faith and love are Siamese twins – separate them and they might both die.' You see, it is possible to have faith without love, and love without faith. James and John, you remember, wanted to call down fire from heaven on those whom they thought were rejecting Christ and His ministry (Luke 9:51–56). I believe that had our Lord not intervened, they may well have done it! These disciples were strong in faith, but weak in love. Faith draws upon on God, and makes full use of all His resources, while love enables us to transmit to others the blessings we receive. We need both faith and love to be daytime Christians.

However, there is one more quality to be considered – hope. This is what enables Christians to remain unaffected by the gloom and pessimism of the age through which they are passing. Non-Christians have to resort to all kinds of pick-me-ups in order to remain optimistic – alcohol, horoscopes, entertainment and so on. All the Christian has to do is to put on the breastplate of faith and love together with the helmet of the hope of salvation, and he is ready for anything!

FURTHER STUDY

James 2:1–26;
Gal. 5:6;
1 Tim. 1:14;
1 John 3:17–18

1. How does James tie faith and love together?
2. What do faith and love produce?

Prayer

O God, when I see what resources You have provided for me in Christ, I feel deeply saddened when I think how little I make use of them. Fill me this day with a greater measure of love, faith and hope than I have ever known. Amen.

Submission to authority

For reading & meditation – 1 Thess. 5:12–13; Rom. 13:1–7

'... respect those who work hard among you, who are over you in the Lord ...' (1 Thess. 5:12)

'Over you in the Lord'. Isn't this a contradiction? The earliest Christian creed is 'Jesus is Lord', which means that He alone is our Master. Surely we serve no one but Him? The answer is that, although there is one Lord, there are many underlings. And those underlings act with His authority so that when we obey them, we obey the Lord. It would be so simple if we had to obey Christ alone – He is so trustworthy. I often get letters from people who say they have great difficulty in submitting to the spiritual authority over them, such as bishops, vicars, ministers, elders, deacons and so on. A woman came to me for counselling, and said that her vicar had asked her to do something which she didn't want to do. I said, 'Your vicar is the God-appointed authority over you. He is not asking you to do anything that is unscriptural, so it would be right, in my view, to do what he asks, and trust the Lord to show him if the way he wants you to go is wrong.' She hesitated, so I enquired: 'Do you have any problem with that?' 'Yes,' she said, 'quite frankly I do. I can trust the Lord, but I can't trust him.'

That's the rub! The Lord can be trusted to get things right – but not His underlings! Nevertheless, if we follow the principle of submitting to the spiritual authority over us, then, even if the counsel we are given is inadvertently wrong, God will quietly work to correct the situation, and bring understanding and enlightenment to all concerned.

FURTHER STUDY

Heb. 13:1–25;
Jer. 3:15;
Acts 20:28;
1 Pet. 5:2

1. How should we respond to those over us?
2. What can we do to help them?

Prayer

Father, help me to realise that one of the ways in which You direct and guide my life is through the authorities You have placed over me. Help me to feel secure in following this principle. In Jesus' name. Amen.

Paul's twelve commandments

For reading & meditation – 1 Thess. 5:13–15; Phil. 2:1–5

'... *Live in peace with each other.*' (1 Thess. 5:13)

Paul lays down some very firm commands for the Christians at Thessalonica. They have been called 'The Twelve Commandments'. Let's examine them one by one.

(1) Live in peace with each other. When you give someone a piece of your mind, you lose your own peace. Remember that peace within is better than position without. (2) Warn those who are idle. The person who steps out of line and dishonours the faith by persistent idleness must be corrected. To shrink from this responsibility is to weaken the effectiveness of the whole church. (3) Encourage the timid. These people can too easily be written off as useless and ineffective, but it is surprising how a word of encouragement can bring people to their full potential. Timid people get that way because of lack of encouragement: they can be helped out of it by making up that lack.

(4) Help the weak. Paul probably has in mind here the weak-willed – those who can never say 'No'. This gets them into one mess after another – bad debts, over-commitment and so on. Don't abandon these 'casualties' to the enemy; give them the help they need. (5) Be patient with everyone. Everyone? Yes – everyone. You get the chick by hatching the egg, not by smashing it open. (6) Make sure that nobody pays back wrong for wrong, but always try to be kind to each other and to everyone else. For a Christian, hitting back is out. Act kindly towards people: they will remember your kindness when all other events slip out of memory.

FURTHER STUDY

Matt. 25:31–46;
Acts 20:35;
Rom. 15:1;
1 Cor. 9:22

1. What did Jesus teach about caring for the weak?
2. What kindness will you do today for someone?

Prayer

Father, help me today to demonstrate such loving-kindness that it will live in somebody's memory for ever. This I ask in Jesus' name. Amen.

Paul's commandments (cont'd)

For reading & meditation – 1 Thess. 5:16–22; James 1:19–25

'give thanks in all circumstances, for this is God's will for you
in Christ Jesus.' (1 Thess. 5:18)

Number (7) is be joyful always. Many do not expect the Christian life to make them joyful. Make up your mind that joy, not gloom, is your birthright as a child of God. If you are gloomy, don't look around you for the cause – look within. (8) Pray continually. Establish a regular special time of prayer and talk to God throughout the day. (9) Give thanks in all circumstances, for this is God's will you in Christ Jesus. If you can't be thankful for all circumstances, you can certainly be thankful in all circumstances. Nothing that happens to a Christian is beyond God's ability to turn to good. There are mercies to be found near the heart of tragedies, and a thankful heart will help you discover them. (10) Do not put out the Spirit's fire. If the fire falls in your church or fellowship, it will inevitably produce some sparks. But don't rush for an extinguisher to put it out, just get a pair of tongs and keep things in place!

(11) Do not treat prophecies with contempt. Test everything. Hold on to the good. Some unconditionally accept every prophecy or word as coming from God, while others unconditionally reject them as coming from man: both attitudes are wrong. Often a word from God is dismissed because we do not like the person through whom it comes. Guard against this. (12) Avoid every kind of evil. Some evils are worse than others, and can be clearly identified as 'off limits', but others are more subtle. Don't stop to differentiate. Avoid the lot.

FURTHER STUDY

Psa. 150:1–6;
100:4; 107:22;
Col. 1:12

1. List some things
for which you can
give God thanks
today.
2. Write your own
psalm of praise.

Prayer

Father, I am thankful that You have given me so many clear and sure guidelines on how to live for You. My willing consent is the only unsure thing. And I make that sure now. Amen.

Motives first – performance next

For reading & meditation - 1 Thess. 5:23–24; Eph. 1:4–6

'May God himself, the God of peace, sanctify you through and through ...' (1 Thess. 5:23)

What did Paul mean when he prayed that his converts might be sanctified 'through and through'? Some believe this to mean that he was asking God to deal a death blow to their sinful human nature so that it would never trouble them again. This, I think, is an extreme view and not at all the meaning of the text. My view is that Paul was asking God to accomplish, by the Holy Spirit, as thorough and cleansing a work as possible. I prayed this same prayer many years ago and experienced a powerful cleansing by the Holy Spirit that turned me upside down and inside out. And what He did for me, He can do for you.

Paul's second prayer for the Thessalonians, that their whole spirit, soul and body be kept blameless, is also intriguing. This raises the question: Is it possible to be kept blameless, surrounded, as we are, by such sinful and hostile forces? Thank God, it is. Had Paul used the word 'faultless' instead of 'blameless', then he would have raised a very debatable issue. We may not be able to get through this world without fault, but we can, by God's grace, get through it without blame. When I was in the USA many years ago, one of my sons, then just seven, wrote me a letter. It was written on paper torn from a scrapbook, in spidery writing and covered with ink blots. Was it faultless? No. Was it blameless? Yes. The performance was not so good, but the motive was perfect.

FURTHER STUDY

John 17:1–26;
Rom. 1:9;
Eph. 1:16;
Phil. 1:4;
Col. 1:3

1. What was the theme of Christ's prayer for the Church?
2. How did Paul usually begin his letters?

Prayer

O Father, I am so grateful that You look at my motives first and my performance next. I do so appreciate this. Others look at my performance and ignore my motives. You are so different. Thank You, Father. Amen.

Immeasurable, inexhaustible grace

For reading & meditation – 1 Thess. 5:25–28; Heb. 4:14–16

'The grace of our Lord Jesus Christ be with you.' (1 Thess. 5:28)

Although Paul was a great man of prayer it did not mean that he regarded himself as above the need for other people's prayers. 'Brothers, pray for us,' he asks. It is our responsibility as Christians to pray for one another – and to pray often.

Paul's last task in this letter is to point his converts to the source of power by which they can overcome all their problems, namely 'the grace of our Lord Jesus Christ'. The apostle had given them much to think about, and they were going to need an enormous amount of strength to put those things into operation. He points them, therefore, to the power through which all things are possible – grace. I am always intrigued by the fact that the writer to the Hebrews, when describing the throne at the centre of the universe, calls it not a throne of power, but a throne of grace. Think of it – at the heart of creation is a throne, from which flows an endless supply of grace.

I read of a man who thought he'd forgotten to turn the light off in his study because he could see light shining from under the door. When he entered the room, however, he found that the light he saw was in fact, the light from the setting sun. Well, you can't turn off the sun – and you can't turn off God's eternal supply of grace! You, whose labours for Christ are unnoticed and unappreciated by others, or unrewarded, don't lose heart. Listen to His Word, tailor-made in heaven for you: 'My grace is sufficient for you' (2 Cor. 12:9).

FURTHER STUDY

Phil. 4:1–23;

2 Cor. 12:9;

2 Tim. 2: 1;

Eph. 1:7

1. What has God promised to supply?
2. What was Paul's declaration?

Prayer

Father, I see that if there are any failures in grace, it is not due to Your lack of ability to give, but to my lack of ability to receive. I open all my being today to that unlimited and inexhaustible supply. Amen.

The God with a face

For reading & meditation – 2 Thess. 1:1; 2 Cor. 4:1–6

'... to give us the light of the knowledge of the glory of God
in the face of Christ.' (2 Cor. 4:6)

Paul's opening remarks are identical to that of his first letter, and are obviously intended to stress the fact that the church at Thessalonica was established, as all true churches are, on the truth that Jesus Christ is God: 'The church ... in God our Father and the Lord Jesus Christ.' This double emphasis was of the utmost importance, for the church at Thessalonica was made up of both Jews and Gentiles. The Jews, by reason of their long history, tended to be God-oriented people, while the Gentiles on the other hand, leaned more toward Christ as the revelation of God in human form. Paul's double emphasis blended these two groups together, and showed them that the God of history had appeared in time, put on human flesh and died upon a cross.

We often use the separate terms 'church of God' or 'church of Christ' to identify the community of God's people – and there is nothing wrong with that – but there can be no doubt that the full revelation of the truth concerning the Church lies in the blending of those two ideas. It is the Church of God and the Lord Jesus Christ.

The term 'church of God', although perfectly valid, somehow takes on a greater warmth when suffixed by the phrase 'and the Lord Jesus Christ'. A great philosopher once said: 'Human beings need a God with a face.' Well, in Jesus, we have such a God. God as cosmic energy or as an eternal force leaves us cold. But the God we see in Jesus warms our hearts.

FURTHER STUDY

Col. 1:1–23;

John 6:46; 5:37;
8:18; 10:30

1. What was Jesus'
testimony about
Himself?
2. What is Paul's
testimony about
Jesus?

Prayer

O Father, I am so grateful that I am not worshipping a faceless being. I look into the face of Jesus and I see the God of the universe – nothing less and nothing more. I worship and adore You, my blessed Lord. Amen.

Staying free of the 'jitters'

For reading & meditation – 2 Thessalonians 1:2; John 1:14–18

'Grace and peace to you from God the Father and the Lord Jesus Christ.' (2 Thess. 1:2)

The Christians in Thessalonica were a thriving community of God's people, surrounded by aggressive and hostile forces. How could they maintain such a lively witness in the face of these depressing circumstances? They got all the grace and peace they needed direct from God the Father and His Son, the Lord Jesus Christ. When Paul says that grace and peace come from God the Father and the Lord Jesus Christ does he mean that there are two separate sources? No. What he means is that the Father is the source and Christ is the channel through which the endless supply of grace and peace flows to His children. When Jesus lived here on earth, He manifested so beautifully those two qualities of grace and peace. So He knows how and when to supply us with these gifts, and thus help us cope with our problems.

It is important to recognise, however, that the supply of grace and peace promised to a Christian does not flow into our lives automatically. It is always available, but in order for it to enter our lives and meet our needs, it must be appropriated. This is why Paul so often begins his letters by making it a matter of prayer that nothing in the lives of his converts should clog the flow. At the moment of writing this was probably the prayer the Thessalonians needed most. They needed the grace of God to keep them going and the peace of God to help them cope with the 'jitters' that would inevitably arise as they faced a cruel and hostile world.

FURTHER STUDY

Isa. 26:1–12;
Rom. 8:6, 14:7;
Phil. 4:7

1. What is the key to continual peace?
2. How can we stay our minds on God?

Prayer

Lord Jesus Christ, I am so thankful that grace and peace were at work in Your life when You were here on earth. Now let them work in me. For Your own dear name's sake. Amen.

Flourishing or floundering?

For reading & meditation – 2 Thess. 1:3–4 ; 2 Cor. 6:3–10

'… we boast about your perseverance and faith in all the persecutions and trials you are enduring.' (2 Thess. 1:4)

In the midst of severe persecution, the Thessalonians' faith, love and perseverance had not floundered, but flourished. A man wrote to me, 'If God protected me more from trials and difficulties that come my way – I would be a better Christian.' I pointed out to him that one of God's primary purposes for our lives is not happiness, but growth. Happiness is a by-product of that growth. God, in setting the goals for our spiritual advancement and character development, often has to steer us into difficult circumstances, for our environment has to be sufficiently hard for our souls to be sharpened upon. We grow through the resistances we receive from our environment – or from the people around us who tend to irritate or upset us.

The Christian life is not a hothouse experience in which we are sheltered from the winds of pressure and persecution, but one in which we are sometimes exposed to every wind that blows. The converts at Thessalonica grew in faith and love despite - or even because of – the conditions of their environment. I know a lady who says, whenever someone asks her how she is coping with her circumstances, 'I'm growing under them.' Believe me, if God permits you to face any trials today, then they will produce far more than they cost. I saw these words on a church noticeboard which contain a truth that is often overlooked. 'A Christian is like a tea bag – not much good until he has been through some hot water.'

FURTHER STUDY

Gal. 6:1–9;

Matt. 10:22;

Heb. 12:1–7;

James 5:11

1. In what ways can we become weary in doing good?
2. How did Jesus set us an example?

Prayer

Father, I realise that hour by hour You are teaching me the right way to live. Help me to seize on everything that happens as a textbook in this school of living. Then everything will further me. Amen.

'That deeper voice'

For reading & meditation – 2 Thessalonians 1:5; Isaiah 26:1–4

'… as a result you will be counted worthy of the kingdom of God, for which you are suffering.' (2 Thess. 1:5)

N ow we come to the real reason why God allowed such persecution: 'You will be counted worthy of the kingdom of God.' I like the way the Living Bible translates this phrase: 'For he is using your sufferings to make you ready for his kingdom.' If there is one lesson that has been brought home to me in my life and ministry, it is this – God only allows what He can use. I keep coming back to it time and time again in my writings, and if I was asked to leave one single statement for posterity it would be that God is working through our trials and our difficulties to make us more like His Son. This truth, I am sure, must have been tremendously encouraging to the Thessalonians, and I trust that it will also be your support – today and every day. If you are compelled to live or work in a situation which is full of hostile forces, then remember that the foresight of a loving God has provided the resources which can enable you to turn the difficulties into discoveries, and help you find meaning and purpose in all that is happening around you.

Listen to His word to you today: God is using the pressures to make you ready for His kingdom. The words of Tennyson come to mind as I write: 'Well roars the storm to him that hears a deeper voice above the storm.' Are you facing some fierce winds of opposition or persecution at this moment? Then listen to what that deeper voice is saying: 'I am using your sufferings … to make you ready for My kingdom.'

FURTHER STUDY

Acts 9:1–43;
Rom. 8:17;
Heb. 11:25;
1 Pet. 5:10

1. What did the Lord say to Paul?
2. Who are people really persecuting?

Prayer

My Father and my God, the next time I find myself in a storm, help me to listen for that 'deeper voice'. For I know that You are there to turn all the bad things that happen to me into good. I am so very, very thankful. Amen.

The disobedient punished

For reading & meditation – 2 Thess. 1:6–8; Matt. 25:31–46

'God is just: He will pay back trouble to those who trouble you.' (2 Thess. 1:6)

C hristians may have to suffer for their faith, but one day the tables will be turned. And what is more, while God's people lose nothing but their sufferings, those who cause their sufferings will lose everything. God holds in His hands the balance of world affairs and will even out the injustices of history to the gain of His people and the loss of those who reject Him. This may sound like triumphalism, but it is nevertheless true. We must not rejoice, of course, in the downfall of sinners and their eternal loss, but we must recognise that one day all wrongs will be righted and justice will prevail.

The theme of punishment is missing in many modern pulpits but it is not missing from the Scriptures. Sometimes we forget that, although God is a God of love and mercy, He is also a God of justice. Those who brazenly flaunt their sins, and laugh at all talk of eternal justice, will one day discover, to their dismay, that God has kept an accurate record of their sin and will punish it accordingly, He cannot be God and do otherwise. One preacher says: 'If God will not punish the liars, the thieves, the adulterers and practising homosexuals, then He will have to apologise to Sodom and Gomorrah.' It would be unthinkable for God to overlook the accumulated sins of humanity, for to do so would be to deny the law which He Himself built into the universe: 'A man reaps what he sows' (Gal. 6:7). The disobedient will be punished. The eternal God has said so.

FURTHER STUDY

Rev. 20:1–15;

Psa. 62:12;

Jer. 17:10;

2 Cor. 5:10

1. How will the dead be judged?
2. Who will be cast into the lake of fire?

Prayer

My Father, as I ponder on the inevitability of future punishment, I do not gloat over it but am humbled. Thank You that my judgment has been taken by Your Son's sufferings on the cross. In Jesus my heart is at peace. Amen.

Admired – in Him

For reading & meditation – 2 Thess. 1:9–10; Eph. 3:7–11

'on the day he comes … to be marvelled at among all those who have believed. This includes you …' (2 Thess. 1:10)

In order to grasp the truth of what Paul is saying in these deeply impressive words we must pause for a moment and take a look at God's original purpose for the first 'holy nation' He possessed – the children of Israel. God brought His people out of Egypt that He might bring them to Himself and teach them the laws and principles of successful living. The Almighty wanted them to be His 'window display', so to speak, at which other nations could look to see the benefits of serving the one true God. That purpose, as you know, was never fully realised, as Israel's continued rebellion and backsliding prevented God from seeing His plan perfected in His people.

God, however, had prepared another plan – a glorious purpose. When Christ came to this world and was rejected by the very people to whom He came, the Jews, God then revealed His divine secret. And what was this? That 'in Christ' He would create a new people, a 'holy nation' consisting of men and women of all races who would surrender to His Son, receive forgiveness for their sins and be built into His divine masterpiece, the Church. Unfortunately, God was not able to be 'admired' in Israel – hence His search for a new people and a new nation. But will He be 'admired' in His people, the Church? Nothing is more certain! Through you and me, the blood-washed members of His Body, God is going to show Himself off to the whole universe. What marvellous mercy! What amazing grace!

FURTHER STUDY

John 1:1–14; 17:5;
Luke 9:32;
Matt. 16:27

1. What are the characteristics of Christ's glory?
2. Are you displaying these characteristics?

Prayer

O Father, when I think of the multitude of things in which You could be admired – the sun, the stars, the galaxies – I am deeply humbled that You chose me to reflect the beauty of Your face. I just can't get over it. Thank You, Father. Amen.

A double glorifying

For reading & meditation – 2 Thess.1:11–12; Luke 9:23–26

'We pray this so that the name of our Lord Jesus Christ maybe glorified in you, and you in him ...' (2 Thess. 1:12)

Paul's flair for orderliness is seen not only in his words of encouragement but also in his prayers. His intercessions for the Thessalonians, for example, have four definite goals:

(1) that God would count them worthy of His calling;
(2) that He would fulfil every one of their good purposes and
(3) every act prompted by faith;
(4) that Christ may be glorified in them and them in Him.

His prayers reveal his tremendous faith, that there are resources in God to meet every legitimate demand His children make upon Him.

Paul's last petition needs special emphasis: 'that the name of our Lord Jesus may be glorified in you, and you in him.' I find this utterly amazing, for it is a double glorifying: Him in us and us in Him. To glorify the name of our Lord Jesus Christ would be enough for any ransomed sinner, but to be told that in the very glorifying of Jesus, He Himself will be glorified in us – that is almost too much to take in. But isn't this typical of the One who constantly surprises us by the wonder of His grace? He overwhelms us with His graciousness. In the glorifying of the Redeemer, the redeemed are glorified. Each saves his life and finds it. Each thinks of glorifying the other, and both end up being glorified.

If that is not enough to make you throw your hat up in the air, then I don't know what is!

FURTHER STUDY

Rev. 22:1–14;
Rom. 8:17;
Phil. 3:21;
Col. 3:4

1. With what does Paul link sharing in Christ's glory?
2. What is another characteristic of His glory?

Prayer

Father, this is too wonderful for words. For me to be glorified in You is something I can comprehend, but for You to be glorified in me is beyond all understanding. Yet I believe it – and I am grateful. Amen.

'A sure word of prophecy'

For reading & meditation – 2 Thess. 2:1–2; 2 Pet. 1:12–19

'… we ask you … not to become easily unsettled or alarmed by some prophecy, report or letter …' (2 Thess. 2:1–2)

Apparently someone in the Thessalonian church was spreading a rumour that Paul believed the 'day of the Lord' had already come. It might have come from a wrong prophecy given by an over-enthusiastic believer, or resulted from someone misrepresenting something the apostle himself had said. However, there appears to be a third reason for this rumour – it might have come from a letter purporting to be written by the apostle, but which, in fact, was not. Historians tell us that there were many false letters written during the days of the Early Church. This caused bewilderment and confusion to a number of God's people. Some began to ask questions about the truth of the Christian message, and it was this that prompted the Church leaders of the first century to put together the inspired letters and documents which today we call the New Testament.

It might surprise some to learn that at the time Paul wrote these letters to the Thessalonians, the Gospels, as we now know them, were entirely unknown to the believers there, for the simple reason that they had not yet been compiled. The life of Jesus and His teachings were passed on by word of mouth, and it was only much later that the manuscripts of Matthew, Mark, Luke and John were copied and distributed to the churches. Just how thankful and appreciative are we, I wonder, of the fact that we have before us today a written record of the life and sayings of our wonderful Lord?

FURTHER STUDY

1 John 3: 1–10;
Gal. 6:7;
Eph. 5:6;
1 Cor. 6:9–10

1. What was John's admonition?
2. In what ways can we be deceived?

Prayer

My Father and my God, forgive me for taking so much for granted. Help me to show my appreciation for Your Word by spending as much time as I possibly can reading it. For Jesus' sake. Amen.

'The day of the Lord'

For reading & meditation – 2 Thessalonians 2:3; Joel 2:28–32

*'... for that day will not come until the rebellion occurs and
the man of lawlessness is revealed ...' (2 Thess. 2:3)*

Before us today is one of the most important prophecies in the
whole of the New Testament – the great Pauline prediction
of what is to take place in the final stages just prior to 'the day of
the Lord'. He speaks first of a general apostasy and secondly of the
appearance of a man of sin, or, as some translations call him, the
wicked one. It is not my purpose in these devotional readings to take
you too deeply into doctrinal matters, but I am bound to point out
that Christians are greatly divided over the meaning of the phrase
'the day of the Lord'.

One theory says that Christ's coming will take place in two
stages; first He will descend to gather His saints in the air, and then,
some time later, return to the earth with His saints. Those who
subscribe to this view believe the term 'the day of the Lord' applies
to the actual coming of Christ to the earth. Thus they see 'the falling
away' and the appearance of 'the wicked one' as taking place after
the Church has been removed from the world, and prior to Christ
arriving on the earth.

<table>
<tr><td>

FURTHER STUDY

Psa. 46:1–11;
Col. 2:16–17;
Dan. 2:21;
Isa. 40:28–31

1. In what was the
psalmist confident?
2. What is his
message amid the
turbulence?

</td><td>

The other main view says that the gathering of
Christians in the air and the coming of Christ to
the earth takes place simultaneously, and as you
can see those who hold that view must believe
that 'the falling away' and the appearance of 'the
wicked one' will take place while the Church is
still on earth. Whichever school of thought you
subscribe to, keep in mind this one thing – God,
not events, are in control.

</td></tr>
</table>

Prayer

Gracious Father, something within me longs to know what the future holds.
But help me to realise that what is more important is that I know who holds
the future. Amen.

The falling away

For reading & meditation – 2 Thess. 2:3; Mark 8:34–38

*'If anyone is ashamed of me and my words … the Son of Man
will be ashamed of him …' (Mark 8:38)*

We said yesterday that the term 'the day of the Lord' is subject to different interpretations. If you believe in the 'rapture' theory (ie that Christ comes in the air for His saints, and then later returns to the earth with His saints), then you will not be expecting the falling away and the appearance of the wicked one to take place while you are here on earth. If you believe, however, that the rapture and the descent of Christ to the earth are simultaneous, or almost simultaneous events, then naturally you would expect to witness this falling away and the appearance of the wicked one. But what exactly do these terms 'the rebellion' and 'the appearance of the wicked one' mean? Let's focus first on the 'rebellion' or, as some translations put it, 'the falling away'.

Many biblical scholars, particularly those who believe that the return of Christ will be one single event, interpret this as being the falling away of nominal Christians who lack a true personal encounter with Christ. Our churches, as you well know, contain many people who give every appearance of being Christian, but have never been converted in the biblical sense of that word. When pressure and persecution come, in the days that lie ahead, these people, because they do not have a living faith, will easily fall away and refuse to be counted as one of Christ's disciples. And if we do not stand up for Him, how can we expect Him to stand up for us?

FURTHER STUDY
2 Tim. 4: 1–11;
Matt. 26:56;
John 6:66;
1 John 2:19

1. Why had Demas
fallen away?
2. What is the state
of your own spiritual
life?

Prayer

O Father, help me to be sure that I am a real Christian – one who is truly converted, truly committed and truly born again. This I ask in Jesus' name. Amen.

'The rise of the wicked one'

For reading & meditation – 2 Thess. 2:4–5; 1 John 2:18–23

'He will oppose and exalt himself over everything that is called God ... proclaiming himself to be God.' (2 Thess. 2:4)

Exponents of the theory of Christ's coming in two stages – a rapture and a revelation – use the phrase 'rebellion', which they interpret to mean a sell-out to the world by nominal Christians who have been left behind at the rapture.

We move now, however, from the phrase 'the falling away' to consider the meaning of the term 'the wicked one'. Both schools of thought are fairly united on the fact that this refers to the appearance in the world of an individual of great and consummate wickedness. Mauro, a writer on biblical themes, says, 'The sin of man has its final outcome and fruition in the man of sin.' It seems that prior to 'the day of the Lord', an evil and wicked personality will arise who will attract great attention and have world influence. His skill at diplomacy and his ability to handle a crisis will be so effective that many nations will be eager to cooperate with him, if only for the security of their own people and the stability of their own economy. He will oppose anything that has to do with the true God and will seek to exalt himself to a position higher than God. It is thought by some that his final act of rebellion will be to occupy the Temple in Jerusalem, which at that time will have been rebuilt by the Jews in readiness for the return of the Messiah, and proclaim himself to be the one they have been looking for. Could such a thing really happen? Yes, of course, it could – and it may well be closer than we think!

FURTHER STUDY

Matt. 24:1–24;

Dan. 11:1–45;

1 John 4:3;

2 John 7

1. How convincing will the antichrist be?

2. Will he deceive the saints of God?

Prayer

O Father, as I ponder these difficult passages, give me not only a clear understanding of Your Word, but a greater sense of expectancy for Jesus' coming than I have ever known before. In His name I ask it. Amen.

'The one who holds it back'

For reading & meditation – 2 Thess. 2:6–7; Rev. 13:1–10

'… but the one who now holds it back will continue to do so till he is taken out of the way.' (2 Thess. 2:7)

'The wicked one' will make a bid for world power and because of his great skilfulness and his ability to handle crisis situations will have great popular appeal. The wicked one is really the devil's rival to Christ, the Son of God (this is why he is described as the antichrist). His method will be similar to Christ's in that he will perform signs and wonders, not, however, out of love and compassion, but with an eye to securing world attention. His power, of course, will not be heavenly but hellish – clever forgeries of Christ's own earthly ministry.

Paul makes the point that there is something that keeps such a world personality from arising at this time. He describes it as 'the one who now holds it back'. Just who is that 'one' of whom Paul speaks? Some think Paul is referring to the rule of law and order. But Paul is not speaking of a principle, he is speaking of a person. Who then is this person? Many ideas have been suggested by biblical scholars in answer to this question. One commentator says it is the archangel Michael who is mentioned in the books of Daniel and Revelation. Most agree, however, that the 'one' referred to here is the Holy Spirit, who, acting in His capacity as the executive of the Godhead, is present in the world to restrict and restrain. At a predetermined time, the Holy Spirit will withdraw His restraints on society, and will allow the wicked one free rein so that he might trip over himself and fall flat on his face.

FURTHER STUDY

1 John 4:1–21;
Rev. 13:11–18;
Mk. 13:22

1. What does John exhort us to do?
2. How do we know the spirit of the antichrist?

Prayer

Gracious Father I see that Your secrets are hidden deep within the Scriptures, and I am grateful that You are letting me discover them. One thing is sure – Jesus is coming soon. Help me to be ready. For Your own dear name's sake. Amen.

The wicked one's overthrow

For reading & meditation – 2 Thess. 2:8–15; Rev. 19:17–21

*'… whom the Lord Jesus will overthrow with the breath
of his mouth …'* (2 Thess. 2:8)

The deceptive ministry of the wicked one will gain him a great following among many nations. Those who follow him and who hope to gain great power with him will discover too late that they have been conned. Instead of climbing to the pinnacle of prominence with the wicked one, they will all be consigned to the depths of despair. Eventually, Christ will return to the earth to overthrow the wicked one and bring in His reign of righteousness and peace.

Paul points out that those who perish with the wicked one will not be able to blame him because originally they refused to love the truth and be saved. The wicked one's victims made the wrong decision before he deceived them so they will not be able to shift the blame on to him. Paul says that when we love false teaching, God will turn away from us and blind us to reality. We will no longer be able to tell the difference between right and wrong. If we deliberately choose lies, we will end up being misled. Error is like a raging lion let out of its cage – once released, its difficult to restrain.

Some Christians may become fearful and apprehensive in the light of these truths so Paul reminds them that the foundation of their security and confidence is that they are '… loved by the Lord …' God chose them to be saved and become His sanctified children. They would '… share in the glory of our Lord Jesus Christ' and knowing this they could stand firm in their faith whatever problems they might face.

FURTHER STUDY

2 Pet. 2:1–22;
Matt. 5:19;
1 Tim. 1:7; 6:3;
Titus 1:11

1 What are the marks of false teachers?
2 What is Peter's graphic way of describing them?

Prayer

Father, help me to keep in mind that although You permit Satan to win some battles, the end is a foregone conclusion – YOU WIN! You love me, save me and allow me to share in Christ's glory. Hallelujah!

God's direct encouragement

For reading & meditation – 2 Thess. 2:16–17; Rom. 15:13

*'May our Lord Jesus Christ ... and God our Father, who ...
gave us eternal encouragement ...' (2 Thess. 2:16–17)*

Paul expresses a great longing that the persecuted Christians will be greatly comforted and encouraged by 'our Lord Jesus Christ himself and God our Father'. Paul had given them all the encouragement he could, but he realised that if they were to stand firm, they needed not only his encouragement but the direct encouragement of God. Does God encourage His people in times of severe stress and trial? Most assuredly so! Paul's words are in the past tense – 'gave us' – indicating that the reason why they had withstood the trials they had been suffering was due to nothing less than the direct encouragement of God. But God had given them not only encouragement; He had also given them hope. No one can live effectively in this world without hope. True hope, of course, is born only out of contact with Christ, and to be in Christ is to be in hope: to be without Christ is to be without hope.

In Romans 15:13, Paul encourages us to 'overflow with hope'. How can we overflow with hope? Most of us have just enough to keep us going – how can we abound in it? We must focus our gaze on the most glorious event that ever took place in this universe – the cross and the resurrection. Calvary, which was seemingly the greatest defeat, became the greatest victory, which means that in any situation there is hope. Is it any wonder that we see a sunrise in every sunset, an oak tree in every acorn and a new beginning in every ending? There's hope – eternal hope in Christ.

FURTHER STUDY

Heb. 6:9–20;
Rom. 15:4;
1 Pet. 3:15;
Col. 1:5

1. To what does the writer to the Hebrews liken hope?
2. What should we always be ready to do?

Prayer

Lord Jesus, I realise that when my gaze is steady my gait will be steady. Keep my gaze on You. Fill me with the same hope that kept You moving towards the cross, so that I see beyond Good Friday to Easter Sunday. For Your name's sake. Amen.

'A gospel with legs'

For reading & meditation – 2 Thessalonians 3:1–2; Acts 8:1–4

'… that the message of the Lord may spread rapidly and be honoured …' (2 Thess. 3:1)

Paul's opening sentence – 'Finally, brothers, pray for us' – shows how humble the great apostle was. Even though he was an outstanding spiritual leader in the Early Church, here he puts himself on the same level as the newest converts in Thessalonica, and asks for their prayers. This is not just a device to get them to pray – he really believes that their prayers will be just as effective as his own. Paul has problems in Corinth, and so he asks for their prayers that 'the message of the Lord may spread rapidly'. The word which Paul uses for 'spread rapidly' is 'run'. It conjures up a mental picture of a gospel which has legs!

Paul is not ashamed to pray for rapid results – and nor should we be. The world is in such a desperate condition that only the truth of the gospel can really give men and women hope. At this very moment there are signs that thousands of people in our nation are beginning to catch on to the message of faith in Christ. All the more reason why we should be bombarding heaven with petitions that, all across the nation, men and women will respond in even greater numbers to the preaching of the gospel. An enthusiastic and alert salesman redoubles his efforts in those areas where a market is opening up. So must we. However, quality is not to be sacrificed for quantity. Paul wanted the Lord's message to spread rapidly but also to be 'honoured'. Quantity with quality must be our prayerful aim.

FURTHER STUDY

Luke 11:1–13;
Mark 1:35;
Psa. 91:15;
Jas. 5:16

1. What was the disciples' request?
2. How did Jesus illustrate His reply?

Prayer

O Father, I am thankful for the people who have come to You during these past months. Let the fire spread, until millions more respond to Your Word. In Jesus' name I pray. Amen.

'Confidence in the Lord'

For reading & meditation – 2 Thess. 3:3–5; Gal. 5:7–10

*'We have confidence in the Lord that you are doing and will
continue to do the things we command.' (2 Thess. 3:4)*

This passage links two things which come up again and again in
Paul's writings – law and grace. If he had left out the words 'in
the Lord', it might have sounded like another law of Moses, only in
this case it would have been a law of Paul.

Paul then focuses their attention upon this important fact:
'May the Lord direct your hearts into God's love and Christ's
perseverance.' The tactful and careful way in which Paul phrases his
words saved these new converts from adopting a legalistic attitude,
and, at the same time, saved him from becoming a lawgiver. He took
them beyond himself and pointed them to the love of God and the
steadfastness of Christ. Now it was no longer between Paul and
the Thessalonians, but between the Thessalonians and the grace of
God, with Paul encouraging them from the sidelines. The greatness
of Paul's heart was never more truly revealed than at this moment,
when he steps out of the picture to make way for God.

The other thing that emerges is that he had confidence in the
Lord regarding them. If he had not introduced them to the grace
of God, then he would have had to say, 'I have
confidence in my influence over you that you are
doing, and will do, the things I command.' That
would have left Paul tense and anxious as every
dictatorial person must be – wondering whether
he could maintain his authority over them. Instead
he was confident in the Lord. He stood aside and
watched God and the Thessalonians work it out
together.

FURTHER STUDY

Isa. 12:1–6, 26:3;

Psa. 37:5; 31:14;

Prov. 3:26

1. What was Isaiah's
affirmation?
2. In what do
you place your
confidence?

Prayer

O Father, help me to take a leaf out of Paul's book, for I see, through his writings,
that the secret of making disciples is to have confidence in You regarding them.
Help me to keep on believing in others, even when it is hard to do so. Amen.

Stern words to the idle

For reading & meditation – 2 Thess. 3:6–9; Neh. 4:6

*'… we command you, brothers, to keep away from every
brother who is idle …' (2 Thess. 3:6)*

Some Christians find the policy the apostle is advocating here a difficult one to accept. Does Paul really intend us to cold-shoulder the idle and lazy? The answer must be 'Yes'. This course of action may seem harsh and confrontational, but there comes a time when, after a number of warnings and admonitions, those who are lazy and indolent must be kept at arm's length. However, we must be careful not to overreact but keep on loving. Paul encourages us to 'keep away' from such people, but we are most certainly not expected to crusade against them. In spite of their disobedience and indolence, they are still brothers. The object of this whole exercise is not to reject them, but to instil into them a sense of self-discipline, and to show them that their wrong behaviour is damaging the cause of Christ.

Sometimes, not always, when a child does not live up to the rules of the home, one way to show him the error of his ways is to ignore him. It is quite clear from these words of Paul that Christian teaching concerns itself, not only with church services, but with our life and attitude in the world. Our faith in Christ should influence our attitude to our work – if it doesn't, then there is something seriously wrong. The truth written in the Scriptures is also etched into every cell of our beings; we are made to be contributive, and unless we fulfil our destiny – ill health or accidents apart – then we do not contribute, we contradict.

FURTHER STUDY

Eph. 5:1–21;
Prov. 10:5; 12:11;
13:11;
Rom. 12:11

1. How are we to use our time?
2. What are the characteristics of drunkenness?

Prayer

O Father God, I am eager to live the life You have planned for me. Take all my powers and put them under Your schooling. I want to contribute to Your cause, not contradict it. Help me, dear Lord. For Your dear name's sake. Amen.

Workers – not shirkers

**For reading & meditation – 2 Thessalonians 3:10;
Ecclesiastes 9:10**

'… *If a man will not work, he shall not eat.*' (2 Thess. 3:10)

When Paul wrote, 'If a man will not work, he shall not eat,' little did he dream that one day it would find its way into the constitution of the Soviet Union. The Communists think they got it from Karl Marx; actually they got it from the apostle Paul. This is a good verse to lay alongside the text: 'Give us this day our daily bread' for there are still some Christians who think that if they have enough faith, God will send them 'bread from heaven'!

We must be clear, of course, about the kind of people Paul has in mind here when he wrote these words. He is not talking about those who cannot find a job, or those who, because of sickness or infirmity, are unable to work. He is speaking about perfectly healthy people who are unwilling to soil their hands, so to speak. He is singling out those who are spongers and are content to live off the welfare state. Notice, I say 'content to live', for there are many who, because of redundancy, are forced into this position.

Those who are obliged to live in this way must watch that they do not lose their desire to work. We are designed by God to be creative and if we are not creative, then we become cranky. Some lazy people are not prepared to listen to a lecture, so if they can't be reached through their minds, they must be reached through their stomachs. If they are forced to go hungry for a while, then perhaps the rumbles of their empty stomachs might speak more loudly and eloquently than words.

FURTHER STUDY
Gen. 2:1–17;
Eccl. 2:24;
Eph. 4:28
1. What was Adam's task in the garden?
2. What was God's clear instruction?

Prayer

O God, I am thankful that You love me enough to be firm with me. You wound me in order to heal me. Help me to be an eager and enthusiastic worker for You – a God-watcher, not a clock-watcher. In Jesus' name. Amen.

Who is your employer?

For reading & meditation – 2 Thess. 3:11–13; Col. 3:22–25

'Whatever you do, work at it with all your heart, as working for the Lord …' (Col. 3:23)

If the words 'never tire of doing what is right' stood alone, we might think it had to do with works of charity and love for others. Set, however, as it is, in the context of physical work, it has an obvious reference to our earthly employment. Does this mean that our daily work must be considered as well-doing? Yes. Jesus said: 'My Father is always at his work … and I, too, am working' (John 5:17). God, Christ and the Holy Spirit are involved in ongoing activity that will not stop until the end of this age. Every one of us is made by God with a drive towards activity, and if that drive is not expressed then we remain unsatisfied and unfulfilled.

A woman once said to me, 'My husband and I used to get along fine when he was working. But now that he is retired with nothing to do he is unhappy and grumpy. He's under my feet all day and we are in conflict'. This is why I often say, don't retire, just change your occupation. You are created by the Creator to create and if you cease to be creative then you will be unhappy and unfulfilled. Life says, create or perish. Honest toil is not something to be ashamed of, and providing our work does not involve us in anything anti-Christian or immoral, then the apostle's exhortation, 'never tire of doing what is right', has deep significance. Surrender your job to the Lord. Tell Him every night before you go to sleep that this day you have worked, not just for an earthly employer, but for Him.

FURTHER STUDY

2 Cor. 4:1–17;
Eph. 3:13;
Rev. 2:3;
Gal. 6:9

1. Why did the apostle Paul not lose heart?
2. How did he view his circumstances?

Prayer

Father, help me to see that although I may work for others, You are really my employer. Let this truth take hold of me so that my work reflects the quality of my love for You. In Jesus' name. Amen.

The final word

For reading & meditation – 2 Thess. 3:14–18; Col. 1:21–23

*'Now may the Lord of peace himself give you peace at all
times and in every way …' (2 Thess. 3:16)*

In these two letters, Paul has dealt with many problems and he
has, at times, spoken quite firmly and bluntly. The question
that might have been uppermost in his mind as he pens these final
words was whether or not the Thessalonians might have been hurt
or offended by his firmness or bluntness. Thus he prays that God
might fill their hearts with His perfect peace. Peace is a favourite
word of Paul's. He uses it time and time again in his letters. The word
means 'harmony' or 'prosperity'. It is that special quality which God
gives His children, enabling them, though they come from different
cultures and different backgrounds, to be fused together into a single
team. Paul draws their attention to the fact that his letter to them is
signed by his own hand. The church in Thessalonica needed to be
sure about this for, as we saw, trouble had risen among them from
a letter which was purportedly written by him, but, in fact, was a
forgery. He suggests that they keep a copy of his signature so that
they will be able to recognise it when they see it again.

His last and final word is a most appropriate one: 'The grace
of our Lord Jesus Christ be with you all.' It is as
if he is saying: don't worry about the future, the
same power that has brought you out of darkness
into light, and has kept you to this moment, will
be there to help you stand unshaken in a shaking
world. And to that I, and I am sure you, will add a
hearty and an enthusiastic – AMEN!

FURTHER STUDY
Phil. 4:1–19;
Rom. 15:33; 16:20;
2 Cor. 13:11

1. List five things you
have learned from 1
and 2 Thessalonians.
2. What are
their practical
applications?

Prayer

Father, thank You for all You have taught me through these two letters. I see that
You are sovereign, Lord, and that everything that happens to me can be used
by You for my ultimate good. I can stand unshaken in a shaking world. Thank
You, Father. Amen.

National Distributors

UK: (and countries not listed below)
CWR, Waverley Abbey House, Waverley Lane, Farnham, Surrey GU9 8EP.
Tel: (01252) 784700 Outside UK (+44) 1252 784700

AUSTRALIA: CMC Australasia, PO Box 519, Belmont, Victoria 3216.
Tel: (03) 5241 3288 Fax: (03) 5241 3290

CANADA: David C Cook Distribution Canada, PO Box 98, 55 Woodslee Avenue, Paris,
Ontario N3L 3E5. Tel: 1800 263 2664

GHANA: Challenge Enterprises of Ghana, PO Box 5723, Accra.
Tel: (021) 222437/223249 Fax: (021) 226227

HONG KONG: Cross Communications Ltd, 1/F, 562A Nathan Road, Kowloon.
Tel: 2780 1188 Fax: 2770 6229

INDIA: Crystal Communications, 10-3-18/4/1, East Marredpalli, Secunderabad – 500026,
Andhra Pradesh.
Tel/Fax: (040) 27737145

KENYA: Keswick Books and Gifts Ltd, PO Box 10242, Nairobi.
Tel: (02) 331692/226047 Fax: (02) 728557

MALAYSIA: Salvation Book Centre (M) Sdn Bhd, 23 Jalan SS 2/64, 47300 Petaling Jaya, Selangor.
Tel: (03) 78766411/78766797 Fax: (03) 78757066/78756360

NEW ZEALAND: CMC Australasia, PO Box 303298, North Harbour, Auckland 0751.
Tel: 0800 449 408 Fax: 0800 449 049

NIGERIA: FBFM, Helen Baugh House, 96 St Finbarr's College Road, Akoka, Lagos.
Tel: (01) 7747429/4700218/825775/827264

PHILIPPINES: OMF Literature Inc, 776 Boni Avenue, Mandaluyong City.
Tel: (02) 531 2183 Fax: (02) 531 1960

SINGAPORE: Alby Commercial Enterprises Pte Ltd, 95 Kallang Avenue #04-00, AIS Industrial
Building, 339420.
Tel: (65) 629 27238 Fax: (65) 629 27235

SOUTH AFRICA: Struik Christian Books, 80 MacKenzie Street, PO Box 1144, Cape Town 8000.
Tel: (021) 462 4360 Fax: (021) 461 3612

SRI LANKA: Christombu Publications (Pvt) Ltd., Bartleet House, 65 Braybrooke Place,
Colombo 2. Tel: (9411) 2421073/2447665

TANZANIA: CLC Christian Book Centre, PO Box 1384, Mkwepu Street, Dar es Salaam.
Tel/Fax: (022) 2119439

USA: David C Cook Distribution Canada, PO Box 98, 55 Woodslee Avenue, Paris,
Ontario N3L 3E5, Canada. Tel: 1800 263 2664

ZIMBABWE: Word of Life Books (Pvt) Ltd, Christian Media Centre, 8 Aberdeen Road, Avondale,
PO Box A480 Avondale, Harare.
Tel: (04) 333355 or 091301188

For email addresses, visit the CWR website: www.cwr.org.uk
CWR is a Registered Charity – Number 294387
CWR is a Limited Company registered in England – Registration Number 1990308

More Every Day with Jesus One Year Devotionals

Each has six themes from *Every Day with Jesus* to stimulate your faith; and each includes 365 undated daily readings, prayers, study questions and an index.

Walking in His Ways

Contains: Changing Times – Unchanging Truth; God's Last Word; The Surprises of God; Bringing the Bible to Life; The Peak of the Epistles; and The Grand Design – Meditations in the Book of Revelation.

£6.99 Softback book
ISBN 978-1-85345-314-4

Bread for the Journey

Contains: The All-sufficient Christ; The Pursuit of Excellence; The Wondrous Cross; The Treasure of Darkness; The Most Excellent Way; and The Care of the Soul.

£6.99 Softback book
ISBN 978-1-85345-224-6

Every Day with Jesus - Bimonthly

One of the world's most popular daily Bible study tools with around a million readers. This inspiring devotional is available bimonthly in standard or large print, and as an annual subscription.

- Get practical help with life's challenges
- Gain insight into the deeper truths of Scripture
- Be challenged, comforted and encouraged
- Study six topics in depth each year

£2.25 each
£12.50 annual subscription
£2.25 large print each
£12.50 large print annual subscription

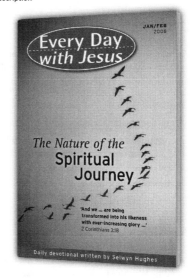

CWR Website and Store

Visit our website store at **www.cwr.org.uk** and you can buy our products online with the safety and security of WorldPay. Offering a complete listing of all our products, our online store gives you:

- Full *Every Day with Jesus* product range
- Fantastic bargains, including entry to our Bargain Basement
- All our publications: seven titles of daily Bible reading notes, over 200 Christian book titles, audio-visual resources, calendars and diaries
- Savings every time you shop
- Your own personalised account
- Forthcoming titles
- Special offers, subscriptions and bestsellers

From the store you can also access the full range of our ministry, including Waverley training courses, news, prayer and forums. Why not visit it today?